The Official Guide to 3D GameStudio

Michael Duggan

THOMSON
COURSE TECHNOLOGY
Professional ■ Technical ■ Reference

ISBN-10: 1-59863-362-7
ISBN-13: 978-1-59863-362-7
Library of Congress Catalog Card Number: 2006908558
Printed in the United States of America
07 08 09 10 11 TW 10 9 8 7 6 5 4 3 2 1

Thomson Course Technology PTR,
a division of Thomson Learning Inc.
25 Thomson Place
Boston, MA 02210
http://www.courseptr.com

Publisher and General Manager, Thomson Course Technology PTR:
Stacy L. Hiquet

Associate Director of Marketing:
Sarah O'Donnell

Manager of Editorial Services:
Heather Talbot

Marketing Manager:
Heather Hurley

Senior Acquisitions Editor:
Emi Smith

Marketing Assistant:
Adena Flitt

Project Editor and Copy Editor:
Kim Benbow

Technical Reviewer:
Felicitas Lotter

PTR Editorial Services Coordinator:
Erin Johnson

Interior Layout Tech:
ICC Macmillan Inc.

Cover Designer:
Mike Tanamachi

CD-ROM Producer:
Brandon Penticuff

Indexer:
Kelly Henthorne

Proofreader:
Sara Gullion

To Jeremy Morriss, who dreamed of this.

Acknowledgments

Thanks to Johann Christian Lotter, George Pirvu, Dan Silverman, David Lancaster, RealSpawn, Exile, Kotakide, GeoMetricks, and the rest of the community at 3DGS for the help they gave me with the software. Thanks to my editors, Emi Smith, Kim Benbow, and Felicitas Lotter, for helping me put this book together. Thanks to my wife and family for their support.

Conitec would like to acknowledge the efforts of the following people in relation to 3D GameStudio A6:

WED Level Editor: Wladimir Stolipin

MED Model Editor: Wladimir Stolipin

Map Compiler: Marco Grubert, Alexej Stolipin

C-Script Compiler: Volker Kleipa

SED Script Editor: Gustav Nordvall

A6 Engine: Johann Christian Lotter

Physics Engine: Marco Grubert

Demo Games: Czeslav Gorski, Dan Silverman, Doug Poston

Game Templates: Doug Poston

Manual: Johann Christian Lotter, Felicitas Lotter

Tutorials: George Pirvu, Felicitas Lotter, Dan Silverman, Doug Poston

About the Author

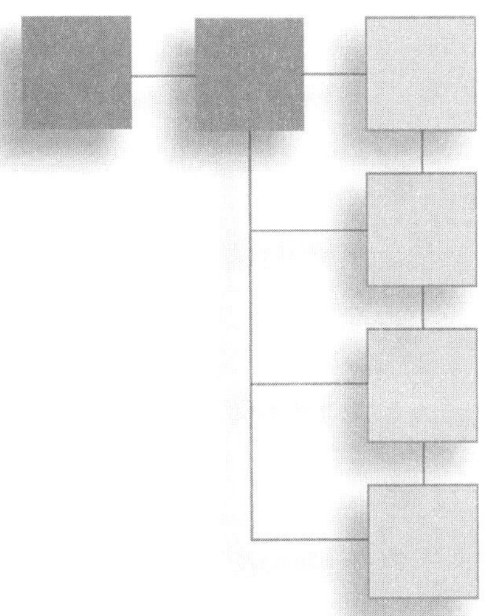

Mike Duggan is an artist and animator with a background in 3D modeling and digital animation. He is primarily a game programmer and motion graphics expert with nearly 10 years experience using Conitec's 3D GameStudio engine. He has taught 3D animation and game design at North Arkansas College for the past three years. He also contributed to the foundations of the Gaming and Robotics curriculum at the high-paced Bryan College based out of Kansas City. Mike is a published author and is currently working on an online magazine about scratchware game development, which will be out in late 2007. Besides 3D GameStudio, Mike uses Adobe Illustrator, Adobe Photoshop, Autodesk Maya, Autodesk 3D Studio Max, Adobe Flash, Adobe After Effects, and SoftImage XSI in his pipeline and knows a number of programming languages, including C-script, Ruby, Java, CSS, PHP, ActionScript, MEL Script, and Max Script.

Contents

Introduction

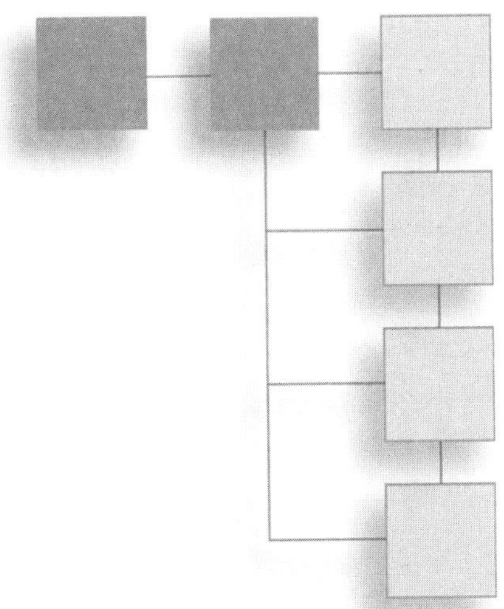

Welcome to *The Official Guide to 3D GameStudio!* Whether you are currently a game developer looking for a new prototype platform or someone looking forward to becoming a game designer, this book will help you learn the essential skills, terminology, and techniques you need to make your very own video games.

When I first began working with 3D GameStudio, the best learning tool I used was to study successful games, which I found at my local video game rental store. Now this may sound redundant, because if you want to make games, you probably play them already. But just because you love sports or army games does not make you a great game designer. You must play all games—and study them for the way they are put together, how the levels are architected, and what story devices are pushed through them.

The lessons in this book are set up with the responsibilities of a game designer in mind, and as such, you will learn how to make a game from start to finish using the most readily found tools in the industry. By the time you complete this all-in-one manual, you will be ready to make your own games for fun and profit—or you might be ready for your first job in the ever-growing and popular gaming entertainment industry!

What You Will Learn from This Book

In *The Official Guide to 3D GameStudio,* you will learn about the game industry as a whole (how video games are made, what job opportunities exist, and how you can break in). You will also learn how to make your own games from scratch—without spending your life's savings doing it! I'll walk you through character animation, level building, and programming various effects; and along the way I give you plenty of details with the hope of answering any questions you might have.

Building games is one of the most challenging and deeply rewarding experiences I can think of. This book will teach you how to make really great 3D games using 3D GameStudio. We will cover a lot of subjects rather quickly, so you had better keep on your toes! You will learn how to create some of the most popular forms of games today. We will start with the first-person shooter game and finish with making a fantasy role-playing game. And this is only the start. Once you have learned the foundations for making computer games, the only limitations will be your hardware, your talent, and your imagination. You can make your own games, publish them on the Internet, or sell them on CD. Or you might make games specifically for demo reels to be a proponent of your career portfolio and to help you land a job in the growing lucrative field of game design—all with the skills you learn right here!

Who Should Read This Book?

Anyone who is inspired and deeply interested in making games, who has recently entered the development field, or perhaps who is interested in prototype possibilities will find the contents of this book very useful. Thus the material is easy enough for a novice to pick up, as well as comprehensive enough for intermediate users. I will go over real-life situations and how to tackle them on paper or using the Conitec software. The software is similar enough to other 3D applications that veterans to map editing and modeling will feel comfortable, and it is practical enough that beginners can get their feet wet for the first time without any trouble.

How to Use This Book

The rest of the content in this book is set up in roughly two categories: there is the academic information, followed by a summary of what you have learned and questions for review, and then there are step-by-step exercises that will help you to create actual games.

In Part I, I focus primarily on providing you with a firm foundation of what games are and how the industry is run (the business side of things). If you are an industry veteran, you might wish to skip these chapters, but there is a wealth of information that can enlighten and serve you, too. After that I start into the meat-and-potatoes of game design.

Parts II and III cover the creation of complete games, including an action game and a role-playing game. The chapters therein are all set up to guide you through exercises in creating these real-life games. Each of these sections begins with developing a strong game outline, then starting on character animation and constructing environments, followed by programming features. The exercises are laid out to give you an introduction to the software tools as well as the process one might expect to find when employed as an actual game developer.

The last of the book, Part IV, shows you how to take what you have learned and publish your games or break into the lucrative design field.

Hardware and Software Considerations

3DGS is a software athlete, ultimately very versatile, and capable of running on many different systems. If you are looking for software specifications information, you can go to www.3dgamestudio.com.

In general, though, faster computers are nicer to run CG programs on: a system with a fast processor, good chunk of RAM (computer memory), and video card are all recommended. 3DGS has minimum requirements, which follow, but it is suggested to get a better system than the minimum for your workspace:

- Pentium III with 128 MB of RAM
- Windows 98 / ME / 2000 / XP operating system
- 32-MB 3D video card
- 3D sound card
- Direct X 9.0

For sound editing, Audacity is the best little program you can have. The number-one reason is that it is fully featured and published free under the GNU General Public License (GPL). You can find out more about it online at their Web site: www.audacity.sourceforge.net.

The Companion CD

The CD contains the setup files for A6 3D GameStudio and Audacity. I have also stocked it with all sorts of useful files for you to complete the exercises included in this book, as well as supplemental materials you might find helpful as you start your own game projects. Here is a general rundown of what's included on the CD:

- **Project Files**—This folder has the images, audio files, 3D models, and other elements used in the exercises in this book. You will need to use these to complete the assignments and make the games.
- **Artwork**—This folder contains the concept artwork, the 2D images for sprites (animated in-game images) and textures, and anything else I could think of. These files can be useful for reference or for activities.
- **Audio**—This folder contains the sample audio files (WAV and MIDI) for use with the exercises, plus some that may come in handy for other projects. They are sound effects, atmospheric noises, and music.
- **3D Models**—This folder contains 3D models and their concept artwork as used in the exercises, plus others that you might want to borrow. The 3D models categories are separated into actors (in-game characters), props, and environment fixtures, such as lights and plants.
- **WADs**—This folder contains the texture packages that 3DGS uses for in the World Editor; there are also extracted textures broken down by type to import and make your own WAD files.
- **Software**—This folder has five major programs for your use: Conitec's 3D GameStudio A6.40; Audacity (the sound editor); A4 Font Generator (for making type fonts in 3DGS); Paint Dot Net (a freeware paint program for converting images, in case you don't own a license of Adobe Photoshop); and GenSurf (a generator for creating instant outdoor levels).

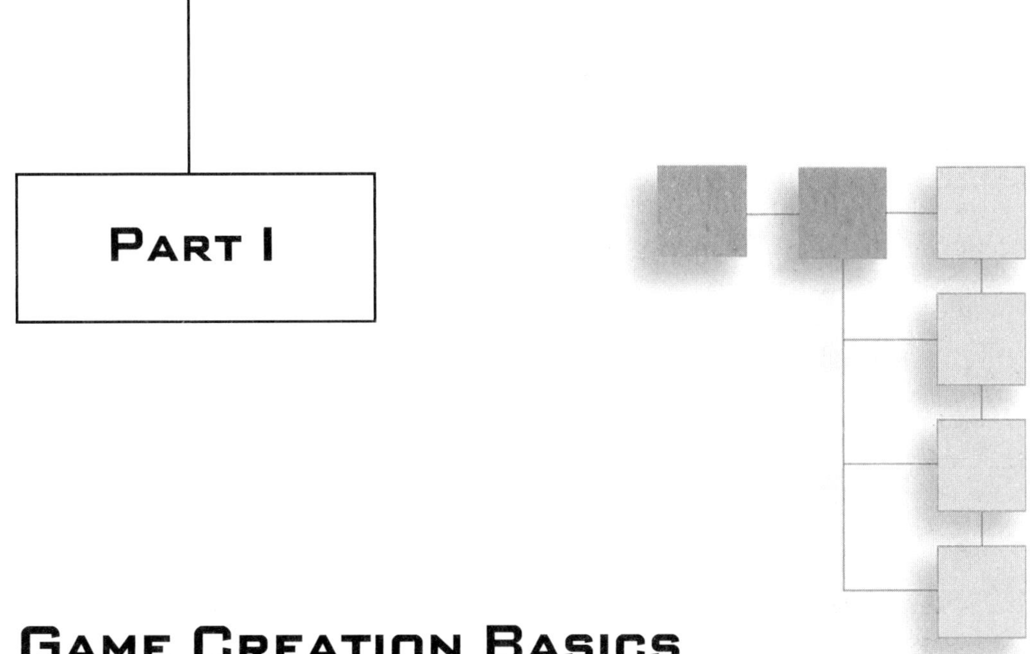

Game Creation Basics

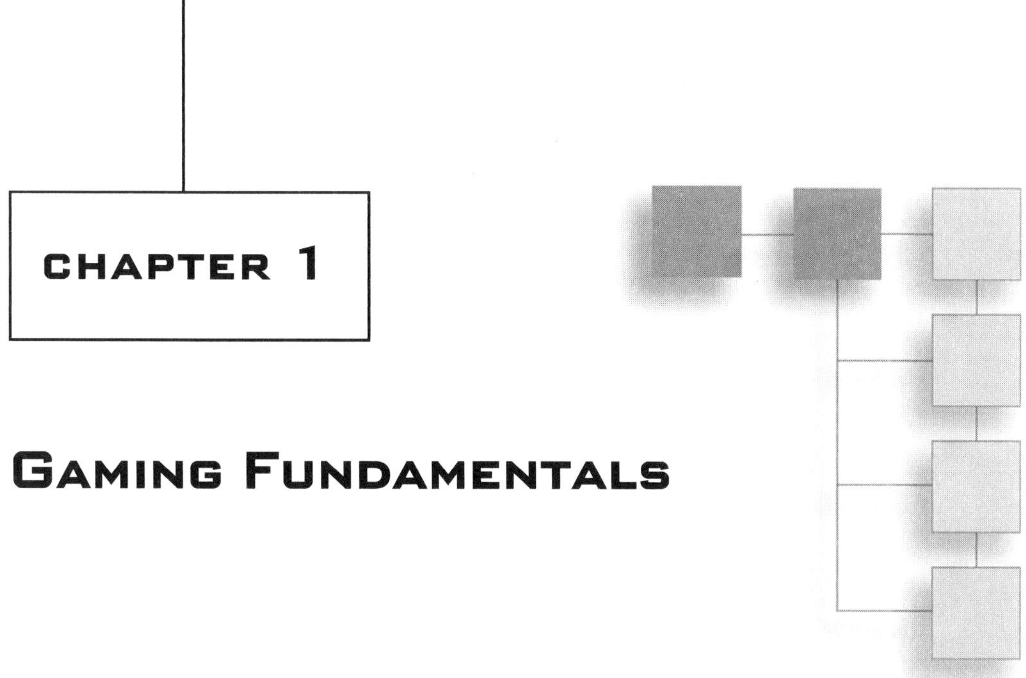

Chapter 1

Gaming Fundamentals

If you've picked up this book, you are probably someone interested in making computer or video games. You probably have some experience playing those games, and you really hate being talked down to like some extraterrestrial not raised on planet Earth during the glory days of Nintendo. On the other hand, this book has been written with the beginning game designer in mind. So I am going to start with the basics and work up to the really good stuff. Along the way, whether novice or sage, you will come out with a better understanding of the key concepts it takes to develop games and how to do so using 3D GameStudio.

Evolution of a Medium

Electronic games are still very new to our society, the same as cell phones, e-mail, digital cameras, and faux-hawk haircuts. Yet electronic games have quickly risen to a competent entertainment medium, peddling right beside books, videos, and artwork—and the game design industry is the largest growing industry today, following in the wake of film and pop music.

Video games got their start in 1961 when MIT student Steve Russell created *Spacewar!* Nolan Bushnell saw the game and turned it into the first coin-op arcade game, called *Computer Space,* in 1971 (see Figure 1.1). *Pong* and *Asteroids* were sure to follow, which they did. (Arguably *Pong* was the first game created, as it appeared in 1958 as a table tennis game on an oscilloscope made by Willy Higinbotham at the Brookhaven National Labs in New York; it was only later

Figure 1.1
Computer Space console (courtesy of Nolan Bushnell 1971)

demonstrated on a console in 1972 by Magnavox and "appropriated" by Atari the same year—but tech historians today agree that *Spacewar!* really started it all.)

Sidebar

After the success of his *Computer Space* coin-op game, Nolan Bushnell left Nutting Associates to found the company Atari (which, roughly translated, means "Watch out, I win!" in the board game *Go*) along with Ted Dabney. Bushnell left Atari to start a chain of pizza parlors with a unique outlook. He wanted to erase the awful public stigma of arcade games at the time and prove them to be family entertainment, so he put arcade games inside his pizza parlors, which he initially named Pizza Time Theater; the company eventually changed its name to Chuck E. Cheese.

What followed was a brief rise in video game console sales, especially remarkable for the Atari systems. Then a curious thing happened: sales plummeted and the future of games went into a slump. Console sales suddenly had the bottom drop in the early 1980s, causing everyone to question whether the industry would ever recover. Several theories for this slump have been put forth—one of which says that with so many competitors and market saturation, development studios were pressured to crank out games quickly, leading to imitative, low-quality titles. The Atari game *E.T.* was a rush job put out for Christmas to tie in to the fandom of the movie, and it ended up with millions of units sent back to the factories and being buried in a landfill—which is totally understandable if you have ever played it! The game had the worst graphics, most confusing rules, and lack of storyline ever. Where was the innovation? Gamers were sick of the games being made.

The video game industry recovered, all right—and how! The year 1985 marked the start of the video game "Golden Age." With the advent of technological innovations—and with Nintendo, SEGA, Sony, and Microsoft entering the console industry—the bar was raised, to the delight of the entire player market. The substance and number of titles with exciting features quadrupled in direct correlation with the rise in sales. Games were good again.

I will offer a case in point. One of the industry titans, Nintendo, was started as a manufacturer of a playing card game called Hanafuda in 1889. Nintendo is the oldest video game publisher in existence today, thanks in part to the legendary Shigeru Miyamoto, who joined Nintendo in 1977 as a staff artist and went on to help create Nintendo's biggest selling games: *Donkey Kong*, *Super Mario Bros.*, and *Zelda* (see Figure 1.2). It was really Shigeru Miyamoto who inspired me to create my formula of the Four F's of Great Game Design, because he was often quoted as saying that all games had to be fun—and if you lost sight of the fun factor you had essentially doomed your product. At the time of this writing the industry is dominated by three console giants: Microsoft (Xbox), Sony (Playstation), and Nintendo (Gamecube), who are all involved in the console wars.

Figure 1.2
Zelda: Twilight Princess (courtesy of Nintendo 2006)

Consoles aside, the first computer game was the text-based *Colossal Cave,* but it wasn't until Donald Woods expanded the idea and made Infocom's popular *Zork* game in 1979 that programmers everywhere were inspired to make their own adventure games. One of these designers was Roberta Williams—one of the first female game developers—who launched *Sierra Online* with her husband. These adventure games were also known as parser games, because players had to type in two-word combinations to interact in the game world (such as "walk north" or "get sword"). As the level of graphic capabilities in games took off (mostly due to the advent of DirectX and Direct3D libraries), so did adventure games—replacing text choices with picture icons. LucasArts launched adventure games into the graphics world with their games, such as the ever-popular *Secret of Monkey Island.*

Networked computer games started when Rick Blomme made the very first multiplayer games at the University of Illinois in 1961. He used a software program popular even today for use with electronic-based education (it is called PLATO). His early games were mostly based on *Star Trek* or Dungeons and Dragons, but they were still not true online games because they were played over a network. It wasn't until 1979 that some fellows in Essex in the United Kingdom, created the first Multi-User Dungeon (MUD) on Arpanet (the system that would later become the Internet). MUDs instantly became popular role-playing game communities among colleges and universities.

By the 1990s, computer games became truly graphical and interactive with lots of online content. Players today can immerse themselves in real-time strategy, fantasy role-playing, and keeping track of "guilds." And with the number of homes that possess computer technology and broadband/DSL technology, computer games are just as popular as ever! There are lots of games with downloaded online content that supplements and extends their replay ability. There are map editors, mod communities, machinima, patches, wallpaper, desktop goodies, and loads more available for fans of these games. Plus, Microsoft's innovative "dev luv"—a relatively new movement—creates a crossover between computer and console development by and for the gamers. Starting in 2007, players will be able to make and contribute their own console games for the Xbox 360 through Microsoft's Live Arcade.

Will Wright, the creative genius behind the popular game *The Sims* and *Spore,* said in an article for *WIRED Magazine* that "games have the potential to subsume almost all other forms of entertainment media. They can tell us stories, offer us music, give us challenges, allow us to communicate and interact with others, encourage us to make things, connect us to new communities, and let us play. Unlike most other forms of media, games are inherently malleable. . . . And more than ever, games will be a visible, external amplification of the human imagination."

Games are evolving from board and tabletop games to the tiny toy worlds of primitive 8-bit graphics to the next-generation photorealistic landscapes of games that make even Hollywood directors envious. Can you imagine what *you* can do with this constantly growing and progressive media form? The limits are endless.

Note

"One way or another, consolidation is all but inevitable. A single, pervasive environment will emerge, uniting the separate powers of today's virtual societies. And then we really will have built the Matrix."

—Steven Johnson, *WIRED Magazine*

Coming Up with Ideas

A great game does not just happen—it takes someone to invent an idea, hash it out as a Killer Game Concept (KGC), and put it to paper. The paper is called a game design document. The designer (if he works within a production company or publisher) finds a development team to make his KGC a reality. The designer (if he is part of a game development team) must find funding to make his game, preferably in the guise of a producer. Games are a tangle of work, and to sort them out I will discuss the finer points of their creation, starting with the steps taken during production.

I bet you have plenty of ideas about games you would like to make. A lot of times these ideas come from playing other games, and you start thinking to yourself, "I wonder if they did this. . . ." or "I could make this totally better if. . . ." Write your ideas down. Personally, I keep several notebooks full of game ideas. They lie around, waiting for the free time to make them happen.

If you have difficulty thinking of a game you would like to make—or you are searching for some fresh ideas—there are several ways to do so. You could brainstorm ideas with friends, do some Internet research, or you could play other games to get ideas.

Figure 1.3
Think it over a while: a great game idea should be wild and fun! (*Atlantis Redux*, image courtesy of Tetraedge 2004)

First, chat with your friends; in this cheap and efficient idea-scouring way, you can hash out ideas for games over some pizza while talking about games that interest you. I have heard several games get their start this way. Say that your friend starts complaining about a movie he saw recently, and you tell him you think that it would make a much better video game. Pretty soon you are both brainstorming ideas to complete a video game based on this premise (see Figure 1.3).

Next, you could search the Internet. If you are completely dry on fresh ideas, there are several Web forums where people post what they'd like to see happen in games. Search for keywords in Google, like "game ideas," and you will be amazed at how many sites you hit where people are posting their own game concepts. Don't just steal someone else's ideas, however! Ideas for games should come from within you. It is perfectly legit to have an inspiration when looking at the sorts of games other people would like to see made; it's just that your inspiration should be yours. Plus, some of the top game producers scour sites such as these to see what the audience wants; when you know what the audience wants, you will have a key to success!

The last trick for coming up with game ideas I can never say enough about: play games! This advice sounds a little obvious, but it is absolutely true. Great games beget other great games. You can make a list of the details you like about games and what you think could have been done better, and then decide to make a game like them, only better. Or you could try the old Hollywood concept of hybridizing media: combine disparate games, like *Gran Turismo* (a car racing game) meets *Elder Scrolls: Oblivion* (a fantasy role-playing game), for a radical new game that busts out of genre placements. Think about it for a minute. How many racing games do you see on the present market that incorporate magic fantasy? Why couldn't they? Or while you are playing *Hitman: Blood Money* you might think to yourself, "Stealth games are so cool. I wish they made one like that movie *Master of Disguise,* where you are a screwball disguise artist.... That would be funny!"

When that little light bulb comes on, and you finally have a Killer Game Concept, never doubt your own abilities. One of the most-often spouted self-defeatist statements that I hear is, "Every idea's been used before! I could never make something new and exciting." Sure, every idea has been used before—but *you* can make it better! Don't doubt yourself. If you have ever played a game, I bet you dimes-to-donuts that you at some time thought, "This bites! Why did the designer's make the game like this?" or "Why did they put this in the game? It sucks." When you do start making critical remarks, write them down and consider them. What would you do differently if you had to make the game over? Every game out there could be made better. You just have to figure out how.

Write down your game idea. There is no greater test for a Killer Game Concept than trying to put it into articulate words on paper. Usually ideas are sublingual, full of images, emotions, and vague details. Try to put your game idea on paper, and then read it out loud. This process, though it may feel awkward at first, will reveal weak spots that made it past your original mental process as you wrote the KGC down. Plus, as you read, you might try putting emotion into your words. You might find there are words you used that don't work where others would work better. After you have your KGC on paper, share it with your friends. Ask them to describe your KGC back to you, based on their own ideas. Don't ask for their opinion or let them cut you down just yet. A concept is a concept and not a finished game, so it is impossible to make hasty generalizations like, "This won't ever work because racing games suck." The point here is that you want them to understand your KGC and find any flaws of misunderstanding you have left to patch up. This seems like a lot of work, but it's really not.

The more you try coming up with game ideas, the easier they will come for you. You will notice that you are watching a new movie or reading a good book and you suddenly stop and think, "Hey—I bet I could make a great game out of this!" Best of all, with the training this book offers, you'll know you can!

Getting Your Game Idea Out There

In the popular electronic games industry, the role of game designer is a difficult one, though many people think they "have what it takes" to perform the job. Almost everybody in the industry has what they believe is THE Killer Game Concept (KGC), and they are just itching to make it happen. It is not easy to have your KGC go from idea to reality, however. There are a lot of people that believe if they just talk convincingly, wave their hands about the air in front of some aging cigar-chomping executive, they will see big money come from their big ideas. Big ideas don't become big money without a lot of elbow grease. Since a game publisher invests between thousands and millions of dollars toward developing a single game title, it's easy to see why they choose their game designers carefully: one or two risky game concepts could end up costing them millions of dollars in revenue. Some companies have been known to go bankrupt because of this. Now game producers are more selective: they choose developers with a roster of hit games in their portfolio and a finger on the pulse of what is "hip." The downside to this trend is that they also choose games they figure will be big hits: sequels to old games or licensed games based on popular movies.

Don't let this scare you. If you love playing games, you probably already have a good idea what would make it and what wouldn't in this cutthroat market—you just need the mad skills and prototype development to make it happen. That is what this book will give you. This is the day and age of personal empowerment because of technology. You can become an independent game designer and (working in your bedroom or garage and on your own time) you can make the next popular game. It is not that hard. All you need is determination, the material covered in this book, and the right software. You can't expect to sell as many copies of your game as EA or Ubisoft, but you have one big advantage that they do not: you DON'T have their costs!

Remember what I said about that Killer Game Concept? Imagine you had an idea for making a great movie instead of a game. How would you make your movie come to life? You could go to film school, become a director, work through several small film projects until you have made a name for yourself; then you have enough clout to work on your own ideas. Or you could become a screenwriter, churning out screenplays and sending them to Hollywood where they could rise to the top of slush piles and eventually have one turned into a film. These are all insider ways to make your film come true. However, this millennium is the age of do it yourself: you could take some cash, buy some costumes and props, talk your friends into becoming stars, and with a digital camera and software like Final Cut Pro for video editing, you could make your movie yourself. It might take you a few months and $5,000 of your own savings, but your idea would be out there: you could put it on the Web, enter it into independent film contests, and get your show noticed.

The exact same thing is true of games. If you have an idea for a great game—one you know would make it bigger than *Prince of Persia*—or even if you have an idea for a game that you or your friends would like to play, you could make it happen.

You could do it the insider way: you could go to school and learn computer programming, game art, and animation, start out at a game house working as a tester or whatever gig you were lucky enough to land, struggle up to joining the game development team, make a few successful games, and when you had enough clout you could launch your own game idea. This is the insider way to make your game come true. The do-it-yourself way is so much faster: you could devote some time to learning the software, talk some friends into helping you (or go solo if you wish), and with the right game engine you could make your game yourself. It might take you seven weeks or it might take you twelve months, but then you would have your idea out there: you could distribute it on the Web, burn it to CD-ROM, enter it into independent game contests, and get your game noticed, all from your own home. Don't think it can happen? Go online and see other gamers that are doing it right now: www.adventuredevelopers.com.

Because of this drive, games are getting easier and easier to make. Independent games (or "Indies") refer to games created independently of the financial backing of a publishing company. These games generally have a small, practically non-existent budget (as in petty cash only) and are often available online for about $10 each download. Independent games are created by a small team of friends, often about one to 10 people. Usually one person is the concept and 2D artist, one is the character animator and 3D artist, one is a pretty decent programmer, one is a writer, and one is a musician, and so on. (If you haven't noticed yet, making games is an incredibly cross-disciplinary activity!)

Figure 1.4
Games are an adventure! *Fable: Lost Chapters* (image courtesy of Lionhead Studios 2005)

These games are often developed in people's spare time and spare space (garages, basements, and such) and with game engines like 3D GameStudio. The amazing thing is the popularity and money-making potential in independent games today, and it is growing monthly. Every single game sold at retail in the last year sold four thousand copies or more . . . all of them, even the bad ones. That may not seem like that much to you, but at $10 per download that comes to $40,000.00 for one year's earnings for doing something that you love.

I am not saying that you have to get a team of 10 of your best friends together right away; you can start building games by yourself, learn your strengths and your weaknesses, and create a few games to advertise your skills. Then if you want to upscale your workforce, you can audition for teammates. The main thought here is that you can do it. You can make great games. Don't wait around. Your game can be out there right now (see Figure 1.4)!

3D GameStudio

Note

"An excellent toolkit to quickly prototype and develop 3D graphics applications. . . ."

—Dr. Dobb's Journal

3D GameStudio (often called 3DGS) is a top-of-the-line 3D authoring software and game engine. It has been around since 1995, and many developers have gotten their start using it or are using it now for rapid game construction. 3D GameStudio is flexible, and therefore it has a lot of potential for making all sorts of 2D as well as 3D computer applications. Yet 3D GameStudio's greatest power is as a full-featured game engine. A *game engine* is the core component of a computer or video game that provides the technology, simplifies the development, and often includes rendering, collision detection, artificial intelligence, character animation, sound, and so on. Game engines are called "middleware" because they provide all the core functionality straight out of the box to develop a game application, while reducing cost, deadlines, and complexities—all of which are critical factors in the highly competitive electronic games industry.

Game engines first arose in the 1990s. The popularity of id Software's *Doom* and *Quake* games caused other developers to license the properties of the software and design their own graphics, characters, weapons, and levels. This saved game developers time and money and changed the way games were made. For instance, *Stubbs the Zombie* is made with the Halo engine and *Land of the Dead* is developed with the Unreal engine and *Vampire: Bloodlines* is made using Valve's Source engine and . . . well, you get the picture. Creating video games takes a lot of different talents and software programs: 3D modeling, sound editing, level building, lighting, and script programming, among others. Developers learned the potential of using these pre-fabricated game engines because it cut their development time in half and allowed them to bring more artistic talent to the field. Advanced game engines (such as 3D GameStudio, the Unreal Engine, Source Engine, Gamebryo, and Microsoft NXA) provide a suite of development tools in addition to reusable software libraries. These tools are provided as an integrated development environment (sometimes called an IDE) to enable simplified development of games.

3D GameStudio is the leading non-proprietary game engine for game designers and prototype development. Game authoring systems such as 3D GameStudio are truly the future of game programming. 3DGS allows users to create their very own video games and publish them royalty-free. It is also legal—as opposed to retro-engineering the latest *Doom* game. 3DGS comes with everything you need: it comes complete with a model editor, a map editor, a script editor, a run-time compiler (built into the map editor), as well as huge libraries of 3D objects, artwork, and template scripts. All you have to do to test your game prototype is hit the Build (compile) button, and then the Run button, and you are playing what you have built!

Figure 1.5
3DGS: the A6 logo

Over 100,000 game developers worldwide are using 3D GameStudio (see Figure 1.5), and this number is growing at a steady pace. 3DGS is for everyone, of all ages and walks of life (and financial resources). You don't need much experience to use 3D GameStudio. In fact, you can simply construct tinker-toy levels, insert models, and add the template scripts—without much experience at all. The engine defaults to a first-person shooter game right away. But if you want to, you can create your own models and designs, textures, and scripts—and you can build any game your imagination can invent, including puzzle games, role-playing games, and fighting games!

3DGS offers three basic levels of games creation:

- Click-together games—for simple games, such as first-person shooters.
- Program games in a C-style scripting language—for ambitious beginners.
- Program games in C++ or Delphi—for experienced programmers.

3DGS Technology

- Six degrees of freedom, multiple cameras, and views
- Supports DirectX 9, DirectPlay, DirectShow, DirectSound
- Binary Space Partitioning (BSP) culling
- Potential Visibility Set (PVS) culling

- Seamless indoor and outdoor support with terrain system
- Static and dynamic point, spot, and directional light sources
- Static and dynamic shadows
- Fog areas, camera portals, reflections and mirrors
- Geometric LOD, detail textures, texture compression
- Softskin models with animation blending
- Animated sprites and decals
- Material properties for static and dynamic objects
- Vertex and pixel shaders
- Layered sky system
- Particle engine
- Physics engine
- Network engine
- Static and dynamic 3D sounds with Doppler effect
- Streaming sound and movie player

3DGS began as an open source engine. In 1993 Larry Myers created ACK (Animation Construction Kit) 3D. It was a Wolfenstein-style open source engine, which is still downloadable online. The next year Johann Christian Lotter improved ACK 3D, creating ACK NEXT GENERATION, followed in 1995 by Acknex-2, which was written for the German TV show *X-BASE*. Acknex-2 was an engine comparable to *Doom*.

Acknex-2 became Conitec property in late 1995 and was renamed 3D Game-Studio; it has since been released in regular upgrades (such as A3, A4, A5, A6, and soon A7 will be released). A4 was the first Windows-based 3DGS software to mimic the *Quake* engine (see Figure 1.6). A6 offers physics, shaders, and bones animation for the first time.

As well as being infinitely flexible, 3D GameStudio has four different editions to choose from. Each edition costs a little bit more, and they each have different capabilities. Use what you want—when you need it. You can publish your game for distribution in all editions (except for the Team editions). With clever thinking, many of the bonus features that are in the higher editions (such as advanced shadows and advanced physics) can be mimicked or faked in the lower editions. The editions are as follows:

- **Standard edition**—The cheapest but lacks a lot of features. It's decent for very simple games or for those with a low budget just starting out.

Figure 1.6
NEON: a game made with the 3D GameStudio engine.

- **Extra edition**—Adds a few more features, like the use of terrains, level of detail (LOD), and losing the watermark (a tiny, transparent A6 in the corner that appears in the Standard edition).
- **Commercial edition**—Has the best features for the money. The Commercial edition has more features than the Extra edition, including unlimited screen resolution and bones animation, as well as the use of shaders.
- **Professional edition**—Has all the available features for 3DGS, and you don't have to display the engine logo when publishing. The file packer makes it more worthwhile as well.
- **Team editions**—There are two Team editions available: Team Commercial and Team Professional. Team Commercial is exactly like the normal Commercial edition. Team Professional is exactly like the Professional edition. The only two exceptions are that you can't publish with a Team edition, but multiple users can use the same software.

Technical Support

If you have problems or don't know how to do something, there are three forms of support available from Conitec. The manual (which is included with the software) explains the majority of controls and features—*and* how to use them. The manual is very comprehensive and should be your first resort of seeking help on something.

Another way to find support is through e-mail, but it's only available for a limited time. The fastest and most popular form of support is the user forums available online. The user forums are very active and helpful. 3D GameStudio's users help beginners out, and you can help others out too. There are also three main online magazines that provide new tips, tricks, and tutorials. Two of them are paid for, the 3AM and 3PM, and a third, Acknex User Magazine (AUM for short) is created by George Pirvu and published once a month online for free.

3D GameStudio will give you all the major tools you need—out of the box—to create your very own custom video games! With 3DGS you are not just "modding out" some pre-existing game like *Far Cry* or *Neverwinter Nights*—you are making your very own standalone game, which you could sell online or on CD-ROM. You will not be on your own; you will become a part of the growing 3DGS community. So get ready to learn the basic foundations and start making games!

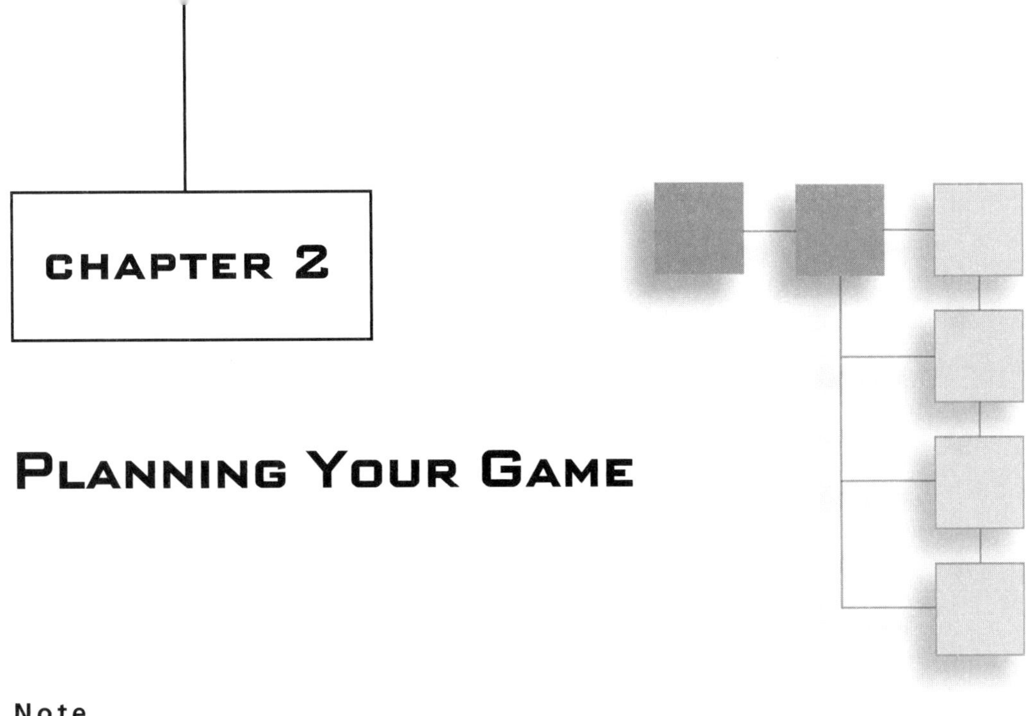

Chapter 2

Planning Your Game

Note

> "Ideas are cheap. A dime a dozen, as they say. It's the implementation that's important! The trick isn't just to have a computer game idea, but to actually create it!"
>
> —Scott Adams

Lots of people have Killer Game Concepts. They stop me all the time to tell me their game ideas and ask if I will help make their games for them. (Somewhere along the line they assume that games are easier for me to make than for them, and that profits will come up and we split them 50/50—or 15/85 with me getting the 15 simply because they came up with the idea.) Invariably, I describe to these people that I have notebooks full of great ideas—ideas that are all my own—and that if I don't have time to make all of my ideas come to reality, I don't have time to work on anyone else's (unless they are willing to pay me).

The key thing with Killer Game Concepts is that all by themselves, they are not games. You could tell me, "My game has this alien spaceship you fly, and there are all these guys and asteroids you have to avoid hitting." However, this does not tell me anything about the game. To make the idea into a game, you have to plan it. Game craft takes more patience and skill than writing novels because it has multiple layers of sound and video, not to mention the player interface. So before you launch into the exercises and build your first game, it's time to take a look at what game creation takes.

Development

You might not work with a team yet, but chances are you will eventually if you continue making games. Most games are created through a working partnership of publishers and developers. Publishers are those wonderful companies that market your games and distribute them to the rest of the country or (through the magic of localization) the rest of the world. Developers are the people—the game design teams—who actually make the games. You are learning, through this book, how to become a developer. There are four basic types of developers to consider.

- **First-party developers**—These are developers who work in-house with a game publisher and make proprietary games for them. Nintendo is a good example of a first-party developer as well as a publisher; they make all their own goods, so to speak.

- **Second-party developers**—These developers have signed contracts with a publisher to make games that will only be published by that publisher; in other words, they sign away exclusive publishing rights on their game titles. An example with this would be Capcom's *Resident Evil:* they have had long-standing contracts with Nintendo that has kept them from publishing to anything but a Nintendo console for any of the *Resident Evil* games. *Resident Evil 4*'s breakthrough move to the Playstation 2 was a sign of change.

- **Third-party developers**—The most common form of design team going; these developers are not possessed by a publisher and only sign contracts with them on a per-game basis. For instance, the game *Grand Theft Auto: San Andreas* appears on many different platforms, such as Playstation 2, Xbox, and the PC.

- **Independent developers**—This is probably where you fall. Independent developers are people who used to be known as "game sages" or "garage gamers" but today have broader titles and more acceptance. These people do not have huge overheads or extraneous responsibilities, but they do find it harder to be taken seriously by publishers and are often left devoting their time to self-promotion and self-distribution.

Developer teams are often composites of 10 to 100 individual designers, which include texture artists, prop artists, technical artists, interface designers, level designers, animators, character modelers, graphics engineers, analysts, concept artists, cut-scene producers, storyboard artists, audio engineers, content editors, sound designers, music composers, motion-capture technicians, pipeline engineers, riggers, programmers, network or service technicians, content integrators, Q/A testers, and so on.

Each of these job titles has significant responsibilities, and depending on the size of the project and the length of the deadline, the more team members will be brought in to complete the game title. The future of game development is moving more and more toward subcontracting labor, because many developers are seeing a loss of profits when they pull in 15 artists for concept artwork, and then spend three months on programming before those artists are needed again, while the artists pull paychecks for play-testing and doing menial jobs around the office. Some of the more forward-looking developers are starting to hire contract artists per job, even telecommuting designers over the Internet, and this leaves the artists to do more to progress their portfolios. Indie game designers will have a heads-up on this new workforce as more work will be done out of the home or per contract.

But typically a game development house is a casual work environment. (Where else do you see office cubicles full of toys and workers playing games? See Figure 2.1.) But hardly anyone gets paid overtime and work days of nine to 12 hours are not unheard of. Around crunch time especially, anywhere from 80- to 140-hour work weeks are common. If you take 140 and divide it by 7 days per week (that is assuming you work weekends, too), that averages 20-hour days laboring to get a game finished before its deadline. By "work" I do not mean people goof off, sitting around playing games all day—because that never happens. Even play-testers do

Figure 2.1
A casual work environment (image courtesy of Lionhead Studios 2004)

not play games all day; there is a lot of paperwork they have to do, and it is real work. It is also estimated that *over* one-third of all game designers burn out before finishing their first game. This usually happens because they don't start making games with a clearly conceived idea of what it takes to make a game. Don't let these numbers scare you. Just be sure that you like making games before you decide to make it your career.

To learn more about game developers and producers, or simply to study the backgrounds of the various largest game companies in the business today, you can go online and read about them at www.gamedeveloper.com.

Spotlight on Johann Christian Lotter

Johann Christian Lotter is CEO of Conitec and the mastermind behind the 3D GameStudio engine. Here are a few of his replies during a brief interview I had with him.

When did you first get started with Acknex? What inspired you to create the program that became 3D GameStudio? How difficult was the process?

"My inspiration to write 3D software was a ray casting toolkit by Larry Myers that I found on the Internet back in 1994. In fact, the first Acknex engine version was a raycaster. While the current version does not contain any code from the early days, the name Acknex still stems from Larry's toolkit."

What sort of programming or design experience do you possess? How did you get your start into the industry?

"I had no previous programming experience; I was (and still am) working as a circuit designer."

What is the most significant element of using the 3D GameStudio that you feel offers users a unique tool? Is there one feature of the software that stands above the rest? How do you feel the game engine compares with others?

"GameStudio's unique feature is its easy access from a beginner's to an advanced level. You can start doing your first games with no programming at all, and then advance, step by step, first into scripting and, later, programming in C++ and shader language."

If you could tell a future game designer, somebody just looking to start in the industry, one thing—what would that be?

"The first advice I would give a beginner who is about to design his first game is start small!"

What is the future of the 3D GameStudio? Can we expect further versions of the software, and if so will it be competitive with the next-generation graphics available?

"GameStudio will be developed further, and with a bigger programmer crew. The next GameStudio generation will have its focus on easier import from all major 3D editors, new templates for creating more game genres without programming, and support of next-generation graphics hardware."

The Game Design Life Cycle

A game design life cycle is what professionals in the industry call the *development time*, from instance of conception to the release of a modern electronic game. It consists of the following stages:

- Preproduction
- Production
- Postproduction

A game is thought out before it ever reaches development. The preproduction stage is often useful for game design teams to find materials and funding, as it shows publishers and/or investors commitment and creative concept.

The Preproduction Stage

In the preproduction stage, a core team member hatches an idea, and then these steps are followed:

- Game design documentation is drawn up.
- Art direction is finalized.
- Technology and the specific tool set are initiated.
- A playable demo or "proof of concept" is created.
- Funding and/or materials are obtained.

The Production Stage

The production stage is where the game is actually made:

- The team is scaled up to full size.
- The producer sets a production schedule.
- Programmers finalize the technology (that is, the code).
- Artists create the characters, textures, backgrounds, sprites, and items.
- Level designers create the levels and implement the event-triggered missions.

- Sound engineers and composers work on music, sound effects, and voice-overs.
- A playable game is tested by play-testers multiple times to work out bugs.
- Approval is met, and the game is released.

The Postproduction Stage

And finally there is the postproduction stage:

- The game is advertised (usually before Christmas); units are sold and distributed.
- Any foreign support necessary is finalized, language localization is accomplished, and the game is distributed internationally.
- Technical support begins.
- Planning is made by the team for doing sequels, patches, or expansions.

Rating the Game

US senator Charles Schumer has been quoted as saying that video games aimed at today's youth "desensitize them to death and destruction." Yet you can ask anyone in the military if real combat is anything like video games, and they will tell you that they are worlds apart. Dire denouncement by the public about games has become an old political token, and one that few people even react to anymore. For years it has been the same: kids embrace some activity (be it dancing, reading comic books, or listening to rock and roll), adults react negatively, and suddenly moral panic and condemnation ensue. Even with that said, games are not anarchic in nature: they have rules that promote proper censure.

It is often during the production stage that most of the game development takes place, and it is also during this time that most teams seek to get an ESRB rating. The ESRB (or Entertainment Software Rating Board) is an independent game software ethics committee similar in function to the film industry's ratings board. Just as movies are given ratings for content, like PG-13 for a show that a teenager only 13 or older should view, games also have ratings: E for Everyone, T for Teens, M for Mature (17 and older), and AO for Adults Only (see Figure 2.2). You might not have realized that an AO rating existed; this is because very few

ESRB

EARLY CHILDHOOD
Titles rated **EC - (Early Childhood)** have content that may be suitable for ages 3 and older. Contains no material that parents would find inappropriate.

EVERYONE
Titles rated **E (Everyone)** have content that may be suitable for ages 6 and older. Titles in this category may contain minimal cartoon, fantasy or mild violence and/or infrequent use of mild language.

EVERYONE 10+
Titles rated **E 10+ (Everyone 10 and older)** have content that may be suitable for ages 10 and older. Titles in this category may contain more cartoon, fantasy or mild violence, mild language, and/or minimal suggestive themes.

TEEN
Titles rated **T (Teen)** have content that may be suitable for ages 13 and older. Titles in this category may contain violence, suggestive themes, crude humor, minimal blood and/or infrequent use of strong language.

MATURE
Titles rated **M (Mature)** have content that may be suitable for persons ages 17 and older. Titles in this category may contain intense violence, blood and gore, sexual content, and/or strong language.

ADULTS ONLY
Titles rated **AO (Adults Only)** have content that should only be played by persons 18 years and older. Titles in this category may include prolonged scenes of intense violence and/or graphic sexual content and nudity.

Figure 2.2
The ESRB rating system is used to rate game content.

game companies allow their game to go down this route for the simple reason that department stores and retail chains (the distributors) do not purchase units for their shelves. AO games do not sell well. There are no federal mandates saying your game (before it is published) even has to have an ESRB rating—it is still optional. But you need to know that distributors are not likely to buy games that do not have an ESRB rating because it could cost them a lot of money and bad publicity in the end if they did and something went wrong.

The process of getting a rating is short and sweet, but it costs $25,000 every time you go through it. You send in a check or money order for that sum along with a questionnaire covering the basics of content in your game, as well as a demo tape of the most questionable content liable to be found in your game. The ESRB appoints three individuals who have no connection with the game industry, and who preferably don't play those sorts of games, to sit down in a closed panel and review the questionnaire and the demo tape for viability. These individuals are not experts in the game industry, nor are they trained at spotting questionable content; a lot of them have kids, but they also have day jobs as construction workers, teachers, and civil service agents. This is meant to provide a purely "outside-interest" reaction that is sure to be objective. Based on those three peoples' unbiased and individual suggestions, the ESRB then awards a rating for the game.

Figure 2.3
Manhunt (image courtesy of Rockstar North Games 2001)

Many popular developers today have to push to keep their game beneath acceptable levels of content. An AO (Adults Only) game will not be picked up by retail distributors, so the developer must reach an M for Mature rating or lower if they want to sell any units of their merchandise. For instance, when creating the game *Punisher*, the developer Volition Inc. had to send the ESRB review copies and $25,000 up to seven times before their content finally merited an M for Mature rating. Some of the outcry is that too many games are squeaking by at the M for Mature rating. Games like *Manhunt* (see Figure 2.3), *Grand Theft Auto*, and *Postal* have frequently aroused the public's ire.

The recent controversy over video game violence and the ESRB's overall effectiveness are nothing new. The first-ever public harping was in 1976 over Exidy Games' *Death Race*, in which players ran over stick figures representing pedestrians in order to win points. The game—inspired by the 1975 cult film *Death Race 2000* starring David Carradine and a young Sly Stallone—was protested until *60 Minutes* ran a story on it, beginning the national controversy over video game violence.

Recently, indictment proceedings began over Rockstar Game's popular *Grand Theft Auto: San Andreas* for unlockable X-rated material discovered by an independent mod community called Hot Coffee in the PC-platform version of *GTA: San Andreas.* This is unfortunate for the game industry, especially since the topic of concern was spawned by an independent mod community. These communities have always had a fringe pornographic coterie, ever since the first game mod developer discovered he could patch a code into *Tomb Raider* to see Lara Croft naked!

Sex and violence are not the only topics for concern when it comes to "questionable content." Drugs, alcohol, cursing, and general bad behavior are all subject to scrutiny. The game developers and producers have reasons for inclusion of "questionable content." Some of these reasons are artistic license, cathartic release, and player acceptance—but the most prevalent reason is because these games sell lots of copies.

Most games have violence as the central conflict. The reason for this is because it is the easiest to impose on dynamic media content like games. Yet it is the way in which the violence is enacted that has most parents concerned. Some games have the players role-playing as evil creatures or villains, and certain people view this as inconsolable. The uncomfortable fact is that people like taboo and cathartic releases; they also like escapism, and for some individuals these games offer the only way to act out their impulses without consequences. Some of these games allow the player cathartic release but set up consequences (although never as dire as in real life). One game like this, named *Fable*, offers players the choice of doing good deeds or doing evil; the more "good" you become the more you look like an angel, with a halo in white light surrounding you; the more "evil" you become the more you look like a devil, with horns and clouds of flies buzzing around you. In a close study done by G4, there were more players who liked playing evil characters than players who liked being good. What was the number-one answer why? "Because it's more challenging being bad," they would say. "It's just more fun."

Game developers were pleased when a federal court hearing made a precedent that games are to be considered the same as artistic media, and as such, they should be protected under the same rights as freedom of speech. Rockstar North and other controversial developers are protesting that their games are pure art and not to be taken so seriously. Artistic license might protect them and the rest of us for now, but with more adult games coming out all the time, the controversy will not end soon.

The controversy continues today, and some legislators are pushing to remove games from the ESRB and place them in a government-sanctioned censorship board to protect parental ratings of the entertainment products. The ESRB counters that they are doing all they can, and that the ratings are effective as far as ratings go. The ESRB says that the problem lies with parents not knowing what their children are playing. In effect, though retail distributors are not supposed to sell M for Mature games to underage minors, they do so anyway, whether or not parents are present, because of "implied consent." In some states there are even hefty fines being wagered for retail stores that sell these games to minors.

Whatever the cause for public outcry, it will continue as a platform for politicians and Christians to poke holes in the electronic entertainment market. However, it has been beneficial because it has caused a lot of game developers to stop and reconsider the kind of content they are producing in the games that they make. It has also caused the sales of games to rise. At the time of this writing, there are equal sums of two sub-genres profiting from the controversy: Christian games (such as *Eternal War: Shadows of Light* and *Dance Praise*; see Figure 2.4) and ghetto games (such as *50 Percent* and *Getting Up: Contents Under Pressure*). There will always be a market for violent and sexual video games, but they are part of a niche market and not a definition for the game industry as a whole. Keep this in mind and try keeping your games clean. It may save you $25,000 somewhere in the near future.

For more information about the ESRB and the ratings systems in place for games, go to their Web site www.esrb.org.

Figure 2.4
Dance Praise (image courtesy Digital Praise, Inc. 2005–2006)

Development Management

Historically game design has been a loose, organic approach with very little structure to it. In fact, the very first game from Sierra Online was made sitting at the kitchen table for the first Apple II computers. In a dream world, game design teams would have every aspect of project management worked out well ahead of time and perform competently on deadline. This invariably never happens. Yet there is method in the madness, and the modern design teams are starting to produce on tighter schedules and with more formal organization. We will look at the various methods of how game development is managed.

Organic Process

Developers eschew formal process and continue to evolve the design of the game over the entire course of development, sometimes called *watershed* development. New ideas and game features are experimented with and implemented at *any time* during the course of development, and the game design documentation remains fluid. In the organic process, there is no clear demarcation between the preproduction and production stages of the game design life cycle.

Rapid Iterative Prototyping

Perhaps one of the best methods for its overall efficiency is the *adaptive software development* or *rapid iterative prototyping* in which the game development again is very fluid: any new idea is added as quickly as possible and then polished later. The polishing is based on what works, what does not work, and what is a priority to change. This process is flag-shipped by industry legend Sid Meier, who believes that getting a game concept or kernel up and running as soon as possible (even using stick-figure graphics) is important to show game publishers that your Killer Game Concept can work—and (most importantly) will work!

Vertical Slice Process

Publishers and investors prefer to see the "proof in the pudding." They prefer design teams using the newer vertical slice process of game design. This process has a very clear-cut preproduction phase, characterized by the creation of a fully featured playable game demo or prototype for the finished game. New features and ideas for the game are put to a committee and usually not introduced after the production stage starts, as it has been shown to slow down development schedule dates (this is the bad habit formally mentioned called "feature creep").

If any new feature or change is made in the game after production has started, then a whole new game design document is written and the old one is shredded.

The Cerny Method

There is a third method—actually a compromise between the organic process and the vertical slice process—outlined by Mark Cerny of SEGA and Atari. It is known in the industry as the Cerny Method. In it, Cerny advises throwing away 80 percent of your work and keeping the best 20 percent for the most entertaining content. So if you have built 10 game levels, you choose the best two and delete the other eight. He says there should be no clear preproduction phase, but that a game demo should be the first thing built. The game demo forms a makeshift game design document so that a clear blueprint is not really needed. He also states that a new game feature can be added at any time, and the game can be altered in any way without controversy. But if it looks as if the new development will be a waste of time, the entire project is scrapped to save money. Because the Cerny Method is a boon to some alternative game developers and a headache to others, it is still being debated.

In Summary

The development life cycle of a game can be short or long, depending on the size and complexity of the game in development. Scope is one of the biggest controversies in game development, and it has been known to make or break deadlines. Oftentimes, a game designer does not take into account the scope of his game (how big it is, how many levels, how many choices or challenges the player might have, and so on), and if the scope grows bigger than the designer anticipates, the game will not meet its deadline. Design companies that consistently meet their release dates (as the developers of *Halo* have always done; see Figure 2.5) satisfy the market and publishers, whereas "feature creep" or poor management choices can upset the market and cause publishers to doubt a company's sincerity in the future.

What You Have Learned

Games are not whimsical devices smart people just "make." They take a lot of additional management and work.

Figure 2.5
Halo 2 (image courtesy Bungie Software 2004)

- You now know that there are developers and publishers.
- You know the different types of developers.
- You have learned the game design life cycle.
- You have learned what it takes for preproduction.
- You have learned what it takes for production.
- You have learned what it takes for postproduction.
- You know a lot more about game censorship and the ESRB ratings.
- You have learned the most prevalent game development processes.

For Review

1. What was the very first game that you ever played, and what was it that appealed to you? Can you imagine that game being remade or given better features or digital graphics? Would it be a better game today? Why or why not?
2. Play a vintage video game, preferably one of the old arcade types. You can find several of these remade online in Flash, or you could play a ROM version on an emulator for educational purposes. (Some examples would be

Super Mario Bros., *Donkey Kong*, *Castlevania*, *Pitfall*, and *Centipede*.) What do you play? Do you actually have a character? What is the level of graphics and how do they compare with today's next-generation gaming technologies? How is the user interface laid out? How do sound effects reflect what is going on? Is the game fun to play?

3. Who are some of the individuals and electronics companies that have been around the longest or made the most significant improvements on the gaming industry? Why have they succeeded while others have failed? How could you apply this knowledge to your own work as a designer?
4. Research and analyze a U.S. or overseas company that is currently involved as a game developer. What are they called? What sorts of games do they make? How did they get their start? What marketing strategies or business model do they use that is successful? What are their current news and events? Do you think they are going to be around for a while?
5. Consider the many types of development strategies (the organic process, the vertical slice, the Cerny Method, and so on). Which would you prefer to use? What if you were running a team of 25 individual developers? What about 100? What are the pros and cons of the different development strategies?
6. Go online to the ESRB's Web site and review their ratings system and the information for parental control there. Do you think that the ESRB ratings system works well for gaming media? Would you do it any differently? Would you add a new rating, or do you think one of theirs does not apply?

What Makes a Great Game?

An electronic game is not unlike other entertainment media adaptations: it must tell an interesting story, it must be visually interesting to watch, and it must draw on the audience's emotions. Yet an electronic game has one thing books and film do not: it is interactive. Players do not consistently move from Point A to Point B like plodding slobs: they are given multiple choices along the way, and they are satisfied when making up their own solutions to problems and having their actions reward them with immediate and lasting consequences in the game.

If you don't understand the process of interactive storytelling, the most rewarding education you can receive is to read a Choose-Your-Own Adventure book or Fighting Fantasy novel. These are examples of interactive fiction. These books can still be found in public and school libraries, mostly marketed toward juveniles. I personally have fond memories for them, my favorite being the Lone Wolf fantasy series by Joe Dever (see Figure 2.6). If you have never opened one, you can find a sampling of them for free online at ProjectAon.org.

In these books, you do not read from start to finish, page after page. The writers do not spend a lot of time on character detail or back story; instead they hit the ground running, allowing the reader to collaborate to tell the narrative. You get to the end of Page 1, and the writer poses the reader with several options, such as, "To enter the right-hand tunnel, turn to Page 33; to leave by the wooden door, turn to Page 102." The paths that the reader chooses will wend him from page to page, skipping several in between, so when the reader picks the book up a second time and makes a different decision, it is a totally different reading experience.

There are also several online interactive fiction sites for adults and special software programs like Game Book Player that allow you to make and share your own interactive narratives. The wonderful reason that I admire these early novels is that they were pioneering games that grew simultaneously with the tabletop pen-and-paper games, such as Dungeons and Dragons, and they taught me a lot about how a game narrative is told.

Figure 2.6
Lone Wolf game book series written by Joe Dever, American edition

You could sit and read a book about espionage, and it would go something like this:

> Daphne looked at the high-rise and realized the only way to get inside would be the roof. That night she cut a hole through glass in a fifteenth-story window and slipped through, dressed in black Lycra. She proceeded down the corridor and hid behind suits of armor as security guards slipped by....

This may seem interesting, but imagine the possibilities when you add interaction.

> You play as Daphne. You walk around the outside of a building, studying it for a way in. If you use your binoculars, you will sight a ladder leading up the building next door to the roof, which runs parallel with the fifteenth story of the building you need to get into. You show up that night after getting the gear you need, and you have your choice of slipping through a window using stealth or blasting the window out with a shotgun and dashing in as fast as you can, leaving a trail of death in your wake. Or—if you did not use the binoculars to start with—you might walk up to the front door, where you would learn there was a tour starting for new employees, and you invite yourself in by stealing some member's badge. You pretend to be a new employee for a while, until you can casually slip away from the group to the bathroom, change your clothes and slide into the air vents to take your own (sneaky) tour of the building....

This second example has a lot more excitement to it; it's fresh—and the reason it is fresh is because you are inviting the player to collaborate in telling the story. You give the player room for exploration, decision-making, and co-storytelling. You are not limiting the direction that the story goes, and you are adding to the player's creativity and sense of wonder. This player interaction makes the game media much more intimate than any other media. In some games, players can actually choose what they want their player character to look like, what abilities they want their character to have, and what their character is called. This intimacy means that the player of a game is much more interested in the outcome of the game, having a direct emotional link that is practically non-existent in fiction, film, or portraits.

Player choice frames the structure of a great game, but it is the substance of that game that will make it or break it. Great games are ones that players tell their friends, co-workers, and family about. Great games have more clout and sell more units in the retail market. Great games have a lasting impact on the behavior of society. It takes no genius to figure out that a game will give players choices, but it takes a more complex nature to understand the substance of great games. We will look now at the substance that makes these games great, and how you can accomplish the same thing.

The Four Fs of Great Game Design

Game industries employ thousands of testers and researchers and spend practically millions of dollars a year in market research to determine what makes a great game. I have a specific formula of what makes a great game. There are Four Fs of Great Game Design (4FOGGD) which must always be present for any game to be great. The Four Fs cannot exist without one another. They are listed here in their order of priority. When I speak of priority, I mean that if a conflict of interests should arise during the development phase of your game, you should always abide by what takes priority in the list.

FUN–FAIRNESS–FEEDBACK–FEASIBILITY

Fun

Games are intended to be fun. Fun is a word synonymous with games. Fun is a simple word, it is easy to spell, and it is innate. Even the smallest child will begin to invent his or her personal game, and the purpose behind this instinct is to escape ennui. Children may count cracks in sidewalks, see how many funny looks it takes to get their parents to laugh, or play with things they are not supposed to. (This last one happens even with adults and forms the motivation behind playing taboo games, such as *Grand Theft Auto: San Andreas.*) The complexity and character of people's games evolve with their age and mental understanding. A game that outreaches a participant's age or understanding will quickly tire the participant and leave her bored. A boring game that is no fun is no game at all.

Give players a fun, fresh, and original experience—one that is sure to encourage replaying and word-of-mouth advertisement. The main rule of thumb is to get people's attention. If your game is offbeat, offers cathartic release, or is irreverent, it will get played. Make players excited about the options you give them in your game. We will look at these options later when we cover puzzles, but always remember that if your choices are unnecessary or stale, the game will lack the luster it needs. Always beware of tedium! Tedium (especially Tedium with a capital T, caused by boring repetitive gameplay) is the Fun Killer. The whole purpose of a game, by its very definition, is fun.

Making your own games can be a humungous power trip. You will notice as you go along that you will be on an ego trip yourself. But I want to caution you before you even get started: don't fall into pride and presumption because these sorts of hubris can kill a Killer Game Concept. The bigger the power trip, the more mind-numbing mazes you start throwing at your players and expecting them to understand where you are going with it. Players will get frustrated; they will consider you a mean master and your game a complete bore. So put yourself in your players' shoes every step of the way, and keep your game fun.

Note

"Good games are good for you. Fun is a vitamin for the mind, essential nourishment for your intellect."

—Dan Bunten with Heidi E. H. Aycock

Fairness

Avoid frustration. Frustration can be a healthy motivator, challenging certain players to achieve greater heights for themselves, but frustration can also lead to anger or worse: Tedium (see the previous section "Fun"). Angry players of electronic games are prone to throwing their video game controllers or beating the computer keyboard, neither of which are conducive to a great game. When designing your game, always remember there are three types of gamers that will be playing a game: casual gamers, who don't often play these games and might find the controls or rules system hard enough without having to jump through too many hoops; average gamers, who are fairly proficient players; and expert gamers, who always play the really difficult levels and still wonder where to find the next hidden Easter egg. Do not force players to repeat complicated moves in the game or learn their lesson by seeing their character die over and over again. Don't kill their characters off suddenly or inexplicably without giving them a heads-up as to why. Provide multiple or universal save points, so players do not have to backtrack or repeat steps. Avoid meaningless repetition, and help the player out.

Duane Alan Hahn (game aficionado) says, "Play is supposed to be the opposite of work, but most video games are just jobs with a little bit of fun thrown in. These games can leave players feeling abused, frustrated, and overly aggressive.... Your game can either irritate or alleviate. Which would you rather do?" These are all good reasons why you should promote Fairness to number two on the list of most important ingredients of any game. Balance is the key to proper fairness. Never shirk from your duty as the designer because in a game you often have complete control over the balance. For example, in *Super Mario Kart* (see Figure 2.7) there is a subtle shifting of balance so that the game appears challenging enough for the player: the computer-controlled racers speed up when they lag behind you, and they slow down when they are way out ahead of you so that

Figure 2.7
Mario Kart: Double Dash (image courtesy of Nintendo 2003)

you—as the player—always think there is a way to beat the game. A designer could program those other racers to be so fast and so smart they'd beat you every single time, but where would the fun be in that?

Feedback

If the player does something right, show him so: give the player a Twinkie! (See Figure 2.8.) If the player does something degenerately stupid, show them that it was wrong to try that particular action: punish them. A game is all about pushing the player's buttons; a game world is little better than a Skinner Box, and if you know anything about psychology you will do fine in the game industry. However, there are two critical rules of thumb to punishments and rewards.

First, you should have your punishments and rewards fit the actions and environment, and be consistent with your use of them: if the player always gets a higher score for grabbing purple jellyfish, and he grabs a purple jellyfish and his score is suddenly lowered—that player will become irate and wonder what sort of mean trick you are playing on him!

Next, you should make your punishments and rewards immediate so the player gets the gist of causal relationships. For instance, if your player has his character walk on lava, the lava should burn the player's character. Similarly, jumping off a precipice and falling five stories should hurt. And beating up the bully should get the player character a kiss from the beautiful damsel he was attempting to rescue.

Figure 2.8
Give the player a Twinkie! (Image courtesy of Hostess Foods)

Instructor Robert T. Kiyosaki began teaching using classroom simulations and games in 1984. He says, "I always encouraged adult students to look at games as reflecting back to what they know and what they needed to learn. Most importantly, a game reflects back on one's behavior. It's an instant feedback system. Instead of the teacher lecturing you, the game is feeding back a personalized lecture, custom made just for you." A player is eager to know that they do something right or wrong so they can adjust their play style and master the game. They listen for the bells and whistles to instruct them in how to play better. You can use this knowledge to your advantage by creating a greater game.

Feasibility

Encourage player immersion whenever you can. To this end, you must avoid inconsistencies and a little terror called "feature creep." Feature creep comes about when a game designer is too close to the project and begins adding "neat features" that really add nothing to the game or do not fit with the original game concept. For instance, if a somber horror game about mutants suddenly introduces to the player a switch that, if he pulls it, drops a bunch of brightly colored soda pop machines out of the ceiling to squash all the mutants, the game has choked: this fun little feature has destroyed the original concept and the player's anticipations of the game being a serious horror game. A good rule of thumb is to develop and stick with a written game design document, which is sort of like a blueprint for your game. Game design teams that stray overly far from their original game outlines find themselves wasting production time and encouraging feature creep.

Keep your games simple. "I would say simplicity is a key factor in any good game design," Thorolfur Beck comments. "Simplicity in interface, game systems, etc. . . .

Simplicity does not have to mean few possibilities (just look at chess), but creating a real good, well-balanced, simple game system is a much harder task than creating a very complex one." Players are notorious for loading up a game and playing it; they hate to be bothered with reading the game manual or having to look up a walk-through guide online. If a player has to use a walk-through and every available cheat code to get through your game with his character alive, you have not done your job. If the player consistently feels lost and frustrated, you have failed to make a great game. As Atari veteran Mark Cerny puts it, "Keep the rules of the game simple. Ideally, first-time players should understand and enjoy the game without instructions."

While you keep things simple, you might want to consider keeping your game flexible because "the next generation is really about choice, and emergence, and continuous experience. It's not about individual levels." Ken Levine, in an interview about Irrational Games' upcoming game *BioShock* (see Figure 2.9), told people, "We want to make a game where a walk-through is useless. That's where games need to go. . . . I'd much rather play a game where I can say 'Oh, I had this experience,' and someone else can say, 'I did that part in a totally different way.' It's about thinking of different opportunities for every play style, and making it interesting for each of them."

Note

"If you take away the fancy graphics of today's games, most of the time you're left with a shell of a game that has been done to death a million times."

—Leonard Herman

Figure 2.9
BioShock (image courtesy of Irrational Games 2006)

I do want to take time to note that, like the planets in our solar system, these Four Fs have a planet/not-so-planet named Pluto that exists on the outer rim; this Fifth F is one that desperately wants to be one of the 4FOGGD (and it is one that developers strive for every time), but because it is not analogous with all games, I could not include it. This Fifth F is Freshness: players don't like to be treated to rehashed games and clones of other games, but it happens; occasionally a new game title will break the ice and sail uncharted waters. Some examples of this include *Grand Theft Auto*, *Doom*, *Prince of Persia*, *Thief*, *Fable*, and *Elder Scrolls: Oblivion*; these are games that—when they first came out on the market—were unique, innovative, controversial (some of them), and offered entirely new game mechanics or ways to play games.

Freshness is not an essential ingredient for creating new games, however. It is a market drive and a potential tool, but great games can hark back to retro years (like the many *Pong* clones still popular today), they can be traditional games (like Texas hold 'em poker), or they can simply be comfortable genre games (there will always be more room for fantasy role-playing games and survival horror games). Yet you will hear a lot of gamers complain about the "Same Old Stuff Syndrome" or SOS Syndrome. But don't worry about it too much right now; just remember to make your games great, not tolerable.

Continue reading, but as you go through the exercises remember the Four Fs of Great Game Design and consider the prospects of each vital ingredient and how it weighs in your decisions. This formula just might save your game!

Game Genres

Game media, being fairly recent, did not originate in a vacuum. It sprang from other media, and so borrows on their categorization by genre typing. In books, movies, and television, genres are distinguished from each other by their subject matter—such as science fiction, fantasy, horror, western, mystery, comedy, and romance. Subject matter is vital to games because the fiction genres appeal to different players. If someone likes horror games, for instance, they will probably play all the horror games they can get their hands on. On the other hand, it is the types of challenges that games offer that distinguish their genre. This distinguishing feature is the *gameplay*.

You must realize that game genre boundaries are still fuzzy. Many games take part in more than one style of gameplay. While this adds broader interest to the experience, it is risky: you run the risk of alienating fans of either genre who are not interested in the new mix of elements. For example, think of the game *Darkwatch*: here you have a horror Western game with a mixture of first- and third-person action. The design team was inspired by the tabletop game Deadlands, but this was still a risky game move on their part. They took the chance that fans of Westerns would hate it and that fans of horror would be turned off by the Western atmosphere. Ideally, the game was targeted at a niche market of people who liked the hybrid genre, like fans of Stephen King's *Gunslinger* trilogy. It paid off in the end for them, but their sales did not reach astronomical projections.

To describe a game's genre appropriately, you must include three basic principles: 1) fiction genre, 2) gameplay type, and 3) playing perspective (a.k.a. point of view or POV). The following are the most common gameplay types (as indicated by genre).

Action Game

This is the oldest of all video game genres and still represents a large portion of the market. In 2005, ESA reported that action games comprised 30 percent of the games sold in the U.S. Most commonly referred to as a "shooter" or FPS (first-person shooter), these games are based around the player's ability to master hand-eye coordination skills in a variety of challenges, such as speed, precision, timing, and aim. The player moves his character through each level, shooting at enemies. These enemies are multitudinous, and so the player has options like upgrading weapons, finding ammunitions, and developing military strategy. Great action games should have good level design with lots of corners players cannot see around, appropriate variations on weapons, surprises around every turn, and smart enemies that make the experience more difficult and therefore more fun. Examples include *Quake*, *Doom*, *Hexen*, *Wolfenstein*, *Duke Nukem*, *Serious Sam*, *Medal of Honor*, *Call of Duty*, *Half-Life*, *Call of Cthulhu*, and *F.E.A.R.*, to name just a few.

3D GameStudio is by default an action game system: if you plug together a level and add the template scripts, you will have an action game similar to *Quake*. There are spaces for weapons, which the player can cycle through, medical kits to improve health, ammo for weapons, and standard AI, as well as path-finding AI enemies. You wouldn't even need to alter the code, unless you wanted to program in better enemy interactions or better explosions. This is the first genre of game we are going to look at making using the 3D GameStudio. We will look closer at the making of a great action game in Part II.

Adventure Game

Adventure games evolved from the two-word combination text parser games of the 1960s and 1970s, the most popular of which was *Zork*. They are about exploring a world and experiencing a story, usually by solving a variety of puzzles. Adventure games do not require action, strategy, or management skills. They move at a slower pace, have better stories, and often include beautiful scenery. *Fahrenheit: Indigo Prophecy* (see Figure 2.10) and *Dreamfall* are adventure games that are sweeping the stage today, changing the style in which adventure games are made by adding tension and suspense through time-based challenges. Interactive story games usually give players the ability to interact limitedly with their environments through a point-and-click interface. Players search for clues, talk to non-player characters (commonly called NPCs), and explore their way from one area to the next until they complete the story. Great adventure games should have the following: powerful storytelling with unique twists and player decision-making that offers multiple endings; obvious puzzles and detective work, often involving inventory items and dialog with NPCs; and awesome artwork to hide the slow pacing and redundant quests.

Examples of these include *Zork*, *Colossal Cave*, *Secret of Monkey Island*, *Myst*, *The Longest Journey*, *Siberia*, *Clue: Fatal Illusion*, *Still Life*, *Legend of the Broken Sword*, *Gabriel Knight*, *Grim Fandango*, and *Maniac Mansion*.

Although, ostensibly, 3DGS can be used to design 3D adventure games (and once you have learned how to do it the process becomes simple), you might consider

Figure 2.10
Fahrenheit: Indigo Prophecy (image courtesy of Quantic Dream 2005)

that the original adventure games are actually made in 2D using pre-rendered backdrops created from 3D applications. You could use 3DGS to create the backdrops, take screenshots, and put them together in a game authoring software program exclusively made for adventure games, such as the popular Adventure GameStudio or Winter Mute Engine. Or you could use the principles of 3D adventure design to make a game like *Fahrenheit: Indigo Prophecy*.

Platformer (Arcade Game)

What used to be called a *sidescroller* (because the background would scroll from one side to the other), a *platformer* is among the oldest vintage gameplay types around. These games are known for their simple complexity: players must traverse from the left side of the screen to the right or from the top to the bottom, while avoiding hazardous obstacles. They must use fast-paced timing to jump and run across moving platforms, wide chasms, and other exaggeratedly difficult terrain. Often they will have enemies that need to be avoided or defeated, but if they do, the enemies almost become another obstacle among the terrain instead of the complicated AI found in first-person shooters. The most well-known examples of these games are *Metroid*, *Crash Bandicoot*, *Sonic the Hedgehog*, and *Super Mario Bros.* 1996 ushered in a much more popular variant today called the 3D platformer: games like *Super Mario Sunshine*, *Spyro the Dragon*, *Jak and Daxter*, *Ratchet and Clank* (see Figure 2.11), *Malice*, *Tak 2: the Staff of Dreams*, the remake of *Prince of Persia*, and the *God of War* game.

Figure 2.11
Ratchet and Clank: Going Commando (image courtesy of Insomniac Games 2003)

3DGS comes with template scripts for physical objects, like elevators and moving platforms, and you can learn to code other bits, like lava or tar pits and terrain obstacles. Technically, 3DGS can be used to create a 3D platformer of your very own. However, it is one of the more demanding game creations you can make because you are forced to take very close measurements of all your steps, gaps, and tangents so that the levels are playable and challenging without being impossible. Also, no one has yet programmed a realistic long jump and climbing routine for 3DGS (although it is certainly not impossible).

Action-Adventure Hybrid

A combination of the shoot-'em-up, the fighting game, the platformer, and the puzzle-solving adventure game, action-adventure hybrids originated with *Tomb Raider* but now form a vast contingent of the best-selling games turning out every year. These games simply share the best of their gameplay types: they have fast-paced timing, hazardous obstacles, hand-to-hand as well as ranged combat, clues to sort through and solve puzzles, inventory items to pick up (besides health and ammo), and tough enemies (with complex AI) to beat around every corner. Sometimes they will also have bits of stealth games or simulations built in as well, which earns them the title of "hybrid."

Role-Playing Game (RPG)

By definition, a role-playing game is any game where the player takes on the role of another person and in doing so goes on various missions. This could practically describe all video games today because the player has an onscreen avatar he plays as. But RPGs are very different. Computer RPGs are an outgrowth of pen-and-paper RPGs that were started by Gary Gygax and his Dungeons and Dragons—and many of them still duplicate the dice-rolling and skill-definition mechanisms. The primary appeal of RPGs is in customizing and equipping an avatar character, taking that character out into the virtual landscape, having adventures, and increasing its skills, strength, wealth, and (sometimes) glory through experience. The downside is that RPGs have been typified by classic quest-driven fantasy games where players beat monsters and get treasure in order to beat tougher monsters and get better treasure. Players complain that they feel more like itinerate second-hand arms dealers, always looting corpses, breaking into treasure chests, and trading with shopkeepers. This has caused hecklers to call such games "monty-haul" or "hack-and-slash" games. Fresh innovative

Figure 2.12
Fable: The Lost Chapters (image courtesy of Lionhead Studios 2005)

RPGs like *Vampire: Bloodlines*, *City of Heroes*, and *Fable* (see Figure 2.12) are challenging the dichotomy. It is time to break with the "monty-haul" traditions.

Great RPGs should have the following: a beginning character who grows into a hero through the game by taking many story-based quests and gaining experience; easy micromanagement of the character's mechanical details and inventory items; hack-and-slash melee combat that is fast or turn-based or some unique hybrid of the two; a strong mythology basis, featuring classic heroic archetypes; and a magical world and system for casting spells or using super powers. Examples of these include *Bard's Tale, Final Fantasy, Chrono Trigger, Baldur Gate, Planescape Torment, Icewind Dale, Diablo, Might and Magic, City of Heroes*, and *Fable.*

The A4 and A5 3DGS came with an RPG demo called *Adeptus. Adeptus* shows you how the 3DGS can be used to make Morrowind-like 3D RPGs. I have used a lot of the original code from *Adeptus* to demonstrate in the exercises how to turn the template scripts into an RPG of your very own. It will be the last game genre I show you how to make in this book.

Strategy Game

Strategy games include both Turn-Based Strategy (TBS) and Real-Time Strategy (RTS) games. TBS games test the player's ability to think ahead and anticipate an opponent's actions. An RTS game involves planning and resource management on a major scale. Players have control of whole armies, similar to old-fashioned war gaming hobbies. They must organize their resources, execute proper actions, and do it all within time limitations. Great strategy games should have the following: well-balanced resources (such as gold and ore mines or numbers of archers) that the player has to manage, multiple teams with an equal choice of winning, a convincing AI for opposing teams, and varied missions for strategy and success. Examples include *Age of Empires, Command and Conquer, Heroes of Might and Magic, World of Warcraft, Colossus, Warhammer,* and *Starcraft.*

Strategy games are not impossible to make with 3DGS, but they are very taxing. We will not go into the ways of doing so in this book. You are free, however, to try it on your own. Simply being able to design RTS games in 3DGS is a testament of its flexibility.

Stealth Game

A rather new style of video game that originated with *Thief* and has expanded to the *Hitman* games is a gameplay type focused on stealth and sabotage. After *Thief* was released, countless clones cropped up, and today lots of games have some stealth feature built right in (such as the action-adventure games *Metal Gear Solid* and *Splinter Cell*). However, there are still games (such as *Hitman: Blood Money* and the *Sly Cooper* series; see Figure 2.13) that are primarily stealth games. In them, the player is usually a sneak-thief, assassin, or pickpocket and must crawl

Figure 2.13
Sly Cooper (image courtesy of Sucker Punch Productions 2002–2006)

slowly through shadows and flatten themselves against walls to look around corners. This is the one genre that is slower than most (even the adventure games they can resemble) because the player must have quite a bit of patience hiding in the darkness and sneaking up on guards. Great stealth games should include lots of contrasting light-and-dark areas that the player can use strategically to hide in; sneak attacks, such as tranquilizer darts or garroting; and lots of wandering guards to avoid.

I will show you how to make a stealth program for your RPG in 3D GameStudio in one of the later exercises. You can expand on this and make an entire stealth game, if you wish. Stealth games still have a growing fan base.

Simulation

The definition of a simulation is "a quasi-realistic simulation of life." Popular simulations include driving race cars (as in *San Francisco Rush* and *Need for Speed*), piloting aircraft or spacecraft, and running small businesses (as in *Diner Dash*). The player must think logically and act as if the game were real. Simulations offer players wish fulfillment by providing interesting role-playing, but they must always form a compromise between realism and casual fun. When a simulation gets too "real," players tend to tune out and turn it off, but when realistic simulations offer additional quirks, options, or fun camera focuses, then players get excited.

One of the most-applauded games ever created using the 3DGS game authoring software was a German driving school simulator, and it remains a fantastic example of the technological prowess of the engine.

Sports Game

Sports games are simulations of athletic competition, where the player wins or loses on the field. Great sports games have the following: realistic motion-captured animation; moves that follow realistic physics; game rules that follow official athletic competitions; referees, cheering crowds, announcers, and those other little touches that make the sport more realistic. Most sports games have very straight-forward internal economy, and so we will not study them in any great detail here. They are rather difficult to make and best left to those people who are sports enthusiasts as well as avid programmers; I am not, therefore, I will not spend a lot of time focusing on them.

Fighting Game

A duke-'em-out arcade classic, the fighting game is where the player competes against other contenders in a virtual arena or ring. Using combination attacks and devastating blows, the player tries to get his opponent down before he loses his own health. Some games that resemble fighting games feature an open arena, like a city block, where your player character has to mow down countless oncoming enemies before moving to the next level (such as *Gungrave*). Great fighting games have the following: a set of stylized characters to choose from, fluid motion-capture (or "mo-cap") animation moves, a smart system of controls, great sound effects, and a heroic victory pose or sequence. Examples include *Mortal Kombat*, *Street Fighter*, *Soul Caliber*, *Tekken*, *Double Dragon*, *Dead or Alive*, and (to a certain extent) games like *Devil May Cry* and *Onimusha.*

I will cover melee combat in RPG development in 3DGS later on, but I will not specifically show you how to make a fighting game. There is, if you are interested, a complete tutorial with the resource files necessary to make a fighting game available online at the Web site for 3D GameStudio.

Construction and Management Simulations (CMS)

An open-ended software toy where the player virtually gets to play God and design his or her own little world, a CMS game is very much like a sandbox with lots of neat building and management tools. These games are about building something and managing some process at the same time. Popular CMS games include *The Sims*, *Rollercoaster Tycoon*, *GhostMaster*, and *Spore.* Great CMS games should have the following: no pre-set win-or-lose condition, an easy-to-learn interface, and open-ended entertainment created by combining and managing the virtual world's building blocks.

Like the strategy games, 3D GameStudio is capable of providing the needed tools for you to develop a Construction and Management Simulation game (there are even some on their company's Web site for you to preview)—and the collision detection and Newton physics make it even easier—but the process for coding one is not recommended for beginners and will not be included in any of the exercises. However, you are free to try it on your own.

Casual Game

Classic games of leisure, such as Solitaire, Parcheesi, chess, *Tetris*, mah-jongg, trivia, and more, have become best-selling electronic games because they are easy for the player to learn and adapt to, while being short enough to be played in a single sitting. The most frequently played computer game in the world is Solitaire, which ships free with Microsoft Windows. Vast numbers of people also play real-world games, like Texas hold-'em poker, checkers, rummy, backgammon, and others over the Internet through game portals. A few games, often called trivia games, imitate the feeling of television game shows. *Who Wants to be a Millionaire?* and *Jeopardy* are good examples. Casual games are time-fillers that appeal to people of all ages and walks of life. Even ex-president Bill Clinton was known to be addicted to *Bejeweled.*

Online Game

While any Internet-connected game is ostensibly an online game, some are intended for multiple players at once and are referred to by those in the business as Massive Multiplayer Online games (or MMOs). Historically, the advent of regular public access to the Internet impacted gaming—spawning non-professional MUDs throughout the 1970s and 1980s. Though primarily text-based, MUDs were the first online representation of RPGs, but they added instant access to games anytime, anywhere, anonymity playing, and virtual freedom. Today MMOs are more graphical and make for huge online communities, fulfilling players' needs to socialize and build bases, and sponsorship of these games and their Web services are a billion-dollar business. Games like *Neopets* (www.neopets.com), *Dofus* (www.dofus.com; see Figure 2.14), and *Habbo* (www.habbo.com) are giant hubs popular today.

Figure 2.14
Dofus (image courtesy of Ankama Studios 2006)

3D GameStudio has editions that make it easier to develop networked and online games, but because you might not have those editions (and because it is more difficult to program them) we will not spend time developing an online game. There are resources on the 3DGS Web site if you are interested in learning more.

Survival Horror Game

Survival horror is a rising gameplay type in which the player has to survive an onslaught of undead or supernatural opponents, typically in claustrophobic environments filled with horror movie elements. The player is usually armed (but not as well-armed as the player of a shooter). The player's goal is generally to escape from an isolated location that is infested by monsters through puzzle-solving and fight-or-flight situations. Survival horror is possibly the only video game genre defined by theme rather than gameplay, and if so it might be a trend that will encompass other themes in the future. From the mechanics described above, the genre sounds like a typical adventure game, but it is also home to fighting games (such as *Nightmare Creatures*), RPGs (*Parasite Eve*), and action/shooters (*Call of Cthulhu: Dark Corners of the Earth*; see Figure 2.15). It is personally one of my favorite game genres.

Figure 2.15
Call of Cthulhu: Dark Corners of the Earth (image courtesy Bethesda Softworks 2005–2006)

Some Lesser-Known Genres

There are some gameplay types that do not get as much limelight as the ones we've talked about so far. They remain in the shadows, not for want of gameplay at all but probably due to their limited description.

- **Artificial life (A-life) games** are about caring for virtual pets. In some cases, such as *Petz* and *Creatures,* the player cares for a number of creatures with a long or even indefinite life span. In other games, creatures have a short life span but reproduce rapidly, enabling the player to breed and mutate them, manipulating the population. *Neopets* and *Nintendogs* are popular examples of a game that incorporates small creatures into interactive and online games, and the niche audience can sometimes be kept up at night worrying about their make-believe animals.
- **Puzzle games** are usually collections of somewhat abstract puzzles based around a certain theme. Puzzle games are distinct from adventure games in that they don't have a story, and they aren't elements of an imaginary world. Most game designers don't pay much attention to these games because they don't offer the same opportunities for creativity that other genres do, but there is a lot of money in the making of such games.
- **Edutainment** is a vast category of serious games that is becoming a market within a market today. Games used to train soldiers for the U.S. Army, games used to define skills for corporations, and games used to teach children their ABCs are all a part of the growing serious game field that got its start in the 1980s with games like *Oregon Trail* and *Reader Rabbit.* These games often have a clearly delineated age group, a simple interface, and an engaging plethora of challenges suitable for their audience. For more information about serious games, you might pick up the book *Serious Games: Games That Educate, Train, and Inform* by David Michael and Sande Chen (Course Technology PTR, 2005), because it really is a progressive new sub-development of the huge game industry.
- **Advertainment** are games that advertise a specific product or company at the same time as entertaining or providing escapism for gamers. Most of the advertainment games that you see are online Flash games located on company Web sites, such as the *Esuvee Challenge* or *Boomerang Grill.* One of the best sites for providing advertainment—as well as setting up community activities—is Joe Boxer's commercial site. If you advertise your services as a

game developer on places like Guru.com, the majority of the proposals you will get from clients is for advertainment. So keep in mind that, though these games can be limited and unexciting to make sometimes, they can provide a steady income for a budding designer.

Playing Perspective

A game genre is not complete without another principle, called *playing perspective*. This is also called point of view (or POV) as in the development of fiction stories. In film, cinematographers have to arrange the composition of all their shots to tell the story, but games utilize cameras—or floating eyes—to witness all the action in the game. The position of these cameras (fixed or not) defines the POV. The following are the most common playing perspectives seen in games today.

First-Person

The approved choice of 3D shooters, first-person perspective enhances the sensory immersion of a game by putting the player in the shoes of the character he is playing. He sees through the eyes of his character, and usually the only part of the player's character that he can see is the hand holding the gun out in front of him. It is important to remember when designing a game for first-person POV that the player will start to think they *are* the avatar character, so cut-scenes that suddenly show them their character or asides where a particularly grating voiceover supposed to belong to their character will take away the player's suspension of disbelief and (worst-case scenario) cause frustration. This POV was successfully used in the Humphrey Bogart film *Dark Passage*, where the first part of the film is seen from Bogart's viewpoint until the bandages are removed from his head and the camera cuts to third-person perspective for the first time.

Third-Person

The third-person perspective is much more cinematic and immediate. The player can see his character on the screen and watch every move he makes. This leads to a greater identification with the player character and greater world immersion. The only restriction is that the character is always on screen, and often seen from behind, so the 3D model must be interesting to look at without having so many polygons that it slows down processors. The demands on modeling a perfect-looking character are getting higher every day, and the avatar is often marketed as a "movie star." Mario from *Mario 64* and Lara Croft from *Tomb Raider* became the first game icons and representatives of their gameplay. There are times you will hear the third-person camera mode referred to as the *chase camera*.

Top-Down (Aerial View)

This is a view looking straight down at the playing field. This perspective is most often seen in games like Solitaire or the early *Ultima*. It limits the horizon for the player, so she has a harder time seeing what obstacles might be coming up, but it does add greater detail to what is on the surrounding map. *Grand Theft Auto* began as a vintage 8-bit top-down game, and to this day in all their versions, no matter how fancy and 3D they get, they offer players a top-down playing perspective if they wish it in homage.

Isometric

This is the favored tilted "three-quarter" view hovering off to one side, exhibited in *Diablo, Baldur's Gate,* and *Planescape: Torment* (see Figure 2.16). This perspective is used to give a fair impression of 3D, even when it is 2D. Isometric games are popular in RTS and RPG but are rarely seen in action/shooters because of the limits to aim and visibility. Most isometric games have simplistic combat

Figure 2.16
Planescape: Torment (image courtesy of Black Isle Studios 1999)

controls because of these limitations. As opposed to the old sidescroller games, isometric games offer player movement in eight directions: north, northwest, west, southwest, south, southeast, east, and northeast to be exact.

From the Side

This reflects the traditional view of SEGA and Nintendo's sidescrolling games as popularized in *Sonic the Hedgehog* and *Earthworm Jim*. This view can be mimicked quite well in 3DGS, even when you are dealing with 3D. In fact, one of the default camera views is a view from the side.

Adventure Scenes

Adventure games are well known for having 3D characters exploring pre-rendered 2D backdrops using an invisible box model. Each scene is like a diorama. The player navigates and clicks through each scene, sometimes having to backtrack many times or click throughout the scene to find elements to interact with. If the designer is not careful, this can quickly degenerate into "hunt-the-pixel" frustrations. The perspective is fixed and unmovable. When the avatar moves to an exact location on the screen, another scene is drawn.

Fixed Cameras (RE Cameras)

This perspective style was first pioneered by *Alone in the Dark* and became the basis for the *Resident Evil* cameras. Later the style was copied by *Silent Hill* (see Figure 2.17) and countless other survival horror games in succession. In this closed-circuit camera view, fixed cameras pan to follow 3D models wandering through pre-rendered settings. When a player character gets too far away from one camera, another one will "switch on" and pick up the action. Unfortunately, players have griped that this perspective style, while maintaining a suspenseful mood, can be frustrating when trying to shoot enemies around corners, and this is the main complaint that players have voiced. If you were the character onscreen, and you could see the monsters approaching from your view angle, then the player should be able to as well! This is one of the reasons that *Resident Evil 4* abandoned the fixed cameras and moved to an over-the-shoulder third-person perspective.

A lot of times, game designers find that their technology limits their player perspective. In the arcade days, games were almost always depicted top-down or

Figure 2.17
When the lights go out, players get scared—with survival horror games! (*Silent Hill 3*, image courtesy of Konami 2003)

from the side because the graphic capabilities were limited. Once you enter the world of 3D, your choices widen to third-person and isometric views. The future will explode as new visual dimensions are explored. 3D GameStudio starts with a default cameras script that sets up most of the above POVs for you automatically—and new cameras are easy to program yourself.

What You Have Learned

To summarize, game genres are a combination of fiction genre, gameplay type, and playing perspective. To fully describe a game genre, all three of these principles must be taken into account. For instance, you would not call *EverQuest* merely a "fantasy game." You would call it a "third-person fantasy online role-playing game."

- You have learned that game craft is more than just coming up with ideas.
- You know what makes a great game design.
- You have learned the formula for making great games (4FOGGD).
- You have learned the gameplay types (Action, RPG, Stealth Game, and so on).
- You have learned the points of view (POVs) used in games.
- You have learned the importance of game genres and descriptions.

For Review

1. Take a popular game that you enjoy and give it a new platform or new genre. If you want to do a new platform (such as PC, Mac, Playstation, Xbox, Gamecube, mobile, handheld, and so on), you would detail the differences and considerations you would have to make in changing your game to that new platform. If you want a new genre (such as RPG, action shooter, adventure, stealth, strategy, and so on), you would detail what new elements you would have to create and what olds ones you would keep intact.
2. Think of a brand new gameplay type (possibly formed as a hybrid between one or more popular game genres). How does your new genre play? Who would play it? What would their major objectives be? What would the main elements of this new genre be?
3. Adventure games have been declining since their Golden Age in the 1970s and 1980s, but recent games (like *Fahrenheit: Indigo Prophecy*) have summoned resurgence in their popularity. What would you do to make adventure games better, more "cool," and sell more on the current market?
4. If you were designing a new game, and its concept was that the player is a shoplifter who has to steal a list of goods for their employer out of department stores while avoiding surveillance cameras and store employees, what would the POV (playing perspective) be? Would it be top-down, isometric, first-person, third-person? If you had to choose only two perspectives (such as first- and third-person, with clicking on key C to toggle between them), what would you choose?
5. Survival horror games and stealth games are theme-based but can have many different POVs and appear as many different gameplay types (such as fighting, action, adventure, RPG, and so on). If you were to invent another theme-based game genre, what would it be? What elements would set it apart as its own genre? Come up with some examples of how it could have different POVs and gameplay types.

Game Psychology

Note

"The next revolution in games isn't technological—it's emotional."

—David Freeman, *Creating Emotion in Games*

A radical new way that game developers are approaching the design of popular electronic games is called *emotioneering*. Marc Echo, creator of *Getting Up: Contents Under Pressure*, coined the term "emotional entertainment products" when speaking of video games: he considered all games to be interactive media that teased player emotions in order to remain viable. This theory is not without evidence, either. Check out the Freeman Group, started by David Freeman, to read more about the power of emotioneering on his Web site: www .freemangames. com.

Typically, you would not think that making a game has anything to do with psychology or playing with people's emotions. You couldn't be more wrong, if that's what you think. You will learn more about why when we look at "Experiencing 3D Space" in Chapter 6. Game developers consistently make use of a psychological gambit called the *emotion gap*. This is where the game developer makes use of the player's expectations and plays upon them to heighten suspense, make the player jump, and further enmesh the player in the mood of the game. It is also great for tugging the player around on a leash or getting him to be more interactive with the game environment.

For instance, say that the developer wants to set up a saw blade trap at the entrances of his dungeons. He has designed it so that when the player comes across one of these entrances, a short cut-scene starts (probably of an unknowing jungle rat running across the threshold and being sliced in half) or cleverly laid clues point out the marks in the floor and the grisly remains of people who attempted to pass the entrance to the dungeon. If the player ignores this warning, he or she gets their character killed (an example of Feedback, one of the Four Fs of Great Game Design from before!).

Later in the game, the player will be chased by a clever monster and come across an entire labyrinth where half of the hallways are covered in these marks. It does not matter if there are saw blades in the floors or not; the player will make a logical association in his mind and start sweating at this point! This is one of many ways to improve the substance of your own game by using the player's emotions against him! You sneaky devil, you didn't know psychology was a useful tool in your game designing kit, did you?

Interaction

Games are not at all like traditional stories. Stories are typically a series of facts that occur in time-sequenced order suggestive of a cause-and-effect relationship.

Figure 2.18
Player choice determines reality in games, as in life. (*Elder Scrolls: Oblivion*, image courtesy of Bethesda Softworks 2005)

A story is a great way to represent reality as a cause equaling an effect. In *Indiana Jones and the Temple of Doom*, we see the archaeologist and adventurer Indiana as good and albeit not good but good enough, the Nazis as misled, and Indiana triumphs in the end. Even a three-year-old can understand the story; the facts, architecture, and background are nearly inconsequential to the audience attempting to understand the story. When it comes to a game, however, the truth of the pudding is in these details, and the audience cannot understand the story from a typical causal relationship but are free to make choices and come at the options from every angle (see Figure 2.18). This freedom of interaction leads to game immersion, which sells games. Indeed, a game that has a lot of immersion is a game that players will want to play over and over again to explore new opportunities and avenues for expression. A story is relatively static—while a game (on the other hand) is dynamic; it moves!

Interaction is important on several levels, but the most important one that you have to focus on is that interaction changes the nature of a game's challenges from being nearly technical dilemmas to being deeply emotional and interpersonal ones. In technically static challenges, a gamer uses logic to solve each puzzle; in an emotionally dynamic challenge, a gamer has to approach each puzzle with surprise, trepidation, and the feeling of having something personal at stake. There is some major emotional significance in providing a dynamic game, one that does not lie cold, but sets the player up for challenge after challenge and keeps the player involved.

Conflict

One of the ways that games keep players involved is through the nature of conflict. Chris Crawford once said, "Conflict is an intrinsic element of all games. It can be direct or indirect, violent or nonviolent, but it is always present in every game." He goes on to describe why: "Conflict implies danger, danger means risk of harm, and harm is undesirable." Every human being and most animals that you care to mention are afraid of harm; no one likes to get hurt. Even human beings who are long-time sufferers, the so-called victims of learned helplessness, are not all keen on being hurt; they get used to greater rewards coming from being hurt a little, not a lot. This element of conflict is simple. In gambling halls and casinos, the way people are hurt is that they lose money at the craps tables and slot machines. It is the conflict that drives them, however, to take the chance and win big or lose it all. The same is true for video games. Most video games feature "life points" where—after getting hit enough times—the player's onscreen avatar will eventually expire. This is why so many games are slammed by the media for having too much violence. When asked if a game could be non-violent, Warren Spector, the creator of games like *Thief: Deadly Shadows* and

Figure 2.19
Conflict implies danger, typically the terminal kind. (*Resident Evil,* image courtesy of Capcom 2002)

Deus Ex: The Invisible War, said that it was frankly impossible. Conflict implies the risk of winning or losing, and in games it is often how many times you get fragged that decides the conflict (see Figure 2.19).

World Immersion

So conflict is necessary to game immersion and creating emotionally dynamic games, but an equally important factor to always remember is the details. Remember before I said that *Indiana Jones* was not about the architecture and background, but about the story? Well, in games the opposite is true. Without an appropriate playground in virtual space, a game could never take place. And one of the key features that players look at when playing games is the artwork. Simply stunning vistas, crumbling mountain ruins, and rusty futuristic metalwork can always astound a player and lead them to further game immersion, especially in first-person games where the player can feel like a tourist. This is the connection between playing a video game and being at an amusement park, like Disney World.

Theme park imaginer Danny Hillis designed ride technology for Disney, but he also makes computer games. He said, "Parks take you out of the every day and re-create that sense of wonder from childhood, the time when nothing made sense, when you didn't know what would happen next and didn't need to. They're wonderful, thrilling, and unpredictable—but safe. That's how I felt the first time I played *The Legend of Zelda.* It was a new thing."

The same is true of the best video games on the market. They will offer you a world—often larger than life—to wander around exploring in, and you are like a kid lost in a department store. There are interesting knickknacks to look at and want, but there are also creepy guys trying to get you off by yourself. The dangers are so subtle as to be negligible. In the day and age of coin-op machines, the loss of your quarters was enough to make the player wag their head if they lost; today, forcing players back to previously saved checkpoints or making them lose experiences they've gained are the punishments developers have to pull.

I often tell my students that designing a game is a lot like being a host at a haunted house theme park . . . or a really good travel agent (see Figure 2.20). You are removing the players from their reality construct and placing them somewhere completely new. You are designing for them a weekend getaway, a retreat, and if you don't think about it that way, then all you will end up doing is creating a sloppy awful place for them to visit and they won't come back. Consider, when designing your game levels, what the visual and emotional impact is of every part

Figure 2.20
The game designer is now a tourism agent! (*ParaWorld*, image courtesy of SEK 2005–2006)

of your level. Put yourself in the player's shoes all the time, and just have fun! If you're not having fun, the player won't have any fun. Have nature trails full of dynamic content, have scurrying animals darting into the brush, have storm clouds on the horizon, and always hint at there being a larger world than the area the player is currently in. This will guarantee game immersion on a deeply psychological level.

Characters

You should also show that the non-player characters (NPCs) are not programmed robots. Players hate it when the NPCs are so stupid that they do not protect themselves or so monotonous they are a bore to listen to. If you bother to put NPCs into your game, at least make them seem like real people. Give them interesting dialog instead of flat drivel. Take the following example:

```
AGENT (to the player): Go see the Boss. He has a mission for you.
```

This doesn't show any emotion at all. It is boring, even though it *does* get the player's mission across. If you were the player, you'd now know that you have to see some other character and get some info from them. But if you were the game's writer, consider jazzing it up a little (while still attempting to keep it short):

```
AGENT (to the player): Boss told me he wants to see you. He has a mission for you to take—one of those few come back from!
```

Now this NPC's dialog has emotion (regretful, sincere), and it tells the player what she must do, plus it sets up the story with foreshadowing. Foreshadowing is a story device that prepares the player for something bad to happen to her later on in the story.

Giving NPCs traits that players can associate or identify with is also very important, almost as important as the traits of the main character (the player's avatar). I prefer giving an NPC three major character traits (what I call the Trait Triangle), but I'll show you how to do it later on, when we get to designing characters. You don't have to tell the player these NPC traits; you show these traits through the NPC's actions. For instance, consider the following interchange:

```
DICK walks up and tells you "I am here to help." You are suddenly attacked by goblin
fighters, and DICK helps you out.
```

This is okay, but it is flat (the speech is, too) and uncharacteristic. If we assume before writing our game that Dick is a swaggering, swashbuckling, vegetarian elf (see Figure 2.21), we should write the same interchange in this way:

```
You are trapped in an alley with no escape. The goblin fighters have you cornered.
Suddenly you hear "Ho! Take this, silly meat-eaters!" and DICK swings in from
a nearby fire escape, kicking three of the goblin fighters and sending them
sprawling. He pulls out a sharp rapier and finishes off the last goblin fighter,
```

Figure 2.21
Swashbuckling vegan elf now 30 percent more enjoyable!

```
and while the fighter is moaning in surprise and death rattle, DICK turns around
and grins wickedly at you. "Hey, mate, I didn't figure you needed a hand, but I
couldn't resist." You are suddenly attacked by more goblin fighters, and DICK
helps you out.
```

Admittedly this interchange takes a little longer and a more extensive cut-scene must be used, but that is a compromise you will face when making a game better. Try giving your non-player characters honestly conflicting emotions themselves, such as hidden motives, secret feelings, and past regrets.

Your player may face groups of NPCs or might be asked to join a group (such as a clan). Do not have basic groups, like Red Shirts and Blue Shirts, with no discernable features. Never let groups, especially a group the player might belong to, appear stale and uninteresting: outfit them with distinctive traits, a shared belief system, and particular goals, and try to make them appealing to the player.

One of the best examples I've ever seen of this is *Thief: Deadly Shadows* where you are a medieval cat burglar in a fantasy setting. There are roughly three major groups of people that you meet during the course of the game. They are the Keepers, who skulk about in shadows and study ancient tomes of lore (they represent man's innate curiosity); the Hammers, who strut around carrying hammers and worship a Builder God (representing Order); and the Pagans, who live in nature and worship a Trickster God (who represents Chaos). Each of these groups has some inkling the others do not. Each is distinctly well-planned by the game designer. (See Figure 2.22.) Each can become an ally of the player during the course of the game. But they only become allies if the player deigns it; this is where the psychology comes in! The player must take open-ended (often purely optional) missions to come to the aid of each of the groups and must often decide between them. The player's decisions change the overall construct of the game, giving the player some powers or immunities he would not have otherwise. The group the player chooses to aid is usually based on which group the player associates with more. This was deliberately planned.

Show that the player's character and these non-player characters cohabitate—that they can love, have fights, or share complex and realistic relationships. You could even have NPCs admire, fear, or respect the player character based on the player's choices in the game. *Fable* (originally called *Project Ego*) is a great example of this: during the game, the player's choices change the world around him. If the player is mean to a few people in one town, neighbors in the next town will react with hostility (characters will scream and run away in fear or actually

Figure 2.22
Sneak-thieves are more than just pickpockets; they now have "issues"! (*Thief: Deadly Shadows*, image courtesy of Ion Storm)

boo him). Yet if the player shows generosity he will continue to be treated with adoration.

Emergent Gameplay

Another way that a player's emotions can be infused in the game is a technique created almost by accident in free-roaming games, like *Grand Theft Auto* and *Thief*: allow the player to create her own stories. This is an example of emergent gameplay. Give the player breathing room and enough random elements with which to interact, and then let them shape the game themselves. This is called *collaboration*—where you are the co-author of the game, and the player creates the other half by his own actions.

Symbols and Myth in Games

Powerful symbols are another way that emotions can take the foray. A lot of people have the mistaken assumption that coming up with ideas for games is a talent that only a fraction of people are born with and cannot be taught. For ages, these same people have thought the same about art and story writing. However, coming up with ideas is not all that hard. Once you begin making games yourself, you will see that inspiration is all around you, and sometimes you will want to make games adapted from mythology or fairy tales.

Mythology holds a wealth of possibilities. The film *O Brother Where Art Thou* (if you did not already know) is based on the Greek myth of Ulysses. Of course, if you watch the film, it doesn't sound like a myth, yet the underlying story structure is a mirror image of Ulysses. Hercules, Cinderella, Robin Hood, and Red Riding Hood have been plumbed to their depths, but many other myths and religious stories can be mined for ideas, as well. The world's leading mythologist, Joseph Campbell, has a book *The Hero with a Thousand Faces* that is a great resource for understanding the relationships between these stories. When considering the story you are telling, be sure to get a copy and read Christopher Vogler's *The Writer's Journey.* Vogler takes an authoritative look at some mythic archetypes set forth by Joseph Campbell and how they relate to books and film. The material in *The Writer's Journey* actually applies to games as much as it does cinema. These mythic archetypes are powerful symbols that go directly to the audience's subconscious, meaning that the audience reacts immediately to such symbols, without having to draw conclusions why it is so.

For instance, some of the character archetypes that have the all-entrenched mythic connotation are the Hero and his Shadow, who represent the ever-enduring battle between good and evil. There are four character archetypes you must remember: the Hero, his Shadow, the Mentor, and Guardians.

The **Hero** is the protagonist of the story, the main character, and classically he has the courage to do what he thinks right, the cleverness to get out of trouble, some special talent to help him, and a strong code of ethics. The Hero is often resourceful and good at what she does. It is imperative to make the player realize that the Hero is not helpless, that the player (through the role of the Hero) can affect change in her game world.

The **Shadow** (also called the Villain) is the Hero's archenemy, the total opposite of everything the Hero is and stands for. The Shadow is a projection of the Hero's dark side, and therefore also has some of the same characteristics as the Hero, except for the Hero's code of ethics. The Hero and Villain will always stand valiantly opposed, as this is the most primal mythic archetype.

The **Mentor** comes across the Gamer's Journey in the **Supernatural Aid** stage; ideally the Mentor is an older, wiser version of the Hero herself—but debilitated in some way so that they don't do any active heroism. The Mentor provides tips, hints, and helps along the Hero's path, and he may sacrifice himself to help the Hero's cause.

Another mythic archetype is the **Guardian**. Guardians are not the Hero's allies. A Guardian shares some relationship with the Shadow, and it stands as an obstacle on the Hero's road, a trial the Hero must pass before accomplishing her quest. The Guardian tests the Hero's abilities, and if the Hero perseveres, the Guardian gives the Hero new items or powers. Of course, in many games the Guardian is represented by all of the monsters the player character must face before she can finally confront the Level Boss or main villain.

Mythic archetypes are a little bit different from fictional stereotypes, but not by a huge stretch of the imagination. Mythic archetypes have been around a lot longer, have sunk into our collective unconscious, and appear in various guises through our imagination and dreams. Stereotypes are flat cliché characters seen in various works, and they include such sundry entities as Enigmatic Strangers, Nerdy Geniuses, Grumpy Old Men, Lonesome Cowboys, Amazon Girls, Magical Teen Girls, Mad Scientists, and more. Stereotypes are around simply because, when people are talking about creative concepts, it is easier to imagine situations and characters by defining them by what they do or the story devices they serve. However, the part about stereotypes that causes rancor amidst the public is how they limit characters (and people).

The story that forms the substance of the game can follow the three-act story framework, or it can be more adequately expressed in the monomyth. In case you are wondering or have forgotten, the three-act structure of storytelling was developed for Greek plays and is still the most-used method of framing plots in screenwriting, dramatization, and novels. The three act structure consists of, obviously, three parts. They are as follows:

- **A Beginning**—Where you get your Hero up a tree...
- **A Middle**—Where you throw stones at him...
- **An End**—Where you get him down out of the tree.

The monomyth—as described by Joseph Campbell in his Hero's Journey—is filled with many steps, more like suggestions, that naturally follow one another in a chain of events common to many legends, fairy tales, books, and cinematic masterpieces. For our intents and purposes, I will revise these steps into the Gamer's Journey, which follows.

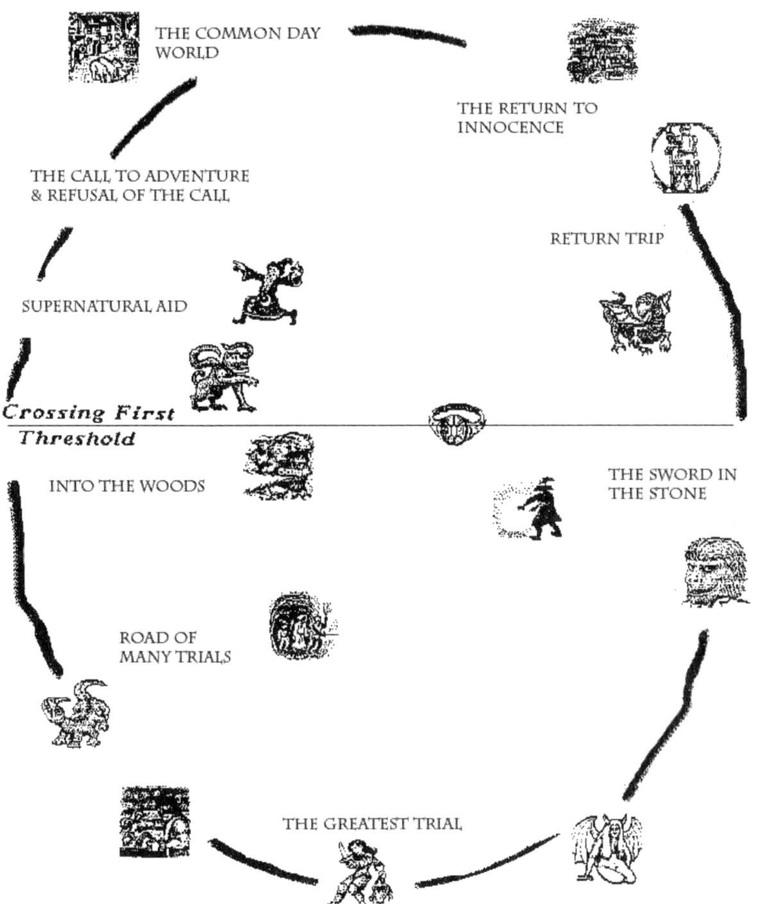

Figure 2.23
The Gamer's Journey

The Gamer's Journey

The Common Day World—This is the "fish out of water" concept, where you see that the player character is taken out of his ordinary space and time and lands in a strange, more challenging world or predicament. This step often takes place in a cut-scene before the game even starts. This step is most notable in role-playing games like *Chrono Trigger*, *Star Ocean*, and *Final Fantasy*.

The Call to Adventure—The Hero is presented with a problem, a challenge, a great quest, that will take her further away from the common day world. Often, this call is refused: the Hero is too busy, uncaring, or afraid to answer the call and usually needs added motivation. This is when the proverbial princess is kidnapped by the bad guy or another character shows up offering big rewards if the player will help them.

Supernatural Aid—The Hero encounters aid in the persona of an advisor (usually the Mentor archetype) or simply by in-game hints in how to play the game, move around in this new more challenging world, and somehow achieve her quest. It is here that she finds the weapons, tools, or abilities that help her.

Into the Woods—Once prepared, the Hero crosses a gateway, threshold, or enters the new and dangerous part of the kingdom, often an underground dungeon scuttling with monsters. Her journey truly begins! Things will start to change the more the Hero advances, creating a darker more fearsome place for the Hero to explore.

Many Trials—Once our Hero has escaped the ordinary and started on her dangerous path, she will face many obstacles and tests. Along the way, she will beat boss monsters, befriend non-player characters, and encounter traders who will supply her with better weapons and health items. These trials form the basis for the largest portion of the game.

The Greatest Trial—The Hero comes at last to her greatest trial, cave of ordeals, the darkest place in the woods, the Shadow's lair. She must face her own fears, deal with her own lingering doubts, and overcome adversity once and for all.

The Sword in the Stone—The Hero has beaten death, cheated her enemies, and now gains that which she has sought all along . . . but is this The End?

The Return Trip—Danger is not out of the way yet, as the Hero must return to the common day world. She has some last foes to defeat, traps to escape, and death to outrace. An example of this is the escape scene at the end of *Resident Evil 4*. Sometimes, this stage includes a rebirth of some kind. Maybe the Hero dies and is resurrected.

The Return to Innocence—The Hero finally returns to the common day world, along with her bounty. The damsel in distress is returned to her rightful station, the healing elixir is given to the dying king, or the Ring of Power ends the mighty feud. Things end happily ever after . . . or do they?

As a game writer, the myths you create through your games, and the emotional tugging that you do through your careful crafting, have the power to change people's moods and affect the experience they have playing your games. Do not fear that by using these techniques your work will become clichéd. As long as you don't overuse tired concepts and you keep your games fresh and original (just remember the Four Fs of Great Game Design), you will not be saddled with undue criticism. Even DaVinci and Van Gogh painted from the same primary color palette—but their works are vastly different, and each is phenomenal! Appropriation is the art of taking an idea from a source (much like the act of adaptation), filtering it through your mind, and giving it your individual voice. While adaptation is usually based on literature (novels, short stories, poetry, nonfiction, and so on), appropriation can be based on anything (for example, American McGee's *Oz* and *Alice* games).

In Summary

Note

"By consuming your daily quota of stimulation, you promote your psychological and spiritual growth. You can also expand your intellectual capacity. Some things have a certain amount of depth that pushes you, makes you think a little deeper than you have, makes you study a little more, makes you connect with things outside of the game environment."

—Dan Bunten with Heidi E. H. Aycock

The one element you should never overlook or forget when writing your game and developing these emotional triggers is why the player wants to play your game. Entertainment, in order to relieve boredom and provide players with a way to escape from the pressures of daily life, is the most prominent assumption game developers make about games. There are different reasons players play games, and only some of them pertain to entertainment. See the "Player Motivation" section in Chapter 3 for more information.

If you can tap into player needs, pull the strings of player emotions, and provide mythic entertainment that will outlast a single play, you will create video games that are fun—not flat! That's what will separate your games from the rest, and what will make you a blockbuster game designer!

What You Have Learned

As David Freeman points out, games are emotional interactive entertainments. You can divide a game into interactive parts and emotional parts; once a player takes on the role of his avatar and has a vested interest in the turnout of the game, it is emotional. The following are the lessons you have hopefully taken with you.

- You have learned to use player psychology to make a better game.
- You have learned the importance of great game writing (dialog, character traits, story devices, and so on).
- You now know how to immerse a gamer in your game world.
- You have studied the Gamer's Journey and its importance in writing games.
- You have gotten what makes a game a legend as opposed to what makes it cliché.

For Review

1. Say that your team leader wanted to have a mansion level that led to a backyard, but he did not want players to wander from the backyard to the woods beyond. The game is a survival horror game featuring alien enemies. Your team leader suggests using laser beams or trip wires in the backyard to keep the players inside the mansion. How would you use the emotion gap (of emotioneering) and some cut-scenes to manipulate the players?
2. Consider the following bit of dialog: "TED: Could you break into the Wizard's Tower and get me the Crystal of Mages?" From what you have learned about putting emotion into games, rewrite this dialog. Keep it short, but show Ted's character traits: he is meant to be strong, forceful, wealthy, and bullying.
3. Invent two major groups that the player of an RPG could join. What are the details of each group? What are their shared beliefs, outlooks, and abilities? What separates them from other people? Why would the player want to join either of them?

4. What are some ways you would force the player to worry about what other characters thought about her? Would you enforce ethical considerations? What about "good citizenship" awards? Would you want the player's character to fall in love and marry NPCs? How would this affect the rest of your game design?

5. The monomyth of Joseph Campbell was used in lots of Hollywood film writing, including the *Star Wars* saga, *Indiana Jones*, and the *Lord of the Rings*. Watch one or more of these film adaptations, and identify which steps on the Hero's Journey were adopted and which ones weren't. Would you have directed the movies differently to follow the monomyth more closely, or do you think they work the way they are?

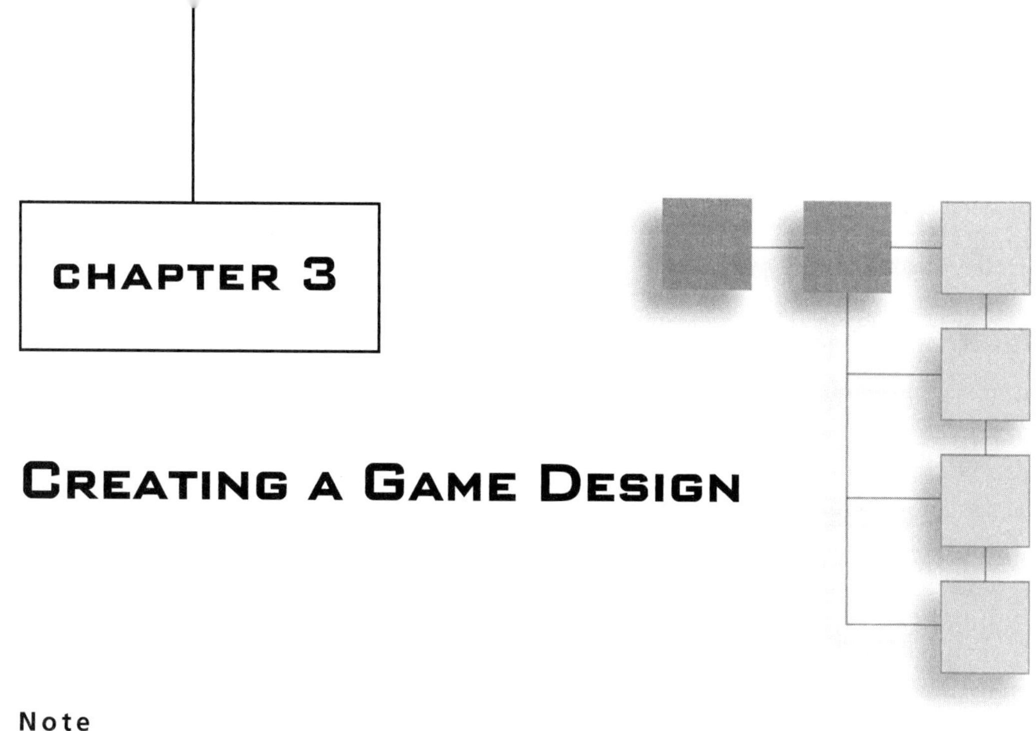

Chapter 3

Creating a Game Design

Note

"The design is not something cast in stone that has to be followed to the letter–it's more of a guideline."

—Jon Freeman

Game design documents (also called *game bibles* or simply "the paper") are used by the production and publishing staff of a game company to complete the project. Essentially, each game design document tells every member of the team the sort of game this will be, what to work on, and when to work on it. The game bible compiles all the characters, illustrations, maps, charts, game features, interface commands, and anything else that might be remotely important for the game design. It leaves no questions unanswered. It is the blueprint for the game design.

As you learned in the last chapter, sometimes the game design document is flexible, and the team adds to or subtracts from it as they go. In other development management methods, the design doc is more rigid. If any alteration has to be done, an entirely new design doc is written up and shared among the team members, and the old one is discarded. When you look at a team running under the "organic process," it is difficult to even find their original game bible because the team members practically work by the seat of their pants and make stuff up on the fly. And people following the Cerny Method will invariably not have a physical game outline, but rather a working game prototype that serves fairly well in its place.

Game Design Elements

Every game team has a different game design document, so no two are exactly alike. I want to repeat that because it is important. *There is no formal outline.* But for our purposes, I will give you the important headings every game outline deserves. A proper game design should include the following headings:

- **Genre**—What kind of game is this?
- **Setting**—Where does this game take place?
- **Characters**—Who does the player play as?
- **Premise**—What is the player's objective?
- **Synopsis**—What happens to the player?
- **Player Motivation**—Why should the player play?
- **Target Audience**—Who would play this game?
- **Game Mechanics**—What are the conditions of the game?
- **Game Graphics**—How does the game look?
- **Game Sound**—How does the game sound?

Genre

Choose a genre from the fiction genres, gameplay types, and playing perspectives (listed in the last chapter). This should stem directly from your Killer Game Concept. You cannot get anywhere in a game outline without a game idea to start with. Be imaginative. There are countless isometric fantasy role-playing games out there today; perhaps the niche market tomorrow will be first-person science fiction Western games. This is why coming up with fresh game ideas is so important, and one way that I mentioned was mixing games and game genres. For one thing, do all role-playing games have to be fantasy? No, they don't.

Setting

Describe the general areas and environments likely to be explored in this game. Give a brief summary of the types of places the player is likely to see. We will cover the details of setting later on, when we look at level design, but I want you to get started right now. Are there going to be any gimmick levels, like lost crypts, crumbling mineshafts, dank dungeons, zombie-ridden mansions, and so on? Gimmicks are often applied to game levels because they are instantly familiar to players. If you want to add gimmicks to your levels, list them here. Also, because video games are part virtual world and part story, you need to know whether your game is going to be linear, non-linear or hub-based. These are concepts we will study later on, but you need to give them consideration when outlining your game setting. In succinct words, a linear game is like a sidescrolling game: the player moves from Point A to Point B, usually blowing up and shooting everything in between. Non-linear games are like the complex adventure game settings, where players wander about at their whim, eventually opening up new areas to explore. Hub-based games return the player to the same place over and over, as a point of reference.

Characters

There are lots of characters that go into a typical video game, but they crank down to three categories. They are the Avatar (the player's character); the Allies/Team Mates/NPCs (those characters that are not the player's character but serve some position in the game); and the Obstacles/Enemies/Bosses (those things that offer the player challenges). Pictures are always better with people's faces in them, and games are always better with strong characters in them. So to reiterate,

- **The Avatar**—This is the player character or protagonist of the game story. Who is he? Is he a nameless warrior, as in first-person shooter (FPS)? Or is she a highly developed persona who is very photogenic? Be sure to add depth of emotion to each of the characters that you create for your game design document, but the most important one to spend time on will be the avatar. It has to serve as the player's thoughts in motion onscreen, the mouse cursor so to speak, and the avatar must be appealing. In some cases, the avatar may even become an icon or spokesperson for your game!
- **Allies/Team Mates/NPCs**—Give full descriptions, including the basic function of any computer-controlled non-player characters who won't

attack the player. For instance, is there a merchant the player can buy weapon upgrades from? What about a healer or innkeeper in your game? And as mentioned in the last chapter, make your NPCs come to life by using emotion: give them character traits that make them more rounded.

- **Obstacles/Enemies/Bosses**—Give full descriptions of the environmental hazards your levels might include, such as poisonous plants, spinning saw blades, or exploding barrels. List and give the functions of any dangerous non-player characters the game might have in store, such as grunts and boss monsters. Artificial intelligence (AI) is most pernicious with enemies, to make them tougher and smarter to provide better challenges. The old enemy concept from *Doom* is a monster that hears the player, stomps slowly toward the player, and ends up getting shot by the player. This has got to change.

Premise

This should contain the most important words in the document because this captivating blurb will form game proposals and submissions for you in the future. It must sell the document, as well as the game, to the reader! Take your Killer Game Concept and write it down. Read it, have others read it, boil it down to its base components, and rewrite it until you have a short blurb. In two or three sentences, describe the game in an excited manner. You need to describe the player's objective in the game—while keeping your descriptions short and to-the-point. Include any meaningful bits of information that cannot wait until the next sentence. What is it that the player has to achieve in the game, and what is going to try and stop her?

Synopsis

Write a detailed synopsis of the game story and plot development as points along the way here. You should also create path trees, walkthroughs, or game flow-charts. Some game teams also list dialog scripts here, much like a screenplay but with target chapters triggered by player actions. Particular story devices must be taken into account, such as the player's collaboration, the interactivity, and open-ended decision-making. The game story should never be static. The player's choices shape the major plot twists, where the story might branch, diverge, or even come out to different endings.

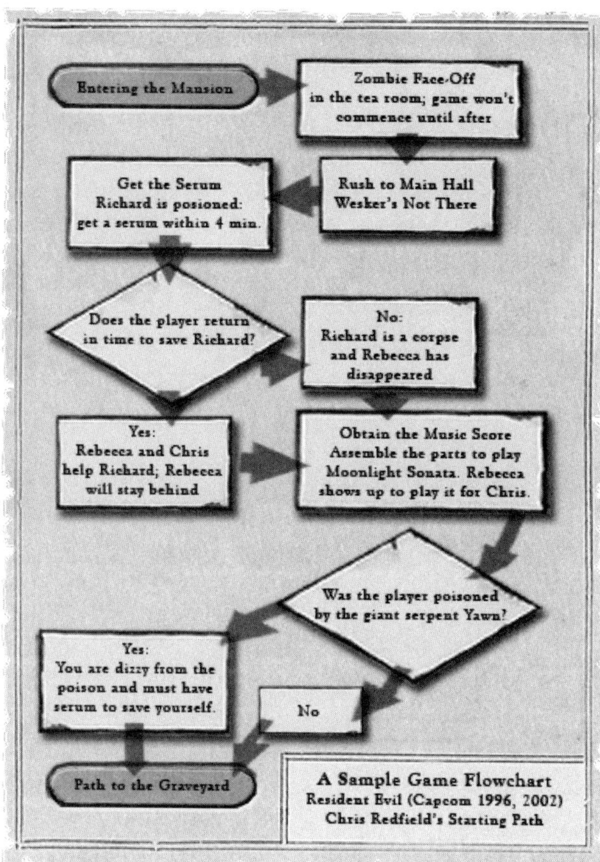

Figure 3.1
A sample game flowchart

If you have ever read a game walkthrough (especially those printed by Brady) you have a strong impression of how a walkthrough is created. Essentially it lists the stepping stones on the narrative path, and the branches along that path. Game flowcharts are trees of action in the game (see Figure 3.1), as dictated by missions to undertake, the player's choices, and areas to explore. Charting scenario variations in your game is a bit like attempting to map the twists and turns of the Amazon River. You can follow one route or another, but usually not both. Many events can only be triggered after the player deliberately performs a certain task, gets a certain item (such as a key or clue), or by solving a situation (such as a boss monster or a puzzle). Game flowcharts are intrinsically the same as algorithm flowcharts, but cover more story fluff. Some designers actually take the game flowcharts (direct from the game synopsis) to programming.

Keep in mind that the player *must* have multiple paths to take to get to the end (or the win solution) of the game. As Brad Wardell said, "Whether it's a strategy game or a platform game, you want players to be able to have multiple ways to win. In *Civilization*, you could win by conquering the world or sending your people to another planet. In *Baldur's Gate II*, you can play as both good and evil, and most puzzles had multiple ways to complete it." Warren Spector spearheaded this movement toward player-centric resolution. The player will have a vested interest and more dynamic emotional entanglement in your game if he feels that what action he takes has an immediate and persistent effect on the game's story.

This applies to replay ability. Too many video games today are built to be throwaway games apparently designed by wannabe or frustrated filmmakers. These games are extremely transparent when they have more cut-scenes than game action. Once you have beaten their games, you might as well trade them in and get another because there is zero difference if you want to play them over again. *Diablo* circumvented this problem by having dungeon levels randomly generated each time you entered them. Players loved it. *Deus Ex: The Invisible War* allows its game players to choose from many different sides and take endlessly different paths before reaching their goals. A truly great game has more than one path and more than one possible ending—it should branch and grow randomly like a carefully crafted Choose-Your-Own Adventure game book.

Note

"When even a simple board game has more randomness and is more fun than most computer/console games available now, you know the technology is being wasted."

—Duane Alan Hahn

Later on, we will cover more about story synopsis and the ways you can set up games to be story-driven or clue-driven when we make an adventure game.

Player Motivation

Tim Schafer—designer of *Grim Fandango* and *Psychonauts*—once noted that all games (in his view) are about wish fulfillment. Whenever a player plays a game, she is put into a fictional scenario that she can't experience in real life. But wish fulfillment is an over-generalization of all players' motivations. There are many factors that motivate people to play games. Let's take a look at just a few. As you're reading through these motivating factors, consider what motivates you to play the games you like!

- **Escapism**—One of the top motivating factors reported by players is escapism. After a long day in real life, it's nice to escape from the mundane world and enter an imaginative, oftentimes "limitless" universe—where your character might either have superhuman powers or be in the habit of breaking the law without facing ramifications! This is known as *cathartic release* and has been shown to improve behaviors of even the most stable citizens. Are you ever motivated by escaping boredom, by entering an artificial world?

- **Competition**—Lots of people play multiplayer online games (MMOs) in order to compete with other players (this is considered player-versus-player or PVP competitions). South Korea, the most wired nation in the world today, is the hub of game competition. The World Cyber Games (a sort of Olympic event for game competitors) got its start in South Korea, and today it still converges for world finals in their country. Players are bigger than life there, appearing on billboards and committing to celebrity ad campaigns. Do you find that the spirit of competition motivates you to play?

- **Social interaction**—All multiplayer games contain strong elements of social interaction—whether they're online, LAN-based, or multiplayer console games. Players can chat with other players over the Internet, even talk through headsets, and communication runs the gamut from teasing to strategy discussion. These games have also sparked a micro-economy of gamers buying and selling in-game merchandise and managing simulated worlds and societies. Do you ever play games that allow you to connect socially with others?

- **Creative expression**—These games allow players to exhibit some form of creative expression. Games like *Def Jam* and *Dance Dance Revolution* allow players to express themselves musically. Games like *Dungeon Keeper* and *The Sims* allow players to build original environments. Then there are countless role-playing games today that allow players to customize their characters. All of these focus on creative expression factors. Some researchers say there are two types of creative expression (which ties in

Figure 3.2
GTA: San Andreas (image courtesy of Rockstar Games 2005)

with Freud's eros and thanatos concepts): creative power and destructive power. Some games offer more creative power, such as *Sim City*, where you have to build a whole city, while others offer more destructive power, such as *Serious Sam*, where you blow up whole cities. Are you motivated to play games that allow you to express yourself artistically in some way?

- **Taboo**—Some games allow players to do things they could never do in RL (real life) without serious repercussions. Stealth games capitalize on this instinct by allowing players to enjoy sneaking around places they are not supposed to be. Other games use taboo elements for cathartic release or to make a social satire. For instance, *Grand Theft Auto* allows players to mug old ladies, steal cars, and sleep with prostitutes (see Figure 3.2). These are all things that society deems inappropriate for citizens to do, even if some of our citizens harbor secret wishes to do them. Video games allow players to do these things—and get away with them—without being patronized, slapped on the wrist, or thrown in jail.
- **Knowledge**—All games are educational by accident (you have to learn how to play the game and then you are expected to learn how to get better at playing it) and some by purposeful intent. These games don't necessarily have to be educational games. On the contrary, these games might be "covert"—motivating players to solve problems, make discoveries, create innovations, and manage resources all in the course of reaching the game's

goal. Do you find yourself expanding your knowledge while playing a game, and does this motivate you to continue playing?

- **Mastery**—Some players are motivated to continue playing a game or play it over and over again because they want to master the game. These players might play one level again and again until they reach the highest score possible or to beat it in the shortest amount of time. In the arcade days, this was equivalent to being the popular kid, and people would crowd around one coin-op game to watch masters at work. Today, players may spend days getting a single mission just right in *Hitman: Blood Money* so they can say they are the Silent Assassin. Do you ever find yourself trying to get the highest score you can when you play a game to be a true master?

- **Addiction**—A motivating factor that is difficult to clearly define is addiction—an intangible factor that results in an almost constant urge to play a game, without a rational explanation. Addiction works on a basic psychological level—consisting more of a feeling than a thought. Many people have criticized games for being addictive substances and game designers as being little better than peddlers of a narcotic agent. Yet this case scenario has always been overruled when psychologists point out that the same traits of game addicts exist in bookworms who cannot put down a new book. Have you ever found yourself playing a game for no logical reason? Was it difficult to tear yourself away, even if you wanted to?

- **Therapy**—For some players, games can be a form of therapy. This does not have to be cathartic therapy, as that is part of escapism. In fact, some hospitals are beginning to prescribe games to patients in order to relax them emotionally and engage in eye-hand coordination for physical therapy. Patients after surgery on their fingers and hands are often encouraged to play console games like the Xbox because it provides physical therapy for their recuperating digits, while at the same time removes the patient from his misery by providing escapism. Another game, called *Re-Mission* (created by Pam Omidyar and the HopeLab) focuses on a real-time cancer simulation, where the player is Roxxi, a powered-up nanobot destroying cancer cells inside the body. *Re-Mission* has shown a small but marked improvement in the psychological well-being of patients who have given it a go. Do you ever find it relaxing and unwinding to play games? Can playing a game sometimes be considered a form of therapy for you?

Spotlight on: George Pirvu

George Pirvu has worked with the 3D GameStudio software since 1997 and has contributed a lot to the ever-growing community of developers who use the software. The Romanian resident runs Randombyte (an application developer) and the *Acknex Users Magazine* online (affectionately called AUM), which can be found at http://aum.conitec.net. He answers questions and helps beginners with coding issues.

When did you first get started using 3D GameStudio? How did you find out about it? Was there anything that told you this was the software you should use to make games with?

"I discovered 3DGS back in 1997, while I was browsing the Net. I was looking for information on how to create my own game engine, but since Acknex 3.7 was already available, I thought that I can save myself a lot of work and concentrate only on the actual game programming."

What sort of gaming experience do you possess? Did you go to school for graphic or game design? How did you get your start in the industry?

"I went to the University of Electronics and Information Engineering and I got diplomas in C / C++ / MFC; however, I have learned about 95 percent of what I know by myself, reading books and examining other people's code. I wouldn't say that I am 'in the industry' exactly. However, I run a small company named Randombyte–www.randombyte.com–and I design all sorts of games and other applications for a living. I made my first game programming money about 10 years ago, when the first client visited my (former) 3DGS-related Web site."

What is the most significant element of using 3D GameStudio that you have learned? Is there one feature that impresses you the most? How do you feel the game engine compares with others?

"I have used lots of engines, and I can tell you one thing: 3DGS is by far the fastest prototyping tool in the world. If you want to get something working and fast, use 3DGS–you won't be disappointed! The engine is a great value for its price; a small team of skilled artists and talented programmers can create high-quality commercial titles with it. Don't take my word for it–visit Conitec's Web site to see how many 3DGS-based projects have gone commercial. I know a small team of only two guys who have made half a million in less than six months using 3DGS. That's impressive."

If you could tell a future game designer, somebody just looking to start in the industry, one thing–what would that be?

"If you aren't extremely serious about it, go find another job. Really! If you want to work in the industry, you need to have a lot of passion for game development, something that isn't required if you decide to (let's say) sell hamburgers."

What are some of your areas of specialty, your interests in game design? What area of game design do you believe has the most room for expansion or might become dominant in the next generation?

"I have built lots of action games, strategies, RPGs, puzzles, etc. Here's some precious advice for the newcomers: you can't create the next *Doom*/*Quake*/*Unreal* killer. Those companies have budgets of millions or tens of millions–you don't. Better find something really original; think about a game concept that was never used before or is a combination of games. What does a backgammon game have in common with *Space Invaders*? I don't know, but if you find the proper link, you will end up having an original game, which might become a hit. Another good idea is to clone a successful game and add many heavy modifications to your clone.

The future doesn't look too bright for many of the big game development companies in my opinion. The competition is tough in the Big Boys' League, but that is an advantage for indies and small companies, who are happy if they manage to sell (let's say) 50,000 copies of their game. Many experienced game developers have gone the indie way in the last few years; some of them are making more money now, some less, but all of them are much happier than before."

Target Audience

Know your audience—that is the number-one rule of thumb with any creative medium, be it art, books, films, or video. Keep in mind that you will eventually be making games for other people, not just for yourself and your friends. These people may have definite opinions about game genres and gameplay. They may have played more games than you or have savvier ideas about the industry. If you don't consider people's opinions you may never be able to sell them your game.

To know your audience, first you've got to find them. Perhaps you like role-playing games, and you spend your personal time surfing RPG forums and Web sites; that's great because you already know the RPG audience! You can frequent Internet message boards and chat rooms dedicated to games like the ones you want to make. You can subscribe to gaming magazines (such as *Game Pro*, *Game Informer*, or *Game Developer*) and read their articles and reviews. You'll be able to find your target audience before long, and you will know what pleases and what bores them.

There are two highly advantageous areas for you to study when facing the question of who your game is aimed at. These are psychographics and demographics. You need to understand the characteristics of the game market—the people playing the games. With over 60 percent of the U.S. alone currently playing electronic games, the player market is much more diverse than it was during the arcade era! For one thing, the average age of the average gamer today is 33—and 40 percent of the people buying games are women. We've looked at why players like to play games, so now let's look at who plays them.

Psychographics

What are the components of players' lifestyles, beliefs, attitudes, and values? How do these components affect these players' choice of games? Game developers are beginning to identify players based on these psychological elements—known as *psychographics.* To understand this, you should try taking the Values, Attitudes, and Lifestyles Survey (VALS) at the following Web site: www.sric-bi.com/VALS/presurvey.shtml.

After you take the survey, your results will appear onscreen. These results will indicate your primary and secondary psychotype—which can include innovator, thinker, achiever, experiencer, believer, striver, maker, or survivor. The terms are pretty much self-descriptive. Once you've begun to take a look at your own psychographics, begin to associate them with the underlying factors that motivate you to play games. Do you see a common thread running through the games that you choose to play? Perhaps you are an experiencer, and you prefer wide-sweeping adventure games because you approve of games with aesthetics. Perhaps you are a maker, so you prefer construction and management simulations that allow you to build whole worlds.

Demographics

A final player market element is *demographics*—which encompasses statistical information related to age, gender, income, education, and ethnicity. There are three major generations of players currently in the United States: Baby Boomers, Generation-X, and Millennial Generation. Make sure you understand the characteristics of these four generations. The newest—and growing—market is the Millennial Generation.

These kids have grown up with overprotective parents, assurances from authority, technology at their fingertips, and the *Lilo & Stitch* saying, "No one gets left behind," as their motto. They are extremely social, cooperative, and active. They are the first ever generation to grow up with computers in their homes and gadgets like cell phones as a must-have. Online games and social interaction appeal to them, as do games that encourage creative expression. Right now, most of the games that are being made are created by the grown-up Generation-Xers, and these games reflect the Generation-X themes of paranoia, abandonment, and do-it-yourself extremism—but this is liable to change as the Millennial Generation starts making games.

What sorts of games do you think you could design, if you were to focus primarily on a specific generation, such as the Millennials or Baby Boomers? What changes would your existing game ideas have to undergo to make them more acceptable for a wider range of generation players?

Game Mechanics

Note

"It's like these developers are trying to invent chess and have created a superb, glossy-looking board and a whole new set of exciting pieces and then sit back and say, 'Look! Look at his new board game we've made! Look at these shiny pieces and this state-of-the art board! What a great game this is!' But they haven't thought about how the game is played. They haven't thought about what pieces can move in what directions. They haven't thought about how these pieces then interact with each other. They haven't developed a set of rules. In short, they haven't thought about the actual game itself. . . ."

—Neil West, "The Way Games Ought to Be" (*Next Generation Magazine*, October 1997)

The game mechanics list some technically dry material about the various game components, all of which you feel will be vital to game design. What are this game's key features? How is the game expected to be played? Is the game fast-paced (like a shooter), or does it require more thought (like a strategy game)? How does the player interact with his or her environment? Are there weapons, ammo, medical kits, or puzzle clues to pick up? What about gate levers or vehicles? What is the player up against? List puzzles this game might offer—and their possible solutions. List all these variables and what triggers them here.

A lot of them are what we call *resources*. Resources are fixed variables that the player can find in-game. Here are some classic resources found in a lot of video games:

- Health, usually measured as hit points
- Lives (more common in older video games)
- Money
- Ammunition
- Fuel
- Population (of computer-controlled people or creatures)

It's worthwhile to remember that not *every* resource is supposed to be a good thing. You could have rates of insanity or crime or damage to your vehicles that would all count as negative resources, ones the player tries to decrease or keep to a minimum. Whichever you are using (positive or negative game resources), you are going to have to set up parameters. Parameters are numeric values that set limits to the resources' variables or have some effect on the rate of change. Consider a laser cannon that is in a fixed location on an alien starship. Among its parameters would be the following:

- Rate of fire or the number of times per minute that it can shoot.
- Range or the maximum distance at which it can hit something.
- Accuracy or probability of its hitting something.
- Power or the destructive capacity of its laser shots.

The distinction between resources and parameters is not clear-cut. Resources are frequently used and fluctuate rapidly, such as health or cash. Parameters change slowly and have secondary traits. Parameters also better define the behavior of objects. The traditional Dungeons and Dragons character attributes are strength, intelligence, dexterity, wisdom, charisma, and constitution. In Dungeons and Dragons, experience points are a resource and often the primary goal of the game. As you see, resources and parameters are defined by mathematical equations. As a designer, it is up to you to determine *what* resources and parameters you are going to put into your game. Be very conservative; remember the KISS principle—keep it simple! (For example, if you don't *have* to have money in your game, don't be stupid: consider leaving it out.)

Parameters and resources have a very unique embodiment when it comes to programming the game. Resources usually boil down to variables, and the digital units of variables are the parameters. For instance, if you were going to program your game to have cash, you would probably start by setting up cash as a variable and define its starting parameter:

```
var cash = 100;
```

The people, objects, or places that a resource comes from are called its *source*; the people, objects, or places it goes to are its *drain*. In some games, they start with a limited amount of one resource and no more come in, so you have no source. In other games, the resource comes in and never goes out, so it has no drain. Some drains convert one resource into another—or into *parameters*. Using the Dungeons and Dragons example, experience points are a primary resource that you get—but then you spend it on your skills and attributes to make your character tougher, smarter, or more clever; this is a conversion of experience points into parameters. This sort of drain is often called a converter. A *converter* is a process that converts one resource into something else. An exchange is a process in which resources change hands between players. The resources are neither produced nor consumed but only moved around, like the Monopoly money in the Parker Brothers game. There are lots of exchanges today, which since the popular days of *EverQuest*, have leafed out into free markets and a new micro-economy.

Don't get flustered thinking about the game mechanics in any big way right now; you can always adjust this section of your game outline, depending on the development management you plan to institute. One of the best ways to handle the settlement of resources, parameters, and more is to open up Microsoft Excel and start filling in the little blanks. Before long, you could have tables and charts telling you exactly how fast your player character is, what his constitution is, and how much money it costs to buy a new war-axe for him.

Remember to be concise, consistent, and realistic with game mechanics. Allow some lateral thinking. For instance, if you can defeat stone golems with your war-axe, why do you need to find a key to open a wooden door? Couldn't you just bust the flimsy door down with your battle-hardened axe? I can't believe the number of games, such as *Silent Hill* (see Figure 3.3), where you are equipped with a flamethrower but you come to a door that says, "The door's lock appears to be jammed; it won't open." The door looks weathered and beaten. What would it take to simply burn the door down?

Figure 3.3
Handgun bullets in a book store? Puh-lease. . . . (*Silent Hill 3*, image courtesy of Konami 2003)

While we are on the subject, when half-naked women drop dead after a battle, they should not drop 35 gold coins and a suit of half-plate armor. I am not kidding. This has been done in so many games that it has become the unthinkable most often-committed design crime. Another example of idiosyncrasy is in Capcom's *Resident Evil 4*, where they had crows that—when you shot them out of the sky—dropped chests of money or ammo boxes. What, did the crows just happen to pick them up because they were shiny? And while we are on the subject, how could a flying crow pick up a 3-pound chest full of money?

Medical kits should not be found lying everywhere, especially not inside a sewer tunnel or abandoned house, so why put them there? Sure, you have to provide the player with conscientious power-ups throughout the levels, but why not make them appear more realistic? On a related note, though *you* may know what you are doing in *your* game, don't always assume the player does. Give her area maps to read, journal entries to deduce clues from, and mission briefings to keep her clued in to just what is going on and what you expect from her next. Letting players flounder unknowingly through your tough game—until they succumb to sheer frustration—is certain suicide for a game designer.

When all these game mechanics interact with one another, they create other systems of gameplay, often unintentionally. Designers call this process *emergent gameplay*, as new mechanics emerge from the ways old ones mix with each other. This creates a whole new layer to game interaction. Using this concept to your advantage is one of the most difficult jobs newbie game designers have. It requires a lot of thought, often looking for tangents and balances. Sometimes designers can't think outside the box because they are too close to their art, but you can bet players will find the loopholes if they exist. For instance, some of the early action games had sections in their levels that had healing pads in them; as long as the players stood next to the healing pads, their health would be renewed. Players soon learned to pick fights with monsters and then run and stand on healing pads—never losing health while taking out all the enemies in the game. This is one example of emergent gameplay.

Here's another example of emergent gameplay: you give the player the ability to move crates around, stack them, and climb on them. If you show the player a level filled with six crates, and you have those six crates there for show or level dressing (and not for intrinsic gameplay) the player might start using his imagination. He could use these six crates to build a makeshift staircase up to a higher area of the level, finding a way to skip past obstacles and scripted events

Figure 3.4
"If there is a crate, I must push it!" (*Legend of Zelda: Windwaker,* image courtesy of Nintendo 2003)

you have waiting for him (see Figure 3.4). If you are smart and take this scenario into account, you might put those six crates in the level and one virtual "Easter egg"—such as a pouch of gold coins—up high enough for the player to reach it (while cutting off his grandiose access to skipping ahead).

Emergent gameplay like this is sometimes hard to divine; you won't discover it's there until the level is play-tested for continuity. Here's one last example that came about when Blue Box and Lionhead Studios were making *Project Ego* (which later became titled *Fable*). Players could fall in love and marry NPCs, and when they did so the father of the bride awarded them a significant dowry. In test-playing, the developers were shocked when players learned they could run around making girls marry them in order to win the dowry, then go off and cheat on or actually kill the girls. The developers had to rethink the restrictions over in-game marriages.

Game Graphics

Initial illustrations, character sketches, landscape paintings, and so on should be outlined here. Later more artistic groundwork will be expected, but the concept forms the rough draft and inspiration. The important sketch and concept art should expand in progression. Miscellaneous artwork to be found under game graphics may include storyboards, environment designs, character designs, character model sheets, and GUIs.

The first bit of game graphics you have to consider and one of the most important is the graphical user interface (or GUI). The graphical user interface is

Figure 3.5
Clear concise heads-up display (*Ghost Recon*, image courtesy Ubisoft 2005–2006)

critical for proper gameplay. A graphical user interface is made up of all onscreen game elements that are used to give the player information or allow him to navigate the game. Because the player sees the GUI of a game almost as much as he does his own avatar, the GUI must be carefully designed to impart the mood and feel of the game while being simple enough for play to be practically intuitive in nature. Text types, patterns, and textures should all reflect the game's intention. Create a sketch of what you think the GUI should look like before you begin building it.

A common GUI element is the heads-up display (HUD; see Figure 3.5) that is imperative in first-person shooters for describing how much health, ammo, and armor a player character possesses. 3DGS has a default HUD akin to *Quake*, but if you want to create custom heads-up displays, that is not only possible but recommended. Heads-up displays, like any other variety of graphical user interface elements, must be fast, intuitive, and reflective of the game's theme.

Another common type of GUI in many role-playing games is the character creation screen. This is usually a 2D panel where players select their characters, assign their characters' skills, and begin the avatar parameters. A character creation screen can be smooth and simple, for ease of its function; or it can have a lot of pattern and texture reflective of the game's mood and feel. Few of them are both. We will tackle character creation screens later when we make a role-playing game.

A *storyboard* is a series of sketches indicating that a sequence of events is taking place. In some ways, storyboards are similar to comic strip panels (see Figure 3.6).

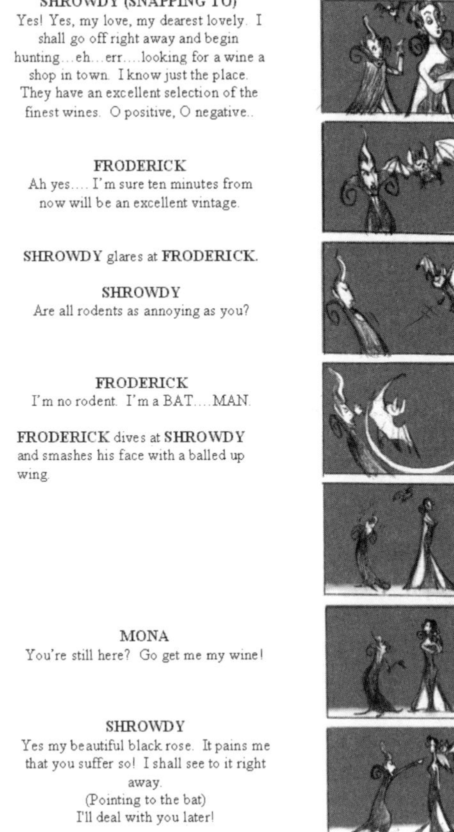

Figure 3.6
A sample storyboard (*A Vampyre Story,* image courtesy Autumn Moon Entertainment 2005–2006)

They reflect the in-game animation, as in cut-scenes for exposition. Storyboards are written similarly to a playwright's script, but with square panels of illustrations beside each section. I have seen some game flowcharts turned into storyboards and then scripted visually, while other storyboards spring from static cut-scenes and expositions only. Learning to storyboard is an arduous task for a beginner, but it can be very rewarding.

An environmental design helps the lead artist (or the concept artist, sometimes one and the same) communicate to the entire game development team what the mood of an area or game level will be. An environmental illustration is often a full-color illustration of a game environment as it will be seen when the game is created. Many of them that I have seen could stand alone as beautiful landscape paintings, while others are more like rough sketches without a lot of detail.

A character design or model sheet is a sketch of a character that will appear in the game. The most important character would be the player's character (the avatar), but character designs must be made of every character beforehand to be included in the finished game. Character designs are vital to the success of a game because they tell you the shape and proportion of the characters, and you take off straight from a model sheet to a 3D build. Monsters, enemies, and NPCs should all be sketched out before they are built in the Model Editor (or MED). Some character model sheets list specifications, such as polygon count, software to be used, and a short list of the character's animation sequences. (See Figure 3.7.)

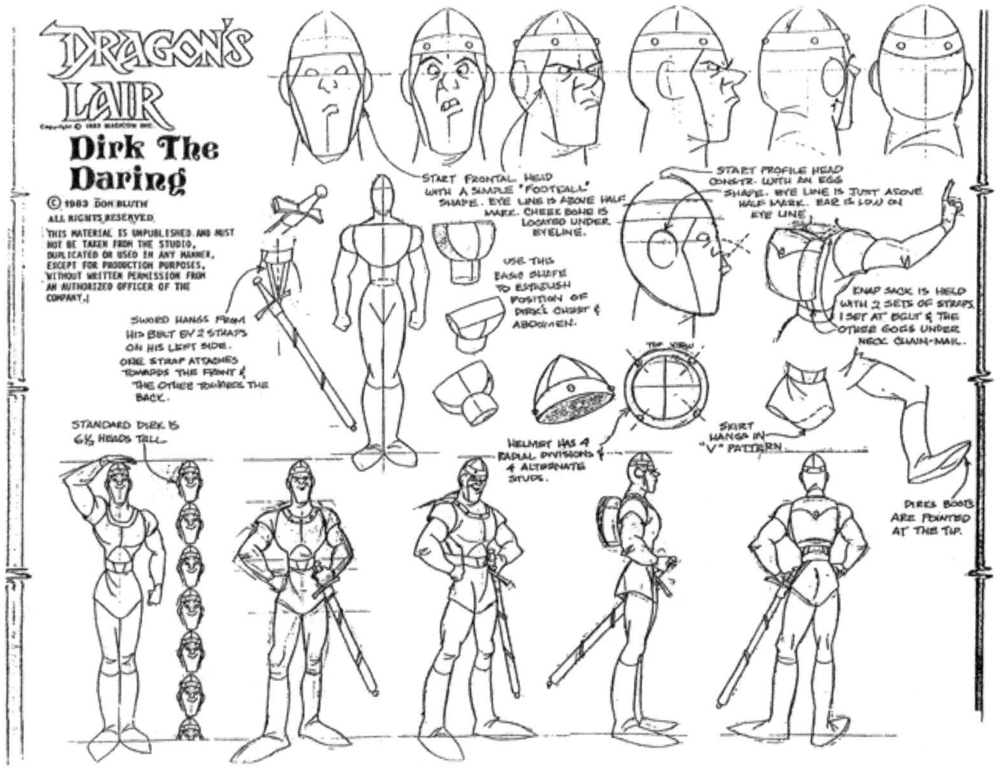

Figure 3.7
Model sheet for the dashing Dirk the Daring, from the coin-op arcade hit *Dragon's Lair* (image courtesy Don Bluth Productions 1983)

Game Sound

The sound engineering, music score, voiceovers, and sound effects must be listed in this section. If the game design team can afford a professional composer or professional voice talent, this should be listed first for investor/publisher eyes. Audio is a very important part of game design because video games are not only graphical; sophisticated sound cards in computers, 3D or Doppler effects, and surround sound speakers have begun to focus the sound aspects of games and make them more vibrant as a result. Sound engineering is further broken into two parts—sound bytes and music—and these two parts are broken down even further:

Sound Bytes

3D GameStudio uses WAV and OGG files for its sound bytes, which can be dropped into game levels when designing them (which is wonderful for the Doppler effects) or scripted in.

- **Character Speech**—Spoken dialog, what are called voice-overs.
- **Character and Item Noises**—Falls, jumps, grunts, groans, and weapon attacks.
- **GUI Events**—Button clicks, beeps, attention jingles, etc.
- **Special Effects**—Such as logs rolling, doors opening, and magic spells.
- **Environments**—Late-night crickets chirping, wind in the leaves, ambient noises, etc.

Music

3D GameStudio uses MIDI and WAV files for its music, although with the higher editions you can also play MP3 or OGG sound files.

- **Level Themes**—Some levels may have their own score, such as those that are more ominous than others.
- **Event Jingles**—Victory songs, sadness from loss, etc.
- **Cinematic Compositions**—For cut-scenes and introductory episodes.

In Summary

There are many other elements you could include in your game design document. After these matters are met sufficiently, you could choose to store all your game notes, maps, sketches, or design changes at the end of your game outline. However, the headings we have just covered house the main necessities you will need to get started making a game. Game outlines not only form a blueprint for your design, they may also serve as a game proposal if you were to take your game idea to investors or producers in search of funding.

Noah Falstein has been a long-time reviewer of game proposal submissions for companies like LucasArts Entertainment and Dreamworks Interactive, and he has a lot to say on the subject of creating game design documents. He suggests that you make *sure* your design is complete but not padded with "meaningless back-story features." Do not work in a void: look at the other games of this genre to compare your material with the competition; it is better to sully your creativity than to miss the obvious. Do not make wild claims that your game concept is unique—especially when it is another Pac-Man clone.

The old adage "think before you leap" is equally valid to game development. Creating a single game is a lot of work (as the game design cycle shows you). Sitting down in front of your computer and trying to spit out a game off the top of your head just won't work. If you try, you will discover you are getting nowhere fast. Even industry professionals—veteran game designers—will tell you they never work in a haphazard fashion. If they did, they wouldn't get anything done. So plan to work smarter, not harder, and write everything down on paper before you start building.

What You Have Learned

A game design document is imperative to making a game. For one thing, it keeps the entire design team on track and on the same page. It also creates a blueprint for the creative process. It allows artistic people to expand and explore their own creativity without going off on wild tangents.

- You have learned all the elements that are common to game outlines.
- You have learned the importance of these various elements (such as player motivations, user interfaces, and concept artwork).
- You have a firm idea of what goes into a game design.
- You could write a game design document if you had to.

For Review

1. Select an original piece of work that you are going to adapt into a video game. Do not select anything that has been turned into a video game before. For instance, you could select a novel, a poem, a song, a painting, or movie—anything that could be turned into a game and makes you think outside the box. Write a Premise (High Concept) that illustrates your decisions, such as who the player plays, what the player does, and what game genre you plan to use.

2. Play three of the most popular (top-of-the-charts) games at your local video store. Study them in terms of content. Who is their target audience, do you think? What demographic and psychographic are the developers trying to reach? What age generations were they intended for? Do you think that the game developers reached these objectives?

3. Discuss three different player motivations and examples of games that address those psychological needs. Then answer the following question: What new motivation might developers have overlooked that could become a popular sub-genre? (The industry was shocked by the popularity of games like *Dance Dance Revolution* that were offered in an age of physical exercise and mastery.)

4. Consider the following game concept: "Using strategy, the player must catch a Gupf. The Gupf is a blob creature that moves around each level, bouncing off fences, and the player can choose from two different kinds of fences: vertical and horizontal. Each stretch of fence costs money, but if the player catches the Gupf inside them he wins a lot of money. The player should be able to choose a type of fence and where to place it on the map, while telling where the Gupf is at any one time and how much time he has left to catch it. This will be a timed game, and with progressive levels of difficulty. The harder the game gets, the faster the Gupf moves and the less time the player has to catch it." Create a rough design, or quick sketch, of this game's onscreen user interface. Display all the elements mentioned.

5. Select a tabletop or board game that you like (examples include chess, Clue, Parcheesi, poker, Monopoly, Risk, Dungeons and Dragons, GURPS, and so on). How would you modify it into an original game design document for a possible video game? What elements would you keep, and which would you change? How would you translate the setting and characters from the board or tabletop to the computer?

6. Construct from scratch your own original game outline. What kind of game would you like to make? Follow the general outline I have demonstrated and come up with your own unique game that you would like to build with the software. Consider every aspect carefully: the genre, the characters, the mechanics, and the walkthrough. For extra credit, sketch some character or environment illustrations or provide maps of the major areas in the game. Keep your original game short (one or two levels) as you would see in a playable demo because you do not want to start big with your first project.

Review of 3D GameStudio by Dan Silverman

Someone wanted to compare 3D GameStudio and its level editor, WED, to *Doom*. There is a bit of a problem with this. *Doom* was not a 3D game and did not use a 3D game engine. Instead, *Doom* used what is known as a *raycasting* engine, which simulates 3D worlds from 2D information. As a result, the level editors for *Doom* and *Doom 2* were top-down only, allowing you to create levels by creating outlines and defining heights via coding or other tricks. I believe that individual meant to liken 3D GameStudio more to *Quake* than *Doom*, but I can only go by what was stated.

3D GameStudio is very advanced, though it is certainly not a *Doom 3* or *Half-Life 2* engine (but, then again, you are not paying hundreds of thousands for it either). The current version is fully DirectX-9 compatible and, thus, fully compatible with today's shaders and the DirectX 9 shader language. Therefore, wonderful effects can be achieved very easily in 3D GameStudio.

Some people may feel that 3D GameStudio is outdated because, in its current rendition, it is a fully BSP-compatible engine. This means no concave surfaces on one single object. While BSP may be restrictive as far as what type or level geometry you can use, it is blazingly fast in terms of the frames per second you get when running a large, complex level. Future editions of 3D GameStudio will allow the user to switch from BSP to Octree and back again, should they need to.

3D GameStudio shines in two areas: ease of use and a fairly complete toolset. When you get 3D GameStudio, you get the 3D engine, a level editor, a model editor, and a scripting environment for programming. Basically the only thing you need to add is a 2D paint program, sound, and your own creativity. This is much nicer than many other engines that force you to build your own tools.

If you are a non-programmer, you can get up and running in no time. There is nothing special that you have to do in order to run and walk through a level you have built. 3D GameStudio even comes with pre-defined templates to help you get various types of basic games up and running.

If you program, there are a few ways to go about using 3D GameStudio. One way is to use the provided scripting language, C-Script. Another way is to create and link to DLLs via the SDK using a programming language like C++, etc. So, you are not limited.

As an artist, I find that 3D GameStudio has an awesome graphical display. Images are crisp, clear and clean. Some of the other engines' displays are sometimes "muddy" (IMHO).

I own my own business creating real-time 3D content. 3D GameStudio is my main tool because I can create content for my clients quickly, and they are always pleased with the results.

Case Scenario: Mama Kat

The following reveals how I came about creating a game outline for an idea I had one day when I was doodling in the margins of a sketchbook and made a female cat with an eye patch. I suddenly experienced the proverbial "Ah-hah!" The idea I originally wrote down was this:

```
A waif—cursed to be a were-cat—struggles to survive in a wharf town, where she
subsists as a pick-pocket...eventually becoming Mistress of Rogues.
```

My basic premise was *Thief: Deadly Shadows* meets *Pirates of the Caribbean*. It would be darkly humorous at its core, with magic and fantasy added for spice. But an idea is just an idea without the proper conceptualization to clothe it, so the outline had to be placed on paper. I knew the name of the main character would be Kat (short for Katrina obviously), so I titled the game *Mama Kat*, with an optional title as *Mistress of Rogues*. Then I merely had to follow the game outline headings as I showed you above.

Genre

I had to choose a fiction genre. It was obvious to me, from the clothes they were selling at local boutiques and the talk amidst the teenagers I met, that pirates were really popular at the time. The fervor might have been incidentally summoned by the movie *Pirates of the Caribbean* and its sequel, Sid Meier's game, or *Puzzle Pirates*, which had been given special attention by the latest gaming magazines. I had loved pirates ever since the time I read (with tongue in cheek) R. Buckminster Fuller's *Operation Manual for Spaceship Earth* and watched *The Purple Pirate*. National Talk-Like-a-Pirate Day (September 19th) had always interested me, as had the *Secret of Monkey Island* adventure games from LucasArts. So I decided on a pirate game for the fiction genre.

For the gameplay type, I was initially drawn to role-playing but settled for a hybrid 3D platformer and stealth game. I wanted the player to be able to use the nimble feline skills to leap to areas of my levels, plus use stealth. I also wanted players who did not want to be nimble or stealthy—but who wanted to be hoodlums—to have some tight action combat as well. This would cover three types of players, as well as evince situational choices for them.

Setting

A wharf town inspired me to create a rough-and-tumble fantasy city called Krawl (because it rhymed with "sprawl" and sounded like "claw"). Krawl, I imagined, would be a character in of itself, and this is what I wrote about it: "The sprawling city of Krawl wraps indelicately around the banks of the Viryl Ocean, and it has since its founding been a popular pirate and smuggler hideout. Krawl is a city of rogues and thieves, barely controlled by brick-headed City Guards, and its architecture is a haphazard maze and mixture of squat and leaning Gothic structures with sweeping roofs, with a full moon almost always glaring down upon it."

I wanted to base Krawl on Merovin, a make-believe place created by C.J. Cherryh for her *Merovingen Nights* book series set in the Alliance-Union universe. The *Merovingen Nights* stories enthralled me as I read them growing up with the twisting alleyways and constant swordplay and skullduggery, and I decided it was just what Krawl needed.

Characters

The three main characters that would grace *Mama Kat* were as follows:

Katrina

The player character, seen in third-person view and heard in first-person view. Katrina is the player's persona, but is a rather noble pirate soul and a creative thinker. She is cunning, quick on her feet, and (for all the trouble she causes) a compassionate sort. Think of a voiceover by Drew Barrymore combined with the face of *Shrek 2*'s Puss In Boots. Katrina dresses in the fashionable puffy-sleeved shirts, dark embroidered vests, and short trousers of a pirate, but she does not wear any shoes so she has more control when scampering up city walls and fighting with feet as well as hands. Kat's trademark eye patch has a mouse skull in place of the Jolly Roger symbol on it, as Kat loves to eat the squirmy mice and rats that hide in back alleys. In her human form, Kat has a freckled youthful face, green eyes, and curly red tresses that never get combed properly.

Katrina uses stealth, night sight, and the impish balancing of a cat to escape from danger. She is one to rely on tricks rather than slashing her way past obstacles, but the player should feel like he has control to handle challenges his own way. Katrina's only real regret (and the deep sadness driving her) is that she never had a very compassionate father. Kat was pushed through the ringer by a bullying father and finally given up for dead (tossed into the canal in a potato sack) by him, for reasons that she only learns later when she goes to confront him. She is rescued by a fisherman and given shelter, but she runs away from him before he can realize her feline powers.

Douglas

The fisherman that saves Katrina's life and is puzzled by her behavior. Douglas misses his wife Charlene and is quick to comfort and adopt the bedraggled young red-haired girl he finds in his net one morning. He gives her food and tries to nurse her back to her former energy, but she repays him by being aloof and eventually running away. Douglas I imagined as a gruff bald man dressed in grays and greens, with a voiceover by Bruce Willis faking a Scottish accent. He stumbles over his own speech and misuses words when he tries to sound smarter than he is really, which only endears him to Katrina. His home is as much a part of him as what he wears, as he has slowly carved every cranny of the wood domicile with Celtic knot work and pretty figurehead-style carvings.

Douglas figures heavily as the Mentor archetype: he takes care of and nurtures Katrina along, teaches her some tricks and survival tips, and tries to impress upon her some life lessons that she learns are true later on in the game. In fact, as his lessons start to hit home with her later, she returns to him and opens her heart. He becomes the father figure she never had.

Whezzle

Katrina's father and the Shadow figure of the game, Whezzle is a poorly misunderstood creature. He had one love in his life: a young tribal woman he met on an island far out across the Viryl Ocean. She was beautiful and stole his heart. They lived in a hut on that island for a long time, but when he found out that she was a were-cat and could turn into a mangy panther at will, he torched their hut and took off with the daughter he'd had with her. He did not know at the time that his daughter was a were-cat as well, and that when she reached puberty, she'd be able to transform into a cat. He set up shop in Krawl and developed a reputation (some of it by accident alone) that made him the Rogue Master of Krawl.

Whezzle is a man trying to make it by hiding his shortcomings. His teeth are rotten, his eyes wide and hollow, and his hair and beard are never combed. He dresses as a pirate would, and sometimes he carries a sword-cane with a parrot knob on top. Whezzle's favorite color is purple, and everything he wears or wishes to look at (including what he thinks his daughter should wear) are purple. Whezzle prefers to avoid confrontation, but when he has to meet a challenge head on, he takes the easier route of stabbing people in the back. He is at heart a coward, and he has made many enemies in Krawl because of his actions. This will lead to later side-quests and story information that comes into play later in the game.

Notice that each of these characters has definitive character traits. They each have at least three, or what I like to call a Trait Triangle. In essence, Katrina is noble, feisty, and impulsive. Douglas is wise, trusting, and solid. Whezzle is rotten, obsessive-compulsive, and cowardly. They each also have funny little quirks. Douglas carves Celtic knot work into the heavy timbers of his home. Whezzle adores the color purple and wears it constantly. And Katrina is missing one eye, never combs her hair, and always seems contradictory.

Premise

My final premise for *Mama Kat* went something like this:

```
Considered a monster by others, you are a feisty girl who changes into a pirate cat
every night. Try the unthinkable in the wharf-side sprawling city of Krawl—and
become the Queen of Rogues! Use stealth, impish balance, pounce attacks, night
sight, and your claws to take over Krawl and rule the Rogues' Guild!
```

Synopsis

The back story for *Mama Kat* goes something like this:

```
The player starts out as the young freckle-faced redhead Katrina, as she is fished
out of one of Krawl's canals by a trawling fisherman. She refuses to recall her
past, but she mentions that a brute threw her in a potato sack and into the canal.
The fisherman takes her home and takes care of her, but she soon runs away before he
can learn that she is a cursed creature: a were-cat, able to change back and forth
from young woman to able-bodied cat. By day she is a pretty redhead with an unruly
attitude—and by night she is a slinky cat creature! She is missing one eye, but
wears an eye patch with a mouse skull on it, and even with this handicap she has
amazing abilities that allow her to escape down Krawl's winding alleys or over
its rooftops. After exploring and getting into and out of several side-quests,
Katrina goes after the brute that threw her in the canal and left her for dead: her
father, the current Rogue Master who controls the Guild of Rogues. Her father ends
up dead (one way or another) and Katrina becomes the new Rogue Mistress, having
proven her merit as well as through inheritance.
```

I do not have room to write everything that I considered happening in the game *Mama Katharina*, but I will write three scenarios for your benefit. In each of these, I placed the player amid a crux of a decision, and the player's choices led to inevitable adventure, some for better and some for worse but all befitting of the player's intentions. I also knew this would encourage replay ability and make for a more prosperous game in the end.

Challenge #1: Escape from the Market

Description: Katrina the cat-girl has just run away from Douglas' hut on the bay, and is in the canal-marked alleys and streets of the city of Krawl. She is hungry, and without thinking, she grabs a vendor's sample of bread and starts chewing. When she turns back around, she sees a red-eyed vendor and his thug buddies with blades drawn glaring at her for stealing. She takes off in a fly of fur, as she morphs into her cat-shape and attempts to escape the market.

Mission: Escape the market place. Avoid the thugs' knives.

Solution #1: The player can try to lose the thugs in the crowd. This has only slight merit, as the crowds in the marketplace shriek and clear the way as the shape-changing cat-girl runs into their midst. However, the player can time the escape right enough to pick up a sword as one of the crowd drops it and use it to fight the oncoming thugs.

Solution #2: The player can use his claws and dexterity to jump up on one of the vendor wagons and vault onto a ledge. A series of platform-style jumps and runs will steer Katrina clear of the thugs, but it will take longer and is tricky.

Solution #3: The player can use guile and money; by talking sweet to the vendor first and passing some gold into the vendor's palms before any bloodshed need erupt. Once the vendor's AI has switched back to neutral, the player can attempt to pick his purse and take the money back, if he or she wants.

Challenge #2: Get the Ronal Ruby

Description: Katrina the cat-girl has just discovered that a very important ruby has made its way into Krawl. It was aboard a plague ship, and her father the Rogue Master wants it *bad*. However, before his minions could fetch it (because they were too freaked out to), the ruby was picked up by the crooked City Guards and returned to their barracks. Now Katrina decides to get the ruby for herself, before her nasty old daddy does.

Mission: Enter the City Guards' barracks. Find the Ronal Ruby. Escape with life intact.

Solution #1: The player could sneak into the barracks through an underground sewage drainage system, but unbeknownst to him, the sewers are infested with giant rats who are not going to take so kindly to a big cat falling into their litter. The player may make it to the barracks, but the Ruby is in the top tower, in the Officer's quarters, so he has to go a long way and back to get it and get out, having to rely a lot on stealth.

Solution #2: The player can bribe a City Guard in order to dress up as the Guard and sneak into the barracks that way. This requires a lot of cunning and dialog decisions that can make or break the player's plans. If all plays out right, the player could have the Officer hand Katrina the Ruby himself, having been convinced she's a secret courier for the Royal Navy. Then she just has to slip out the same way she got in, and breathe a sigh of relief.

Solution #3: The player could buy a grapple line and find a clever and high enough roof spot with coverage to launch the cable at the City Guard barracks tower. This will immediately set off multiple alarms, as Guards see Katrina breaking in by slinking along the wire, but she will end up in a room across the hall from the Officer's quarters (and the ruby inside). The player will have to be quick to snatch the ruby and get out, or else fight lots of armed Guards as they burst into the tower.

Challenge #3: Befriend the Bats

Description: Katrina the cat-girl has learned that the bats of Orkley cave have amazing gifts, including the ability to think and speak to humans. The cute cartoon-looking bats can give her far-sight, or the ability to see things going on from far away. She needs to see the plans of her father, the Rogue Master, and to do so, she needs to get one or more of these bats to help her. So she travels into the Orkley cave and prepares for anything.

Mission: Get the bats to help Katrina.

Solution #1: The player finds the bats deep on the other side of the caves, after multiple arduous platform-style challenges. However, he rushes in and the bats have seen Katrina coming and have fled to a place that she cannot climb. The player may attempt to climb the sheer cave walls after the bats, but in so doing fall down a steep face and end up hurt. This causes one of the bats, named Itchy, to come to her aid out of compassion.

Solution #2: The player could find out from a local hermit, living in the cave, that the bats have been driven farther and farther into the cave and away from their natural food source by a great black bear. The player might decide to find the bats' natural food source, and when Katrina finally encounters the bats, the food becomes a bribe. This is a tricky task, as the natural food source is a type of gloom-fruit that grows by the treacherous rocks of the bay on the shores of the Viryl Ocean.

Solution #3: The player could find out from a local hermit, living in the cave, that the bats have been driven further and further into the cave and away from their natural food source by a great black bear. The player might decide to find and stop the bear at all costs. A huge fight ensues, and the player better be lucky enough to have found a powerful inventory item or weapon before entering this fray.

Player Motivation

Escapism would have to be the primary purpose behind *Mama Kat.* Mastery and addictive qualities might enter into it as well. Plus, the player is essentially role-playing as thief, so there are taboo elements that might motivate the player.

Target Audience

Players who love to experience and explore will enjoy the many winding alleys and twisted walkways, nooks, and crannies of Krawl. Players who like puzzles and thinking will enjoy the locks that have to be picked, the goods that need rifled, and the fat merchants that need weaned from their golden tributes, all of which will take strategy. So the basis for many players is already taken care of. When it comes to action, the game will keep players who enjoy action games on the edge of their seats with adrenaline and suspense during chase scenes and swordplay.

On the demographic side, I imagined this game would attract those players who enjoy fantasy, do-it-yourself bravado, and the pirate theme. This applies to Generation-X as well as the Millennial Generation, with a brief nod to the Baby Boomers. That covers a wide scope.

Game Mechanics

The player's character would have resources like Health (which depletes whenever the player is hit by a weapon or singed by fire), Weapons (such as blackjacks, garrote wires, tranquilizer darts, poisons, and explosives), and Nine Lives (which are reduced every time the player wants to reload the game from the last check point without having to reload from the last saved game). Health could be regained by eating mice, which would have to be caught running around in game levels. Weapons could be found, bought, and upgraded, mostly through underground black market dealerships. Nine Lives would have to be discovered, as a sprite of a kitty cat face with a halo and wings, in Easter-egg locations hidden throughout the game—and would be the rarest of the resources.

I know right away that there would be parameters to playing the clever feline, and that they would consist of Impish Skill, Picklock Skill, Aim Skill, Stealth Skill, and Claw Attack; the rates of these would go up as the player earns experience in them, and the only way the player earns experience in them is by practicing them consecutively throughout the game. The more the player picks locked doors, the better he gets at the Picklock Skill, and so on. . . . This rewards system would be tempered by the player's failures, as well.

Instead of the light orb in *Thief: Deadly Shadows* or the blue-colored screen as in *Chronicles of Riddick*, a Cheshire cat smile would be permanently fixed in one corner of the screen. Whenever the player was crouched over a door, picking the lock, the smile would shift from happy to frowning, depending on whether or not any other person could see the player. If the player was hidden in shadows, the Cheshire grin would be fixed in a rictus grin. Thus there would be a stealth program handling how crafty Kat was being, and part of the system would depend on environmental factors, such as obstructions and shadows, and part of it would depend on Kat's skill parameters.

Game Graphics

See Figure 3.8 for a model sheet of Mama Kat.

Game Sound

Besides getting some quality RPG music for this game, it would be advisable to record some voiceovers and mix digital sound for the effects.

Here are some sound bytes for use with the game by category:

- **Character Speech**—Spoken dialog by Katrina, Douglas, and Whezzle, as well as mutterings made by City Guards, merchants, vendors, and other NPCs.

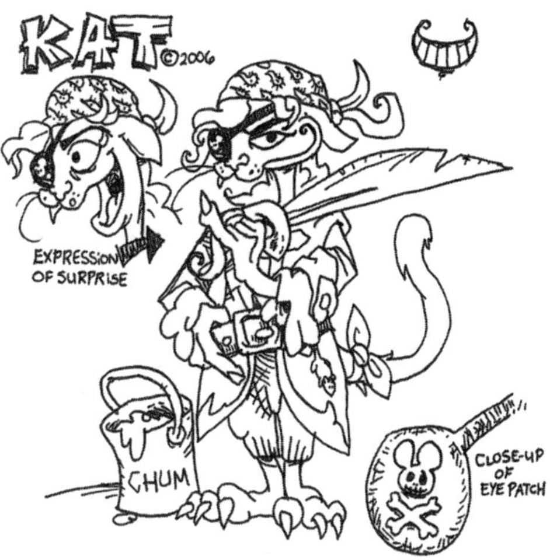

Figure 3.8
Mama Kat herself—the player's character model sheet.

- **Character and Item Noises**—Falls, jumps, sword swings, mouse squeaks, meows, pounce attacks, claw rake attacks, picking locks, etc.
- **GUI Events**—Button clicks, beeps, attention jingles, and so on.
- **Special Effects**—Magic spells, picking up Nine Lives, summoning the bat Itchy, etc.
- **Environments**—Ambient Krawl noises (day and night), ocean waves, and so on.

Here are some samples of music that will be used in the game:

- **Level Themes**—Especially surrounding the hazardous levels and at night when Katrina is out on the prowl.
- **Event Jingles**—Making it past missions, failing terribly, using Nine Lives, etc.
- **Cinematic Compositions**—Recorded music especially surrounding late-night taverns.

In Summary

This is by no means a complete game outline, but I want it to show you the meat and potatoes of what goes into a game design document when you decide to start your own. You can use this one as an example of what to do, what to think of as you start writing, and what not to do. You could even take off from here and build your own game narrative. Consider what else you might add to the *Mama Kat* game. Would you change the characters? Would you add different resources and parameters? What sort of scenarios can you come up with for the walk-through? What more would you like to see? This could be a great exercise for you to brainstorm by yourself on your own time or with friends or classmates.

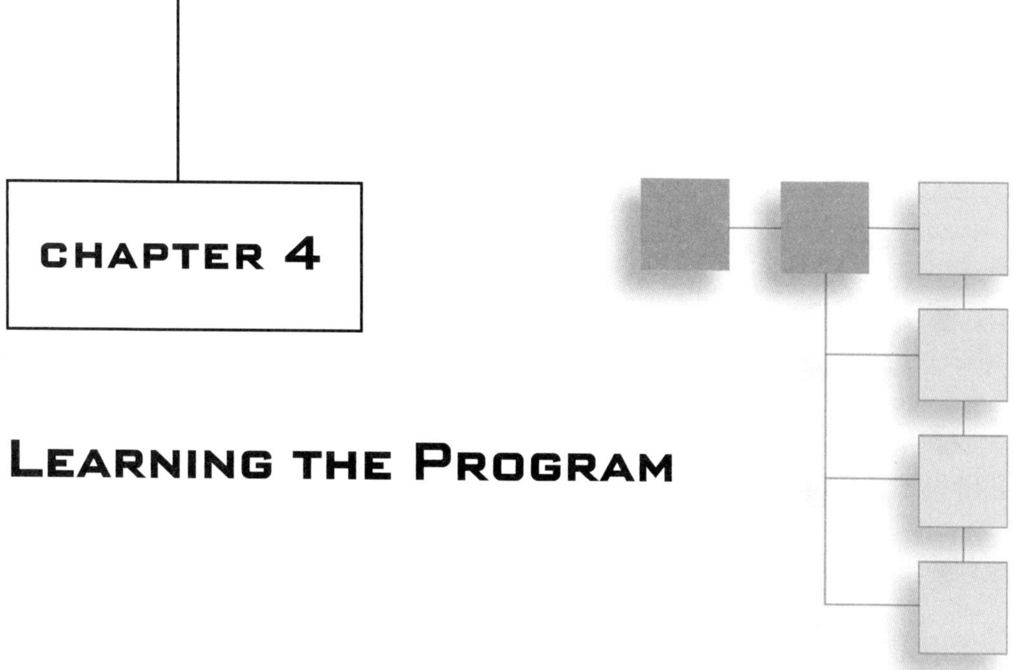

Chapter 4

Learning the Program

3D GameStudio is an IDE as well as a rapid game engine. It has everything you need to make and distribute your own 3D computer games right out of the box, including a built-in Model Editor, which is used to make the distinctive video game characters, weapons, props, and furniture for your levels; a Level Editor, which is used to make the sweeping vistas and unexplored terrain for your games; and a Script Editor, which is used to program the behaviors and actions of the game characters and scripted events.

Before you begin making your own video games, let me take a moment to familiarize you with the programs you will be using. You will have more of a solid foundation before creating a first-person shooter game or role-playing game if you understand the software that it will be built on.

MED: the Model Editor

Animated 3D models, terrain height-maps, and other elements are created for 3DGS by using the Model Editor (or MED). MED is conservatively importable. This means you can import models created with popular 3D editors, like Milkshape, or any models with common 3D file formats (such as X, 3DS, MDL, MD2, WMP, OBJ, ASE). You can find a lot of MDL and MD2 files (common for *Quake* and *Quake 2*) for free online at different modding communities. As long as you are not creating a game intended for commercial use (which means that you do not plan to distribute it with the intent to make money) and you contact the original modeler to ask if it is okay to use their models, you could borrow their mod content and manipulate it until it works in your game levels. You can find several of these models online at www.polycount.com.

If you are used to the heavy-hitter commercial 3D editors, like 3ds Max or Maya, you can alternatively create your animated models and import them with the GameStudio plug-ins, which are available online. Though I mentioned that some designers prefer to use external modeling programs, 3DGS' own Model Editor provides all the capabilities for designing models—and sometimes it's even used to make levels with. It has two major functions: a 3D Editor and a Skin Editor for applying a skin to the model. Let's look briefly at those now.

3D Editor

MED's layout has a central section with three grid panels (2D orthographic portals) and a 3D window for previewing the end result (see Figure 4.1). When right-clicking on the 3D window and selecting GXL Properties, its lighting and view range properties can be adjusted. Models are made of wire meshes, a group of vertices and triangle surfaces that are called polygons. MED is intended to be used to create low-polygon models for use with games. In the grid panels, you will see the model's wire mesh, and the model will appear see-through. In the 3D panel you will see the blocky shape of the model. Open the warlock model in the Work folder to preview MED and see how it works. Click on File > Open (or you

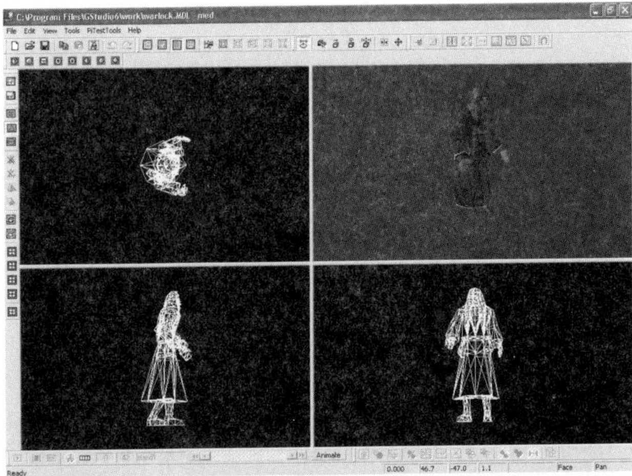

Figure 4.1
3D GameStudio Model Editor (or MED)

can hit the little folder icon at the top) and browse until you find warlock.mdl in the Work folder.

Go to View > 3D View < Textured + Gouraud because it turns on the texture-mapped 3D view, so you can preview the model with its skin on. Notice here you have also turned on Gouraud shading, too. You can also put your cursor over the center of the four panels, where they all meet, and click and drag the widths of all the panels at once. This fluid panel construction will aid you a lot as you model and animate characters. I prefer to have my 3D view take up about a third of the total view when I am previewing models in MED. You can reshape the view panels at any time that you wish, and it makes editing faster.

Click on the Position button; it is the icon that looks like a blue double-ended arrow over a blue ellipse close to the center of the top menu bar. If you are ever unsure about the names or function of any of the icon buttons, you can mouse over them and their names will appear. Once you have selected the Position tool, notice that you can now click and drag your mouse cursor in the 3D view to rotate the camera's eye around the model. You can click and drag the right mouse button to zoom in and out. All of the view panels are relatively controlled by the little icon buttons above, namely the Position, Select, Move, Rotate, and Scale buttons. We'll get to those later.

Skin Editor

MED also has a Skin Editor, which allows the model to be professionally textured. Textures are created in external 2D graphics editors and imported from a BMP, TGA, DDS, or PCX image file. MED can do skinning all by itself too; it uses UV mapping to texture the model and has an assortment of color palettes and brushes. For you to view the Skin Editor, go to Edit > Manage Skins to open the Skins window. Here you can preview available skins, make new ones, set them, and open the Skin Editor. Click the Skin Editor. Don't worry; it opens in another window (see Figure 4.2).

Now you can see the warlock model in the central pane. It works similar to the 3D view in the other window; you can drag the right mouse button to rotate the view around the character model. You can see the 2D skin, unwrapped, on the left side. The skin, as you might notice, is an unwrapped packaging that goes all the way around the model. By itself it does not look like much. In fact, it looks like a jumble of face, hair, cloth, and leather. But if you go to View > Draw Lines in the Skin Editor you will suddenly see the wireframe underneath the 2D skin that

Figure 4.2
3D GameStudio Skin Editor

MED maps to. This is because the Skin Editor is a UV skin mapper. U stands for "horizontal axis" and V stands for "vertical axis," and the two together make a decent 2D skin texture to cover a 3D model. From the Skin Editor you can export the image, fix it in a paint program, and import the image back in to create a whole new skin for the warlock. We will come back to that useful feature in another chapter. For now, go ahead and close the Skin Editor. Click the X in the upper right-hand corner to close the window.

Animation

MED offers you two methods to animate a model. If you have the A6 Commercial or Professional editions, you can use bones animation. In bones animation, you create a skeleton (literally a framework of bones), with each bone controlling a number of model vertices. In essence, an arm bone may control the vertices of the arm, and if the elbow rotates, the arm and wrist rotate with it. This is by far the best way to animate bipedal characters like humanoids, but it consumes system memory and processor power when doing the final rendering.

On the other hand, all the 3D GameStudio editions can do vertex animation. In vertex animation, mesh vertices and model shapes are moved, rotated, scaled, and so on, and the new positions are stored in key frames. This is typically sufficient for creating mech-warriors or androids, but it is pitifully hard to create realistic humans. Most of the exercises that I will present later are vertex animation, but I will describe how to do bones animation in brief for those of you with the Professional or Commercial editions.

Key frame animation is how lots of animation programs (including MED) store model poses and timing. Depending on what you name the frames, they will sequence together to create a scene. The 3DGS engine animates the model by calling up scenes, and it interpolates frames of the same naming convention in order to do so. So when your warlock has to walk across a lawn, only the frames with names like walk1 to walk7 are brought up, in order of hierarchy. The number of scenes that 3DGS can use is limited, just like all game authoring systems, because the action choices that a player can have are limited—but other than that there are really no limitations to what you want to animate the models doing.

The template scripts that come with the 3D GameStudio are designed to handle nine different basic animation scenes: `stand`, `walk`, `run`, `jump`, `duck`, `crawl`, `attack`, `swim`, and (finally) `death`. The code selects which scene to call upon and display based on the character's state at any given time. So if the player is pressing the up arrow key, the state is set to walk—and the engine calls up the `walk` scene. If the player is pressing the up arrow key and the SHIFT key at the same time, the engine recognizes the state is run and calls the `run` scene. Likewise, if the player's character falls into a water block, the state comes up as swim and that scene is showed. You do not have to animate every single state of animation. It would be really silly for a two-ton mech to want to swim, so you could leave off animating a `swim` scene. If you choose not to animate a scene for a state, know if that state should come up (perchance even by accident) and the engine cannot interpolate an animated scene for it, the model will simply freeze in its last frame of animation before it entered the state, and it will continue to hold that frame until its state has changed to a scene it can accommodate.

Look down at the very bottom of the 3D Editor window. To turn on the animation function, you have to click the button about dead center that says Animate (see Figure 4.3). Once Animate turns yellow, you have control over the warlock model's animation. There is a scrollbar you can drag left and right to reveal the various key frames of the warlock, and their names and position number show up left of the scrollbar. There is a film-tape icon beside the scrollbar that allows you to Go to Frame (given that you want to jump to a specified frame in the animation). Try it now. Click on the film-tape icon and, in the selection window that pops up, choose duck1. You should now see the warlock hunched over. Beside the film-strip icon you should see a Play button. If you click on the Play button (go ahead and do it now), you will see the warlock loop through all his animated scenes in the 3D view. To make him stop (which you will want to do

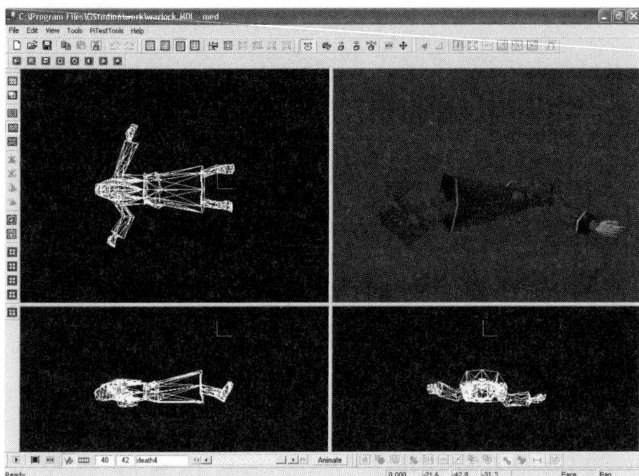

Figure 4.3
The warlock's final days

before any more editing, or else you will cause your processor to suffer), click the Play button again. The animation speed of the warlock might look off to you now, but wait till you see him in the virtual world before making any alterations to it because the program code sets his animation speed.

You might not have noticed, but the warlock model has a built-in flaw. His death scene is all wrong. If you were to let the warlock die in the game world, his final death key frame would freeze onscreen as his final visage (thereby leaving a convincing corpse). Check out the warlock's final death frame by using the Go to Frame button and selecting death5. See how he looks like he's reclining in a Barcalounger, sans the Barcalounger? He's lazing back, up above the ground plane. Use the scrollbar at the bottom to move back one frame to death4. This should be his final frame. It looks more natural.

Use the animation scrollbar to advance one frame of animation to go back to death5. To fix this little problem is going to be easy. Go to Edit > Manage Frames and make sure that death5 has been selected before pressing Delete Frames. Voila! Our irritating death snafu has vanished into the void where meaningless bytes go. We no longer have a lounging corpse, we have a better corpse. See how simple that was?

Of course, we might have needed that frame of animation for some unknown reason. You cannot undo Delete Frames to get back the death5 frame. You can get rid of death5 without having to erase the key frame, however. How do you do that? Remember I said that the engine interpolates animation based on scenes?

You could simply rename death5, and it would still be there, but it would not show up when the warlock dies. Select Edit > Manage Frames, select the frame that you want (in this case death5), and press Rename Frames. In the text field that shows in the pop-up window, type **lounge1**. Click OK. Now you still have the key frame that was death5, but the frame's name has changed and will no longer show up in the final rendering.

In-Game Rendering

Now we are going to take a look at the functions built-in that allow the model to interact in the game world. Go to the stand1 frame of animation. This is the first frame of the warlock's animation, which is the most important because it sets up the model's bounding box. The *bounding box* is what the engine uses to provide collision detection, which keeps the warlock from flying off into virtual space. He bumps into walls, and they bump back, because he has a bounding box. The first frame of his animation sets up the values for his bounding box—such as minimum and maximum x, y, and z values.

The bounding box also sets up the hull for the model to define whether or not the warlock can squeeze through doorways or under fallen tree limbs in your game levels. The hull is invisible. Imagine that this hull is a fixed size box, a little smaller than the warlock himself, that is centered on his origin. The warlock's origin is indicated by the small green-blue L or cross shape that does not appear to be attached to the model's mesh in the center of the warlock. You might have noticed it in MED before you loaded the warlock model. Because hulls can penetrate world maps or other geometric objects, it is imperative that the warlock's origin stay roughly in the center of his character. Unfortunately for you, the template scripts set the weapons that the warlock picks up to weld themselves to his origin, which means that they will be stuck in his belly. The warlock will also appear to shoot his weapons from his belly. This is always good for a chuckle, but we are going to fix this later when we program the game.

You might be wondering, "If the hull sets up the bounding box, which sets up collision detection, is there a way to view where the warlock's feet would touch the ground when I put him in the game level?" The answer is no, not necessarily. In fact, the template code does not use the model's hull to place him on terra firma; instead, it measures the distance of its feet to the ground, based on the very first frame of animation (again). This constructs a virtual ground plane that the model is standing on. The ground plane is a plane running in Cartesian space through x and y—and set beneath the model by a fixed distance z from the model's origin (if you are not familiar with geometry, coordinate z is how you tell things to position themselves up and down within virtual space). In other words, the ground plane is based on the model's lowest vertices in the first frame, like the stand1 frame. By looking at stand1, you can run an imaginary line across the warlock's feet at the bottom to get a mental picture of this ground plane. Use the scroll bar to advance the animation forward to view the walk and run animations and see that they are constructed to touch this ground plane, too. In fact, `stand`, `jump`, `walk`, `attack`, `death`, and `run` all use the ground plane as their basis for horizontal motion.

The only scenes that can break the ground plane are `duck` and `crawl`. Due to the unique way that the scripting handles these states, you should move the imaginary ground plane up 16 units. This is because the script causes the model to sink into the floor a fixed z distance of about 16 units to allow them to duck and crawl under objects that they wouldn't otherwise. This is great when your character has to scoot through a small hole in a wall, but it can be tricky to model correctly. Go to the warlock's duck1 frame and notice that he has been raised up above his original ground plane about 16 units. This goes the same for all of the `duck` and `crawl` key frames. If he wasn't, part of him would disappear through the floor when you put him in the game level and press the END key to crouch.

The last state to break the ground plane rule is swim. When the character is in the `swim` scene, it needs to keep its center (right about where the gut of the warlock is) on the origin but rotated up, like it is fanned out and swimming frog-style. Just imagine a straight line to represent the surface of the water. The `swim` cycle is called only when the model is inside of a passable block or terrain in the game world. The model will wade in shallow water. His wading height is set to be any water that is under his center of origin; anything over the origin, and it is assumed that he should be swimming. Anything deeper than wading height will cause the model to switch to a swim state. When the player surfaces or dives deeper (using the HOME and END keys, respectively), the model will actually rotate up and down accordingly. Go to the warlock's swim1 key frame and study how he was laid out to swim. You can drag back and forth on the scrollbar to watch him swim in slow motion.

You have now learned the basics of modeling in 3D GameStudio. Now we will look at the Level Editor interface. Go ahead and close the Model Editor, and if you want to you can save the changes you made to the warlock model. You might need it for later.

What You Have Learned

The Model Editor is the modeling program that comes with 3DGS, and it has a 3D editor and Skin Editor. The following are lessons you should have learned:

- You have learned how to get around in the MED interface.
- You have learned the significance of some of the menu bar icons.
- You have learned how to play the model's animation.
- You have learned how to see (and alter) key animation frames.
- You now know the significance of the model's frame names.
- You should know what a hull, bounding box, origin, and ground plane are.

The WED Interface

The character must have a virtual space to exist as a part of. What this virtual space is will be determined by you. You – as the designer – will construct a whole world (if you wish it) for the player to explore. This world might be as small as a bedroom or as large as the galaxy. Whatever the scope of the game, your world is created using the 3DGS Level Editor.

The Level Editor (also referred to as the World Editor or simply WED for short) is the main editor of 3D GameStudio. WED is a map editor and compiler in one. In it, you position the various objects, assign actions to models (also known as entities) which are created through scripts, assign textures to the level geometry, and build your levels using the Binary space partitioning (BSP) tree technique. WED functions a lot like a computer-aided drafting program. You do not have to be the most proficient mathematician to be a game designer, but some preliminary experience in geometry might come in handy.

Open the Level Editor. For your first tour of WED, it is advised that you open one of the example levels found in the Work folder. Go to File > Open (or press the Folder icon), and browse to the Work folder. There are several game levels here, but I want you to select techdemo.wmp; just remember not to save any of your changes. Notice that WED has two options: you can open GameStudio levels (WMP file extensions) or level files made with other editors (such as QLE, MAP, and so on).

View Windows

The layout for WED is simple (see Figure 4.4). WED has four portals (or view panels) in its central section: one 3D View window and three orthographic windows. They are set up different from MED because they are not fluidly controlled. Each is a Microsoft Windows window, so you can minimize, expand, and close them separately. You will have to keep your eye on the windows' name bar to make sure which window you are operating in at any given time, especially when you get to the tricky positioning and scaling of level geometry.

The orthographic grid panels are arranged on a grid that is generated by Cartesian coordinates: three points, called X, Y, and Z. Each orthographic grid panel is 2D and defined more simply by the following: Top (X and Y coordinates), Back (Y and Z coordinates), and Front (X and Z coordinates). The grid views are split into multiples of 128 units and further split into multiples of 16 units to help with snapping and spacing. The grids will automatically resize when you zoom out a bit and in steps of multiples of 8. Whenever an object is placed in virtual space, you will see it in all four windows and from different angles.

You can preview the objects as they will appear in the final game in the 3D window. Similar to the way you textured the 3D view in the Model Editor, you can see the objects in the Level Editor as fully textured—but first you have to turn it on. Go to View > Textured or press the F7 key. You can also use the 3D window to zoom and pan around the game level. Click on the 3D panel's name bar to

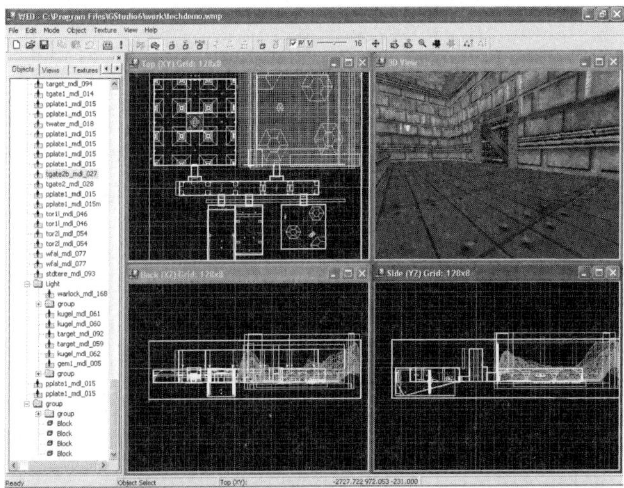

Figure 4.4
3DGS Level Editor (or WED)

select that window, and go up to the Menu. Select Mode > Walk-Thru. Now you can control all of the motion in the 3D View window with your mouse, so try it out. Move the mouse left and right to pan your view. Left-mouse click to move backward and right-mouse click to move ahead. To leave the Walk-Thru mode, press the ESC key.

The objects placed into WED are easy to tell apart: the background color defaults to blue. The white wire frame objects are called blocks (that turn red when you select one of them), the megaphone-looking things are sounds, yellow light bulbs are lights, the blue wire frame objects are 3D models, the yellow lines are plotted pathways for enemy AI, and the green cameras are positions used for viewing. This easy color-coding is a default preference set up in WED; you can change these colors later by going to File > Preferences, but I do not suggest you do that until you are more comfortable with the program.

There are considered to be two main elements used throughout WED: blocks and entities. *Blocks* are textured wire frame objects that make up the level geometry, like floors, walls, and ceilings. When the level is compiled, it takes longer for visualization controls to cover blocks than it does entities, as entities exist as external elements. *Entities* include terrain height-maps, 3D models, and sprites. This is why the basic level geometry is developed with blocks, but all the "dressing" and props, like trees, picture frames, dirt, and more, are created with entities. When creating the hallway of a house, for instance, I like to make the walls, ceilings, and floors all out of blocks. I might even make some trim for the top of the wainscoting out of smaller blocks. But when it comes to the wallpaper, chairs, bureaus, and picture frames, I prefer to make those from textures, sprites, and models.

Toolbar Buttons in WED

Here you can find the basic instructions found in WED. First, look at the menu toolbar. You will find that most of the functions you will use have been condensed to icons. From left to right these are as follows:

- **New**—Creates a new game level from scratch.
- **Open**—Opens a previously saved level.
- **Save**—Saves your work. Do not save your file as "untitled," as any level called this will not be programmable. Likewise, always keep your file names short and lowercase, with no unusual characters like spaces, dollar signs, or hyphens.
- **Copy and Paste**—Duplicates selected objects.
- **Undo**—The Undo feature is limited when adjusting Object properties but is otherwise unlimited in capacity.

- **Build WMB**—Compiles the WMP level into the binary WMB ready for running.
- **Run**—Used to test-run the level; opens up the level in the engine, along with the program script. You enter further command line options here.
- **Select**—Used to select objects that you click on with your mouse; if the object you tried to select did not turn red, it is not selected and is probably covered by another object that was; continue clicking until you get to the object you desire. You can also click and drag a yellow frame around multiple objects in one of the orthographic portals to select multiple objects at once.
- **Move, Rotate, and Scale**—Alter the orientation and shape of selected objects when you click and drag them; alternately, you can use the arrow keys once the object has been selected. You can click the top bars of each of the orthographic windows to adjust the object from multiple angles. When using the Scale mode, you can scale vertically and horizontally simultaneously by holding down the Ctrl key while scaling.
- **Vertex Move, Edge Move, and Face Move**—Alter these aspects of the selected object. In each case, yellow dots will appear that you can click and drag to move the selection to a new position. When compiling your map, you cannot have any concave areas, so WED will alert you if you move your selection in a way that would create anything but a convex.
- **Add Object**—Add blocks and entities to the virtual space.
- **Delete Object**—It's faster to select the object and press the Delete key.
- **Snap On/Off, Snap Mode, Snap Size, and Axis Restriction**—Don't worry about these right now.
- **Eye Move, Eye Rotate, and Eye Zoom**—Used to orient the orthographic and 3D View windows. These will change the position or orientation of the virtual "eye" to fix a new focus point.
- **Camera Move and Walkthrough**—Used to explore the level through the 3D View window.
- **Scope Up and Scope Down**—Moves up or down when dealing with groups of objects.

Project Window

On the left-hand side of the screen, you will see several tabbed columns with information necessary for your level build; this is called the Project window. In the Project window you will find the following:

- **Objects**—This is a tree list, or hierarchy, of all the groups, blocks, and entities used in the level. To select one of the objects, double-click on it. To immediately focus on one of the objects in the view windows, right-click on the object and select Go To. If you click on a group's plus sign (+) it will turn into a minus sign (–), and all the objects within that group will be displayed and managed.

- **Textures**—This will be the most important Project window tab you will use (see Figure 4.5). In Textures, you can view (in descending order) the currently selected object's texture, the most recently applied texture, and the WAD or

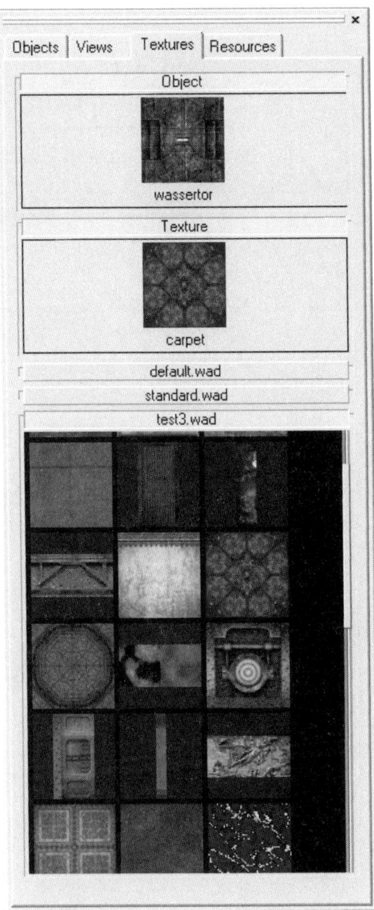

Figure 4.5
Textures in WED

WADs you currently have open and are using. I will describe what WADs are and how textures come into play later on. Also note that you can right-click inside open WADs to open the Texture Manager, and that you can also Save WADs or Add Textures here. Textures must be of a power of 2 (such as 256 × 128, 1024 × 256, or 64 × 64) for best effects; odd ones (like 394 × 213 or 723 × 1280) are often rejected and, if not rejected, are slower at rendering. You can right-click in open WADs, go to Show, and select the size of the textures you want visible in the Properties window, such as 1:1 ratio or 16:16 ratio. This will help you manage your textures.

- **Resources**—Here you will find all of the files, such as the program scripts, that are currently a part of the game. If you right-click on a behavior script and select Open, the source code will be displayed automatically for you in a separate window.

Note

At the very bottom of the WED screen, you will notice that the system traces your mouse position (and objects you may be placing or dragging with it) in the view portals above. It is tracing your position in Cartesian coordinates, going in order: position X, position Y, and position Z. This allows you further control of your placements and better handling when it comes to programming items like teleporters.

Running Levels

Now you are ready to test-run techdemo.wmp. Click on the menu icon that looks like a red exclamation mark. If you are unsure about any of the menu icons, mouse over them and their names will appear so you can read what they are called. The red exclamation mark button is the Run button. Click OK when you are ready to run the level.

This tech demo was created by Conitec in 2001 to illustrate the capabilities of the A6 3D GameStudio Commercial edition. It has several areas that you are free to explore, including a Static Light Room, a Water Room, a Shooting Range, a Weather Zone, and a Dynamic Light Room. Your onscreen avatar is a model that comes free with 3DGS, called fempunk.mdl. To see what she looks like (as the tech demo starts in first-person POV) press F7 to cycle out to the third-person perspective (see Figure 4.6). You can continue pressing F7 to cycle through all of

Figure 4.6
The tech demo in action

the POVs 3D GameStudio includes by default. You might want to take note of them now, as we will come back to them when we start setting up our camera angles when building our very first game. They include first-person, third-person, orbiting, and from-the-side. You can move the girl character around using the arrow keys on your keyboard. Hold down the SHIFT key while pressing the arrow keys to run in any direction. Press HOME to jump up and down and END to crouch; while crouched, you can use the arrow keys to crawl.

When you enter the Water Room, you will notice that it is full of water (including fish for added realism). Make sure you are in third-person mode and wade into the water. Notice that your character's walking will slow down. When your character walks in to where the water reaches just over her knees, your punk girl will start swimming. This is because the water has reached her origin and switches to the swim state. While swimming, you can use the arrow keys to move around, the HOME key to swim to the surface, or the END key to dive down.

As soon as you enter the Shooting Range, the programmers lock your view mode to first-person again. It will make more sense why later on when we create our first action game. For now, walk up to each of the weapons. You will automatically pick them up. Try them out by aiming and shooting at the targets (see Figure 4.7). Special physics programming causes the targets to react differently. You have your choices of various weapons, and you can cycle between them using the number keys on your keyboard.

Figure 4.7
Try different weapons in the Shooting Range.

The Weather Zone includes lightning and rain, and if you wait long enough a tornado will appear. These are examples of particle and sprites effects. The tornado will not harm your character, but it could be programmed to pick the character up and throw her—or cause health damage—if you wanted it to. The water puddles are not water blocks like the one in the Water Room, so you can't wade or swim in them. This is based on the way the designer created them. We will look at the difference later when you create your own game.

When you are ready to leave the tech demo, press ESC. This will bring up the default game menu. The menu allows players to save their game, load a saved game, open and make changes to screen options, view helpful hints, and quit or resume the game. Use the arrows to go down and select Quit—or right-click to turn on the selection cursor (a red arrow) and use your mouse to select Quit. When it asks you if you really want to quit, select Yes. You have now test-run your first game map in 3D GameStudio!

What You Have Learned

The Level Editor (or WED) is the main engine of the 3DGS software, and it is the main one you need to learn to use. The following are lessons you should have learned:

- You have learned how to get around in the WED interface.
- You have learned the significance of the menu bar icons.
- You have learned the significance of the Properties window.
- You now understand the Cartesian -based windows.
- You know how to use the 3D View window to Walk-Thru.
- You have learned how to test-run a game map.
- You have been shown the default 3DGS game functions.

SED: the Script Editor

We can create a game by clicking together a level from prefab geometry pieces (much like Lego blocks), placing players, props, weapons, and monsters (and attaching behaviors to each of them), adding a game menu, and then publishing the whole shebang in a standalone EXE file. So why would you need to do any programming? One reason: games "clicked together" from predefined bits are boring. You have to program to customize your game, bring to life the player's experience, and have your individual vision bloom. However, the main goal behind programming is not to spend all your time doing it—the main goal is to take the task of making scripts fast and easy for you, the designer. That's what 3D GameStudio excels at.

I just want you to know that programming does not have to be difficult, time-consuming, or scary. I am still more of an artist than I am a programmer today—even after programming my own games in 3D GameStudio. Part of the reason this is true is that 3D GameStudio's wonderfully simple program language (call it WDL or C-script) is very user-friendly. There are several levels of programming language. Essentially a programming language is a translator for a human to talk to a computer and vice versa. Since we can't speak machine code, we use syntax-based languages with object-oriented and Boolean logic. C-script is closer to human speech than it is to machine code, so beginning programmers *can* wrap their brains around it without having to learn a whole new way of speaking. The 3DGS Script Editor (also called SED) is a lovely syntax editor that makes the process even more painless and fun for the user.

But before we take a look at SED, I want to give you a brief overview of what programming is to bring you up to speed. If you are already a programmer or have worked with higher-end languages like C++ or Delphi before, you might not need this refresher. If you don't, feel free to skip down to the section "C-Script Syntax," and start reading again from there. If you would like to read about programming, then please continue.

Programming

Note

> "I wrote my first game on a remote terminal using APL/360 as the language. My first micro-computer game emulated a complete tank war game on a home-brew system I built that had a whopping 4K of memory and a 512-byte operating system. The point is, a good writer need not blame his tools. He'll make do!"
>
> —Scott Adams

To get a computer to do something—well, anything really—you have to come down (or up) to its level. A computer cannot process information in human language; it can only communicate in binary machine code. This numeral code

Figure 4.8
Binary machine code

(really just a positional notation with a radix of 2) is a bunch of 1s and 0s, forming a pattern of switch-on and switch-off. A line of machine code might look like 010011000101011 (see Figure 4.8). This is not only the language of machines, starting with electronic switch-boarding, but it is the way that computers get things done. A computer cannot—insofar—read a human being's mind and interpret what we want it to do. There are scientists in the fields of cybernetics, robotics, and nanotechnology that are currently making hypotheses about computer-human interaction, and if you have the free time to study haptic technology it can be very rewarding. But for the moment let us assume that the only way you are going to make your game work the way you want to is to actually sit down at the keyboard and have a chat with your PC.

To have this little chat, you are going to have to use a translation device. This is where syntax language comes in. Core programming languages (of which C-based languages are a part) are syntax languages that narrow the gulf between human programmers and the machines. The syntax is nothing without a compiler, however. Compilers chop up the syntax into understandable parts and then in turn convert them into binary. In this fashion, the programmer can tell a computer what to do and when.

By now you might be curious, how would a programmer know what to tell the computer? For instance, if you are programming a game like *Hitman: Blood Money* and you want your bald-headed model of assassin heroics to slip unseen, crouching in shadows, what does the programmer have to type into a script editor to make the computer understand that? The human language, you might be thinking, is full of innuendo and inferences that a computer just won't be able to comprehend. Very good, you are absolutely right. Let's take a look at this for a minute.

You can tell a teenager at the DMV to start the car and back out of the parking lot, but how would this translate if you wanted to tell a computer to? First, you would have to break down every segment of the command. Then you would have to break down the logic so that the computer understands what it is doing as well as what not to do. You would have to tell it something like this: "Walk up to shiny metal box with rubber tires under it. Walk up to the side door where you see plastic wheel attached to dash. Grab and pull up on metal handle on outside of door to open car door. Climb into the car, settling on seat first before closing the car door. Pull car keys out and aim them in correct position before inserting into side of steering column. . . ."

This could go on and on, and you would even have to go back to finish identifying "What is a steering column?" "How do I climb into car?" "What is 'car keys'?" and so much more. Imagine that this process is the same as describing the operation to a Neanderthal that has just woken up today out of a big block of Nordic ice flow. He has no idea what you are talking about and has extremely limited concepts of the vocabulary you use. You have to be succinct, direct, and definitive about everything you try to communicate.

Algorithms and Human Logic

Algorithms are not our normal way of thinking about problems. We do not naturally solve problems in our daily lives with the use of algorithms. There are several reasons for this, and it helps explain the human-to-computer gap:

- We tend to start executing as soon as we start thinking about a problem.
- We tend to tailor our solutions to the problems at hand; in other words, we do not often have standard solution protocols.
- We rarely think about the individual steps it takes to solve a problem. Minor problems we solve automatically, and other ones we make automatic inferences about.
- We don't write down our solutions to problems in step-by-step fashion.
- Some things just seem obvious to us because of our upbringing and shared experiences, which a computer wouldn't have.
- We tend to make minor adjustments to our solutions and change our plan of tactics automatically, without consciously realizing our evaluation process.
- We act most of the time based on emotions and intuition, which machines don't have.

A programmer has to come up with an algorithm. An algorithm includes the solution to a problem, such as this, and the steps by which the machine can solve it. To create an algorithm, a programmer has to identify what the problem is, define a solution, turn the solution into an algorithm, program the algorithm, and finally check to see if the algorithm works. Solutions to algorithms generally come in three flavors: sequential, conditional, and looping. Let's take a brief look at them.

Sequential Algorithms

These algorithms continue along a set course. The example given about getting into a car and starting it would be an example of a *sequential* algorithm. You are telling the computer what to do, step by step, and you do not expect any deviation from the norm. Unfortunately, sequential algorithms are dull in games because games are about randomness and interactivity. If you were simply going to code an animated CG movie, you could have it done in sequential style. For games, you are going to have to work with conditional and looping algorithms as well.

Conditional Algorithms

These algorithms follow the logic of British mathematician George Boole—what we call Boolean logic. *Conditional* algorithms (sometimes called *selective logic*) are most often identified by their instruction code syntax, `if...then/else`. By `if...then/else` statements you can set up whole subroutines to check for interrupts to your sequential algorithms. For instance, say that you are creating a finite state machine (FSM). Finite state machines are most prevalent in games as enemy monsters that the player has to beat. The simplest FSM is a monster that is given a set path to wander, such as "go to tree, then to rock, then to barn, and then back to tree." This is a sequential algorithm. It is also a looping one, but we won't worry about that right now. Now let's say the hero comes across the monster. We will want to interrupt the algorithm. If the hero is bleeding and unarmed, we might want the monster to attack the hero. If the hero is armed and loud, we might want the monster to act frightened and run away. This is where we would program a sequential logic function. We would write a bit of code like:

```
{
  if (player_bleeding==true)
        {attack;}
  else if (player_bleeding==false)
        {
        if (player_armed==true){run_away;}
        else if (player_armed==false){attack;}
        }
  else {return;}
}
```

Looping Algorithms

These are logic functions you want to continue into perpetuity or until some measure has been met. Looping algorithms are most often noted by their syntax

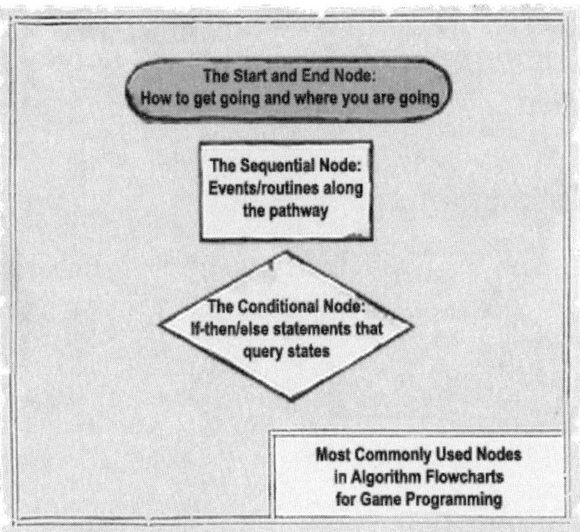

Figure 4.9
Nodes represent instructions in the algorithm.

`while`. For instance, every player's character must have a `while (alive)` statement placed somewhere in its behavior code, or else the machine would play right through the rest of its commands and then crash, and the player would wonder where his character went. To keep the player's character in the virtual playground, we have to use a `while (alive)` statement to keep the character around so the player can use him as a serviceable avatar until such time that the character is fragged and dies.

Perhaps the easiest (and most visual) way for us humans to conceive of an algorithm is the flowchart method. With flowcharts, you construct graphical representations of how an algorithm should work based on the logic you are using (see Figure 4.9). Flowcharts are similar to descending trees, as they begin with the Start of the algorithm and continue on until they reach the End (or in a looping algorithm, until they reach the `wait` that brings the routine back to the Start again). Along the way nodes represent sequential steps, conditional statements, and looping commands. Creating flowcharts is in itself a craft and area of study, which could aid you in the development of programs. See Figure 4.9 for the most commonly used nodes in flowcharts, and turn back to Chapter 3 (Figure 3.1) for a representation of how flowcharts are arranged.

C-Script Syntax

I have probably given enough hype about C-script, but I have not defined what it is exactly. C-script was originally called World Definition Language (which is why the script files carry WDL file extensions today). C-script is easy, flexible, and just as powerful as many of the BASIC-based 3D languages that it originates from. It is an object-oriented language that is a simplified version of the language C++. If you do not know how to program in C++, C-script can teach you all the basics of computer programming. If you have ever programmed in JavaScript or the C-languages, you will already have a foundation for the syntax.

The syntax consists of definitions and functions. Definitions set object names and starting properties. For instance, you can define a screen image by setting a bitmap panel; this would be done through a definition. We will do several of these as we learn about setting up user interfaces. Functions determine the behavior of world objects by making them run through instructions during game play; this causes an object's settings to change dynamically. For instance, you would set an action of `player_walk` to the player's character, and the player character (being an entity) would run through various subroutines, including looping logic, to check whether the player character is still alive or whether he has been killed.

Definitions

An example of a definition, as I stated before, could be a screen panel that would show up on the user's computer screen and overlay camera views. Let's take a look at one and the common definition syntax used:

```
BMAPscreen1 = "my_screen.pcx"; //defines a bitmap, named screen1
PANEL first_screen {bmap = screen1;} // sets up the bitmap to be used
```

Objects usually consist of one or more of the following elements:

- **Variable**—(`var`) Usually a variable is given a fixed-point number of up to 6 digits, with up to 3 digits after the decimal (for example, 123456.123). Due to its fixed-point accuracy of up to 0.001, it is more than sufficient for most applications.

- **String**—(`STRING`) Usually a string is a fixed text string written within quotation marks, often intended for in-game dialog. Various line feeds can be implemented by placement of `\n` such as "this is my first and \n second line of text."

- **Flag**—Flags are fixed binary switches, which you can imagine as a light switch, where 1 means "on" and 0 means "off."

- **Color**—Colors are addressed as blue, green, and red values between 0 and 255 (0 being black and 255 being white). 255 must never be exceeded.

- **Angle**—Angles are given in degrees between 0 and 360. They count counter-clockwise. Euler angles are used for 3D: `pan` is 0–360 horizontal along the z-axis, `tilt` is –90–+90 vertical along the y-axis, and `roll` is 0–360 rotated and tilted along the x-axis.
- **File name**—(`"filename"`) The file name represents the content of the file. The file name is limited in the program to 20 characters, all lowercase, and must not contain a path or unusual character besides the underscore (_) character. Valid extensions for files in 3DGS are PCX, BMP, DDS, or TGA for bitmaps and sprites, MDL for models, WMB for map entities, MID or MP3 for songs, WAV or OGG for sound effects, AVI or MPG for movie clips and cut-scenes, and WDL for code scripts.

Functions

Functions control the behavior of game objects and especially the entities. 3D GameStudio is a multi-tasking game engine, so it allows a lot of routines and subroutines to run simultaneously. Functions are instructions that execute in-game. Some, called actions, run on start-up, while others (such as keystroke functions) run only when triggered by the player.

The following is an example of a function:

```
// this will set up the player's character
action my_player()
 {
        my.fat=off;
        my.narrow=on;
        my.trigger_range = 24;
        my._movemode = _mode_walking;
        my._force = 0.05;
        my._strafe = on;
        my._bob = on;
        my._health = 100;
        drop_shadow();
        player_walk();
 }
```

You will work on code scripts in the chapters dealing with making games based on their genre; there you will learn the basics behind the code and what the functions mean—as well as how to make them your own!

The Interface

Open up the Script Editor (or SED). SED is useful for creating your own custom scripts and programs for 3D GameStudio (see Figure 4.10). To help you along the way, SED is a syntax editor, which means that it provides special syntax highlighting, code completion, bug testing, and other useful features that will improve the performance of your coding. You could very well use Microsoft Notepad (which comes free with the Microsoft Windows operating system) to code your WDL scripts, but SED will offer you a lot more functionality out of the box that a simple text editor will not. I just want to show you some of them while you have SED open.

First, open up a default script, such as the main program for the tech demo we created earlier. Go to File > Open (or click the Folder icon) and browse to the Work folder, where you will find techdemo.wdl. Notice that game scripts match the name of the level they were created for. I will show you how and why later. For now, open techdemo.wdl. Now you can view the script, line by line, which runs

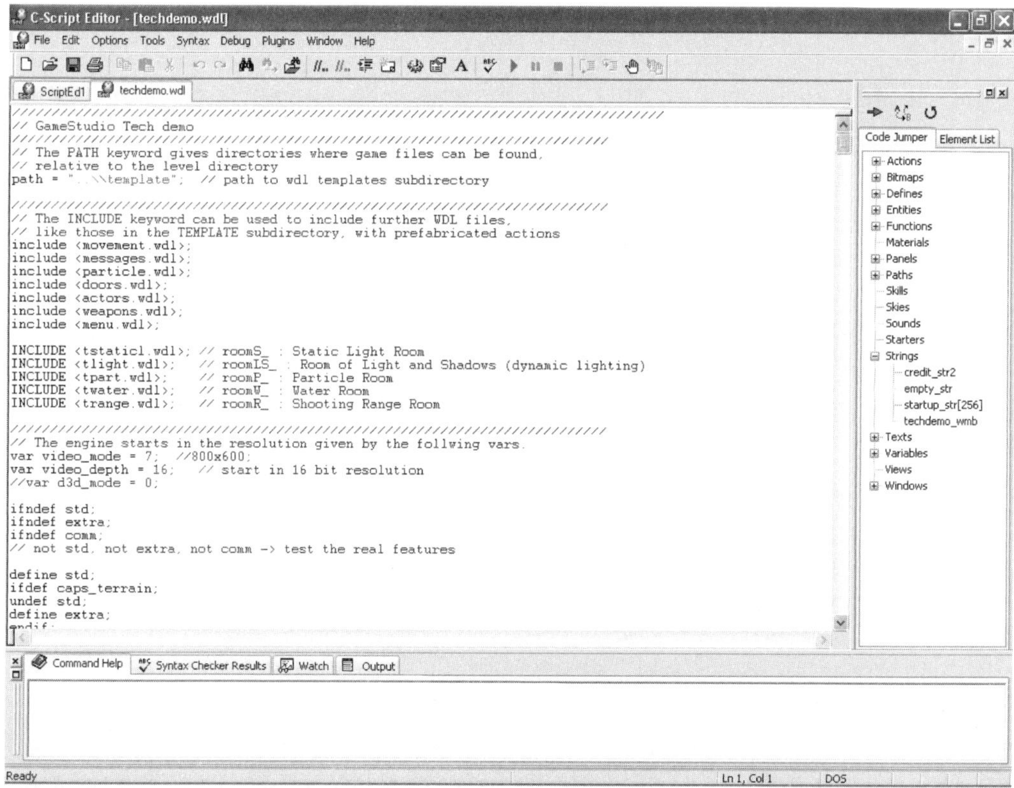

Figure 4.10
3DGS Script Editor (SED)

the tech demo that we tested earlier. Any line beginning //... is a comment. Comments are not parsed (or translated) by the compiler and do not get run through machine code; comments are merely good for one programmer to leave notes for himself, as well as programmers who follow him, to indicate the process the script took to build. The tech demo script starts with several comments.

Just beneath the comments, you will see a set of operations called *includes.* Includes are operations that load other various scripts into the current script to run their definitions and their functions as a part of this one's. You have to be very careful in what order you include significant code scripts, as well. You would not want to load the enemy AI code before you loaded the code that governs basic character movement, such as walking, running, and attacking. So you see that `include<movement.wdl>;` comes first and `include<war.wdl>;` comes after.

SED has an ultimately friendly user interface. The central window shows you the code, line by line; the menu bar has functional icon buttons that make coding faster; and the Properties Panel on the left side of the screen gives you helpful elements, such as the Code Jumper and Element List. At the bottom of the screen, you will see several tabbed window panels for debugging your scripts. We will look at most of these later. For now, I want to bring your attention to the most impressive tools in SED.

Inserting Commands

If you wish to insert a command, press CTRL+SPACEBAR and a pop-up will bring you a list of commands from the database and functions from the included scripts as well. You can press the first letter of the command you wish to add and the list will automatically scroll for you, but you can also move up or down the list by pressing the up and down arrow keys. Press ENTER when you have selected the command you want to insert.

Commenting Lines

Comments, as mentioned above, are very useful when you want the computer to skip part of the code (for instance, when you are writing production notes). To comment a line, select the line or lines you wish to comment and click the blue //... icon on the menu toolbar (or you can press CTRL+ALT+C). This will automatically add //... comment bars to each of the selected lines. To uncomment lines, select them again and click the red //... icon in the menu toolbar to remove the //... bars from the lines of code.

Code Jumper

The Code Jumper can save you time, and time is money in any software development. The Code Jumper contains all the scripts' functions, actions, strings, and so on, and by simply expanding the list, you can view all of them. Try it now. Expand the Actions section of the Code Jumper to find `my_player` and click on it. The cursor position in the central window will jump to `my_player` directly.

Element List

The Element List contains all the script's elements, such as the WDL, BMP, PCX, and MDL files that are included in the script. To open these files, go to the Element List and simply click on the item you want. If what you click on is another script, such as movement.wdl, it will open up inside SED. Otherwise, the associated application program will launch. Try it now. Select one of the included WDL script files, like movement.wdl. Click on it and see if that WDL file opens in SED.

Test Run and Syntax Check

You should always do a test run before a syntax check. Press F5 for a test run of techdemo.wdl—then press F6 to do a syntax check. This is the easiest way for you to check if there are any errors or leaks in your scripts to provide you with the correct warnings. You can further control debugging processes by selecting Debug in the Program menu.

Smart Syntax Editing

SED has a smart function built right in. Notice that whenever you go to the end of a code line and press the ENTER key, an auto indent function automatically indents your lines. If you press the open curly brace ({)—which opens a routine—a closing brace (}) is automatically added to close the routine for you. You can turn these smart functions on and off by selecting Options in the Program menu.

What You Have Learned

The Script Editor is the place where you will be doing your programming for 3D GameStudio, and C-script is the friendly object-oriented programming language you will learn to use. The following are lessons you should have learned:

- You have learned how to get around in the SED interface.
- You have learned the significance of the menu bar icons.

- You have learned the significance of the Code Jumper and Elements List.
- You now know the helpful functions of the syntax editor.
- You now understand programming and what an algorithm is.
- You know what sequential, selective, and looping logic algorithms are.
- You know how to set up an algorithm flowchart.
- You know what definitions and functions are in WDL scripts.
- You know what comments and includes are in WDL scripts.

In Summary

3DGS is your one-stop software development kit for creating amazing 3D and 2D games. The only thing it does not come with is a 2D paint program or sound editor, but that is why the companion CD to this book has the software programs Formati and Audacity on it (both are freeware programs). I prefer using Adobe Photoshop for making my BMP and PCX files, and I retool my sound WAV and MP3 files with Audacity, but feel free to pick up and use any software that gets the job done and that you find helpful to the production pipeline. You should now know enough about the three programs that compose 3D GameStudio (MED, WED, and SED) to feel fairly confident enough to get started making your first game.

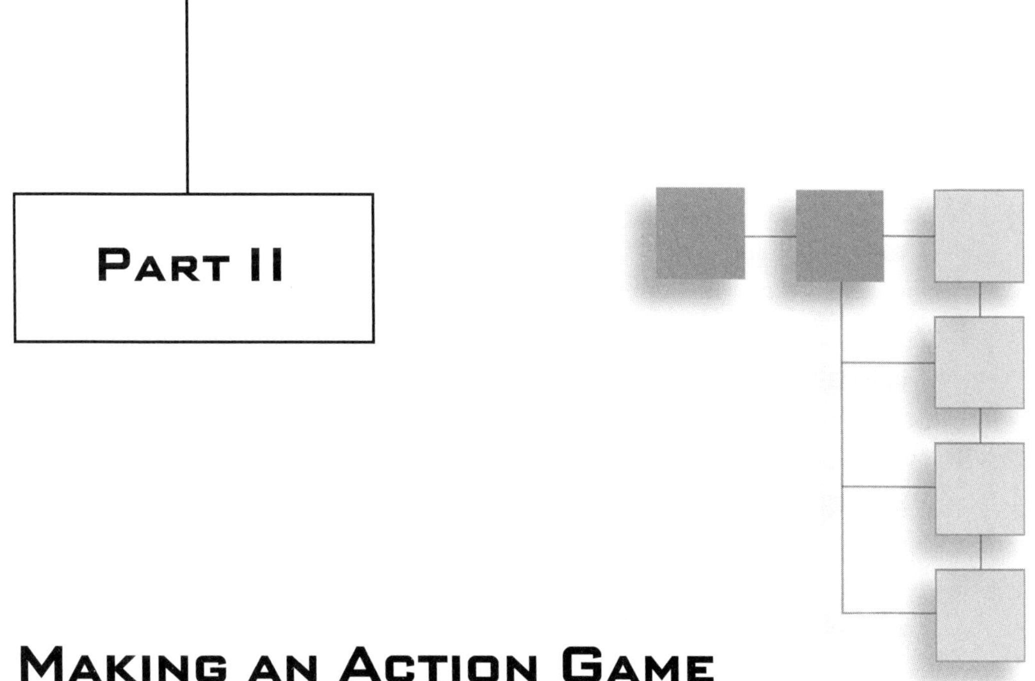

Part II

Making an Action Game

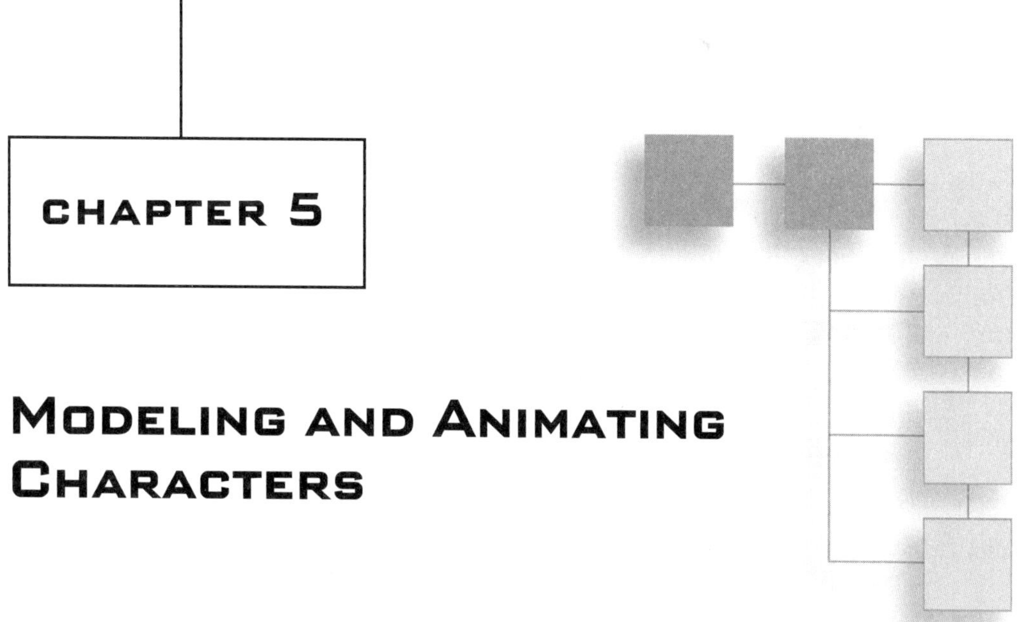

Chapter 5

Modeling and Animating Characters

In this part of the book, you are going to construct an action game. To refresh your memory, an action game is usually typified by hard-hitting action, fast-paced motion, and lots of obstacles or enemies to overcome. Action games, in essence, are the game media equivalence of action movies. They offer audiences the same fighting, shooting, chasing, flying, exploding, and stunt-defying scenes as action movies do.

Action games encompass a wide range: because most games have action in them, several subgenres fall under the heading of *action game*. These include shooters, fighting games, and platformers. However, the action game market is highlighted by the first-person shooter (also called FPS), with games like *Wolfenstein*, *Duke Nukem*, and *Doom* revolutionizing the game market. Action games today have become more detailed, both graphically and through their choices of weaponry and tactics. These games include popular shooting games like *Call of Duty*, *Brothers in Arms*, and *Medal of Honor*. The ones I mention here are all examples of military-themed action games. The U.S. Army even produced its own military-themed action game, which is intended to gain recruits. There are also action games that do not have military overtones, but they still have weapons, ammunition, and plenty of targets to blow up.

Action games have also taken the majority of slugs when it comes to the violence issues in the media. This is because action games try to realistically (and sometimes unrealistically) portray violence. Action movies have done the same for years. Look at the Clint Eastwood, Charles Bronson, and Arnold Schwarzenegger films that have epitomized the action genre for decades. With "action" in the blurb of any film, you can instantly imagine blood and bruises and chase scenes and bullets flying. The action game we will make will be less violent. Our target audience will be a younger one. Even though the violent overtones will be dimmed, in-game destruction and damage will still take place.

Almost all action games have the following definitive characteristics. The player usually plays as one character, the avatar, which is pretty simple and straightforward (no micromanagement of the character's skills, items, or powers). There is often a straightforward script; the game does not dwell on the plotline but instead forces the player through action scene after action scene. There are rarely any puzzles, except the aim-and-shoot kind or the gymnastic platform-jumping kind. There are very few locked doors, and those areas the designer wants to prevent the player invading before their time they place blood locks on. *Blood locks* are an industry mechanic, where the player finds his character locked within a room or area and has to battle umpteen monsters before the doorway opens and she can exit to the next area. Some of the older action games use straight-through levels, and at the end of each level is a boss monster, which has to be beaten before the player can victoriously continue to the next level. Next-generation games are modifying this some because the standard blood lock or boss monster have become cliché. In all action games, there are things to shoot and things with which to shoot (targets and weapons). Inevitably, the industry is moving toward completely destructible levels, but the programming behind that is still a long ways off. Games like *Black* may prove to be the future of action gaming or a flash in the pan.

Technically, you can create a character, a room, and plug a prefabricated script from the templates into your level using 3D GameStudio, and you have an action game. A simple short action game, the makers of 3DGS purport, can be whipped together in a week, with a slightly more complicated game or game of another genre taking slightly longer to make. 3D GameStudio was primarily inspired by great action games, like *Wolfenstein* and *Quake*, and is ready-made to snap together action games. If you have ever used the Quake Editor, you are way ahead in learning 3D GameStudio because a lot of the tools will be familiar to you. I am going to show you in the following step-by-step tutorial how to make an action game, and not only any action game, but your very own game, custom-created by you! I will also show you some of the insider secrets on getting the most out of your action game.

We will start with a game outline. I have provided the outline here, for the sake of the tutorial that you will go through. This will be a spoof game, one with some hilarious childish toys rather than rocket launchers, and it will be campy gothic fun. The target audience is for kids aged nine years and up, but you will find it can be addictive to play for anyone. First, we will look at how to model the characters in the Model Editor. Then we will build three levels in the Level Editor, including a death-match arena. Then I will show you how to program scripts of your very own that will make your action game run even better. So get ready for some creepy fun, and let's get started!

Game Outline for Action Game

Title: *Hector & Hex: Blood Relatives*

Genre: Action Game

Setting: A great big spooky Victorian house

Characters: Hector and Hex, who are two mischievous monster siblings.

Premise: Hector and Hex are usually inflicting pranks and torture on others, but Hector is livid when Hex steals his teddy bear and threatens to destroy it! Now (as Hector) you have to get your teddy bear back, using any and all weapons at your disposal.

Synopsis: A vampire and a werewolf met and had two kids, Hector and Hex, and they live in a creepy house on the outskirts of town, much like the one in *The Addams Family*. The two kids carry their sibling rivalry to actual blows, sometimes inflicting medieval torture on one another; but since they are practically invincible, these little monsters' squabbles have few repercussions. Today is just one more fight between the two!

Player Motivation: Hector needs to get his teddy bear back from his sister. He will chase her all over their mansion and knock her out with his fatal arsenal.

Target Audience: Generation-X, or anyone who might still remember *The Addams Family* with any fond memories will enjoy this short game—as well as anybody who has a soft spot in his heart for Halloween.

Game Mechanics: Hector will have medieval weapons, such as an axe, a crossbow, and a garlic-launcher (the stinky fumes will hurt any ghoul who comes close!). Power-ups will include Boo-Coo cola health drinks lying around the house and Nanny Spiders who stitch up the worst of the kids' ouchies.

True, the older text-based games are virtually an artifact of the past, but players still use cursors (now in the forms of pointers or tiny hands) to manipulate the game interface; and players interact with the storyline as an onscreen avatar (the main character) by use of the keyboard and mouse. The avatar exists in a virtual space, the game world that you create. If the game is driven by a first-person

Figure 5.1
Hector & Hex: Blood Relatives

POV, then you never actually see the player's character, only his hands holding the weapon out in front of him. If the game is driven by a third-person POV, you always see the player's character, as it is usually centered onscreen. In the latter case, the character's appearance and the way it is animated matters more. . . . And besides that, plot without character is a grocery list. As the slogan goes, "What people are interested in is people." Your people have got to have jazz; your characters have got to have appeal!

Creating Memorable Game Characters

Note

"Our character is what we do when we think no one is looking."

—H. Jackson Brown, Jr.

Mario. Luigi. Link. Samus. Squall. Agent 47. Sonic. Kirby. Lara Croft. These names evoke whole feelings, memories in gamers—not only their own but those of imaginary people whose eyes players have looked through. Each of these characters, plus so many more besides, has become a truly memorable character in their own right. They transcend the visual screen into iconic figures of the games they serve. Sometimes a memorable character appears to become a legend overnight, but indeed it is the struggle and vision of the designers behind the characters that lead to their ultimate success. No character starts fully-formed.

First, the designers sit down together and brainstorm a character. What would they like to play as? What would they like to see? What has never been done before? Then character concept sketches are drawn up. Amid countless variations, a sketch will be chosen and launched into the 2D and 3D computer software. Artists perform color comparisons and editing. Many possible variations are made over time, until the image is perfected. Animators breathe life into the game characters. Voice actors provide the noises behind the characters. And finally, when the game starts up and the player takes the controls, they discover themselves locked into epic battles in the persona of a new-formed legend. In the end, it is the player's decision-making skills and actions in-game that define the character for who it is.

Many designers today don't want to create a strong central figure. They report that the player's own personality and choices should always take central stage, and that the player's character—if given too much life—might rob the spotlight. Flat nondescript characters usually result from this way of thinking, and I have never seen a game win popularity contests with these sorts of amorphous characters. Role-playing games tread the line between having no set character (just an ambiguous "you") and having fantastic idiosyncratic characters that become rock stars in their own right. If you glance at the ratings for games in the Final Fantasy series, you will see which type is more popular. People like to watch James Bond or Indiana Jones, but they also wonder what it would be like to *be* these popular characters. This sort of make-believe governs the central hub and the defining emotions of the most popular games on the market today.

Before you go gallivanting into the wonderful world of make-believe character generation, we need to take a look at the concepts that form the substrate of what makes a truly great hero. What are the common attributes of the making of a legend? Let's look at the work that goes into making a memorable character.

Personality

Note

> "Character cannot be developed in ease and quiet. Only through experience of trial and suffering can the soul be strengthened, ambition inspired, and success achieved."
>
> —Helen Keller

Creating a memorable player character that players want to play over and over again is definitely rewarding (from the commercial end as well as the artistic and

Traits Triangle

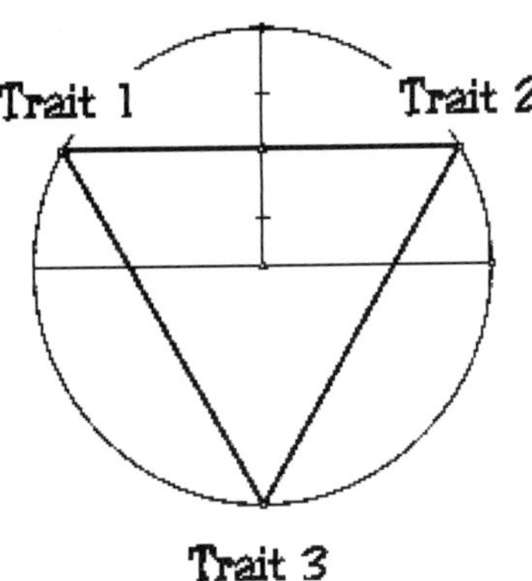

Figure 5.2
A Traits Triangle

technical end). One of the most important elements of a character's particular appeal is his personality. Character traits are important, not only because they influence the player's reactions (as we talked about in "Game Psychology" in Chapter 2), but also because they can shape the character's looks, actions, and dialog. All the most successful game heroes have well-defined personalities. So before you finish making up a character, you have to make sure you know at least three of its character traits and what skills it possibly has. Some designers take the "old school" approach to this and use character sheets full of information about each character, much like the paraphernalia used for role-playing games such as Dungeons and Dragons. I prefer to use a Traits Triangle to describe the character (see Figure 5.2).

Giving your character three major traits, you can immediately see how they would interact to form the character's behavior and the choices he or she would make. Whatever you do, don't choose boring or agreeable traits. Making your character strong, loyal, and handsome is fine and dandy if you are tailoring a stereotypical Prince Valiant, but stereotypes are boring to play. Mix it up more. Try making your character heroic, ugly, and clumsy, and you instantly have a winner on your hands. Trust me.

Note

"Personality is born out of pain. It is the fire shut up in the flint."

—J. B. Yeats

As biographer John E. Mack wrote in *A Prince of Our Disorder*, "A vital ingredient in hero-making is the resonance that the follower finds between the conflicts and aspirations of his own and those he perceives in the person he chooses to idealize. . . ." In other words, try to find problems that we all share as individuals in the struggle of life, and let the player fantasize through your hero character about the ways we can actually solve them, real or not. This is one reason why *Rolling Stone Magazine* has said that we are living in the age of the slacker-hero: people like to root for the underdogs that reflect the underdog in all of us. This has been one of the key ingredients to the ghetto *Grand Theft Auto* game series.

In traditional film and literature, the worth of the plot is measured by the character growth, or how far the character has to go to get what he wants most. Films such as *Nacho Libre* and *Napoleon Dynamite* reveal humanity's ever-present desire to rise above the contentment state and reach for something better. What are the challenges that define such characters? What approach to these challenges exemplifies their personality? How does what happens to the character change him into a different person? On the opposite side of the fence are those stories where events happen—but the character doesn't change or grow at all, he merely survives. Doctor Who, James Bond, and Conan are perfect examples of characters that we can count on to be the way they are, no matter what story we watch or read with them as the central figures! It is a fact that considering characters like this, if they were to dramatically change, we would actually be disappointed beyond belief.

Today's games reveal character growth most often in the form of experience points and level upgrades. This is a paltry simulation of the emotional growth of literature and films. Seldom are less trivial acquisitions ever had in the course of a game. This is one of the limitations of the game industry. In a game, all the choices lie in the hands of the player, and unless the game world is so carefully crafted to react to every decision with emotional impact (such as the morality conditions in the game *Fable*), then character growth will probably always prove flat dreams in the interactive universe.

Create a strong and vibrant character for your game, one with a defined sense of prejudice, style, emotion, and idiosyncrasy. If you do that, you might well avoid the whole issue of character growth or lack thereof by creating another James Bond or Conan!

Note

The word "avatar" comes from ancient Sanskrit and is defined in that language as "the incarnation of a Hindu deity in human or animal form." One of the most popular examples of this incarnation would be Buddha, considered to be an avatar of Vishnu. In this sense, an avatar in a game is an extension (or incarnation) of the self of the player. It's no wonder players identify so strongly with their avatars!

Name

Another element of character appeal that you must concentrate on is the character's name. So far there has been only one game with a Nameless One as the main character or protagonist for a game (*Planescape: Torment* by Black Isle Studios), but it is a practice that is discouraged in game creation. Your character's name is really important, as it reflects the character as well as the player.

The choice of a name should not be made lightly. It will influence the player and how the player acts as the character. If you have a character named Duke Nukem or Dirk, the player has a pretty good idea without even having seen it that he is playing a tough macho character, whereas a Guybrush Threepwood sounds like a total dweeb. A character's name should fit the character. It should also fit the game, and it should be short enough that the player can become instantly familiar with it.

Avoid making names that are too similar to one another or homonyms in a game; you run the risk of confusing the player or causing her undo frustration if she has to remember some character based solely on his name. For instance, you would never tell the player to go back 10 levels in order to find one merchant named Quentin, if you have another merchant named Quint and another named Quentis. The player will not remember which merchant is which. Set each of your names (as well as the characters) apart. Use a baby name book, which you can find at any library or book store (or even online), to come up with unique names, and make sure you pick ones that fit the characters' personalities.

Appearance

So far, every detail of creating compelling characters that we have discussed so far applies equally to books as it does to games. However, video games by essence are a visual media, and so every character in a game has to make an appearance. Designers find the greatest challenge to making a character is evincing a strong reflection of the character's name and personality in a single visage that can be glorified in full 2D and 3D. Game characters are expected to look cute, handsome, winsome, clever, beautiful, elegant, grungy, powerful, tough, lithe, bouncy, dashing, and a string of other adjectives that put them above the stratosphere of ordinary. Mario and his team appear as cartoon characters. Squall and Cerberus appear as ethereal fantasy figures. Lara Croft appears as a bouncy athletic female version of the extraordinary Indiana Jones. What are some dramatic and telling features that will draw and hold the player's attention for level after level of gameplay? What if your character was brought to film and appeared larger than life (as opposed to the pixel version you see onscreen)? What would attract your attention to the character then?

Take a look at the Traits Triangle I told you to create for your character. How would each of those traits show up or be represented in the character's appearance? If you wrote down "slovenly," what visual cues would you use to reveal that he is slovenly? Create a crafted visual hook by selecting one or more specific traits about your character and accentuating them. Indiana Jones has his fedora and his bullwhip. Ash Ketchum from *Pokemon* has his blue vest, green gloves, and cap. Mario has his black mustache, red cap, and overalls. Link has his pointy ears, green cap, and tunic. Spock always had neatly trimmed hair and large pointy ears, not to mention his upraised eyebrows that always made him appear to be questioning. Color schemes and noticeable details should remain consistent. Set your character apart from the rest by developing habitual stances, looks, and visual traits.

In third-person games, displaying the look of a character is relatively simple. The hero is always right there on the screen in front of the player (although most third-person games force a player to look at the player's backside for nearly the entire time). Through the proper animation, proportion, dress, and habitual attributes of the player model, the player will get a good impression of the character.

In first-person shooters, the gameplay takes the character off the screen and forces the player to look through the character's eyes. This makes the action more intense but makes mental imaging of the character more difficult for the player to pull off. The solution that many of these games have used is to create graphic cut-scenes where the player sees his character onscreen for a little bit while the camera moves outside the first-person perspective to reveal some dialog or NPC exposition. This is clever, but it can also be disorienting for gamers who find that the break destroys the believability of the game immersion. This "coming up for air" technique can actually backfire if the designer does not handle it right.

In-game sequences are not the only place characters will show up. Cover art on the box, the manual that comes with the game, magazine ads, trailers, posters, desktop wallpaper, goodies, and other marketing angles will also establish the look of the character—sometimes even before the game is released or becomes well-known. Whatever you do, don't sell your work short by overusing the same images or screenshots of your low-polycount models in obtuse poses. If you are not a great concept or character artist, hire one to do some sketches or paintings for you, and frame them in the published materials that support your game. You will be glad you did.

The appearance of a character must be thought out at the conception, the same way his or her personality and name are—but the appearance must then be further developed by sketch artists and finally rendered into a model in the game. The first impression a player will have of the character is its appearance. Often, this impression is formed before the player has ever picked up the controls—likely in a trailer or demo that the developer releases. The character's first impression must encompass its personality, voice, expression, and dramatic flair. Look at current trailers for upcoming releases on sites like GameSpy.com to understand the intricacies of how this is accomplished.

Voice

Finding your character's voice should not be an arduous task, but it can end up a costly one. Most all game characters to this date are silent heroes. Most of the dialog appears in static dialog windows or dialog option trees, without the support of auditory clues. This is just fine, but many gamers are getting tired of it. Some games give voices to the main characters. These can work cleverly, or (in the case of some first-person shooters) they can backfire by alienating the player from his own character. If you want to have quality voice talent, you can find some good friends to supply voices for you for free—or you can hire actors for a professional product (and higher cost). The latter choice is not suggested if this is your first game; however, once you get a few games published, you might consider spending some of your profits in hiring quality voice talent. If you want to do voiceovers yourself, it wouldn't hurt to gain some theater or drama experience first because understanding acting will benefit your game experience.

Regardless of whether you have vocals in your game or not, the words with which the character speaks will tell volumes about his personality. Dialog gives tremendous insight into what sort of character this is, what accent or education the character might possess, and what respect the character shows for the people he is busy talking to. Consider the writing of dialog carefully. Keep dialog short because of space constraints in a game, but keep dialog filled with emotional cues as to the impression of the character speaking.

Other Characters

Not all the creatures and characters you find in a game reflect the player avatar. We looked at these in Part I of this book, but besides the obvious ones, like the monsters the player must defeat to gain treasure, there are two types of creatures and characters that can bestow the player with unique interaction depending on the game genre you are using. They are non-player characters and parties of adventurers.

Non-Player Characters

Non-player characters (often referred to by the industry as NPCs) play an important role in the story. In traditional story structure, NPCs (called *bit characters* in fiction writing) are those people the main character interacts with on a consistent basis to expose story details and information and dynamically shift story emphasis based on dialog and interaction. In game structure, NPCs fill the same important role. The most obvious NPCs in games are the enemy and the aide. The enemy (or villain) plots something that the objective viewer admits is purely diabolical or misguided. The enemy in a game is the character the player must triumph against. Often the enemy is the mythic Shadow character. The aide in a game is the character that the player must talk to, interact with, and gain guidance, new weapons, or abilities from. We looked at the role of the Mentor archetype and the player ally in Chapter 2, "Planning Your Game," but NPCs also encompass the merchant, tradesman, a character in danger that needs escorted or rescued, guardians, and so on.

NPCs can reveal all the emotions and personal reactions that the hero can't show, for whatever limitations of the game engine or limits placed by the designers. A hero facing off with a villain would not be nearly as satisfying without a pleading helpless populace needing to be saved from the villain! As Warren Spector said once, "We need better actors. We can count on players to do interesting things. Wouldn't it be nice if NPCs behaved (and looked) more interesting, too? Wouldn't it be nice to get a sense of what an NPC is feeling through facial expression, posture, or subtle changes in the way they move based on circumstances? Let me see a tear or a smile or a frown, caused by my choices.... And how about characters who speak believably, rather than in the stilted branching tree dialogue we're stuck with today? Give me all that, and we'll really be on to something special."

One of the most remarkable things to come out of the game *Vampire: Bloodlines* by Troika Games was the fact that the game's designers spent the majority of production getting the NPCs just right. They hired professional voice talents. They pioneered new ways to model NPC faces and gave them subtle emotional cues through face morphs. Depending on the static branching dialog tree (you still never heard yourself or watched your character's emotions because there were none) and what choices you as the player made in what you said and how you responded to them, you would see the NPCs go from content to terrified to begging to hateful, all in rapid succession. None of them actually cried, but many of them came close. This little-known game broke several game design conventions and the naysay crowd that said that it could not be done. If one game can effectively recreate human emotions on 3D-constructed "puppets," why can't more games do the same?

NPCs in any game can be defined by their relationships with the avatar, their functional role in the game, and their fictional role. Let's look at these three characteristics of NPCs in detail. To define an NPC, identify the character's relationship to the avatar. In most cases, this will fall into one of three categories: helpful, neutral, or hostile.

- **Helpful**—These are characters who support the avatar and provide information or resources. In action games, helpful characters are often found only in particular locations in the game, and they have a limited number of things to give the player, like the Merchant character in *Resident Evil 4.*
- **Neutral**—These characters interact with the player, but they don't provide help. You have to obtain something for them in exchange for their information or assistance. A character whose only function is to impede the player in a passive way, such as a doorkeeper who won't open the door until told the password, can be considered neutral. Consider whether your NPC could be removed and an object put in its place, like a keypad that needs a password; if this is so, the character is probably neutral.
- **Hostile**—These characters actively oppose the player's progress. They attack the avatar or do other malevolent things to impede the player. The avatar must defeat hostile characters (often through combat). Unlike a

neutral NPC, who may appear simply as an obstacle, hostile characters add the risk that the player may lose the level or the game.

Sometimes you might want to create a character whose relationship with the avatar changes over time. The player's actions can cause an NPC to become more helpful or more hostile. In this case you need to define a scale of affinity and think about the kinds of events or actions that change that affinity. Can the avatar attack the NPC or harm it in any way? Can the avatar assist the NPC or make friends with it in some way? How would you script these things to happen? This will help you establish a more immersive relationship between the avatar and the NPCs.

After you've decided whether the NPC is helpful, neutral, or hostile, you must define its role within the game world. The role of an NPC implies how the character serves the gameplay. Roles include the following:

- **Physically opposing the avatar**—This is the oldest NPC functional role, going all the way back to *Pac-Man*.
- **Providing the player with information**—This can happen either continuously within the game as it progresses or at intervals along the way. This information could just as easily be supplied using a dialog box, but it's good to have a character supply it.
- **Giving the player missions to fulfill**—Many games start with a briefing of some kind about the player's mission; this can often be delivered by a character that plays no other role. The RPG genre is full of people who offer quests to the hero.
- **Trading with the hero**—These characters' role is to exchange one kind of resource for another that may aid the player somehow. For example, blacksmiths buy and sell armor and weapons in exchange for gold. They don't typically dispense information or assist the player in any other way.

Parties of Adventurers

Most of the strategy or role-playing games on the market do not stick to one main character. This complicates matters for a designer engineering the game characters. Since the earliest days of *Final Fantasy*, there have been parties. Parties of adventurers were inspired by the tabletop role-playing games that video games modeled themselves after. In the popular fantasy role-playing game market, players could create their own characters and join together in parties of adventurers to seek their fame and fortune in abandoned mines and webbed dungeons. *Final Fantasy*'s creators brought the same concept to video games with the inclusion of player parties. Ideally, one character would play the role of the main character and would form the inception point for the player—but as the player progressed through the game story, she would gain new allies who would join her party. These new allies formed additional game characters, each with their own personalities, unique names, attributes, and abilities. Usually, allies in the party would be different enough that they could build each other up by combining their talents. However, the main character (or player avatar) would form a central nimbus, a melting pot for the whole team, and would be the deciding vote on all matters.

If you find yourself planning to create a more complicated role-playing game and want to institute a whole party of adventurers, remember to keep each member separate from the others in terms of name, traits, and personality. You might want to laud the natural elements and have one party member represent Earth, one Fire, another Water, and finally Air—while the player avatar would represent Spirit (the hub of all the elements). This is, of course, a hasty and over-simplified example, but you get the idea.

Also, today's push toward online gaming makes parties of adventurers more common-place, but harder to predict, in an ever-growing virtual community where players can log on and join parties or whole guilds in an effort to team up or vie for title, fame, or treasure. These games do not share the emergent dichotomy of the solo role-playing games of classic gaming, so it is unsure yet what can be learned or emulated by them.

Five Lessons of Creating Game Characters

There are five lessons about creating memorable game characters that you should take to heart; I call these "lessons" because some legendary game designers have learned them along their paths to success. If you want to be a successful game designer yourself, it is important to learn from the hard-earned lessons of others who have come before you. These lessons are as follows:

1. Accept and capitalize on lucky accidents.
2. Exaggerate the character's motions.
3. Use an appealing colors palette.

4. Make use of your own artistic style.
5. Never use stereotypes.

Accept and Capitalize on Lucky Accidents

Shigeru Miyamoto of Nintendo fame said that most of the character quirks he created that made them memorable were accidental. The only reason Mario has a mustache today is because in the old 8-bit graphics it was difficult to tell the difference between Mario's nose and his jaw, and so Miyamoto wanted the artists to put a mustache in to separate the two. Today, Mario would not be Mario without his signature mustache.

Exaggerate the Character's Motions

Miyamoto had other life lessons he was willing to share about creating game characters with appeal. The first of these was exaggeration. Players respond better to game characters with exaggerated animation. For instance, Mario is short but can jump three or four times his own height. He squishes a little when he falls to the ground. And his spurts of "Woo-hoo!" and "Let's-a-go!" have delighted players for decades now. This does not mean that you have to exaggerate your character or turn your game into an interactive cartoon if you are attempting photorealism, but it is worth thinking about.

Use an Appealing Colors Palette

Next, Miyamoto said that the number one thing he wanted Nintendo's artists to remember when making memorable game characters was color. He wanted strong primary and tertiary color palettes, with high contrast and real visual power, so that the characters were recognizable even as blurs on the screen. This is really something you should think about when skinning your avatar's model. Pick a color palette that appeals to you. If you have to, look at a painting or photo that has really nice color composition, and then sample it as you paint your character's skin (in Adobe Photoshop, you can use the Color Picker to sample colors like this).

Make Use of Your Own Artistic Style

Every major talent in the world will tell you: impersonation is the sincerest form of flattery, but don't impersonate me. Plagiarism is rampant in the new Internet

Figure 5.3
Imaginative use of artistic style (*Psychonauts*, image courtesy Double Fine Productions 2005)

world that we find ourselves struggling to create in. Some designers will emulate great works of art, others will emulate the Saturday morning cartoons, but regardless, all major talents must seek to get their vision across to the public. You must do it, too. Don't shirk from becoming renowned for expressing yourself through your game. Just because you want your game to look just like *Medal of Honor* and appear uber-realistic with photo-quality textures and faces on all your characters doesn't mean you *should*. There are lots of games out there, and lots of game developers out there right now trying to accomplish that very same goal. Why not go off on a tangent? Why not do what *you* are good at?

The creator of *Earthworm Jim* and *Messiah* said that creating a character with a strong silhouette was important; this is imminently visible in *Earthworm Jim*, as no other character shares the side profile that Earthworm Jim does. Similarly, Tim Schafer, the creator of *Grim Fandango* and *Psychonauts* (see Figure 5.3), says that original artistic style and having unusual flair in designing key characters is important to the success (and audience recognition) of your game. This line of thought is what has made Tim Schafer, as well as film director Tim Burton, successes in their industries. Do you have a particular artistic style you could apply to your game characters?

Never Use Stereotypes

One of the lessons that should be learned in creating memorable characters is never to go for stereotypes. If you remember, I mentioned stereotypes in Chapter 2 in the section "Symbols and Myths in Games." I said, don't do it: don't ever use stereotypes. Archetypes are okay, but stereotypes are very limiting when it comes to storytelling and critics taking your work seriously. When creating characters—even when it comes to 3D modeling and animation—it is never a good idea to make stereotypes. One of the worst stereotypes is the Big-Breasted Bimbo. Big-Breasted Bimbos are apparent in games such as *Tomb Raider* (Lara Croft) and *Bloodrayne* (Rayne); they have exaggerated assets that target juvenile horny males but do very little to engender play for the rest of us. In fact, there are many women who report that these games initially scare them away from gaming altogether because they appear so juvenile and reflect poorly on the industry. They are a carry-over from the game industry's early connection to the comic book industry. Other stereotypes that are perpetuated include growling military generals, shifty-eyed thieves, and studious bookworms. Don't use them, unless you are poking fun at yourself or the media industry.

The Principles of Animation

There's a common misconception that because digital artists (such as 3D artists) use a computer to do their dirty work, that it's quicker and easier. Let's shoot that notion down right now. Computers do make certain tasks easier, but creating digital art and animating 3D models is deliberately slow and tedious. You have to own a lot of patience to work in the digital art field.

There's this really great saying in computer animation that goes, "Moving stuff around is NOT animation!" Let's study that for just a second. Making an animated character is not quick or easy, as I have already explained. If you just want to move objects around the computer screen, then that *is* quick and easy; you can think yourself a great artist and wait for the clients to roll in. But it is not going to happen. Anyone can learn the basics of the software and move stuff around, but no one is going to buy a product anyone can do. They want what *you* can do, or what you will soon be capable of, which is real animation. Animation is about bringing characters to life in a virtual world. Life is never easy, so why should replicating it in Cartesian space be?

If you are setting out to design games, you must get some fundamental lessons about animation under your belt. I'll summarize the animation basics—most often called the Principles of Animation. These were first listed by Frank Thomas and Ollie Johnston in the book *The Illusion of Life: Disney Animation* and ratified in the 1930s by Disney Studios. These principles apply to all forms of animation, and they are still as useful today as they were then. Let's look at the essence of each.

- Timing
- Emphasis
- Secondary motion
- Anticipation
- Follow-through
- Overlapping actions
- Arcing motions
- Squash and stretch
- Weight distribution
- Appeal

Timing

Timing pulls everything else together. The number of frames for each pose impacts the overall feel of the animation. You have to find the right balance between allowing the action to register and creeping along so much that you bore your players. Generally speaking, when animating in 3D GameStudio, faster is better. But too-fast animations can make the character appear as a blur when you play it in the game. Fast animations can look good, but they also cause disorientation if everything you animate is too fast.

There are a number of ways you can control the timing in 3D GameStudio. In the Model Editor, you can set poses and frame-by-frame animation. You can hit playback and view the animation as it should appear and make adjustments as needed, while you create your character. Then you import the 3D model into the Level Editor and test-run your game. If the animation still looks wonky, or you realize that there are some minor adjustments to the timing, you can use the Object Property panel in the Level Editor to change the character's animation speed for walking, running, jumping, standing, and so on. This makes timing easier to control for the user, rather than having to go back to the Model Editor and import a new model all over again. Another way you could change the model's timing is to program the model by creating a custom action for its behavior and setting its animation frames by hand by scripting line by line.

Timing is referred to as *pacing* because it helps to frame an overall animation; ask any professional speaker or comedian what pacing is, and they will help to illustrate this difficult subject. Essentially, think about Wile E. Coyote (the Chuck Jones variety): when the Coyote was chasing the Roadrunner and dashed off the edge of a cliff, Jones knew it was funnier if the animation slowed down, and then held the moment when the Coyote realized his precarious predicament. As a final touch, the Coyote would hold up an "Uh-oh!" sign before suddenly plummeting to the canyon floor far below. This moment of suspended animation (literally) made for barrel laughs because of the pacing.

Emphasis

I have been to karate championships where the moves were so lightning fast, legs and fists so stiff and speedy, that I could barely keep up with the direction of attack or what was going on. On the other hand, you watch Jackie Chan action movies, and he (and the other martial artists) slows down the action so the viewer can keep up with what's going on. *Emphasis* is literally the process of slowing down and over-exaggerating the action you want to perform in order for audiences to keep up with and understand what is going on (see Figure 5.4). For instance, you could create a basic jumping animation for the player character that has the character go up and back down again in under four frames. But for the player to understand that his player character is jumping when the player presses the jump button, you have to set up the shot better: have the character bend her knees slightly, wave her arms about, and then push off into the air, where she hangs for a frame or two, then drops back into a slightly exaggerated crouch position. This jump animation has better dynamic emphasis for the action than moving the character straight up and back down again.

Figure 5.4
Emphasis makes for exciting animation. (*Kya: Dark Lineage*, image courtesy Eden Studios 2003)

Secondary Motion

It is not the finely grilled cheeseburger they slap on your plate; it is all about the condiments, the cleanness of the plate, and the overall service that make the presentation. Secondary motions are smaller actions than the whole that take place during the main action and add emphasis, character, or overlapping action. When Lara Croft walks along a mountain path, her ponytail bounces side to side, doesn't it? Her walking is the primary action; the bouncy hairstyle is the secondary action. Even when a character is idle or at rest, he does not stop moving: his chest rises and falls, he may scuff the toes of his shoes, he may turn his head and look side to side. Other examples include the flopping ears of an alien beast as it pounces on you, the recoil of an enemy fighter after blasting his shotgun, and so on. Secondary actions should always add to the primary action, not distract from it. If secondary motions become too prominent, they override the primary motion themselves, and may perplex the viewer as to what is going on. Great character animation should clearly communicate to the audience what is going on at any one time.

Anticipation

Remember those Tom and Jerry cartoons, where the bulldog would be about to hit Tom in the face with a fist? He would lift Tom by the scruff of his neck, then wind up his arm so that it became a blur of motion and then BAM! And Tom would be stuck in a piano with the ivory keys dangling from his mouth like teeth. This is a fantastic example of anticipation. The bulldog would not have been able to send Tom flying across the room if he had not wound up his arm. It would not have been as funny. Similarly, a soccer player would have to pull back his foot before kicking a ball across the field; if he just walked up and immediately tapped the ball with his toe, it would not roll very far.

The unfortunate detail of modeling with 3D GameStudio is that it is harder to communicate anticipation. Most game creation engines have a similar problem. This is because the instant the player communicates to the game that he is taking a course of direction, the input becomes translated into output. A game character that is standing still might suddenly start running to the left, jump over a fallen log in the road, or attack a would-be fatal enemy. The game states are fluid. It is much harder to program transitions between these states. This is why the first frame of a character's "attack" scene has to show the character already laying the smack-down on somebody; the rest of the frames are considered follow-through.

Follow-Through and Overlapping Actions

A baseball batter does not quit swinging as soon as his bat touches the ball and knocks it into orbit over the stadium; the bat continues arcing down until the batter drops it to run to base. A guy leaping across a vast chasm does not land gracefully on his toes every time; he tumbles forward and has to catch himself on hands and knees before picking himself back up. These are examples of follow-through and illustrate a single point: avoid stopping everything all at once. Consider that by Newton's law, all things have mass and all objects with mass have momentum. If energy is applied in any given direction, the object will continue in motion until another object repels it or the object runs out of energy. There should always be some continuance of motion, something indicating life in your animation. Otherwise it will just look wrong.

Arcing Motion

The best things in life have curves, and the same goes for animation. Arcs tell us that nothing moves in a straight line; the natural motion of life is set along a curve. The way women swing their hips when they walk, the way arms swing at your side, the natural lift when jumping to the sidewalk . . . these are all examples of arcing motion. Try turning your head from side to side. Notice your head dips slightly on center, and your eyes almost close at the same time, barely blinking as your head passes the curve. Now try keeping your head still and your chin level. Slowly rotate your head like a robot to look from side to side. Notice how strange it feels and how much more effort it takes? It's moving in a straight line, so it is unnatural! Whenever a character lobs a grenade or opens a treasure chest's heavy lid, he is moving in arcs. Anything else just looks . . . wrong. (See a trend developing here? If something looks wrong, the viewer will recognize it—at least on some gut level—and your animation will appear flawed.)

Squash and Stretch

"This isn't rocket science, folks. It's more like rubber ball science," as Gary Leib would say. When something (let's say a rubber ball, because it is the most redundantly used object to illustrate this point) hits the ground it squashes flat. When it bounces back up, it stretches out again (see Figure 5.5). It turns spherically round (or whatever its normal state is) before it starts back toward the ground, in which case it elongates again. Then it hits the ground and squashes flat again. This cycle continues until the ball loses enough energy to remain still or

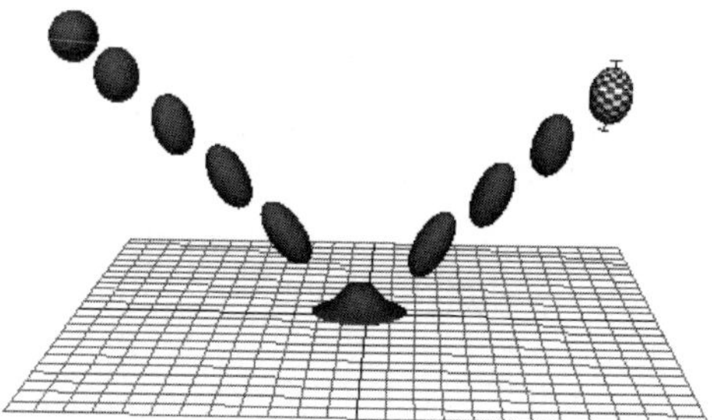

Figure 5.5
Squash and stretch

your hand reaches out and stops it. The natural path for the bouncing rubber ball is an arc. The repeated process of squash and stretch has resulted in this Principle of Animation. It applies to all cartoon characters that are meant to appear flexible, fluid, bouncy, and jolly—but if the object is meant to be rigid, like a brick wall or heavy anvil, it does not apply.

Think of Miyamoto's Mario character: whenever Mario would land on the ground, he'd squash. Whenever he'd leap high into the air, he would stretch out his body. Miyamoto wanted Mario to have the same qualities of squash and stretch to make his animation more believable and appealing, like having a large squishy toy that you could move around. But there's a catch: Mario never once loses volume. He stays the same mass, but he is either being stretched out or squashed. No matter how fluid or flexible the object is you are animating, it will never realistically lose or gain mass.

Weight Distribution

Every existing object shares space, volume, and mass. Even if these values are negative, allowing the object to float through the air like a balloon, the object still has them. When animating your game characters, keep in mind that they have to behave like real objects. Allow your game characters to shift their weight from foot to foot as they walk, to lean forward and back as they stand idly at rest, or to land hard from a short jump; this will give your animated characters tangible qualities that will make them seem more real.

Plus, always keep in mind that every character is going to be different. Some characters will be smaller and more lithe, while others will appear thicker and heavyset. Animating the actions of each will have different challenges: the smaller, more dexterous characters will have to almost appear weightless, while the thick heavyset characters will be ponderous and labor in their motions, and each move they make will take longer. The more emphasis and exaggeration you can give to these differences, the more appeal the characters will display.

Appeal

This takes us back to the previous five suggestions for success. Frank Thomas and Ollie Johnston in their book *The Illusion of Life: Disney Animation* wrote, "While a live actor has charisma, the animated character has appeal." What they meant by this is that audiences go to movies to see handsome actors strut and say lines, their eyes twinkling and showing visual charisma. Animated characters (of cartoons and games) have to ooze appeal: the audience must not mind looking at them and must have a psychological connection with them as the story progresses. I am not suggesting that every female game character has to have the curves and bust line of Lara Croft (see the previous section, "Never Use Stereotypes," for my particular rant about Big-Breasted Bimbos). I am also not suggesting that every alien critter be cute and furry with big eyes like Ratchet from *Ratchet & Clank*, either. Use your best judgment to give your characters appeal.

In Summary

Making memorable characters—whether the player's character, the countless NPCs, enemies, or allies the player might run across—is one of the most important lessons a game designer must learn. Half of the game the player sees is his player character; the other half is the game's levels. Creating a unique and fun character will spell success, while making a flat or boring one will spell failure.

What You Have Learned

Now you have all the basics of character animation. The successful applications of the five suggestions for creating memorable game characters, as well as the Principles of Animation, could spell the difference between the $10 bargain-bin games and the blockbuster games everybody's got to have!

- You have learned to make a Traits Triangle for characters' personalities.
- You now know how important it is to name characters correctly.
- You have learned what it takes to make memorable game characters.

- You have learned the importance of great character design.
- You now know the Principles of Animation and their importance.
- You could create a memorable game character with appeal.

For Review

1. Name three of your favorite game characters of all time. What is it about them that you think makes them appealing? Why do you like them? Is it any of the things we have talked about?

2. Turn yourself into a game character—but exaggerate it. What costume would you wear? What skill sets or abilities would you have? What amazing super powers would you have? What other characters from your real life would you have to add? Do you have a Shadow or Mentor character, for instance?

3. Create an original character for a game. The game genre doesn't matter; make your character for any gameplay type you like. What would you call your character? (Remember that the character's name has a lot to do with the player response.) What would your character's traits, skills, and powers be? How would you dress or color your character? Now think about the animation. How would you translate this character into a 3D model and animate it? What would its walk, jump, and attack animations be like?

4. Imagine that you are going to animate a martial arts wizard picking up a wounded comrade off the floor of a warehouse, then leap and kick to open an air vent, and jump out the chute before bad guys shoot him. In this short scene, what Principles of Animation would you have to take into account, and how would you show each of them?

Exercise 5.1: Modeling Your Avatar

First of all, take a look at the game outline for the action game we are going to make. It will be called *Hector & Hex*. In it, notice what avatar the player is going to play as (Hector) and what the player's objectives will be. Consider what directions you could take for the player's main character, and how you could put your own artistic style on it. If you do not feel artistic yourself, consider other

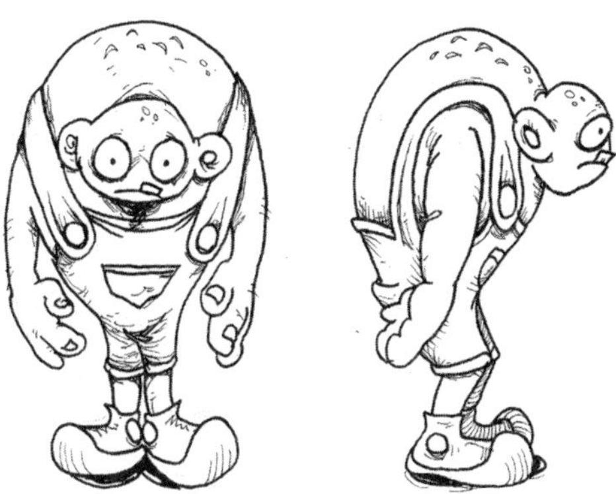

Figure 5.6
Character concept of Hector

game, comic book, or movie characters you have seen before and which ones match this avatar best. Why do you think you make the decisions that you do? Is it in response to the character's archetype or because of your past experiences with the media?

Hector—as I imagine him—is a big lovable brother ghoul, who is mentally slower but meatier and, therefore, stronger than his sister Hex. Hector and Hex both have vampire blood in them, so they cannot withstand the sunlight, garlic, or receiving wood splinters. Due to their werewolf blood, they are possibly cowardly when it comes to silver, so their weapons might shoot silver bullets at each other. All of these ideas (which come from brainstorming) may lead to further character identification and game development. See Figure 5.6 for my character concept artwork of Hector.

Note the artistic style used here. We are dealing with a youthful and Gothic cartoon style (rather than a photorealistic one), similar to the Claymation characters of the popular Tim Burton shows *The Corpse Bride* and *The Nightmare Before Christmas.* We will have a lumpy male character with overly large eyes and tiny dots for pupils. His clothing I conceive of being loose and simple in detail. We will have to do something clever in the skinning of Hector to make him appear white and clammy like a corpse. I will provide the models for Hex and the other creatures and items Hector might find, so all you have to do is model and animate Hector.

Now that we have some concept artwork to go by—so we are not working in a creative void—we can start to develop his character model for 3D GameStudio. Open up the Model Editor, and let's begin.

The first thing you will notice is that the Model Editor opens to a blank (or new) model screen. It also does not store the preferences or changes you might have made before when we worked with the warlock.mdl. Go to View > 3D View > Textured + Gouraud so you will see the shape of the character in the 3D View window as you create him. Also, click in the middle of all four view windows where the panels meet and drag to resize the view windows. Once they are all equally visible and of roughly the same size, you will be ready to start.

Modeling a Leg

Select the Cube from the basic geometry panel, located in the menu bar. The Cube icon looks like a 3D cube. When you have clicked on it, you will have the cube primitive selected.

Click once in the top-left window (it is one of the orthographic view windows), and a cube will appear. You will be able to see it in all four windows. You cannot click again to create a second cube; as soon as you click in the screen and create one, the Model Editor immediately switches your tool setting over to the Move tool.

Move the cube (by clicking on it or on one of its direction arrows, and dragging the mouse) to roughly about the position of the object origin (remember, that's the cross or L-shape that was in the Model Editor before you started creating the cube). Now look on the menu bar, to the left of the Move and Position tool icons. It may take you some time to memorize where all the tools are on the menu bar, but if you have any doubts, simply hover over the icons and pop-up text will tell you the icon's description and which tool you are looking at.

Move your mouse cursor seven icons to the left of the Position tool. You will be in the middle of three distinctive buttons: each is framed with yellow, and they are Group mode, Vertex mode, Triangle mode, and Bone mode. Select the third one, Triangle mode. Triangle mode allows you to select and influence individual triangles (sometimes called *polygons*) on the model. You will be switching from Vertex mode to Triangle mode and back again frequently as you complete this exercise, so try to get comfortable knowing which mode you are currently in and where to click to turn the next one on.

If the cube is still selected (showing red in the 3D View), deselect it first by clicking elsewhere in one of the windows. Now select the top two triangles of the cube by holding down CTRL and then clicking on the triangles in the top-left

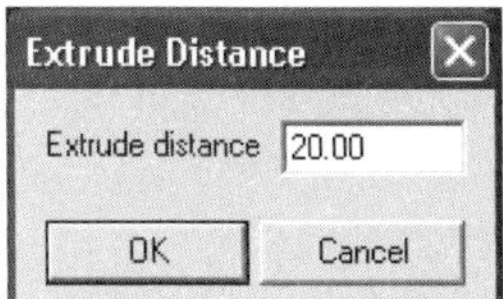

Figure 5.7
Extruding the cube by 20 units

orthographic window. You will see them selected in the 3D View window immediately to the right because they will turn red as you select them.

With these two triangles selected, click the Extrude button in the menu bar. Extrude should be three icon buttons over from the right and looks like two overlapping triangles. Extrude allows you to extrude (or stretch out) planes of the 3D object you have selected.

When you click Extrude, a dialog box will appear asking you how far you wish to extrude the plane selected. Type **20.0** into the field, and click OK (see Figure 5.7). You will see that the cube has extended upward 20 units. It has also developed more vertices (the little ticks where lines intersect) and more visible lines. This is exactly what we want, as we are going to turn this cube into a leg.

Click Extrude by 20.0 five more times. You shouldn't have to type anything more in. As long as the integers do not change, the text field will remember what you typed in last. Just click Extrude and OK, and you should be just fine. When you are through, you should be able to look at the two bottom orthographic view windows, and your object should resemble a seven-story high-rise building.

Now select Vertex mode from the menu bar. Once you have Vertex mode selected, you should be able to select and make adjustments to individual ticks (or vertices). You can select multiple vertices by clicking on the Move tool and click-drag your cursor somewhere off to the side of the object in one of the two bottom view windows. You will see a green selection marquee box appear as you drag your mouse cursor across the view window.

Use this method to select the second row of vertices on the object. You can preview what you have selected because the vertices will turn red. You should have four vertices selected. You can use the 3D View to explore your object and make sure which four you have selected. It should look like Figure 5.8.

Click the Scale button and stretch this row way out. You will notice that with the Move tool, you have to grab the vertices by clicking directly on one of the ticks

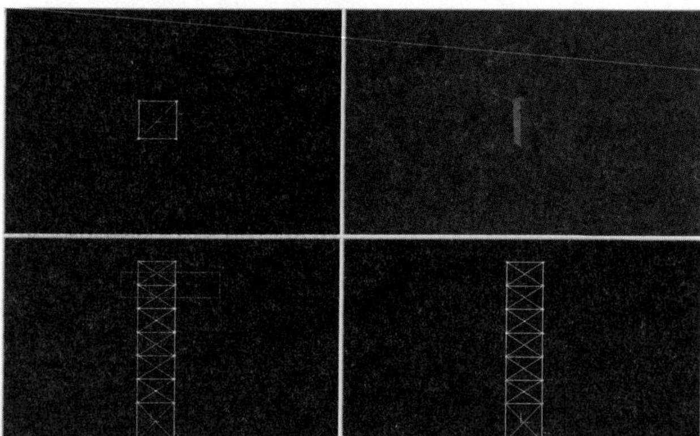

Figure 5.8
Selecting one horizontal row's vertices

and dragging, but with the Scale tool, you can click anywhere near the selection you have made and drag left or right or in and out, and it will respond. Try to get the hang of it before you move on.

After you have the selected row stretched to about one and a half the size of the original cube, move down and select the next row of vertices. Stretch this row out using the Scale tool, but not nearly as far out as the one above it.

The next row you will want to leave alone, as it will form the knee of the leg. Skip down to the row after it, and use the Scale tool to make it a little wider—but don't make it nearly as wide as the first row that you stretched out. The idea is to taper them down, until you reach the foot.

The foot will be the last two rows of vertices, and you will select them together by clicking Select and click-dragging your mouse over them, grabbing those vertices with the green marquee. Altogether, you should have eight vertices selected. Once you have them selected, use the Scale tool to shrink them in just a little. See Figure 5.9 for an example.

Zoom in to get a closer look at the foot. To zoom in, you can either use your mouse wheel or click on the Position button. It is the one that looks like a blue ellipsis with the rays right above it. After clicking on Position, you can right-click and drag your mouse to zoom into and out of the view. You can click-drag as normal to pan around the point of origin. Try it now. Zoom in to the bottom-left view window to get a much closer view of the foot region of the leg.

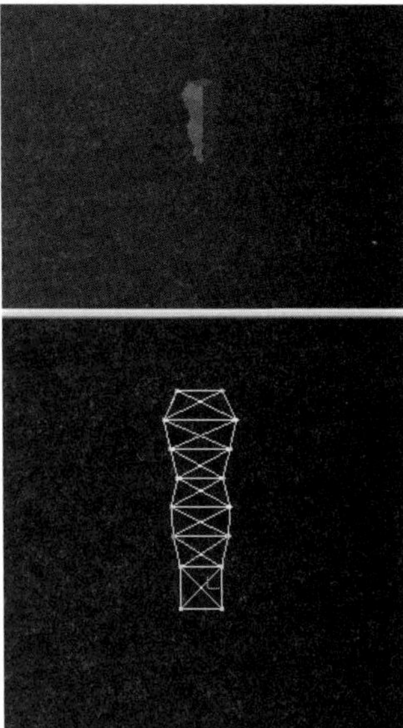

Figure 5.9
The leg as it should be proportioned.

Click Select now and choose Triangle mode again. You are going to select the two triangles on the front of the foot (it is the bottom-most box of the leg) by holding down CTRL and clicking on them in the bottom-left view window. Inspect your work in the 3D View window for accuracy. If you see any red other than the front of your foot, you have made an error. Simply let go of CTRL and click on one of the triangles of the foot to deselect any others you have inadvertently selected.

Once you have the front plane of the foot selected, click Extrude and type **30.00** in as the number before clicking OK. This will stretch out the foot, making it look more like a real foot and less like a peg leg!

However, this foot needs a lot of work. Right now it is little better than a box, and unless Hector is wearing shoeboxes on his feet, we need to make the top of his feet curve more.

Switch to Vertex mode and select the top two vertices on his extended foot (we shall call these his *toe ticks*). You can grab both toe ticks by click-dragging your marquee over them in the bottom-right view window. Now that you have the toe ticks selected, click Scale and move them in closer to one another. Next click Move (be sure to click on one of the ticks, or you will deselect them instantly!) and move the toe ticks a few units down to give a gentle rise to the foot as it meets the leg. Your foot should look just like the one in Figure 5.10.

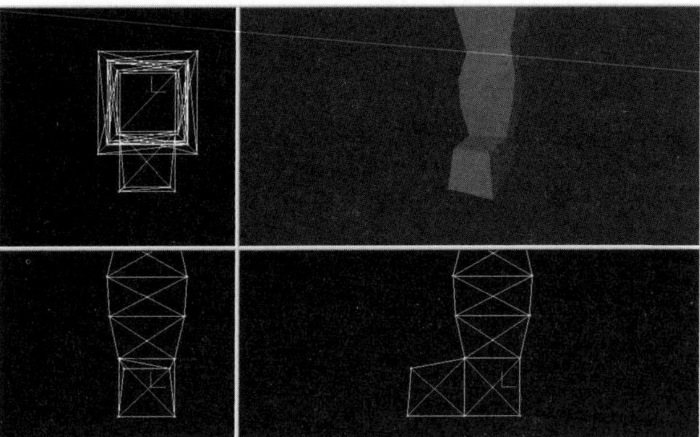

Figure 5.10
Hector knows these boots were made for walking!

Save it as leg.mdl by going to File > Save and typing the word **leg** in the Name field. You will need to create a new folder to store all the items you make for the *Hector & Hex* game. Right-click in the C:\Program Files\GStudio6 folder and select New > Folder, then name it **hector_hex**. Save the leg.mdl in the hector_hex folder.

Note

Before we go any further, I want you to know the different parts of a model that is made in 3D. First of all, any 3D model will be made up of triangles (often referred to as *polygons*, but in MED they always have to be in the shape of a triangle). Every corner of a triangle is referred to as a *vertex*. Vertices are essentially where lines intersect. The outward surface of each of these triangles is called its *face*. Multiple triangles, connected together, make up a wireframe surface of a model—what is called a *mesh*. A mesh can be seen as a wireframe, or it can have a material applied to it to give it a solid shape. This material is a *skin*. The skin can have a painted texture or just a color, and it can be given a mathematical formula for handling light absorption, called a *material*, or even its own little render program, which is called a *shader*. Some 3D models are animated, and the common practice now for quick 3D modeling is to create a hierarchy of underlying structures, which make posing the model in various frames more expedient, called *bones*. Make no bones about it, but there are lots of vocabulary terms to learn before becoming an animator!

If you cannot create a folder in the GStudio6 folder, try making a folder in My Documents or on your external storage device; sometimes access to the Program Files folder is restricted on a network, and a path to the templates folder has to be entered in the code anyway. Now we are ready to model Hector's body.

Note

Have you noticed? You can use Select or Move to select faces or ticks in the Model Editor; you can also use Scale or Rotate to make selections. You must be careful about what you click and drag with the Move tool because you might inadvertently make a new selection instead. If you should lose your selection when working with the Move tool, simply go to Edit > Undo. The Model Editor has limitless Undo capabilities.

Modeling a Body

You have one leg already made, so serviceably you have two legs made. Now you need to make the body. Instead of using a cube, we are going to use a sphere for our basic geometry and stretch it. The cube would be a great starting place because it makes sure that your model stays low in poly count. But for this exercise, I want you to experiment with different shapes and ways of modeling.

Open a new model file by selecting File > New Model, by pressing CTRL+ N, or by clicking the New icon on the menu bar.

On the geometric shapes menu bar, select Sphere and click inside the bottom-left view window. A round sphere should appear.

Make sure that you are in Triangle mode. Use the Select tool and the green marquee to select the bottom third of your sphere. See Figure 5.11 to make sure you have the correct area selected before continuing.

Use the Scale tool to shrink this part of the sphere in, making it about half the original size. Then use the Move tool to drag the bottom third of the sphere down, elongating the body. The body should now look a little like a hot air balloon. Hector's back is humped and his bottom small, so we have the general construction for his body done. Now we can curve it.

Figure 5.11
These are Humpty Dumpty's formative years.

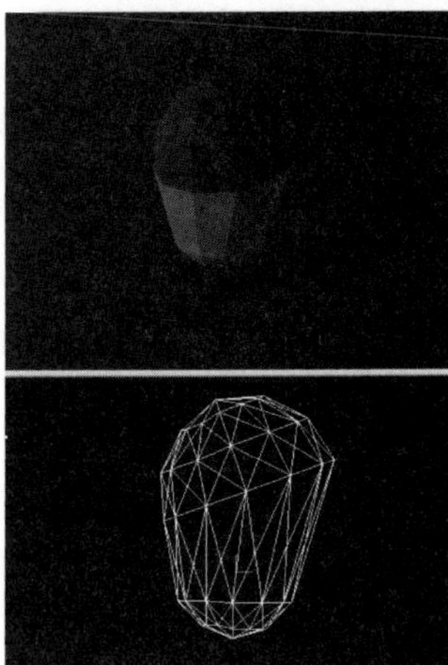

Figure 5.12
Hector was born with this hump.

Select the faces that form the top third, just above the longest planes.

Use Rotate to rotate the whole area forward at a slight angle. See Figure 5.12 to make sure that you have this done correctly.

Modeling Arms

Now you are ready to give Hector some arms. You will have to select the needed faces on either side of his bulbous body, one by one. It is easier to use the 3D View window to make your selection, because you can right-click and drag your mouse to rotate your view around Hector's body.

Hold down CTRL and, in Triangle mode, select two triangles forming a square on one side of his body, about halfway down (see Figure 5.13).

Click Extrude and enter the number **10.00** before pressing OK—at least five times.

Just as we did with the legs, use the Select and Scale tools alternately to squeeze in the part of the arm that will be the elbow, then taper out in either direction. To do this, you will have to select individual vertices of the elbow in Vertex mode while holding down the CTRL key because simply dragging your mouse and using the green marquee won't cut it anymore.

Do the same on the opposite side of Hector's body, until you have two suitable arms (see Figure 5.14), then Save As **body.mdl**.

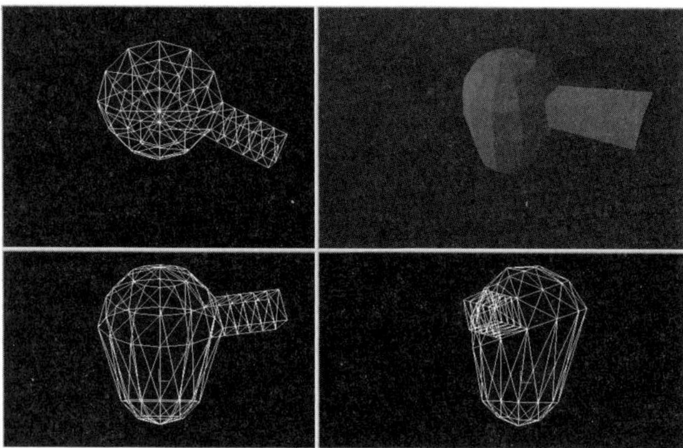

Figure 5.13
Expanding one arm at a time

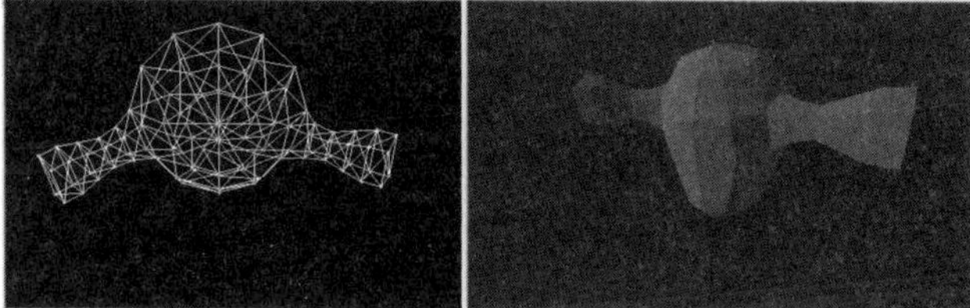

Figure 5.14
Hector bears arms.

Most of the time, arms drop to a person's sides. However, before rotating the arms to point downward and animating Hector, we are going to have to skin him; so leave the arms up in the air where they are, as if someone said to Hector, "This is a stick-up!" Open up a new model file. We are going to work on Hector's head now.

Modeling a Head

Place a sphere close to the origin. Grab the top half of it in Triangle mode; remember that to grab half of it, you will have to drag your marquee a hair's breadth over the median to adequately grab the polygons within the region.

Use the Scale tool to enlarge the upper portion of the sphere. Hector's head is supposed to be shaped roughly like a football, so we are halfway there now.

Select the back half of the sphere from the top-left view window. Scale it so that the back half of the sphere is shorter than the front half.

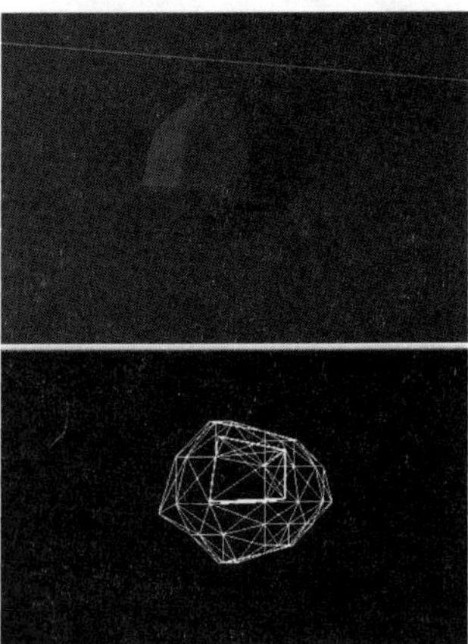

Figure 5.15
Hector's head

Select two triangles making up a square on the side of his head, and Extrude to 10.00 points. Do the same thing on either side of his head, for these will be his ears.

For an added touch, you could switch to Vertex mode and select the four external vertices of each ear, then Scale to stretch out the ears so that they taper into his head.

Last but not least, grab the vertex in the front and center of Hector's face, where Hector's nose would be. Using the Move tool, pull this vertex out a little ways and pull it down just a few units to make it appear that he has a nose. Save this model as **head.mdl**. Your head should look something like Figure 5.15.

Now you are ready to put all of these together again so you can skin them and make Hector ready to animate.

Putting the Model Together

Open up body.mdl, then go to File > Merge and pick head.mdl. The head will appear inside the body because they share the same origin.

Use the Move tool to drag the head up and out of the body; in your front view window you do not want to see them touching. You might have to Scale them to make the head fit the body better.

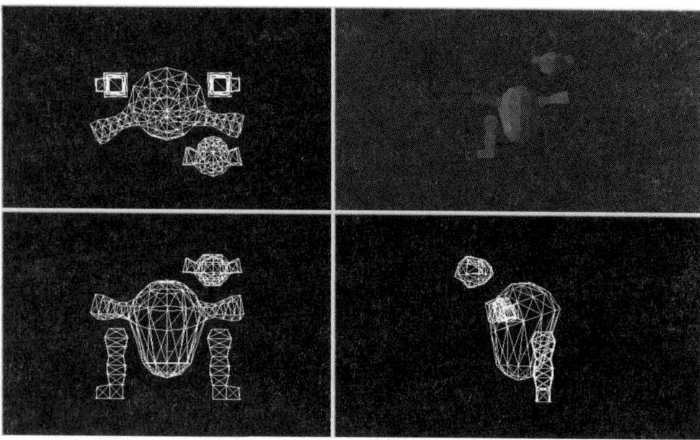

Figure 5.16
Hector is ready to get skinned!

Next, go to File > Merge and select to add the leg.mdl. Resize the leg with the Scale tool and use the Rotate tool to move it into position for skinning.

Go to Edit > Copy Selected and press CTRL + V, or select Edit > Paste to duplicate the leg. Now you should have two legs. Arrange them on the screen so that they do not touch each other, the body, or the head.

This layout will provide the best visibility when you want to skin (or add texture to) the model (see Figure 5.16). Save your new file as **hector.mdl**.

Exercise 5.2: Skinning Your Avatar

A *skin* is an image and/or a material applied to a 3D model usually to match its wireframe. Skinning your models in 3D GameStudio can be done in a variety of ways. The Skin Editor comes with many tools, including paint and palette options: you can use the Paint Bucket to drop paint right onto polygons, or you can use the Pencil tool to draw details in the program itself. However, the Skin Editor is rather clumsy when painting fine details on the models; most developers export skins into a paint program, where the real color and contrast are added. For the following exercise, I will be using Adobe Photoshop (see Figure 5.17). The most comprehensive commercial paint program on the market now is Adobe Photoshop or Jasc PaintShop Pro—but since you are just starting out you can use Paint Dot Net, which is an open-source program you can download off the Internet and comes with some of the built-in features that Photoshop

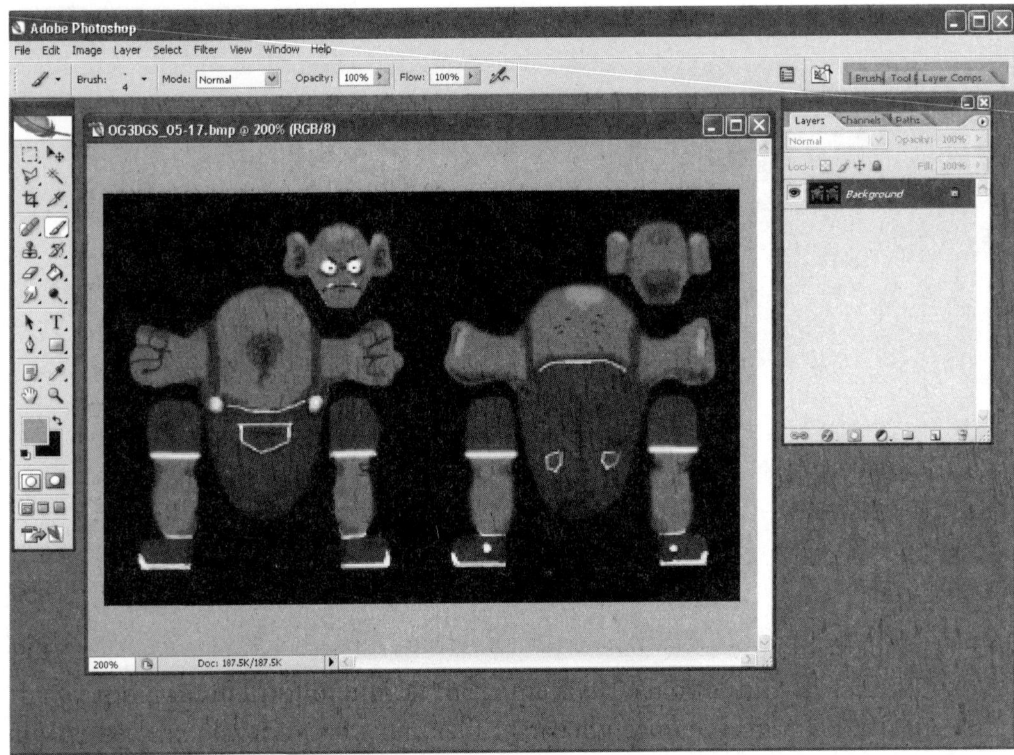

Figure 5.17
Adobe Photoshop is the standard in 2D art.

possesses. Whatever program you prefer to use, open it up because we are going to look at what it takes to give Hector a skin.

Note

Notice that the Skin Editor does not have an Undo function built-in. You must be a perfectionist when it comes to drawing a surface on your model, or else you will not be able to retrieve lost information. The Skin Editor works in real time on the model, so your changes show up immediately in the 3D Editor for you to preview.

Creating a Skin

Make sure you have hector.mdl open in the Model Editor.

Go to Edit > Manage Skins and, in the Skin Manager, click to open up the Skin Editor. There is no skin, so the box on the left should appear black, and the model's various pieces should appear black on a blue background. You familiarized yourself with the Skin Editor when we messed around with the warlock.mdl, but this time you will actually use it.

First, create a skin for Hector: in the Skin Manager, go to New Skin. The Skin Settings window will pop up. We want a textured skin, so click the Texture check box and close the window. Now you should see a new skin (Skin0) in the Skin Manager. Click Skin Settings and, under Texture Format, select 256 × 256, 24 bit, with mipmaps. Now click the Skin Editor button again, and you should see a black skin in the left window. To create the actual skin mapping, let's produce the back and front projection of Hector's mesh: In the 3D Editor, go to Edit > Create 2-Sided Mapping > Front, then click OK. If it worked right, you should now see a projection of Hector's front and back side in the Skin Editor. Note: a skin map that shows only the front and back is not the best to work with because it lacks composite sides; the skin will be infinitely stretched on the side faces. We could correct this by editing the skin mesh and inflating the side triangles; however, this should not bother us for now. We will use pure colors and bleed them over the edges so black should not creep up and mar Hector's sides.

Open the Skin Editor. Go to View > Draw Lines, then click in the left (skin mapping) window for the lines to show up. This allows you to see (and export) the character model's planar lines but hides the vertices of the model. You do not need to see the vertices of the model when you are painting its surface, but when you first start painting the model, you will have to know where the general lines are on it. You can hide these lines later, as you start importing skins, by simply coming back to View > Draw Lines and clicking it to remove the check mark.

Click Select All, and then click the Fill Selected button in the paint palette bar. This fills your texture and the triangle borders with the colors set up at the beginning of the palette bar. You'll need this for making the triangle borders visible in the exported image. Now go up to the menu in the Skin Editor and select File > Export > Current Image to BMP. Notice here that you can save skins as BMPs or PCX files. I chose BMP for this exercise. Save your BMP skin image as **hector_base.bmp** in the same folder you put your body parts, the game folder hector_hex.

Minimize the screen windows for the Skin Editor and Model Editor and open hector_base.bmp in the paint program of your choice. For this exercise, I will use Adobe Photoshop CS2 because it is the one that I am most familiar with.

With hector_base.bmp open, I arrange my toolbars to match my preferences in Photoshop.

Make sure that your Layers Panel is open (it defaults to the right of the screen). Right-click on the background layer, which should be the only layer available, and from the list of options that come up, choose Duplicate Layer. Name the Duplicate Layer **wireframe**.

The wireframe layer will need to remain your top-most layer, as you will use it to gauge your paint margins. In order to do so, there is a drop-down list at the top of the Layers Panel; these are your Blending Options. With the wireframe layer highlighted, drop down the list and choose Overlay. From now on, you should be able to see all the paint that you place on the background layer, while your lines on the wireframe layer should still remain faintly visible. You can turn the wireframe layer's visibility on or off by clicking on the eyeball icon out to the left side of its layer in the Layers Panel.

Click on the background layer to select it to work in. This is where you will be painting.

Now select the Paint Bucket tool, which is sometimes hidden behind the Gradient tool in the Tool Bar.

You will have to select your colors in the Color Picker. To bring up the Color Picker, click on the Foreground Color field on the Tool Bar. Once your Color Picker window is open, you are free to choose colors to apply to your skin image.

Use the Paint Bucket Tool to drop whole swaths of color in the background layer. Merely click once to drop color; the more you click the Paint Bucket over a pixel field, the more paint expands, and it can blur your margins. You might occasionally hide the wireframe layer to view the changes you are making to the background layer. The lines that show up in the background layer you can take out with the Brush tool.

Now select the Brush tool and, if you haven't already, cover up the lines in the background layer (you will have to hide the wireframe layer to do this). You can change the width and settings of your Brush Tip by clicking on its shape options in the menu bar. Remember to change your Brush Tip often to fit the area you are working in.

Paint details, such as Hector's eyes, nostrils, teeth, and such, using the Brush tool. Alternatively, you could use the Clone Stamp tool or bring in other images to make his face and clothes. The real character appeal comes across from the details that you place on the skin. Fine details, like the pattern of the cloth that makes up

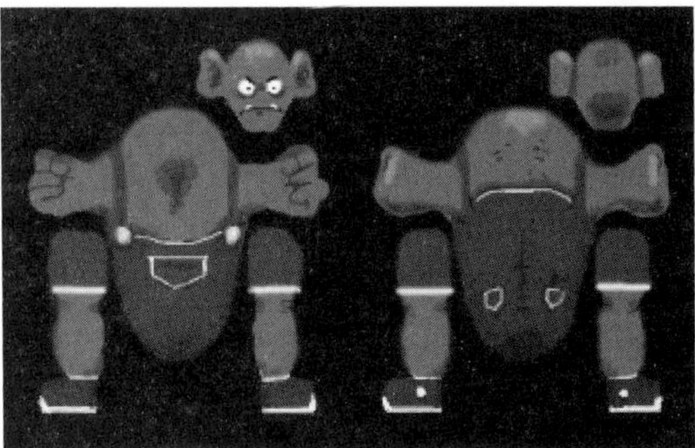

Figure 5.18
The finished Hector skin

his overalls and the faint blue veins on his flesh, will add further appeal and make the character more believable. However, do not make too many small details—they might never show up in the final render.

Lastly, set your Brush to 35% opacity and, using black as your foreground color, you can paint in shadows. Use white as your foreground color to paint in highlights. Imagine the light source coming from above so that the lightest highlights are hinted at on the upper planes, and the darkest shaded areas are on the lower planes as well as below or under the arms or chin. Lighting is tricky, even when using dynamic lighting in-game, so estimating lighting on the perspective of the character is crucial.

Save it as **color_skin.psd** to preserve your layer organization (in case you have to return to it). You can also go to File > Save As and save it as a BMP file, such as **color_skin1.bmp** (see Figure 5.18).

Applying the Skin

Test your skin image in the Skin Editor. Maximize the Skin Editor and selectFile > Import to find the color_skin1.bmp image that you just saved. The skin image will wrap around your model immediately, and you can view it in the central view window. Use the scrollbars or click the Position button and use your mouse to pan around and zoom in and out to view your model from all possible angles. Get a really good view of your model and how the skin looks on it.

Don't close the Model Editor just yet. If you leave the Skin Editor and Adobe Photoshop open, you can continue making adjustments to the skin image and

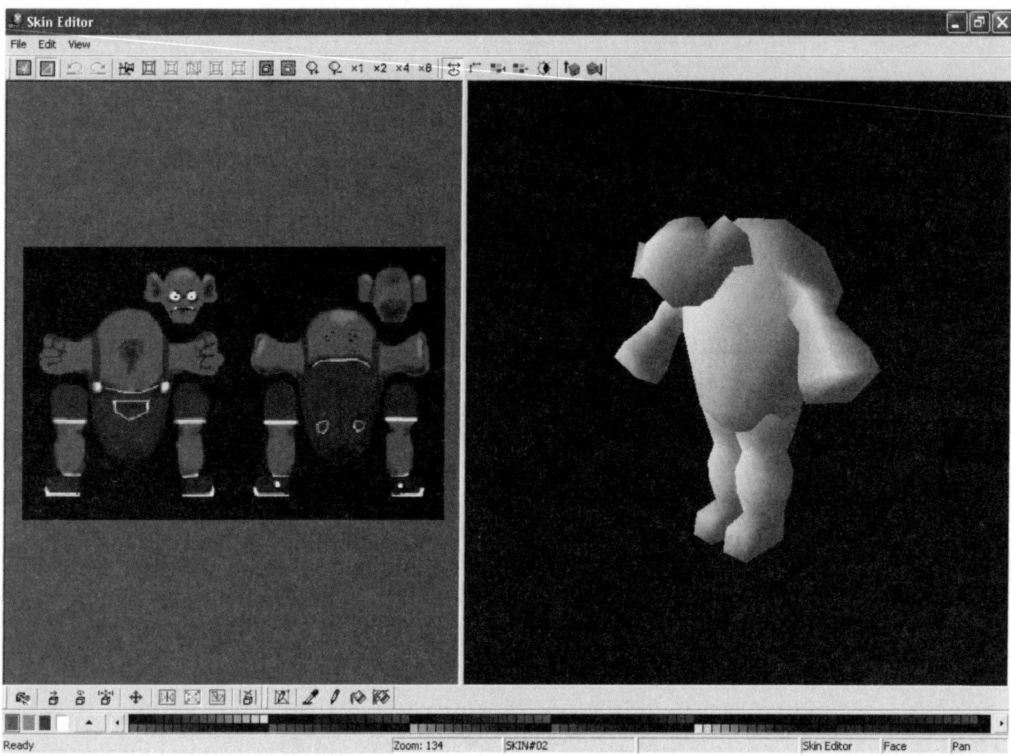

Figure 5.19
The Hector skin brought into the Skin Editor

applying them in the Skin Editor to test it. I suggest that every time you finish making adjustments and want to test the skin again, you rename it with a new number in the sequence at the end, so the next one would be color_skin2.bmp, then color_skin3.bmp, and so on. This saves you time if you suddenly realize you have to roll back to a previous version of the skin image.

Once you get the skin just the way you want it to look on the Hector model, save it as **hector.mdl** (see Figure 5.19).

Quick Skinning Tip

When using the MED of an old GameStudio version (A5), I had difficulty getting my RGB image back to Indexed color mode and reapplying the skin image to the model in the Skin Editor. Almost every time the colors are stripped because the Skin Editor has a very picky built-in color palette. Most RGB images at 24-bit color work, but some colors are not represented well. Because of this, I like to capture the Skin Editor's color palette, and open it inside Photoshop to pick all my colors from. Here's how to do it.

1. In the Skin Editor, maximize the window and scroll to get the most colors available from the color palette at the bottom of the screen. Next hit the arrow button to the left of them to open the Color Picker panel. Then use the PRNT SCRN key on your keyboard to take a snapshot of the screen.
2. In Photoshop, go to File > New and make sure that your presets are set to Clipboard, then click OK.
3. When a blank white Photoshop image comes up, simply press CTRL+V or go to Edit > Paste, and the snapshot you took will drop into the Photoshop image window.
4. Next, use the Crop tool to crop the Skin Editor color palette, deleting everything but the palette.
5. Go to Layer > Flatten Layers to place everything on a single layer.
6. Save the file as **color_palette.psd** to preserve the correct colors. Then you can open and use it anytime you are skinning images.
7. You could also make a custom color palette from samples you take from this image, and then save the custom color palette so you can use it over multiple skin jobs.

Try it! You merely have to use the Eyedropper in the Color Picker window in Photoshop when you are working on a skin image and pick colors right off the color_palette.psd file as long as you have that open in a separate window. There will be some blending because of the Brush tool that you may be using, but overall your image colors will come off looking closer than ever before.

You should now have Hector looking like Hector should. He's creepy and kooky, and he looks fairly ghoulish. He has enough character appeal in his overall appearance that players will find him entertaining to play as. Unfortunately, his body parts are all over the screen, and he has no animations. If you were to throw him in a level and give him the `player_move` behavior, the results would be disastrous! It is now time to make Hector move—though not just move, but be fun and exciting for the player to move around the game world as. Let's look at how you do that.

Note

At any time, you can check your model's properties. 3D GameStudio has a limit of 65,000 polygons per single model. Additionally, models with vast triangles will hog the end-user's processor and make the game slower. This is why you must keep your poly count down to an agreeable limit (in other words, make only low-poly models). In the Model Editor, you can go to File > Model Properties, and it will read off to you how many faces and vertices your model currently has. When I checked the Hector model, I come up with 244 vertices and 472 faces. This is an incredibly low-poly model and just right for the game we want to build!

Exercise 5.3: Animating Your Avatar

The first step to animating Hector is to stitch his body parts together the way they need to be for your first frame of animation. The initial animation state you are going to create will be the stand animation. Look at Figure 5.20 to see how you should place the body parts together in the Model Editor in anticipation of animating them. The head must rest down the body—overlapping with the area you painted as a neck. The arms lie at rest at his sides. Do this by selecting the vertices and using the Rotate and Move tools. Rotate the legs and place them side by side under his body, the upper fifth of each leg overlapping his hip region. The most difficult part of aligning his body parts will probably be the deforming of Hector's arms. Be careful here; know that what you learn by practice in one area of development will carry over to others later on.

There are two more tasks you must accomplish before you can start animating. One is to orient Hector correctly. Rotate Hector so that he is facing to the right in the top-down view (the top left-most grid window). If—when you open up the Model Editor and load Hector from scratch—he is facing down in the top-down view, then when you animate him, he would be walking, running, and jumping in the wrong direction, which would be very annoying. So rotate him so that he is looking to the right in the top-down view.

The second task is sizing Hector correctly. Go to File > Merge and select warlock.mdl from the work folder. You should see the warlock model appear in the Model Editor. He should be already selected (a completely red shape). The warlock is a standard model that comes free with 3D GameStudio, and it comes

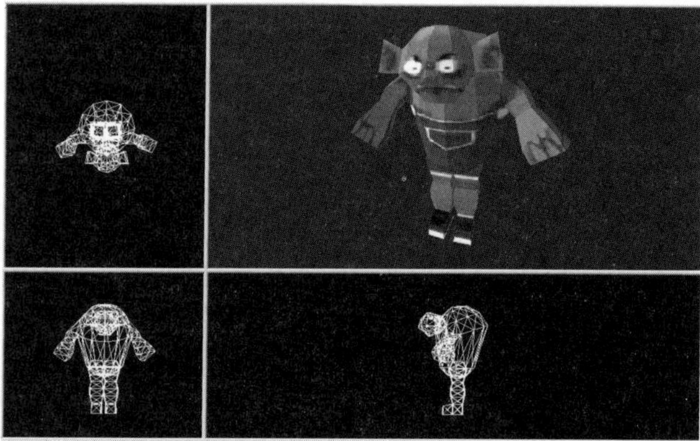

Figure 5.20
Putting Hector together

in really handy for comparison work like this. If the warlock is shorter than the Hector model, you need to shrink Hector. If the warlock is taller than the Hector model, you need to enlarge Hector. Either way, you need to make Hector a half-head shorter than the warlock model. To do this, first delete the warlock model (or Edit > Undo your Merge), then choose Select All so that every bit of Hector is selected. Using the Scale tool, you are going to size him where he needs to be. Once you are through, you are ready to begin animating Hector!

Animating the character model is broken down into each of its states: stand, walk, run, jump, attack, duck, crawl, swim, and death. You are going to start by performing the stand animation. Then I will show you how to create the walk, jump, duck, crawl, and death animations. Run is not necessary because you will duplicate the walk animation for it, as he will naturally speed up when you speed up his animation. Attack will not be called into play because we will switch Hector to first-person POV when he starts hitting targets. Hector will probably never need to swim either, so we are going to ignore that state for now.

You will see immediately why we made Hector out of individual parts, like Lego blocks. You are going to do some fast (and some would say dirty) animation. If you had made Hector out of one seamless mesh, then you would have to zoom in and select parts of the mesh vertex by vertex to do your translations and rotations. You can do it that way. It takes a lot of patience and skill. This is why we are going to make the animation simple, so you get the hang of the animation process first.

Stand Animation

This animation is the one the player sees on the screen when she starts a new game, and it is the state that will resume any time the computer does not sense input from the player. So the stand animation controls the player character for over 75 percent of the animated screen time, and this makes it the most important animation state.

When you have the parts aligned correctly for the first frame of his stand animation state, go up to Edit > Manage Frames > Add Frames and call the first frame **stand1**.

Now you have to create a second frame of the animation. To do so, select Edit > Manage Frames > Add Frames. The dialog box that comes up will allow you to insert the new frame wherever you want it, call it whatever you want, and even base it (copy it) from any frame in the frames list. Call the new frame **stand2** and assign it the Source Frame of stand1. It should place the new frame automatically after stand1. From now on, all you should have to do is click Edit > Manage Frames > Add Frames, then click OK, and it should continue to copy and create new frames on the fly!

Select some of the vertices of Hector's hump with the Vertex mode on—or select one of the faces on his hump with the Triangle mode on.

Between the Vertex and Face modes and the Position, Move, Scale, and Rotate buttons at the top are several selection choices. The middle one (which looks like a blue square overlapping a black square) is the Select Connected button. Click it, and you should see that Hector's entire body and arms are selected. They should all turn red at once.

Now you can press the Animate button. This will switch you into animation.

Slide the frame slider until you are in stand2.

Using the Move tool, slide Hector's body up ever so slightly. Using the Scale tool, expand the width of his body in a very subtle manner, one that would almost be imperceptible. You are going to animate him so that he looks like he's breathing when he is standing in place.

Click on Add New Frames, calling them **stand3** and **stand4**. Make stand3 a copy of stand2 and stand4 a copy of stand1.

Note

Be careful! When you create a new frame of animation and base it off of a previous one (as we will be doing in these exercises), you will notice that if you go back and edit the source frame, it alters the other frames–sometimes most dramatically! This is because each frame of animation that is duplicated off of a previous one will store any changes made to that one at a later date. You have to think ahead and be very frugal when editing earlier frames of animation (even in entirely different animation cycles) so that you don't deform a later frame of animation.

You can add minor details as you like to the four standing frames. For instance, you can make gradual shifts between stand1 and stand3 with subtle changes in the translation and scale of Hector's body. You could have his arms flair out on the intake of breath and droop on the exhalation. You could have him wiggle his ears. The more secondary motions you can add, the more realistic Hector will become. (Note: the more subtle shifts you can give to Hector's cycle will make him a better model; too large a shift will make him look "jittery.")

Walk Animation

Walking is essentially like standing, except that all of Hector's limbs must be in motion. His legs will pump and his arms will swing in tandem. We must pay careful attention to secondary motions and arcing motion with this animation state.

Go to Edit > Manage Frames > Add Frames. Add one new frame, called **walk1**, and use as its source frame stand1. This will begin your new state.

Select one of Hector's legs. To do so, select some of the vertices (if you are using Vertex mode) or some of the faces (if you are in Triangle mode), and then click the Select Connected button.

Rotate it slightly so that his toes are moving up and away from the body, as if he is going to punt a ball. You should rotate only in the side view portal window. If you rotate in the top view portal window, or any other, his leg will rotate at a weird angle. Be sure only to rotate the leg a short space at a time. Don't worry, because we *are* going to add more frames for his walk cycle.

Now that you have rotated the leg, notice that it is not connected to his hip socket any longer. Use the Move tool to shove the leg back into its socket and make it appear correct. If you don't want to move it back all the time after having rotated it, you can also select a different rotation center with the Options button next to the Scale button.

Select Hector's other leg the same way you did the first. Rotate this leg going the other way. This will create a swing in his step. The rotation that you apply will create an arcing movement.

Move this leg to sit on the pelvis the right way, where it appears natural.

Create a second frame, called **walk2**, by going to Edit > Manage Frames > Add Frames and clicking OK. The frame should be created for you, and it should mirror the settings of the first frame in the walk cycle. Rinse and repeat everything you just did.

Create a third frame, called **walk3**. This time you will rinse and repeat again, but I want you to take the legs all the way to their fullest extension, where one is pointing directly ahead of Hector's body in the direction he is facing and the other is pointing directly behind. This will be the peak of his walk animation.

Now you can go back through each of the three frames that you have created and clean up your image. For one thing, legs do not naturally move stiffly. Usually the knees are bent slightly when a person walks.

Starting in walk1 you are going to select each of Hector's arms. Click on the button marked Select Touching until his arm is selected and highlighted in red all the way up to his armpit or near enough. Then you are going to use Rotate and Move to swing the arm the opposite direction of the leg on that side of his body. Do the same with both arms so that they are swinging along with his steps.

When the legs are at their fullest extension, I want you to select only the lower portions of his arms (that is, from his elbow to his meaty fists). Rotate the lower portion of his arms closer to his body, as though he were bringing his arms in. Don't rotate them too far because you don't want to make his body appear to "jitter" in the middle of his walk cycle; just rotate them enough so that there is a glimpse of him starting to pull his arms up toward his chest. Use the Move tool to place them where they look most natural because you don't want the mesh to deform.

You are going to make a fourth frame and call it **walk4**, but this time you are going to set the source frame to walk2.

You are going to make a fifth frame (called **walk5**) and base its source frame on walk1.

You can test your walk cycle (if you wish) by clicking the Play button. Notice that the Model Editor, in the 3D View portal, shows you all the animation you have created so far. It looks like Hector is taking a step, and then stopping to take a breath. Great! Click the Play button to stop the preview and let's continue.

Repeat these steps to create walk6 through walk10—making sure to do just the opposite of last time. For instance, if you swung his left foot forward and right foot back in the first part of this exercise, switch them so that his right foot goes forward and his left foot goes back. The same goes for the swinging arms.

When you are finished, you might consider making secondary motions: his head bobbing or his body swaying side to side as he walks. When you get done, pat yourself on the back! You have just made Hector walk.

Run Animation

The previous animation—the walk cycle—will be used to make Hector run as well. Using the template scripts to build your game, Hector will immediately start running if the player holds the SHIFT key while moving with the arrow keys. If you do not define a state for run, the character will freeze in motion while zooming across the level—and that does not look very realistic! So I will show you the fast (and easy) method for creating a run animation, without having to animate a single frame.

Move your frame slider until you have walk1 selected.

Go to Edit > Manage Frames > Add Frames. Call this one **run1**, and set its source frame to the current frame (which should be walk1). Automatically, a run1 frame will appear at the end of your walk cycle, thus beginning a run cycle, and it will look like the first frame of the walk cycle.

Move the frame slider back until you see walk2.

Repeat the process, but this time the Model Editor should recall your intentions from before. All you should have to do is click OK, and a run2 frame will appear based on walk2. If it does not look anything like walk2 something went wrong.

Continue in this venue, until you have recreated all of the 10 frames of the walk cycle as the new run cycle (see Figure 5.21). This is a cheap and efficient way to create a run cycle for Hector. You could tweak the two so that the run cycle is markedly different in appearance from the walk cycle, but the run cycle will look different anyway when you test your game level later on because the run cycle looks like the walk cycle speeded up. Similarly, if you are importing original *Quake* models, *Quake* does not use walk—it uses run. You would create a walk cycle from the run cycle with the same process, just in reverse.

Figure 5.21
Run, Hector, run!

Jump Animation

Now Hector is going to take a flying leap, straight into the air and back down again. It might be somewhat disappointing that we are not going to animate him jumping a chasm or doing any double-jumps, but what do you expect when he is a half-ton of ghoul flesh? So get ready to make Hector hop!

Go to Edit > Manage Frames > Add Frames. Add one new frame, called **jump1**, and use as its source frame stand1. This will begin your new state.

You are going to want to use Rotate and Move to get Hector to pull his meaty fists up closer to his chest, just as you did with the walk cycle. Remember you can select just his lower arms by selecting a face on the end of his fist and pressing the Select Touching button until his lower arm has turned red to show that it is selected. If you mess up, remember that you can always go to Edit > Undo.

Next you will want to bend Hector's legs at the knee so that he looks like he is kneeling. If you bent his legs slightly during the creation of the walk cycle, you should already know what to do. Otherwise, select a face on one of his toes and hit Select Touching until his leg is red all the way up to the knee.

Use Rotate and Move to bend Hector's legs at the knee—but make sure that it looks perfectly natural and does not get too deformed!

When you are on the last leg and still have part of it selected, press Select Connected so that the entire leg is selected.

Rotate and Move it so that the foot is flat on an imaginary ground plane and the leg reaches the hip socket.

Start the same with the other leg, but this one you are going to make where his knee is touching the ground plane. He should now appear to be kneeling on one knee. You can use this state for his crouch position as well, but it makes an excellent start to his jump cycle because he could push off from the ground better this way; this is an example of anticipation (see Figure 5.22).

Select All so that every single face and vertex of our dear Hector are highlighted. This is where having a good eye and being able to see imaginary lines are going to come into play (of course, you could drop a grid if you wanted, but I prefer to eyeball it).

Slide the frame slider back a few frames. Notice that Hector is no longer touching the true ground plane. If you go all the way back to stand1—which you can do

Figure 5.22
Hector kneeling and getting ready to spring

using the Go to Frame button—you can view the true ground plane because he is, in essence, standing on it there. Go back to jump1. Using the Move tool, slowly nudge the entire Hector model down until he is touching that imaginary ground plane. When you think you have it right, go back to stand1 and test your guess.

Go to Edit > Manage Frames > Add Frames; call this one **jump2**, and base it off of jump1. With the entire Hector model selected, use the Move tool to raise him up in the air several units of measurement.

Go to Edit > Manage Frames > Add Frames; call this one **jump3**, and base it off of jump2. Move Hector up a little more into the air. If you like, move him forward just a few units to make it appear as if he is moving forward a little. Remember that this is a hop. The actual jumping motion is carried out in-game thanks to the script, not how far you model him in the Model Editor; essentially, he should stay in place when he jumps, and he should move up and back down with ease. Repeat this process to create jump4.

When you do jump5, you will start moving Hector back down to the ground plane. He should move down faster than he did going up; the physics behind this are related to the squash and stretch principle of animation, as well as basic momentum and energy factors. It should take him longer to get airborne than it does to hit the ground again—especially with this half ton of ghoul!

In jump6 he should be just about to hit the ground again. In jump7 he should already be on the ground.

Now slide the frame slider back to jump2. We are going to make all the difference in his animation by placing secondary motions throughout. For one thing, his legs will rotate back to center and his arms will fly out. His head should bob a little.

First, select one of his legs by clicking a face (in Triangle mode) and clicking Select Connected. If you still have every bit of Hector selected, you might want to press Select None first before you select anything else.

Rotate and Move the leg so that it is closer to center and his toes are starting to point toward the ground.

Move to jump3 and finish the motion by pointing his toes right at the ground and having the leg centered with his body. When you make changes in one frame, any frame using that frame as its source is also altered. You can slide ahead to jump4 or even to jump7 and see what I mean.

Go back to jump2 and do the same thing with the other leg, finishing in jump3.

In jump5, jump6, and jump7, you are going to do the opposite: you are going to Rotate and Move his legs so that, once again, he will land in the position that he started from in jump1. Keep the two legs straight in your mind. Make sure the leg he was kneeling with is the one he ends up kneeling on when he comes back down (see Figure 5.23).

Go back to jump2 and select one of Hector's arms. Use Select Touching to reach from his knuckles to the top of his arm, where it meets his body.

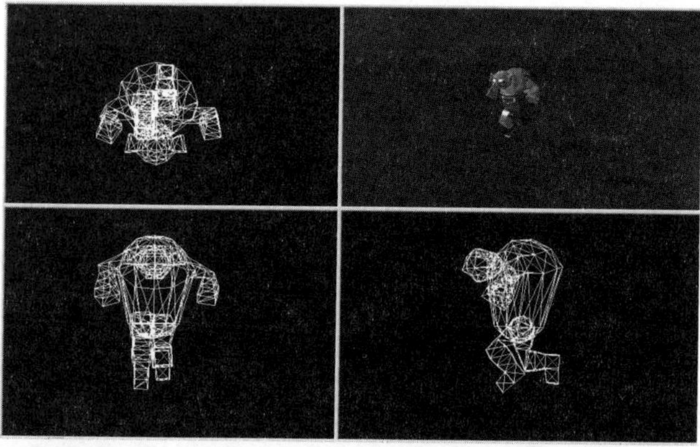

Figure 5.23
Keep the legs separate in your mind.

In jump2 and jump3, use Rotate and Move to swing the arm up, out, and away from Hector's body. You want to make it look like his arms are flying out as he leaps into the air.

In jump4 and jump5, bring his arm back toward his body, like it was at the start.

Do the same thing with the other arm so that they match. You will also have to fix the arms in jump6 and jump7 because they will have been altered due to the changes you made.

Now for Hector's head. Select a face on his head, and click Select Connected. Once his head turns red, go to jump2 and Move his head so that it appears one or two units lower than jump1.

Slide the slider to jump4, and raise his head back up to its normal position.

Make any minor adjustments that you can see need fixed throughout the jump cycle, until Hector looks pretty good and goofy going airborne. The player will thank you for it!

Duck and Crawl Animation

Hector and his sister Hex love to sneak around the manor house and play pranks on their parents (and any unlucky visitors!), so they have become experts at ducking and crawling. Their mother even swears there is some snake in the family bloodline! So let's look at how well Hector is going to crouch.

Go to Edit > Manage Frames > Add Frames. Add one new frame, called **duck1**, and use jump1 as its source frame. This will begin your new state.

Now you have to select the entire Hector model and move him up approximately 16 units. You are going to have to use your best judgment (and a fair eye) to approximate the distance. The model's origin (the central cross or L-shape) should show up just under his body mesh. You are doing this because—as I have mentioned before—duck and crawl states are programmed differently in 3D GameStudio, as the model will be dropped 16 units into the ground plane. The model will also have a drop shadow applied, so *where* the model sinks into the floor might not show up as harshly as you think.

Now go to Edit > Manage Frames > Add Frames and click OK to make duck2 based on the current frame of duck1. Hector essentially appears as if he is kneeling on the floor.

You could add more frames of animation and make Hector appear to be breathing (using the Scale and Move tools on his body, as you did in his stand cycle). That is entirely up to you. As it is not imperative to the proper function of the game, having two frames of Hector kneeling should do just fine.

Occasionally you will have approximated the 16 units incorrectly. If you do, it will show up when you test-run your first game level. Simply re-open the Model Editor and the hector.mdl, use the Move tool to approximate the distance better, then save it. The model will be automatically updated in the Level Editor.

Death Animation

With such a strong word used as "death" in the cartoon-based game we are constructing here, we are not going to go for gory or realistic dying animations. Hector is not going to explode into bits or groan and faint away. It's just not in his nature.

Go to Edit > Manage Frames > Add Frames. Add one new frame, called **death1**, and use stand1 as its source frame. This will begin your new state.

We are going to pose the Hector model until he looks absolutely stricken. To do this, first select his right arm up to the elbow by selecting a face on his knuckle and clicking Select Touching until his arm turns red up to the elbow. Use the Rotate and Move tools to turn it slightly.

Now hit Select Touching a couple more times to select his arm all the way up to his (nonexistent) shoulder. Use Rotate and Move to make the arm come up, as if he were shielding his face from a blow.

Select his right leg up to the knee and Rotate it so that his leg is bent. To make rotations to his legs in the Model Editor, use the bottom-right view portal.

Hit Select Connected to select the whole leg and Rotate and Move it so that it looks like he is partly lifting his leg up in the air.

Select his left foot up to his ankle and Rotate and Move it so that it looks like his foot is bending upward.

Hit Select Touching a few times until his left leg is selected up to the knee, and then bend it slightly.

If you did this correctly, his left foot should now be flat against the ground plane again. Move the frame slider ahead (which should take it to stand1) to double-check the placement of Hector. He might need to be nudged down or over to touch the ground plane again.

Figure 5.24
Hector has been struck!

Go to Edit > Manage Frames > Add Frames, and make a new frame, called **death2**, based on death1.

Click Select and drag your marquee over the upper half of Hector (his head, arms, and body). Hit Select Connected to grab his whole upper body. The only items you should NOT see in red are his legs.

Use Rotate and Move to make it appear that Hector is back-stepping. See Figure 5.24 to understand what I mean.

Select his right leg (the one that is lifted in the air), and lift it even further.

Go to Edit > Manage Frames > Add Frames, and make a new frame, called **death3**, based on death2.

Select the entire Hector model and Rotate him one-eighth turn CW (clockwise) in the left view portal (the top-down view). We are going to make Hector appear to spin around on his heel.

Make two more frames, and in each have Hector Rotate another one-eighth turn.

Now you are going to make death6, but you are going to base it on stand1. Hector is back to standing again. Rotate him 180 degrees so that he is facing backward. This completes Hector's half-turn.

Figure 5.25
Fatality!

Select each of his arms up to the shoulder, and Rotate them out so that he looks like he did when you initially modeled him.

Make the frame death7 based on death6. Select the entire Hector model, and start to Rotate and Move him so that he looks as if he is falling flat on his back (which is what we want him to do). Continue this through death8 and death9 until Hector is 100 percent prone (see Figure 5.25). The most important point of reference you have for each of these poses is his back heels: make sure that the heel of his foot matches in each of the animations (pin it in your mind's eye if you have to).

Create a new frame, called **death10**, that is based on death9. You will touch up the model to put Hector's body at rest. First, select each of his arms up to the elbows and Rotate and Move them, then click Select Touching to select his entire arms and Rotate and Move them again—until his knuckles are almost touching the invisible ground plane (but watch out for deformations or dimpling of the mesh).

Select one of Hector's legs and Rotate and Move it until the toe is pointing away from Hector and the leg is splayed just a little.

Lastly, select Hector's whole head and Rotate and Move it until it lays limp to one side and appears to sink into his body a ways. There we have it! Hector has just died (or passed out, or fainted, or whatever you will).

In Summary

Now that you have successfully created Hector, you are practically done! Later I will talk about the application of bones animation, but you now have your feet wet with vertex animation. I have supplied you with the remaining 3D models that you will need to start building the levels and programming the game. On the other hand, you should practice with 3D modeling, especially if you found you have talent at it, and you could create other characters to go in this game (see Figure 5.26). For instance, there could be spiders, carnivorous plants, tanks of squid, weapons of all types, and props for Hector to find along his warpath. Perhaps you can experiment with the Model Editor and find new ones that have yet to be imagined—or re-skin and customize existing ones. Have fun, use your imagination, and apply the lessons and principles you have learned herein to make whatever you desire with the 3D GameStudio!

Figure 5.26
Try creating all these unique creatures if you dare!

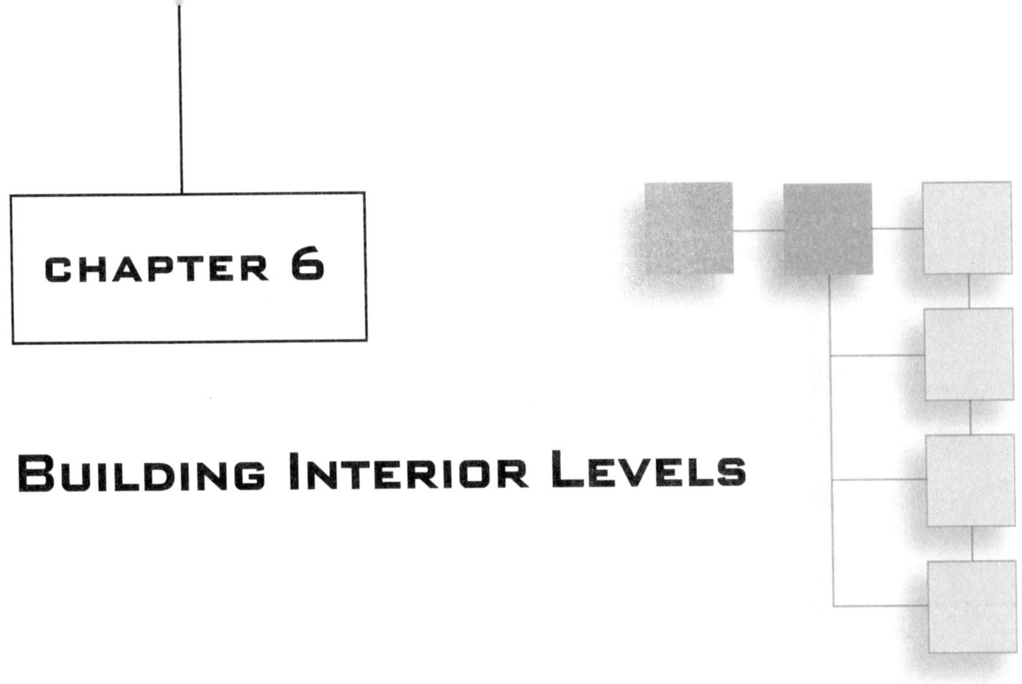

Chapter 6

Building Interior Levels

Note

"Most often, when you think of game art, it is the characters and creatures that come to mind—even though it is the environments those creatures inhabit that really create the illusion of a world. . . . You want your game to be convincingly real to truly inspire mood and drama—and yet you have to be inventive without straining credulity. It's a matter of combining and synthesizing, keeping the aspirations in your head, but looking for new ways to fit it all together."

—Marc Taro Holmes, Obsidian Entertainment

We have covered the creation of game characters, but these characters have to exist somewhere. Without an appropriate frame of reference—evidenced in a game world—the players are just so many random pieces without a place to be. Gameplay also has to have a background for reference, a playground for the player to explore, find resources, and beat combatants in. If we use the analogy of a theater, the game world provides the stage for the action, and the players are the actors on the stage. Inside this game world there are several scenes (or chapters) that we call levels. Each level has a set of objectives that the player must reach before they can travel to the next level. *Level design* is formally defined as the creation of environments, scenes, scenarios, or missions in an electronic game world.

3D Space

Note

"Even though it's fun to crawl inside a computer and play with its potential, it's really important to look at other aspects of your life as well. That's where ideas for programs will come from."

—Marcia Burrows, *K-Power Magazine*

The art of replicating objects and scenes that we see all around us in the form of computer-generated images is the essence of 3D design. In order to create a virtual world, a 3D space can be a near-enough replica of the real world or a complete figment of imagination. If you've played a lot of games before, you probably know what a virtual world is—but if you need a refresher or the term is totally alien to you, I will describe it for you. Most 3D games contain virtual worlds; take for example the game *Myst* or its counterpart *Riven*, both of which contain the characters, sets, landscapes, and scenes that don't exist in our real world. All these images are put together by graphic artists and create a composite computer-generated 3D world. Some games like *Rez* do not even compare to the real world because they are so abstractly removed and alien. A world builder needs to visualize her virtual worlds before attempting to create them.

All of the space inside a virtual world is referred to as the *3D space*, and the objects inside this 3D space are created from geometry and have textures mapped to them. Suitable positioning of objects in the 3D space generates the player's illusion that the game world is a large, immersive world similar to the real world. Some games can represent the real world very closely. The key phrase here is "very closely" because, in order to simulate anything as complicated as the real world, you have to spend a lot of effort, time, and thought; but given the limitations of the software today it will never be "perfect."

We looked at WED in a previous chapter, but there are basic 3D concepts that you are going to have to comprehend before you can continue to build worlds. They are

- Spatial dimensions
- Units of measurement
- Textures
- Level of detail (LOD)
- Entities

Spatial Dimensions

In the real universe, every object has three dimensions. They are length, height, and width. To create 3D worlds, you must define these dimensions for the 3D space. They are called X, Y, and Z dimensions. Placing and orienting objects in a 3D scene involves establishing a spatial relationship between the objects using these X, Y, and Z dimensions.

You must have studied geometry during your school years. This geometry used the Cartesian coordinate system, which is also used in 3D space to orient and define objects. The Cartesian coordinate system has an origin from which every object is referenced. From the origin, three lines run at right angles to each other—one side to side, one back and forth, and one up and down. They are referred to as the X, Y, and Z axes. Any object in the 3D space can be located by measuring its distance from these axes. These distances are called the X, Y, and Z coordinates of the object. Thus the origin is 0 units X, 0 units Y, and 0 units Z (0, 0, 0). Assume that an object is placed at (22, −100, 65) in 3D space. This implies that the object is 22 units away from the origin of the X-axis, −100 units away from that of the Y-axis, and 65 units away from the origin of the Z-axis. In other words, (22, −100, 65) is the distance from the world origin (0, 0, 0).

Consider a painter and a sculptor at work. A painter uses paints and brushes to draw on canvas. This painting is on a 2D plane. There is no third dimension on the surface of the canvas. The sculptor works in three dimensions. The sculptor is able to go around the sculpture and feel it evolve in all three dimensions and make it look good from every angle. The painter brings out the effect of textures and lights with the judicious use of colors, whereas the sculptor uses some tools to skillfully carve textures on the model and live light sources will provide the lights and dynamic shadows. The difference between 2D and 3D software can be compared to the difference in the work done by the painter and the sculptor. 2D software (such as bitmap/raster programs) recognizes a picture with the help of the X and Y axes. 3D software recognizes objects with the X, Y, and Z axes.

The curvature of the lens of our eyes enables us to see things in perspective instead of in a flat plane; as a result, objects located far away appear smaller than the objects located nearer to your face. The same effect is generated in 3D GameStudio by displaying your objects in the 3D View window—enabling you to gauge depth on your monitor screen. If you were to observe the 3D View closely, you would find that two parallel lines seem to meet at the horizon; the same effect is observed in the real world. Artists call this the *vanishing point*, and it rests on the horizon line. The exact same geometry lessons you learn here are what artists have used in painting and sketching for years, which they call *perspective.*

In addition to the perspective view, 3D GameStudio uses three orthographic views to display objects. Two parallel lines in an orthographic view always run parallel to each other. This does not represent the real world; however, it helps estimate relative sizes of the objects accurately. You can also place the objects along the grid lines or resize them accordingly based on the grid lines. To do this, you must understand about units of measurement.

Units of Measurement

Distances are measured in the real world by using units of measurement, such as inches and feet or centimeters and meters. Similar units are used in 3D GameStudio to define and locate 3D models. The units of measurement in 3D GameStudio are referred to as *quants.* The maximum number of quants that can exist in a single map are 100,000 with the coordinate origin set at the center of the map. Unfortunately, quants are not equivalent to a fixed size, such as the centimeter or inch. There are some really good reasons for this.

Look around, and you'll find that each object is three-dimensional: this book, your chair, your computer, the room you are in, and so on. The world around us is 3D. No, I am not talking about the sort of 3D you have to wear the red-and-blue specs for; that is a holographic representation of 3D space using a visual trick. Because we are used to our 3D environment, we do not find it necessary to study every object in terms of its height, width, and depth. We just know they exist and the scale they exist in relation to us. Similarly, choosing a scale in 3D GameStudio is up to you—and it should be determined by the scale of the player model. If you have a player model 86 quants high and you assume (for example) she should stand five feet tall in the virtual world, then 86 quants should roughly equal five feet. To work out just how big 1 quant is, all you have to divide is 5 by 86 to come up with an approximated 0.059 as the size of 1 quant. Then you can estimate the size of one room or one car based on the new unit of measurement. This may seem like overdoing it, but it is actually pretty handy to do it this way. Say you decide to have a game where the player is a giant. You can measure the size of objects in comparison to your lumbering giant so that the world appears much smaller than the player model. Or you could make the player a mouse and have fun creating larger-than-life kitchen counters and dining room tables for your playing field.

Don't let the math scare you. As any designer knows, shortcuts are the only way to get projects done under deadline and on time. 3D GameStudio does not force you to measure every little thing. I will show you how—just by plopping your player character into the Level Editor before getting started building—you can measure rooms and doorways effectively by how many heads tall your character stands!

You might be wondering, How big does a quant look in the Level Editor? You might even assume that one little square on the grid in one of the orthographic views on the screen would be one quant. This is not the case—you can see in the window title bar how many quants are one little square and how many little squares are one big square. You can zoom in and out of the orthographic view windows using the middle mouse button and see the scale change size. You will zoom out far enough where the little squares become big squares again and on and on into infinity (there are normally 8 × 8 of them in every larger square, but you can adjust this value under File > Preferences > Grid Hi). Don't let the grid lines mislead you! Always place your player character or a character placeholder into your level before you begin building so that the level stays in proportional relation to the creatures and characters.

Textures

The width and height of textures should be some power of 2, such as 64, 128, or 256. PCX- and BMP-based textures are displayed with 16-bit color depth, and TGA-based textures are displayed with 24 or 32 bit. The size of your textures is dependent on the maximum video memory you and your customer are running on your video card. Some of the older video cards have only 8 MB memory. Some old 3D accelerator cards (specifically the Voodoo series) don't allow texture or sprite sizes greater than 256 × 256. Textures that don't fit are automatically scaled and resized by the engine, which will hog computer memory and decrease load times. The game will still run, but it might swap textures, slow down, or cause jitter in some of the places in the map. Sometimes you will see an error message when testing out a level that says you are trying to use a texture that is the wrong size. If this happens, just choose another texture for your blocks, or you can extract the texture, resize it, and import it again (overwriting the original).

Textures set in the Level Editor come in the form of WADs. *WADs* are packages of textures, and you can use WADs that are compatible with 3DGS, the Quake Editor, or the WorldCraft Editor. Naming conventions are important in WADs, as the textures are supplied in alphabetical order. You can bookmark specific textures that you like or plan to use over and over again, as well modify WADs by extracting, renaming, removing, and adding textures at will.

Textures can be turbulent (appearing as though made of liquid) or be turned into a sky. Sky textures move at an angle, so their tiling should be perfect before you set them to sky. Sky textures can be applied to sky boxes in the level and give a fairly perfect representation of a cloudy racing sky. Textures can have other settings applied to them, some depending on the edition of 3D GameStudio you possess.

Level of Detail (LOD)

Levels of detail (LOD) are not supported by all editions of 3D GameStudio. LOD is used for increasing the frame rate in large outdoor levels. The difference in rendering speed is remarkable when you develop outdoor levels where lots of different entities are visible at one time. If you spent a lot of time on your player character and end up with a huge number of polygons, the computer might render the character pretty well in the close-up but will churn harder to get a good view in an outdoor level.

To compensate, entities can switch between four files, depending on their distance away from the camera. If an entity's file name ends with "_0" then the engine assumes that similar files ending "_1" or "_2" or "_3" are the three further LOD settings for that entity. For instance, if you have player_0.mdl then the engine assumes player_1.mdl all the way through to player_3.mdl are the model's LOD files. LOD uses the distance from the camera, set in the script by the value `camera.clip_far (clipping)` to shift between the various LOD files. If there are dynamic shadows applied to the entity, the shadow will turn off or not render at all after the entity is more than 50 percent of the clip_far distance away from the camera. You might have witnessed the same LOD technology used in the large outdoor levels of popular games such as *Fable* and *Elder Scrolls IV: Obsidian.* A hill that looks like a green blob will switch to a lush verdant hill the closer you get to it, and when you are right up on top of that hill, suddenly blades of grass, mushrooms, and other 3D touches appear to cinch the visuals.

Entities

Any construct that is not part of the level geometry is referred to as an entity in the Level Editor, but there are many types of entities. Entities are external files found in the work directories or subdirectories therein. There are four basic types of entities to be found.

Map Entities

A map entity has a file extension of WMB and was originally created in the Level Editor, saved and compiled to a WMB file. Map entities are rigid 3D objects used for level parts that move as a whole and can have behaviors applied to them (as opposed to level geometry, which cannot). Map entities are typically used for doors, platforms, gates, and so on. You can make your own map entities by creating an object in the Level Editor and performing a Build as a map entity. Many level objects can be found in the prefabs directory in the GStudio6 folder. You will find many subdirectories under prefabs, including predefined portals, furniture, vehicles, and the like. It is not wise to scale prefabs without creative thought behind it because some of the predefined objects were made with smaller articulate angles and intersecting planes that can corrupt your level's compiling if you are not careful.

Model Entities

You have already been using the Model Editor to create 3D models for the 3D GameStudio. External model files share the extension MDL and are composed of a 3D mesh with an attached skin or skins. You can convert 3DS, X, ASE, OBJ, or MD2 files into MDL files using the Model Editor. There are also plug-ins you can download to import Caligari TrueSpace, Maya, or 3D Studio Max models. Model entities make up the majority of furniture, props, actors, and objects in the Level Editor. They are also the only entities to which you can apply shadows. For myself, I find it is handier to build the details in the levels with MDL files than with basic geometry—but you must have underlying geometry, or else the player model will escape past the level or float out into empty space.

Sprite Entities

Sprites are flat 2D objects that can be placed into the Level Editor and used as a decal, particle, or object in and of itself. You would not use sprites for any object that is meant to have substance, but they work great for items that are supposed to be thin, such as paper, posters, billboards, signs, plants, grass, leaves, and so on. Sprites will turn to face the camera at all times if their three angles are set to zero. If you want the sprite to stay stationary and not turn to face the camera, you must set one of its angles to something besides zero, like 0.1. Sprites can start out as external PCX, BMP, DDS, or TGA files and are created by paint programs, such as Adobe Photoshop, Jasc PaintShop Pro, or Paint Dot Net. 32-bit TGA files contain a separate alpha channel that allows you to set transparencies if you have the Extra edition of 3D GameStudio or better. A sprite is rendered as an overlay, so its black parts are completely transparent, creating unique sprite shapes. Sprites are always rendered faster than map or model entities, and can also be used for particles. Particles create the really neat effects, such as flares, fire, explosions, smoke, and so on. Some old 3D accelerator cards (specifically the Voodoo series) don't allow texture or sprite sizes greater than 256×256.

Terrain Entities

Terrains are not supported by all editions of the 3D GameStudio. Terrain entities are texture images mapped to a rectangular grid of height values, resulting in a mesh that can be used for irregular outdoor terrain. Terrain entities carry an HMP file extension, and are commonly referred to as *height-maps*. Several small terrain height-maps are better for the computer processor during rendering than one gigantic terrain. Terrain is very fixed. It cannot be rotated, but it can be scaled. Terrain cannot have extremely steep slopes (less than 45 degrees, and the slopes will suddenly look stretched-out and unnatural). Terrain height-maps look better if the camera is farther away and does not intersect with the terrain's polygons. For the most part, try to build your outdoor levels with blocks—but if you have an exceedingly great need for more realistic terrain, incorporate height-maps.

Light Sources

3D GameStudio fills its levels with pure global lighting, keeping everything everywhere well lit, until you place your very first light source. Light sources can be placed in the Level Editor, and their colors and ranges can be adjusted. The engine supports both static and dynamic light sources. Dynamic light sources are created by the code script when the level is run; they can move, wave, flicker, change colors, and the like. Static light sources can be placed in WED and typically look better than dynamic light sources because they are able to cast shadows. Static light sources do not affect the frame rate, so you can place as many light sources as you like throughout your level without worry. However, light sources should be placed with a lot of creative thought to provide just enough illumination while maintaining the mood and theme of the game. Designers will also tell you that you must place lights on the go, or else you might end up testing a level that turns out really dark and suffer frustration.

Sound Sources

External sound files, such as WAV or OGG files, can be placed directly into the Level Editor, and their range and volume can be applied to match your design. Static sound sources cover the same sort of range as light sources, but instead of bathing areas in illumination they provide looping sound effects. 3DGS supports both static and dynamic sounds. Dynamic sound sources are created by the code script whenever the level is run; they can change amplitude, move with other entities, play once and quit, and so much more. With plug-ins that you can download online, 3D GameStudio allows MP3 files to be used for dynamic sounds as well. We will look at creating dynamic sounds later. Static sounds can be dropped directly into WED, and wherever they are placed, they will set a Doppler effect when the game is run. The Doppler effect means that when moving toward a sound source, the sound will appear slightly higher pitched, and then slightly lower when moving away from it. This makes the 3D space appear more realistic because it immerses the player on an auditory level and provides non-visual clues as to spatial orientation.

Level Architecture

Level architecture has an important role in game development. Architecture creates space. It defines the virtual reality, provides a point of reference for the player, and sets the stage for the game action—but only at specific costs to the designer.

Speaking of costs, developing 3D spaces is similar in some ways to developing architecture for buildings. Designers with some construction experience will find that building levels is amazingly similar. There are inherent costs in building the environments. For real-life construction, there are costs for materials, labor, and real estate. In the development of 3D games, designers have to know that simple shapes, square objects, and straight lines cost less in number of polygons, time to compile or render, and memory usage by the computer—but humans discern such sparse surroundings as unnatural and even appalling. Specific spatial tricks must be used to cut down on these costs while emulating organic curves and round objects, a feat that is still difficult in 3D art. The rules that govern 3D construction are different from architectural construction; however, there are no limits to 3D like there are in reality. Game levels do not have to comply with user compatibility, so they don't have to include doorways people can walk through, windows people can see out of, or even toilets for people to get their business done. Game levels can twist and wind and ignore the laws of physics or gravity. Impressiveness and decoration are usually the only ways that real-life architecture influences game architecture. Such details as protection from the weather are irrelevant because weather (if it exists in a game at all) is purely cosmetic.

Outdoor game levels often feel sterile in the same ways that indoor levels can appear sparse—and often for the same reasons listed previously. Sweeping vistas and rocky terrains are nearly impossible to recreate in 3D due to screen resolutions and memory limitations (even with advances in LOD terrain). Natural objects carry even more organic curves than human-made objects, so game developers tend to avoid using them in games or "dumb them down" so that they can include them without sacrificing space. This causes outdoor levels to appear even more fake to gamers than indoor ones. Often game scenes will appear little better than a theatrical stage with cardboard props.

Therefore, level architecture is more about gameplay than it is about perfect simulation of the real world. Level architecture compares to movie sets in that it supports the narrative and gameplay by putting certain details in graphic context. It does this through the substrate level by mimicking real-world buildings and objects, but it does so only as necessary. If the golf course needs to have alligators and sandpits, you can drop them in; otherwise, you can leave them out.

First, let us look at the three main functions that level architecture serves in games.

Game Flow

The primary function of level architecture in games is to support the gameplay. When working off of a game outline, a game can be long or short, depending on the built-in challenges, obstacles, and resources. It can also vary based on the detail of level architecture. A game where each level is the size of a small dormitory will be very different from a game where each level is the size of Las Vegas, obviously (see Figure 6.1). The pacing of the game action, what is called *game flow* by industry professionals, can be short and sweet or long and meditative and is often dictated by the size and complexity of the game's levels and their content. You can read more about game flow in the section "Game Flow and Level Layout" later in this chapter.

Figure 6.1
Pacing can be determined from the size of each level. (*Elder Scrolls IV: Oblivion*, image courtesy of Bethesda Softworks 2005)

Industry Insiders Dos and Don'ts

From the leading industry designers today, here's a compiled list of the things to keep in mind at all times.

- Avoid areas that look important but aren't because they can frustrate players.
- Don't put all your monsters or power-ups in one area; proper placement pacing is important.
- Don't forget to give your player enough power-ups to survive.
- Don't design levels that are so difficult they create a "choke point."
- Don't design levels so confusing the player has to get a walkthrough online to finish.
- Don't forget to accommodate the three types of players.
- Don't reveal all your eye candy in the first level.
- Don't keep fiddling with a level; design it and move on.
- Don't forget to test your level as you go.
- Don't frustrate or make the player mad; provide players opportunities to avoid the most difficult parts.

Setting the Mood or Theme

The secondary function of level architecture is to support the story, mood, theme, and so on. The reason that mood or theme gets a back seat to game flow is because there should be a careful balance between each, and if there is any dispute, then game flow should take priority. It is far too easy to create a beautiful game level but not think to make it serviceable to the player. Kevin Saunders of Obsidian Entertainment says, "If a level plays well, you'll find a way to make it pretty, but the reverse isn't necessarily true."

Buildings in game levels are analogous to movie sets: they are composed of false fronts and "dress up" the scene rather than serve the virtual people so-called "living" there. There are no right and wrong ways to engineer game levels, and sometimes doors and houses can be made realistically to fit human beings and sometimes they can be made eight times larger, as if for giants; when it comes down to it, it is all up to you. Sometimes irregular and asymmetrical level engineering is curiouser or more enjoyable than stodgy "realistic" engineering. Just remember that the game levels have to set the stage for the action later on.

People also respond emotionally and reactively to familiar places and styles of architecture. For instance, a creepy candle-lit castle has a vastly different atmosphere than a bright cheerful glen where birds are chirping in the trees. Game architecture—when used appropriately—sets up game atmosphere, and game atmosphere should set the stage for the gameplay and reflect the mood and emotional string-pulling you, the designer, want to do. Think about the game that you have in you, which you have planned to build. What sorts of areas would you include in it? One of the most cleverly contrasting examples comes out of fantasy role-playing games. The game starts in a homey inn or tavern, with a large warm hearth and chattering friends. Eventually, the player enters the nearby nameless dungeon and the place is foul, with water dripping from slimy stone walls and a gloomy music ambience. Even the least-experienced player knows that one area is set for recuperation and buying equipment, while the other is for fighting terrifying monsters and grabbing as much gold as possible. Level terrain can entertain and set the atmosphere for a game, immersing the player in the world, making her feel like she's actually hiking through steep mountain trails or hacking up monsters in dank dungeons (see Figure 6.2).

Make your terrain as realistic as you can, given the limits of the game engine, and make it appropriate to the story and characters your player meets. If you can do that, you have the underpinnings of a truly great game!

Fencing the Player

Architecture also serves to hide the fact that the player character is actually inside a box. The box must have virtual constraints as to how far, and where, a character

Figure 6.2
A monster and a dank dungeon. Nothing could be homier, right? (*Elder Scrolls IV: Oblivion*, image courtesy of Bethesda Softworks 2005)

can explore. Without a frame of reference, the player would not be able to get around in the virtual world you are creating. Without appropriate level architecture, the player's character might well float off into virtual space.

This last point is one of the reasons you must be very careful when you create your game levels. Nearly every player has found a glitch in a game before. One of the most common glitches found in games is that of a game level not having a tight hull or having leaks to it. The player is exploring an area where mountains hem in the level and suddenly the player finds his character floating outside of the level build in empty space. This is not only annoying, but it also destroys the suspension of disbelief and kills immersive play. You will notice this as you test the levels you build, and you will learn to correct these oversights.

Keeping players from wandering off the world that you have built or wandering where you don't want them to go (sometimes for reasons of game challenges or story script) is called "fencing the player in" by game developers. Your fences will be frustrating for the player as a general rule of thumb (nobody likes being told they cannot go somewhere or do something that they want), and so you have to make your fences clearly recognizable. The player must understand that the fences are part of the game and not merely thrown in by the whim of the level designer. Many games do not advertise that their game world has boundaries or that the game world is limited, but there has not been a game yet built that can contain a single limitless world of infinite exploration. Essentially, the level architecture puts these boundaries into graphic context.

Note

"The very best games are the ones where you have to figure out what the object is. The trick is to provide direction subtle enough that it's not perceived immediately. Theme parks have that, too. When you enter Disneyland, you don't know the Sleeping Beauty Castle is your objective, but there's no doubt when you're in Town Square that you should be walking up Main Street USA. Just like in a great game, you always have an idea that you need to go this way or that way. Eventually you catch on to the themed worlds and the central hub."

—Danny Hillis

Elements of Levels

Every game level should be composed of the following:

- Basic geometry or architecture
- Details (such as textures or sprite decals)
- Stage props (models of the furniture, trees, rocks, and so on)
- Lights (sunlight, colored lights, or ambience)
- Gameplay elements (items to be picked up or looked at)
- Non-player characters
- Enemies, monsters, and obstacles
- Environmental teasers
- Gimmicks

I will show you the importance of each of these and how to put them into your levels as you build your first action game. Two of them, which you may be unfamiliar with completely, I will describe here: environmental teasers and gimmicks.

Environmental Teasers

One of the most difficult but definitely one of the most rewarding of the items listed previously is the *environmental teaser*. Environmental teasers give the player an overall illusion of depth, that there is an entire world just outside the level the player is currently exploring. Even indoor levels are better if they have some windows or skylights that give the player a glimpse of the outdoors or the weather. You will succeed in making your player more curious about, and inspired by, the little details you put into your levels, and the player will explore more of the game map. Environmental teasers include

- A few awesome background shots in the distance.
- Architectural details sweeping out past the playing area.
- Cracks in the walls or windows sharing glimpses of another area outside.
- Sound effects of things going on just outside the level.

Fast-paced action games, such as the *Devil May Cry* series, are well-known for the briefest glimpses of environmental teasers, such as where Dante runs across the foreground and the camera cuts in low for sweeping shots of awesome background artwork. It makes it appear as though the Dante character is just a small part of a much larger world. That is exactly the kind of thing you want to impart to the player when you place environmental teasers in your levels (see Figure 6.3).

Figure 6.3
Yes, but look at that background! (*Devil May Cry 2*, image courtesy of Capcom 2002)

Gimmicks

A lot of games—from the early years of SEGA and Nintendo onward—contain gimmicks. Gimmicks make levels immediately memorable for players, similar to the use of mythic symbols. They can become clichés, but gimmicks give character to regularly dull game levels, which is why gimmicks are still used with regularity. Some examples of gimmicks used in games include

- A lava level, where one wrong step hurts.
- A sewer level, full of noxious fluid to wade through.
- An underwater level, where the player swims with the fishes.
- An above-the-trees level or cloud city level.
- A wind tunnel level, where the player might get blown away.
- A graveyard level, where the dead start coming back to life.
- A mine cart ride, where the gaps can be fatal.

Regardless of whether you use gimmicks in your game design or what areas you choose to represent in your game, it should all be tagged to the game's story. Don't throw a graveyard level crawling with undead monsters into a level-headed science fiction game unless you are absolutely sure you can explain it through the story. And according to industry veterans, you should put these levels on paper before starting to build them. And when you do so, come up with as many ideas as you can, and then keep the best eight out of 10.

Try to make your level gimmicks fresh rather than parodies of clichéd games. For instance, if you do plan on having a cemetery full of the marching undead, consider what is making them leave their graves. Are they hungry for brains? Are they dissatisfied with the necromancer who has taken residency in their crypts? Or are they unhappy with the local construction crew making enough noise to "wake the dead"? If you plan to drop the player into a level filled with dangerous goop where one wrong step makes the avatar toast (see Figure 6.4), consider what makes the goop so deadly and *why* it is in the level to begin with. If the goop is lava, why doesn't the player's character spontaneously combust or suffocate in the sulphur-choked environment? If the goop is a toxic spill, who created the nasty chemical mixture and who dumped it there? When you ask questions like these about your gimmicks, you will

Figure 6.4
One wrong step . . . and poof! You're got by a gimmick. (*MediEvil Resurrection*, image courtesy of Sony Computer Entertainment 2005)

discover a wealth of fresh ideas that have been untapped by previous game designers.

Adding Style

Most level designers copy real-world concepts of architecture and nature. Many actually go location scouting and take photographs or make sketches of unusual and interesting objects, buildings, textures, and scenes. They incorporate their photographs or sketches into the environments they build in 3D. The most difficult design component of working on levels in 3D (opposed to a picture) is that the level must look good from many different angles—the player will be able to explore the level and by so doing will be able to view the level from many different angles. This is one of the key characteristics of great architecture and room decor. Think of the places that you like to visit because the environment inspires you. Think of places you would like to vacation at. These places are fun, they're breathtaking, and each of them has that special feng shui. You must learn to integrate feng shui into your level design. We'll get back to that in a moment, but one of the ways you do this is through the use of artistic style.

The level designer's artistic style will carry throughout the level and create a rhythm and mood that pulls it all together. The style influences everything, including the way characters will dress, the game interface, the architecture and way structures look, the level exteriors, and the rules the game follows. American artists tend to be rather conservative in nature, but many of them have been influenced by global trends, such as the Japanese style of animation called manga, to create cutting-edge games that push the boundaries. Tim Schafer's game *Psychonauts* is well known for its Milkman level, which actually recreates an M.C. Escher art piece in a third-person game; it is unique because the laws of physics no longer apply. One moment you might be standing upside down, above the area you were just moments before!

Cultures can affect the style in a game, as well. Dusty Western shooter game levels are affected by the pioneer days of America's Wild West and may feature dust-swept towns, rowdy saloons, iron-horse engines, clapboard wagons, and ranch-style farmhouses. Games like *Voodoo Vince* and *Shadow Man* utilize the romance and superstition surrounding New Orleans and its voodoo atmosphere to evince a spectacular cultural style their own, entirely motivated by jazz and magic. They are very distinct in their cultural style. The same is also true of made-up cultures in fantasy role-playing games. Each can be more distinct than the next, and the application of their cultural style can change the look and feel of one game to separate it from all the rest. I will give an example.

The Norse believed that elves fell into two categories: Light Elves (of tree and lake) and Dark Elves (of tunnel and shadow). Popular fantasy fiction has applied this folklore to manufacture two distinct cultures, one of the green nature-loving elves who play music while tripping lightly through oaken groves and another race of elves that live in the Underground and worship the powers of darkness and cruelty. Each culture may have a shared history, but neither would look like the other. The Light Elves might have golden skin and hair, while the Dark Elves might appear as polished jet with snow-white hair. The Light Elves dress in brown leathers and bark, green leaves and vine-whirled patterns. The Dark Elves might dress all in black, with silver filigree and blood-red staves. This split between two similar societies form naturally distinctive cultures—each with their own unique style. You could liven up a normally dull fantasy game by embellishing the two cultures even more and adding further details and patterns around them. For instance, the Light Elves might carve oak leaf patterns on the wood timbers of their homes, while the Dark Elves might trace the likeness of spider webs and poisonous snakes on the cold stone of their dwellings.

One of my rules of thumb when developing levels for a game is to consider the game world as a giant amusement park or vacation resort and the player as your client, the tourist. Players like to play games, watch movies, and read books about far-off locales, pretty landscapes, and places the players themselves wish they could take a trip to. This is one of the main components of escapism—and one of the most well-known motivations for gamers. If you have a game that is decent to play, has a great story, and unique characters, it might still suffer on the player market. You might not know why, but it might be because the levels are plain and the areas the player has to explore and fight in are insipid, boring, or uninteresting. Get it in your head that, as a game designer, you are delivering a whole package: treat your players as tourists and set them up for thrills in lush and exciting game worlds!

Experiencing 3D Space

Note

"Reality is merely an illusion, albeit a persistent one."

—Albert Einstein

There is a buzzword in game studies called ludic space. Essentially, *ludic* means relating to or characterized by play, and *ludology* is the study of ludic systems. Ludic systems are so broad as to encompass the many virtual media of games, from computer games to tabletop and board games. Ludic systems are the systems of experience, including elements of gameplay and experiences related to gaming. Ludic systems incorporate any game, its rules, and the experiences thereof, and ludic space is the imaginative space (or virtual environment, narrative, or immersion factor) that is entered into in order to enjoy a game. Ludic systems are difficult to understand and ludology is all very high-brow, but essentially ludic systems are based off of temporal mechanics and interactive concepts. These concepts or levels (as many ludologists call them) are described as follows:

- **Discourse level**—The level at which the player experiences the game.
- **Performance level**—The level at which the player interacts with the game.
- **Simulation level**—The level at which the player's actions have direct cause-and-effect relation, creating a realistic-seeming environment.
- **Substrate level**—The level where the natural underpinnings and rules create an engineered game world.

When you are developing game levels, you must think of the timing constraints when you consider pacing. You must consider the substrate level when you build geometric objects that take physical shape. You must consider the simulation level when you code your level. You usually never even think about these levels; they are innate to people who are born game designers. Yet if you find you are having trouble creating an immersive game environment, you might want to take a moment to make sure you are fully developing each and every one of these levels. The ludic systems bring together an environment where the player can experience your game.

Take a skip-and-a-jump down the ludic space pond, and you are facing the ways in which players experience your game. Most video games are inherently visual, so players will always count on experiencing your game through its graphics. Most video games are auditory; in other words, they have awesome sound effects and voiceovers by paid actors. Haptic systems are interactive devices where you can feel—or get direct sensation—from your video game; when I describe haptic technology used in the console market, I am discussing the popular rumble mechanic that controllers have so that they vibrate whenever the player's character's health sinks too low or the avatar gets slammed by an oncoming bus. Some science fiction writers assume that eventually we will all be plugged into a matrix and get direct virtual play shot into our brains. *Star Trek* has featured a holodeck, where a room creates nearly real 3D environments that can be as small as a private eye's smoke-filled office or as grand as the peaks of Mount Vesuvius, and you can dictate what sorts of enjoyment or escapism you want to experience. These wild imaginings are not that far off.

You must keep in mind the sorts of engine limitations that you will have to compete against to bring to life emotionally deep games. Let's take a look at some, and how you can think around them.

We simple human beings have 250 million receptor cells in our eyes, 120 to 140 degrees of visual field scope, a depth that discerns hue, saturation, light, and darkness, and fully stereoscopic and constantly shifting visual focus. Viewing a computer monitor severely hampers our visual field. For instance, a monitor only has a 45- to 60-degree angle of visibility, a low light intensity range of about 255, and flickers at 50 to 100 Hz. Absolute darkness is impossible. The monitor is also fixed and cannot shift its focus as rapidly or in as stereoscopic a way as humans can. 3D video cards are trying to raise the standard for a computer, but there are always going to be some limitations. And that is just a look at the visual handicaps.

Let's look at the auditory ones. Humans can detect fully 3D sounds, react to minute echo clues, can speak or even sing any time at will, and are not normally followed around by a music soundtrack (with the exception of people who walk around with iPod buds glued to their ears). In opposition, a computer has only limited reflection of 3D sounds, cannot accurately simulate echo sounds yet (so the clues are not perfect), does not allow gamers to speak or sing at will into virtual reality (and even if they can, it is never guaranteed there will be appropriate feedback), and often force onto gamers music soundtracks meant to heighten emotions. University-funded game development teams are experimenting right now with games designed for the blind that focus on sound alone with a state-of-the-art Doppler system built into 3D game engines, but this is still in the experimental stages.

When it comes to touch receptors, we humans are sensory animals. The touch spectrum in games has been limited to haptic technology devices, as I mentioned previously, in the form of vibrations arising from game events. We humans can detect surface textures of objects, relative humidity and wind pressure, ambient heat, and the hardness of the surface we are walking on. These are all elements that have (as of this writing) never been experimented with or have never proven possible in a virtual reality. I won't even mention smells because, although humans are enabled with several complicated olfactory systems, none of them has ever been put to use by a composite computer game so far, (although scratch-and-sniff handhelds might not be too far off base). Games cannot portray the scent of a flower-strewn field or the stench of death on the battlefield after combat (and probably for good reason!).

There is one thing that games are good at. Games can play with people's minds, manipulating the tenets of psychology to further gameplay or story progression. However, there are vast boundaries of psychology that have never been tapped in games. There are some dungeon and stealth games that have emulated feelings of claustrophobia before. There are some cliff-top 3D platformers that have come near to arousing agoraphobia (the fear of heights), but only when the sensation of height is an exaggerated one. Fierce combat scenes or scaling steep cliffs never makes the players feel weary or exhausted. Other fears, such as the fear of the unknown, dread, and phobias of certain animals like spiders or snakes, have only been grazed by game designers without any intent to push the boundaries. Most of the time, game developers will tell you that these sorts of immersive sensory tricks are only possible if the interface is right—if the player is sitting in a darkened room at night with surround sound speakers and a bass that rumbles the house when playing games. Gamers approve of these set-ups, but few have the sort of income to afford them.

Given that you are limited to audio, visual, and psychological exploration, construct game levels that take players somewhere exciting. Glue your players to a computer, using a mouse and keyboard, by planning ahead and using psychology. Develop your game world to play, look, and sound good—and keep in mind the levels of ludic space necessary for an exciting game time!

Game Flow and Level Layout

You must have a clear concept of your game levels before you start making them up in the Level Editor. You should consider the four Ws: Who? What? Where? Why? The answer to these, in association with each of your game levels, will clarify the concept for you. "Who?" is a question that refers to the player, as in "Who is the player playing as, and what is her avatar?" "What?" is asking the avatar's goal, as in "What is the player trying to achieve in the level?" "Where?" asks where the action takes place, as in "Where is the level set, in what region?" And lastly, "Why?" asks why the player is willing to go to this particular region, and what does he hope to win by going there. All of these questions, taken into account long before you ever start developing a game level, will make your levels more prosperous. They will also set the flow of the game and the balance in each level. Game flow is dependent on proper pacing, balancing of resources, and the ways levels can be laid out.

Pacing and Balance of Resources

Proper pacing in a game is even more important than how the game looks. Proper pacing is imperative—a real sink-or-swim mark for the game creator. A balance between player resources and challenges is one of the keys to pacing the game. If you have too many player resources in a game level, such as health or ammo, then the challenges will seem too easy, or the importance of gaining game resources will seem needless. If you have too many challenges (or those challenges seem repetitious) without resources or places for the player to stop and take a breath, you will merely frustrate the players and lose potential sales. Balance is imperative. Alternate between forcing the player to struggle to stay alive and reflectively exploring or solving puzzles; this will increase the playability of your game.

The best games start the player out slowly, letting the player "get her feet wet"—learning the game system and the expected rewards and punishments—before ramping up the difficulty. Some games start the player off with training levels, where the player suffers no adverse repercussions such as life-or-death consequences for her actions. Training levels can be filled with mentors or hint boxes to help the player learn what kind of controls the game uses. Most games made today allow the player the option of training levels while letting the action of the game start right away.

Level Layout

The level layout can also influence a game's flow. Let's go back to feng shui for a moment. Feng shui is used by some Asian and American architects and contractors to create an atmosphere in a building. This atmosphere follows the flow of chi through the building. Essentially, when you are creating game levels, think of the potential player camera as the chi, and keep in mind where it will be at any one time during the game. In first-person shooters, this camera is always where the player character is—so the principle of feng shui is even more like reality; you must consider which way the player is facing and where you want him to look next. Games that do not take this into consideration are often easy to spot because players complain about getting lost or not knowing where to head next. The level layout should always make the player's goal apparently obvious, unless you expect him to get lost as part of the gameplay (such as in maze games). There are roughly three or four ways a game can be laid out:

- Linear levels
- Non-linear levels
- Hub-based levels
- Death-match levels

You might be wondering, What is the difference between a linear, non-linear, or hub-based game? It is simple: the game story might (or might not) support backtracking, or there might be a central location that the player keeps coming back to. These are the sorts of considerations taken into account when the game flowcharts or walkthroughs are constructed.

Linear Levels

Linear games do not have to be sidescrolling platformers. However, they are games where the player never has to stop or backtrack. In linear games, the player has to practically run from Point A to Point B while overcoming any obstacle in-between. These games are often action games and are incredibly fast-paced. A good example of linear games is *Half-Life 2.* The only thing with linear games is that you have your work cut out for you: you have to put more levels in them to satisfy the player's speed and the story's fast pacing. You also have to make each of these levels look good and carry immediate emotional weight (because most of the time players will not slow down to enjoy the scenery, and they will be first-person games, so the textures and terrain must stand up to closer scrutiny). The only problem with designing linear games is that the level designer might put a lot more into each level than the player is apt to spend the time to look at. The player is more focused on getting to Point B, and if there are any obstacles along the way, the player looks for the most expedient way to overcome them (for example, shooting enemies, solving puzzles, finding the key for the locked door, and so on.). This does not give the player a lot of time to lollygag around and enjoy the scenery.

Non-Linear Levels

Non-linear games not only allow but also demand backtracking during the game, and sometimes a player can be kept in one level for hours on end while she seeks to solve a single challenge. This is a primary component of adventure games. There do not need to be as many levels because the player sees more out of each one. Sometimes a doorway between two or more levels is not opened until an event is triggered later in the game, making passage easier and backtracking less redundant. After the player finishes everything that he has left to do in a non-linear level, then he is transported to another section of the game, but never in a fashion like the linear movement from Point A to Point B. The main problem with building non-linear games is that it is too easy to lose the player. The player might not be able to see his goals clearly, or he gets lost in large levels where his direction is not marked. On the other hand, non-linear games allow for emergent gameplay and further exploration.

Hub-Based Levels

Hub-based games have one pretzel-like level that forms the hub; this level is the place the player comes back to after exploring other levels. Usually there are blocked doors or rooms within the central level that let out into all the other sublevels, and each and every one of the sublevels has specific goals to be met. Often the blocked doors or rooms are opened only after the player completes an

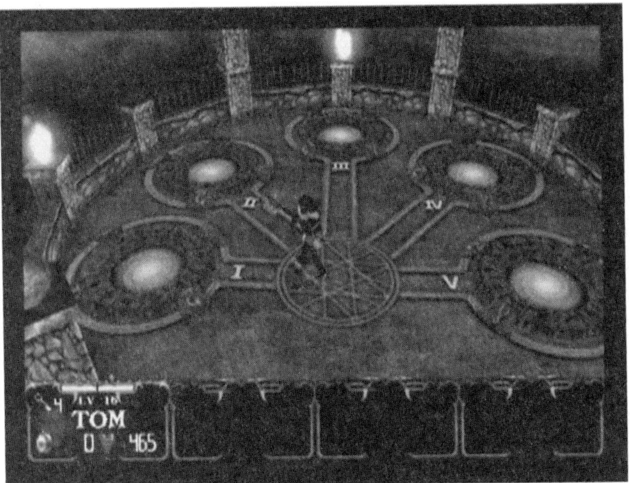

Figure 6.5
Multiple paths from a central hub: the Tower exemplified hub-based games. (*Gauntlet: Dark Legacy*, image courtesy of Atari 2001)

objective or gains enough keys. *Gauntlet: Dark Legacy* and *Mario 64* have popularized hub-based games (see Figure 6.5). For instance, in the *Gauntlet* game, the player and his friends start out in the Tower, and, after she gets so many gems of a certain type, she can unlock doorways that will take her to new, more difficult levels. Each level has a major goal, and once that goal is met the sound cues up victory music, and she is transported back to the hub in the Tower. This is repeated until every doorway has been unlocked, and the player opens the final door in the Tower and faces the boss monster Skorn.

Death-Match Levels

There is a fourth type of game level construct, called a death-match level, which has the primary purpose of being self-contained, often circular. A death-match level goes nowhere, but it sets the stage for an arena-type competition. This is common to online player-versus-player (or PVP) games, such as *Unreal Tournament*. Death-match levels belong in only specific types of action games, so they are optional when it comes to setting up your level architecture. The only time that they are seen in solo action or role-playing games are in boss-monster areas or places set for blood locks. Blood locks are part of a tradition in such games that have met with ill-favored review lately; the player must beat an enemy or number of enemies before she can move on.

In Summary

Build game levels that fence in the player, give them challenges, and flow really well so that the player never gets lost in them. Your levels should never take the player out of the perceived reality you have tried so hard to construct through your artistic style and manipulative use of psychology. Careful consideration of the pacing, balance of resources and challenges, and level layout will make the difference in game flow and improve the way a game is played. Put all this together, and you could have a best seller on your hands!

What You Have Learned

A game level supports the gameplay first and foremost. Secondly, it supports the game story. The following are things you should have learned about level architecture:

- You now understand the principles of 3D space and components.
- You have learned that game levels are practically movie sets, full of false fronts.
- You have learned that game levels are virtual cages that create boundaries to keep players in the 3D world.
- You have a firmer grasp of why artistic style and cultural influences are so important in level design.
- You understand ludic space and how to present a better game experience.
- You have a better understanding of game pacing and game flow.
- You know the differences between the types of game levels, such as linear and non-linear layouts.

For Review

1. What are some popular spatial tricks that level designers have used that you think overcame the limitations of the 3D environment or software? Take a look at really low-poly low-portal games, such as *Nightmare Creatures.* Can you identify some tricks that you could incorporate in your level building?
2. Many games have been targeted by critics because they overuse the same gimmicks or familiar level design, that they are too imitative, especially

fantasy role-playing games. Critics say that the designers did not create worlds distinct enough from each other. If you were to develop a fantasy role-playing game, what are some ways that you would add a new artistic style and new gimmicks, and make the world really distinct?

3. Play any popular game on the market, and study the way the pacing and game flow sets up the gameplay. If the game is split into individual levels, do they ramp up in difficulty? Does the game follow a linear, non-linear, or hub-based layout? Is there a fair balance of resources and challenges?

4. Games can have distinctive cultures in them. *Voodoo Vince* and *Shadow Man* share a New Orleans magic culture, but they exhibit the culture in different ways. Choose a single culture (whether real, romantic, or made-up), and discuss how the culture might influence the look of buildings, interiors, characters, objects, and rules of your game world.

5. There have been a lot of experimental games that have used time as an actual element. All games have time as a pacing factor, but there have been many (like *Prince of Persia* and *Max Payne*) that have used time to slow down action, rewind mistakes, and capture motion. What are some compelling ways you could use time as an element in your game?

6. The real world is the perfect inspiration for game levels. Select an area you feel comfortable with or attracts you in your local neighborhood. Study it for at least 15 minutes, perhaps even take pictures of it if you have access to a digital camera, and then make a level map on paper based on it. Include notes about possible textures, sound effects, and light sources. What is it about this area that is compelling? How would you work it into a game?

In regards to your own level construction, you can create level flowcharts on paper to illustrate through your game design document what sorts of environments you are going to use. Then later, concept artwork, including environment illustrations and maps, and finally 3D world-building can take place. The Level Editor is best suited for world-building. It makes creating landscapes, placing light effects, defining patrol paths, and setting local sounds a straightforward and easy process. A huge library of over a thousand prefabricated textures, building parts, furniture, vehicles, weapons and actors is included with the 3DGS software. You can drag elements into your game levels and instantly click together a game, or you can create custom behavior scripts to give the game a really cool style. As soon as your levels are ready, a button click generates an EXE file ready for distribution via the Internet or on CD-ROM.

We are ready to begin world-building. Do not worry if you do not have everything memorized yet, or if you still have questions. The purpose of this guide is to teach through example, which is the best way to learn how to make great games. So read on, and begin by building your very first level.

Exercise 6.1: Building Mansion Floor 2

According to our game synopsis, Hector will have his teddy stolen from him by his sister Hex, and he has to get it back. To do so, he will chase after her from the mansion's second floor to its first floor and (finally) to the basement, which we will make a death-match level. His sister sets the goal as Hector chases her, so the levels will be laid out in a linear (yet maze-like) fashion. The player has to get the teddy bear back. To do so, the player has to chase Hex. Unbeknownst to the player (and Hector), Hex will create distractions along the way in the form of obstacles, including biting spiders, poisonous plants, and other (more mundane) obstacles. This is an action game, so Hector will be able to pick up certain weapons and fight some of these obstacles, but the real importance of gaining weapons is fighting Hex in the death-match level we will build at the end.

So first we have to construct each of the game levels. We are not going to make them in Level Editor as one single game level, but as three separate game levels that we will then stitch together in our main script. The reason for this is the compile times for the Level Editor: the larger a level is, the longer it will take to iterate each of the map portals and compile each block. It is not unusual for really large levels or levels with an ungainly amount of obtuse angles to take a longer time compiling; some can even take up to several hours. We want to keep the compile time for each of our levels down to a few minutes. The only factor we cannot control in this is your computer processor. Your computer's processor (and its available RAM) will affect the time for map compiling as well.

The first level you build is the first level (or starting point) of the game, and what you name it will determine the name of several subsequent files, not the least of which is the name of the main programming script. There are many naming conventions to recall when working in the Level Editor. For one thing, your names must be short (otherwise 3D GameStudio will truncate the names, and your file might become lost or damaged). They must *not* contain any spaces,

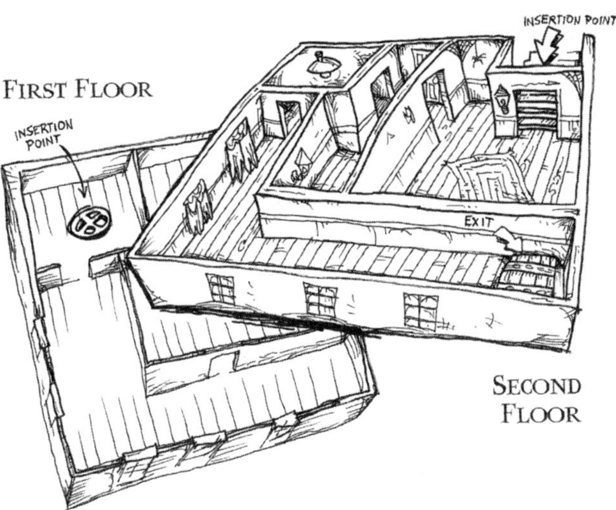

Figure 6.6
Map of Mansion Floor 1 and 2

dollar signs, periods, hyphens, or other wild card symbols—so only use standard characters to name your files. If you follow those few rules, your levels should load and run just fine, and there should not be any severe command-line breaks.

Take a quick gander at the level map for the Mansion Floor 2 in Figure 6.6. Generally, you want to make maps when developing your game design document, and the maps should spawn from the game story and walkthrough. Maps need to convey the layout and placement of objects in the level, as well as "hot spots" where scripted events happen (such as loading the next level or picking up health power-ups). Maps should be fairly consistent and include a basis of measurement. You can create maps using a ruler, pencils, and a pad of paper—or you can use your computer and make maps in vector programs like Adobe Illustrator. Indoor levels are like house plans. They reflect the floor layout of a building. Dungeons can be purely random in their layout, but looking at blueprint and house plan books at your local library can inspire you when laying out maps of interior game levels.

I don't expect you to be a carpenter or mason before picking up the tools of the Level Editor and framing a house. Yet the same skills and knack for engineering—understanding the distribution of weight, balances, laying foundations, and so on—will definitely be invaluable if you know them. Level geometry is virtual space. This means that nothing you make has intrinsic physical shape or weight. Planes can intersect planes, rays can wander off to nowhere, and primitives can be placed anywhere. You could build a house that would never stand up in reality. However, the player of your game will get a subconscious notion that some vital element is not right in the game world—and you could potentially shoot your goal in the foot of providing an immersive environment if you were to make such treacherous transgressions. So think like a builder. Imagine that there is gravity in your virtual world. For every ceiling, provide a supporting structure. For every house, provide a firm foundation. For every roof, provide a house under it. You do not have to carry this out in detail, but you should give the illusion that the game world could be real. (Of course, as with Schafer's *Psychonauts* game, there will always be contradictions to this rule, but understand that games like *Psychonauts* are sacrificing immersive belief in a virtual world for the sake of finer artistic style.)

Note

WED considers everything you create in it to be an object. An object can be a block of geometry, an entity, or a group of objects. Grouping allows you to make collapsible lists of elements to build complex structures, such as archways, bridges, rooms, and staircases and edit them separately from everything else. Only an entity can have a behavior or action applied to it that supplies dynamic content to your levels.

Starting a New Level File

So let's get started. Go out and find the CD-ROM files intended for this project, located in the hector_hex folder that came on the CD-ROM. There should be three folders: a models folder, a bmaps folder, and an sfx folder. Copy and paste these four folders directly into your hector_hex project folder on your hard drive. The models folder has a hector.mdl file, but because you placed the hector.mdl that you created in the upper hierarchy and not into a subfolder you will preserve the hector.mdl that you created!

Open up the Level Editor (if you have not already done so). You will notice that, unlike the Model Editor, WED does not automatically start you at a new map. You have to go to File > New or click the New icon button to open a fresh level map. When you see three graph windows and a 3D View window in the central area and a Project window on the left containing a root file list, you know that you have a new map open. If the Project window does not appear, you can go to View > Toolbars and make sure they are all check-marked.

Go to File > Preferences to set your initial settings in WED. You can adjust the color and appearance of selected, unselected, and entity objects, as well as the appearance of the WED layout here in Preferences. For now, you are going to

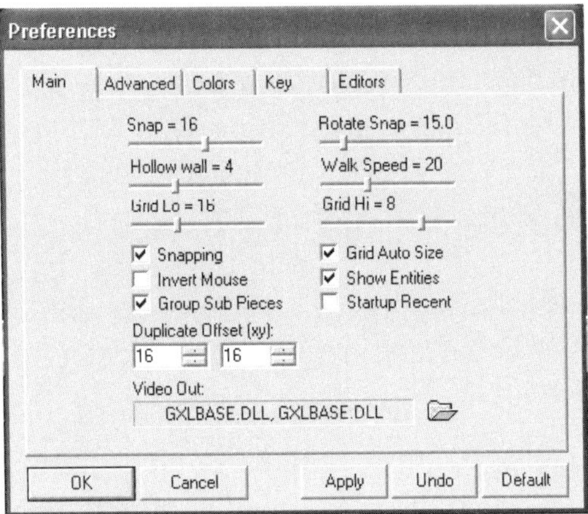

Figure 6.7
The hollow wall slider set to 4

adjust the slider under Hollow Wall to 4 (see Figure 6.7). If you build a hollow wall (which we are about to do to construct a room) and then scale it, WED does not put limitations on the thickness of the walls. If you set Hollow Wall to 4, the walls will resize in proportion but stay at a width of 4 quants, which is sort of thin but not bad. You can make thicker and thinner walls to add variety to your level by coming back to File > Preferences and changing the Hollow Wall slider. It will not overwrite earlier changes. Before leaving Preferences, set the slider under Snap to 1. Snap controls the objects you move and scale so that they snap to the grid whenever you move. If you set Snap to 1, it will allow you to move objects incrementally and give you further control in editing.

Go to Texture > Texture Manager to bring up the Texture Manager dialog box. Notice that the dialog box calls itself the WAD Manager; it's the same difference. Here you can add, remove, and create WAD texture collections. Click Add WAD and browse to the wads folder. Select Interior.wad. When you are done, click OK to exit the Texture Manager dialog box.

Select the 3D View window by tapping it on the name bar. You should be able to tell that it has been selected, based on how you have your Windows Desktop set. Press F7. This makes your 3D View texture mapped so that you will see actual texture mapping rather than wireframes. Objects that are selected will appear as red shaded objects.

Now you are ready to save your level file before continuing. The reason you are going to save the file is the same reason that you set a root folder when developing a Web site: it creates folder recognition and directory hierarchy so that you will be able to load entities later. Go to File > Save As and call your file hex.wmp in the hector_hex folder. WED automatically adds the WMP file extension. The name you give files should not be longer than 20 characters and must not have any spaces or weird characters (although underscores are acceptable). You will want to save as often as possible so that you don't lose any information. Now you have completed your preproduction settings, and you are ready to start the production process.

The Project Window

Let's take a moment to review one of the most important windows you will see (besides the basic view windows). The Project window is on the left of the screen. By default the Objects tab is active. Under Objects, you should see every object composing your level all laid out in a directory tree. Root is at the top of the tree, so maybe it's an upside-down tree because the tree grows from Root. The tree will reveal models, lights, sounds, blocks, and groups. Groups are whole collections of objects, similar to subfolders, with a plus (+) or minus (–) sign beside them to indicate expanded lists. If your level ever becomes a chaotic mess and you still want to locate and adjust a single block or particular group, you can double-click on that object or group in the Objects tab and that object or group will be selected (turn red) in the view windows. You can right-click and open that object or group's Properties panel here, too. In the Properties panel, it is best to rename the object or group to give them unique and fitting names so that you can find them more easily later on based on their file name. As you shall see during the exercises, grouping and ungrouping objects makes for a neater approach to editing your maps.

The next tab—Views—helps you to set and manage various view positions you might want saved for later. In case you are in Camera Move mode, a red square and a green square connected by a red line will appear on the map. The red square is your camera and the green square is your focal point, or where the camera is looking. By moving these points around, you can quickly find the camera view position you want and save it for later.

The most useful tab in the Project window, hands down, would have to be Textures. Here your level will spring to life when you add surface materials to its walls, floors, ceilings, and grass planes by applying textures. You create tiled textures on the faces of your blocks with computer graphics you simply have to click on. Textures are brought up from collections called WADs, which you can manage and design yourself inside the Textures tab of the Project window.

Lastly, Resources is another directory tree, but this one is full of all the script files and functions you have running in your level. Double-clicking on the name of the script file will open it in the Script Editor. Since we are not ready to start programming scripts, we will not go into this one just yet.

Basic Geometry

Go to Object > Add Model > Models > Hector.mdl. You can do this in the menu or click the Add Object button (it looks like a cube with a yellow star on its corner). You should see the Hector model that we created in the last chapter appear in all four view windows. If you go to Object > Add Model and see an <empty> there, it means you did not copy the models folder into hector_hex. We want to put the player model in the level so that we can accurately measure doors, windows, walls, and the rest in proportion to the scale of the model rather than measuring quants.

Go to Object > Add Hollow Cube > Large to create a large hollow box. This is not a single geometric cube, as you would get if you selected Add Cube. Look on the Project window for Objects, and you will see that you have just added a Group. Click the plus sign (+) beside the Group to reveal the hierarchy beneath it. This Group is made up of six blocks: four blocks for the outside walls, one block for the ceiling, and one block for the floor. You can hollow anything, not just cubes, by creating a primitive and selecting Edit > Hollow Block; blocks will become hollow with a wall thickness in quants equal to the slider you set under File > Preferences.

Just as in MED, WED has position tools. Each of the position tools has an icon button with a cube on it and a blue arrow (or arrows) that shows what the tool does. Click the Scale button (which has three blue arrows coming away from a cube). If you have difficulties finding the correct button, you can hover your cursor over each button and it will tell you what it is called. Another option is to go under Mode on the menu and you will find the tools you need there. Scale—just as in the Model Editor—is used to resize objects. However, these tools work differently in each of the orthographic view windows, and you have to make sure a view window is selected (click on its name bar) in order to work in that view and along those coordinate axes. Scale the hollow block in the Top (XY) grid view. You might have to use the mouse wheel to zoom out far enough to see the entire group. See Figure 6.8 for how far to scale the hollow block.

Now click Move and use the arrow keys on your keyboard to raise the group up until the floor is touching the green lines representing the XY axes (and the ground plane). Hector's feet should just about touch the floor of the hollow cube.

In the Project window, switch to the Textures tab to reveal the controls for textures in WED. You can click the name bar for Interior.wad to drop down and view all the textures in that collection. There is a thin scroll bar to the right of the textures that allows you to scroll up and down to preview all the textures in

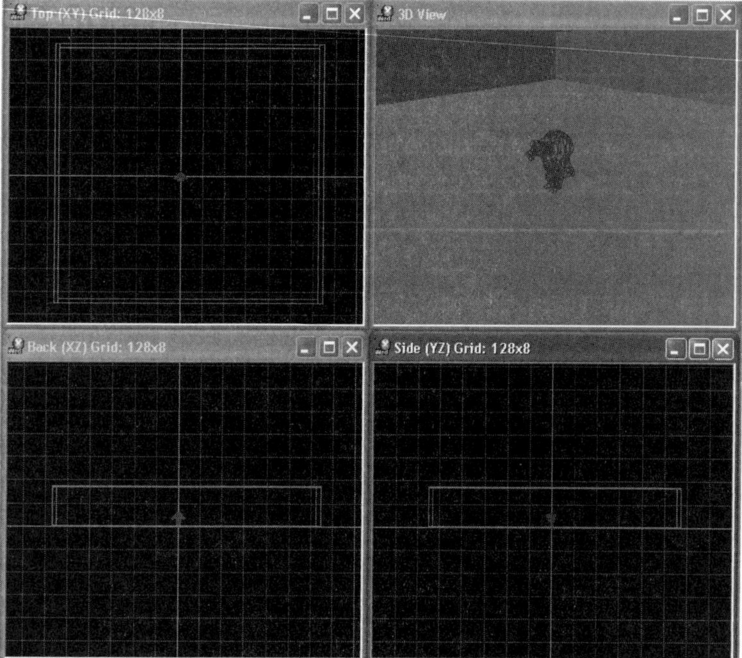

Figure 6.8
Laying out the second floor

Interior.wad. I also like to put my cursor at the very bottom of the preview window and stretch out the visible panel for previewing textures (see Figure 6.9). You can right-click on any of the textures to pull up settings, add, rename, extract, remove, and so on. You can also select Show Texture and set the thumbnail sizes for the textures.

With the hollow block selected, find and right-click on the texture called Wall38_512x256. Remember that if you have problems finding a texture, they are in alphabetical order. In the list that comes up when you right-click on the texture's thumbnail, select Apply. You can also double-click on a thumbnail to apply the texture to the selected group. You can go to Edit > Select None or click off the object to deselect it and preview the textures in the 3D View.

You might notice that this is a wall texture. It works great on the room's walls but looks sort of funny on the ceiling and floor. Select the group again because now we are going to fix these. Go to Object > Scope > Scope Down or click on the Scope Down button (it is the icon button on the furthest right end and appears to have a triangle and blue down arrow). Optionally, you can press CTRL + PAGE

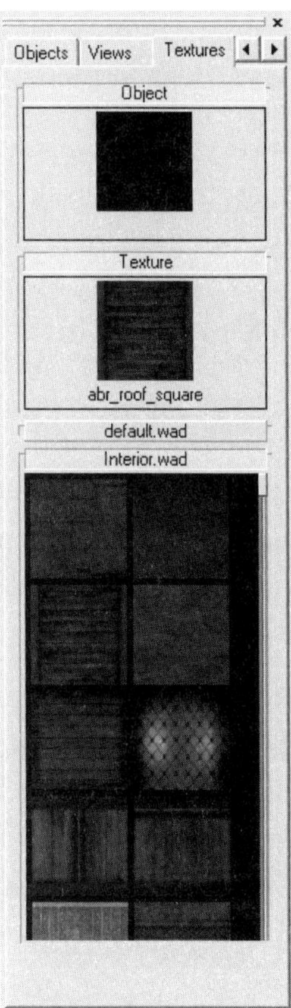

Figure 6.9
Previewing textures in the Project window

DN. The Scope Down button takes you into the group to work with its individual parts, which includes six blocks right now.

Select the floor block and apply the texture Wood16c. Notice that the easiest way to select the floor block by itself is to click over it in the Top (XY) grid window. Depending on where you click, you might select the ceiling block first. Click again in the same spot to select the next object down, and so on. This way, if you lose a block in the middle of a group of blocks, but you can see its outline in one of the grid windows, you can click in the same spot on it until (eventually) you will reach it. Applying Wood16c will make the floor appear to be made of hardwood boards. However, the texture size is too large. I will show you how to take it down a notch. With the floor selected, right-click and open Properties. Click on the Surface tab. Surface is the place you go to alter and adjust the orientation, scale, and position of surface texture maps. Right now the surface plane selected will turn yellow. Click the arrow buttons supplied on the panel until the surface facing into the room (the actual floor surface) turns yellow.

Set both the X scale and Y scale fields to 0.5. This will shrink the texture to appear more realistic. Once the texture is set, click on the Properties tab, and then select the check box that says Texture Lock. Texture Lock freezes the state you have set for textures on an object so that if you were to Move, Scale, or Rotate the object later on, the textures would stay where they are now. Exit the Properties dialog box when you are through.

Select the ceiling block and apply the texture abr_roof_square to create wooden beams along the ceiling. We are not going to worry about the outside of the mansion floor and getting it looking right because the player will not be leaving the interior of the second floor—but if we were, now would be the time to select the out-facing surfaces and apply different textures to them.

Make sure that your textures fit the surfaces they are on and look appropriate. Study Figure 6.10 to see what I mean. If any texture does not look quite right, open Properties and under the Surface tab, you will see an X offset, a Y offset, and an Angle setting. You can adjust the X and Y offsets to change the position of the texture on the surface, and Angle adjusts the rotational angle of the texture on the surface. These can really come in handy when working with various sizes and shapes of blocks.

Figure 6.10
The second floor in 3D View

Right beside the Scope Down button (which should no longer be available) is a Scope Up button; you should click it or go to Object > Scope > Scope Up or press CTRL + PAGE UP. We have left the introspective work on the group, and Hector was not a part of the group, so Hector will reappear.

Now we will start to make walls within the second floor, following our map. First select Hector and place him on the insertion point we have marked on the map. This should be in the upper-left corner of the second floor. Then click Add Object and select a large hollow cube. Use the Scale tool to stretch it out to make Hector's bedroom surround him. Make sure that the walls of his new bedroom touch the ceiling and floor that we have already created and textured. Make sure the red lines of this new hollow block neatly overlap those of the old in the orthographic grid windows.

With the second hollow block selected, click on Scope Down. Select the floor and ceiling block and press DELETE. Also delete the northern and western wall blocks. This leaves only two walls of the hollow block. Scope Up and Scale/Move the two walls until they finish Hector's bedroom (see Figure 6.11).

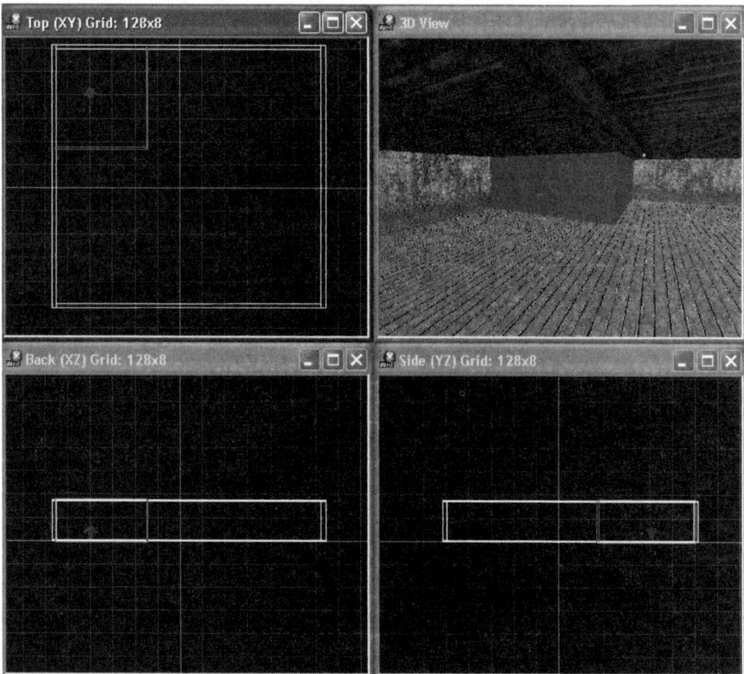

Figure 6.11
Creating a bedroom

Apply the Wall38_512x256 texture to the group with the two walls.

Now you might notice that Hector cannot get out of his bedroom because he does not have a door. We will have to make him a door. Scope Down on the group with the two walls because we will work intimately with the southern wall.

Next click on Add Object, and this time you must add a medium cube. Scale it carefully to make a doorway, using Figure 6.12 as your guide. Do not worry about its width, but know that it must surpass the wall's width. If you are concerned that your doorway will not be wide enough for Hector's large shoulders, Scope Up to preview and then Scope Down to continue resizing the cube.

When you have the cube at the right scale, apply the Wood05b texture to it, then go to Edit > CSG Subtract. With the cube still selected, hit DELETE. Voila! You now have a doorway. The reason that you add a texture to the cube (or whatever you are using to erase blocks) is obvious: wherever you CSG Subtract from will inherit the texture from the block you are using to CSG Subtract with. In this case, the door frame now has the Wood05b applied to it. If you did not add a

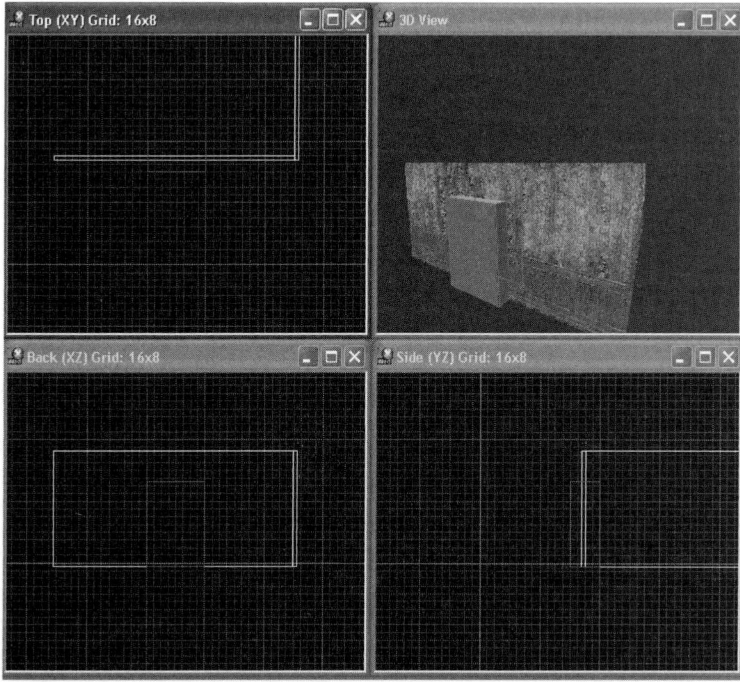

Figure 6.12
Object for CSG Subtract

texture to the cube first before you CSG Subtract, then there would not be a texture on the surfaces where you erased.

As you can see, when you CSG Subtract, you are not making a hole inside the block that was the wall; you are actually creating an intersection of three blocks where there was only one before. These three blocks now make up the wall and the doorway. This is the way in which CSG Subtract works. It is ill advised to use anything other than simple blocks to erase with. And try to avoid round blocks because they will create curved nooks with many small angular pieces that will clog the BSP tree when compiling. Now that you have a doorway, it is time to make a hallway for Hector to jog down chasing Hex. Before clicking on Scope Up, select the one straight wall in this group, and go to Edit > Copy or press CTRL+C.

Scope Up and press SHIFT+INSERT, or go to Edit > Paste to duplicate the wall block. Now this block is not part of any group yet. We will fix that in a moment. The way that you do that is to manage your hierarchy in the Project window. Go to the Objects tab in the Project window so that you can view the hierarchy as it currently exists.

There is one small group with a group inside of it. This is Hector's bedroom, and the doorway you've just created. Right-click on the group inside of it and go to Properties. The very first tab—Properties—is where you are headed. Here there is a text field that says Group; you can click in this field and rename the group whatever you would like. This group is the doorway, so for simplicity's sake (other designers will thank you!) name it **doorway**. Do the same with the group it is enclosed in, naming that group **bedroom**. Last, name the larger group **second floor**. Now click-drag the bedroom inside of the second floor group, and it will join that group. Click-drag the new wall block that you duplicated into the second floor group as well. See Figure 6.13 to make sure that you have performed this task correctly.

Scope Down and select the new wall block that you created. You are going to use the grid windows to move it into position. Once you are in Move mode, remember that you can use the arrow keys to make snap translations. If you find that it is not lining up correctly using the Move mode by itself, let me show you a trick. Right-click and open its Properties dialog box. In the panel go to the Position tab. You will notice there are coordinate settings for Position, Rotate, and Scale. Although the fields beside each do not tell you what they are, you should know by guesswork: they are the Cartesian coordinate system and reflect

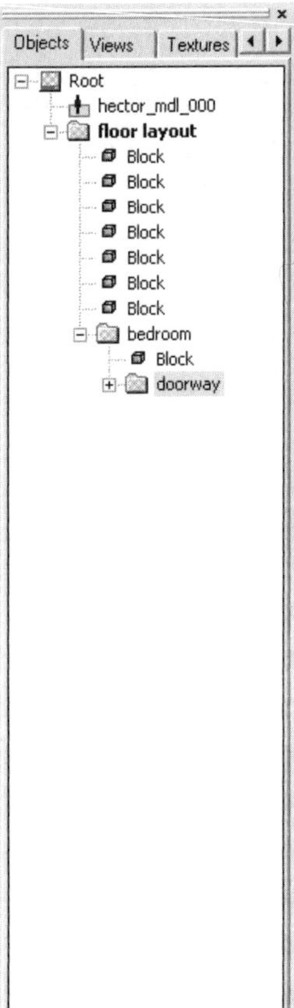

Figure 6.13
Constructive hierarchy of objects deserves proper naming.

the three points X, Y and Z, in that order. You can perform point-size translations in the Position tab to get the wall block into the correct placement. This also comes in handy because, unfortunately, the same trick that you use to select objects placed on top of or next to each other by clicking in the same spot until you reach them also means that when you are using Move, Rotate, or Scale you might accidentally select another object—or worse, the object you want to select is so small that it resists you selecting it through larger objects. Once you have an object like this selected, you can use the Position tab in its Properties panel to move it incrementally around the 3D space without any time-consuming mishaps.

Now that you have this wall where you want it, go to Edit > Duplicate or press CTRL+D. This will clone the wall (automatically copying and pasting the object). Position the new wall at a 90-degree angle to the original, completing the turn in the hall. Scale it so that it reaches the end and still butts up on the original wall. It is all right if this wall stretches out past one of the outside walls because no one will see outside the second floor.

Go to Add Object > Cube > Medium, and give it the Wood18 texture. Position part-way down and close to the end of the hall, intersecting the wall block. You want this one to come out only about a hairsbreadth from the wall block and drop into the floor. It will be a larger cube than what you used to carve the doorway earlier. You are going to make the trim to go around the door frame.

Use Edit > Duplicate (CTRL+D) to duplicate this cube, and right-click to enter the Properties panel. You are going to incrementally shrink this cube in the Scale fields of the Position tab. It must be smaller than the door trim, but it must stretch out past it a little along the Y-axis. It must also not touch the floor block—not by any means. When you get it into position, go to Edit > CSG Subtract and press DELETE. You now have a doorway with a door frame around it. This is the approved way to model doors in the Level Editor because it adds depth and realism. Keep this in mind.

You will notice that on the inside of the door frame the wood texture of the door frame and the wallpaper texture of the wall are competing. This will be evident in the 3D View window and in the final game when you run it. It is considered unprofessional to leave bleeding like this; although it can be time-consuming, we can fix the issue. First select the wall. Scope Down and select one of the blocks surrounding the door. Right-click and bring up the Properties panel. Under the Surface tab, you can click the right or left arrow buttons until you reach the surface facing the inside of the door, and then change it to the Wood18 texture. Do this for the rest of the blocks surrounding the door, then Scope Up to see your work. Notice that the bleeding has stopped.

Select the bedroom group and duplicate it as well. Rename this group **exit**. Rotate it 90 degrees clockwise, and stick it against the upper northeastern corner of the second floor.

Select Add Object > Hollow Cube > Large, and give it the Wood18 texture. Scope Down and delete the roof off it, then Scope Up. Rename this group **stairwell** and place it under the floor of the exit group.

Go to Add Object > Cube > Large and also give it the Wood18 texture. Move it over the top of the stairwell group but not touching it. You want it to intersect the floor of the mansion's second floor. See Figure 6.14 to see what I mean. When

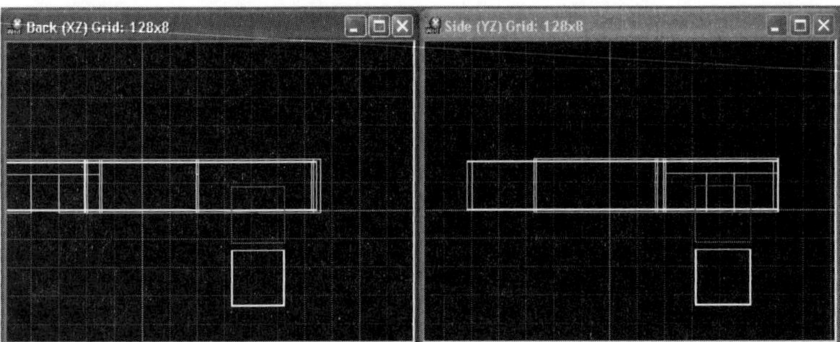

Figure 6.14
Getting ready to CSG Subtract an opening for the stairwell

you get it scaled and positioned how you need it, go to Edit > CSG Subtract, and then delete the cube. You should be left with a hole in the floor block.

Raise the stairwell group back up to meet the floor block. Use the 3D View window to make sure there are no obvious gaps. If there are, you can proportion the stairwell group.

Select Add Object > Add Prefab > Upstairs > Steps06 to drop some prefabricated stairs into the level. Apply the same Wood18 texture. Move it into the stairwell group, and resize it and position it until it fits inside the stairwell without losing the appearance of the steps. It should blend in pretty well, since we are going to use the same texture we used on the rest of the stairway contraption (see Figure 6.15).

Create a stair rail that goes all the way around the top of the stairwell. The easiest way to do this is to select Add Object > Add Primitive > Misc > Lumber > 4 × 4 and apply the Wood18 texture to the block. Place it upright, next to the top of the stairs as a banister, then press CTRL+D to duplicate it several times over. The clones you space out evenly, going all the way around the stairwell. Lastly, select one of them, rotate it so that it lies horizontally again, and move it into position to be the railing. Try this on your own and see what you can create. You might come up with a better way to do it, such as using a cylinder for the banister. However you decide to construct the rail, keep it simple.

You might also want to create wooden support beams going down the hallway outside of Hector's bedroom. These can be easy to add, and every touch adds more realism to the game level.

Before you call it quits on basic geometry, let's look at adding some windows. Hector and Hex are not the types to enjoy sunlight. Far from it! So though we are

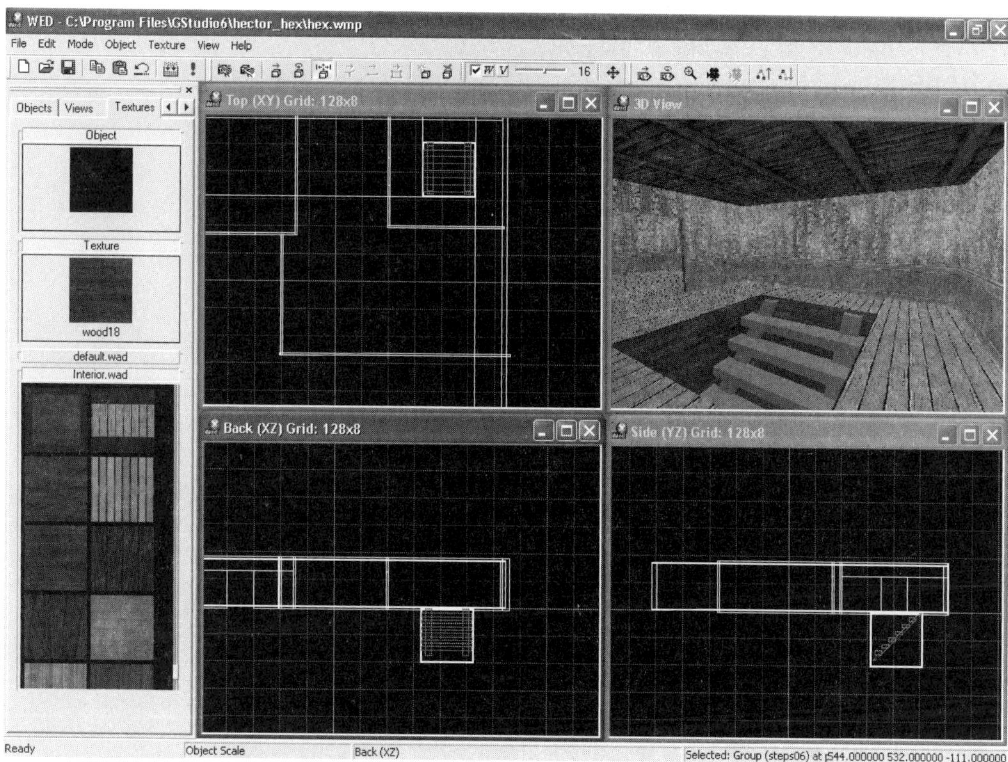

Figure 6.15
The staircase going inside the stairwell

going to add some windows here, we will be covering them up in the next section with boards. The windows will add to the gameplay, however, so they are an important addition. First create a medium cube and apply the Wood18 texture to it. Size it so that it is smaller than the doorways and higher off the floor, and place it along the outside wall just south of the bedroom. Make sure it intersects the wall, passing through.

Use Edit > CSG Subtract to make a hole in the wall, but do NOT delete the cube. Using the Position tab in the object's Properties window, move the cube south an interval and select Edit > CSG Subtract again. If you do this correctly, you will not make more than five cubes out of the single wall.

Rotate the cube 90 degrees clockwise, and move it to next intersect the southern-most outside wall. Make sure that it is placed roughly a third of the way along the wall because you are going to make three windows along this wall. Do the same as you did on the western wall, using CSG Subtract to make three windows here. Once you are finished, you can delete the cube you've been using this whole time to make the holes. You should have five windows in all.

Pat yourself on the back! You have just created the first part of the second floor. It's taken a while, so you probably want to save your file before continuing. Take a breather and use the Walk-Thru mode in the 3D View window to explore what you have built so far. To do so, make sure you have at least one object selected, and then go to Mode > Walk-Thru. Alternatively, you can click the camera-like icon button or press the W key with the 3D View window selected. You will be able to pan the camera in the 3D View using your mouse and zoom in and out and strafe left and right with the arrow keys. You can also go up and down, like riding in an elevator, by pressing the HOME and END keys. The PAGE UP and PAGE DN keys make the camera tilt up and down, respectively. Before you start into Walk-Thru mode, you could even expand the 3D View window by tapping the Maximize button in its upper-right corner so you have better visibility. Besides the windows, you should not see any leaks in the hull of the level. If you do notice any glaring gaps, you might want to think about fixing them before moving on. When you are through with Walk-Thru mode, press ESC.

A Quick Tip on Textures and Sprites

Textures and sprites are both 2D images that are mapped into our 3D scene along the X and Y axes (relative to the image itself). When applying a texture to an object, not every available surface has to have the same texture applied. Right-click in your scene with your object selected and open its Properties panel. Click the Surface tab. Here you will be able to apply textures to individual surfaces of your object. The panel will display how many surfaces in total there are and which one is currently selected (often the surface selected will appear in yellow or pink by defaults in the view windows). You can apply textures by browsing to the surface you wish and double-clicking the texture you want in the Textures tab of the Project window on the left of the screen. You can then move the texture on that surface left and right or up and down using the X and Y offsets. You can spin the texture on the surface by changing the value of its angle. You can make the texture appear smaller or larger using the X and Y scale fields.

Similarly, when you place sprites into your level, they can be mapped to the X and Y axes. Create sprites in your favorite paint program, and optimize your render time for your level by creating sprites that match a power of 2 (like 128 x 256). Paint areas dead black (RGB 0, 0, 0) that you want to be invisible when the sprite is loaded. The engine ignores black and is tolerant enough to erase pixels with a value up to 5 or 6.

If you notice egregious black edges around your image when it is displayed in the engine, it is because any pixel that is not completely black will be displayed in full without transparency. In a BMP or PCX file, every pixel is defined as full opaque or as invisible; there is no in-between. You can correct this oversight by creating an alpha channel and saving as a 32-bit TGA. With our alpha channel, as colors get darker they are displayed with more and more transparency until they are fully invisible. You can save your files as TGA and tell the difference. (Some paint programs require you to assign an alpha channel to the image first.)

Sprites will always turn to face the camera, unless you do something to counteract it. Select your sprite and open its Properties panel. Under the Position tab, you will see three angles set for Rotate: in order, these are X, Y, and Z. Make sure that there is not a single 0.00 in any of the three fields. If you want, you can create a safe margin for error by placing a 0.01 in all three fields, although as you will read in the exercise, I caution you to put a 0.10 in at least one or two of the fields. This is entirely up to you and the sprite that you are working with. A minimal angle will do.

Some sprites you will want to always face the camera. Study games like *Hitman: Blood Money* and see that the waving tall grass is actually a series of sprites that turn to face the camera at all times, implying natural order. You might also consider that a full moon in the sky would look better if it rotated to follow the camera. However, be watchful for plane intersections. If the sprite has to rotate too far to face the camera, it might disappear behind blocks forming the ground or the sky, and that would disrupt the image.

One more thing: sprites are not truly physical. Some may stop the player from crossing his hull when the physics engine runs. Others will have "leaks" that let the player run right through them at certain angles. Sprites also do not cast shadows. If you want a sprite to appear to have substance or act like a solid object, you must give the sprite a solid object to back it up. You can place geometric blocks into WED and arrange them where the sprite will be. Then in the Properties window, you set the blocks to Invisible. The player will not be able to cross the sprites. However, the sprites will still not cast a shadow. If you must, you can combine sprites with geometric blocks textured to match the sprites to generate some shadow maps. Or you can duplicate the sprites in a paint program to be close to black, blurred, and saved as a TGA. Then in WED, you set their values in the Properties panel to Transparent and rotate them to lay on the floor or ground. Those are two ways you can get sprites to cast shadows!

Note

Primitive blocks can appear sterile and, with such straight lines and no capable curves, they can appear wholly unnatural. You can add objects besides cubes, and some of these will appear more natural by default. However, any block you throw into your level you can give a more asymmetrical look that you find most common in nature! Under Mode in the WED menu, you can select Vertex Move, Edge Move, or Face Move. Selecting any of these allows you to move a block's edges and vertices around to appear more natural-looking. Just remember to watch out for those pesky concave blocks! You can distort any block's edges and vertices in such a way as to deform it however you like, but WED must make allowances because of the rule that there not be any concaves in your level. Simple spheres can be distorted into odd-shaped boulders, chairs can be made more curvaceous and elegant, and tree trunks can be warped to appear like root-bound testimonies to the capriciousness of Nature's whim.

Adding the Details

Now you are ready to start adding the decorations, such as furniture, rugs, picture frames, cobwebs, and so on. I will show you how to add models and sprites to the level and how to create physical objects out of model entities using invisible geometry. This will go much more quickly than the last part of this exercise, but with some creative thought it can take longer. The reason for this is that I will show you how to scratch the surface, so to speak, but the more details you add to a level the more character it has and the more immersive it may seem. Adding details is tedious work, but it can be very rewarding. Plan ahead, and your levels will be sumptuous.

Found in the project files for this tutorial are several folders, called bitmaps, sounds, models, and code. You are going to copy all of these to your hector_hex project folder you are working in. They include all the files that you will need to place and move in your levels. You already have a models folder, and it contains the hector model you created. You do not want to overwrite the hector.mdl file, unless you are dissatisfied with the way he looks.

Once you have the folders placed in the project folder, you now have libraries that you can use. Go to Object > Add Object > Add Model, and you should see a list of available models. If you do not see a list there, either the duplication process of the libraries was not done correctly, or it might not be in the Level Editor memory yet. WED sometimes takes a while to register changes to its directories or code, and if that happens, simply save your current file and re-open it. This will refresh all attached resources.

When you re-open your file, if you get any error messages such as "Damaged at line −1," your file is damaged. You can attempt to open its backup with the file name extension .bak instead of .wmp. Otherwise, you might have to start over again, following the steps laid out in the last exercise. This is an unfortunate problem that can happen when your PC crashes or is switched off while you are editing your level. Remember to work in steps, saving often, and remember the special naming conventions you have to follow whenever saving files in 3D GameStudio: keep the names short, all lowercase, and do not put any wild card symbols in them (such as hyphens, dollar signs, and so on).

Go to Object > Add Object > Add Sprite and find the sprite called lights.bmp. This is a string of Christmas lights, like one would see strung outdoors around trailer parks. It will go nicely in Hector's bedroom and makes a fitting first start to your sprite handling (see Figure 6.16).

You cannot see the picture in WED. Instead, it appears as a transparent wire-frame billboard. Notice at the base (or bottom) of the sprite, there are little feet;

Figure 6.16
The Christmas lights

this is so you can tell which way's up and which way's down on a sprite in WED. Of course, there is no clear understanding which way the image is facing. If you have a sprite you plan to use with writing on it (say a poster or sign), you will have to test-run the game to see if you placed the sprite correctly; if it needs turned around, you can go back into the Level Editor, use the object's Properties panels to perform Rotate angles along the X-axis and put it right as rain. As lights.bmp does not have any writing and does not change whatever side you look at it from, we won't have to bother with this for now.

You will probably have to scale the lights.bmp to fit the bedroom wall, and you will move it up near the wall's surface plane but not right on it. You do not want to place sprite decals directly on the same plane as the surface of the wall that you want to affix them to because, if you did, the engine would have the sprite and the wall surface compete for visibility. This leads to bleeding between the two, which also happens whenever you have two blocks with different textures applied competing for surface plane (you might have seen this happening in the door frame that we created). You want the lights.bmp to be positioned near the top of the ceiling, maybe two squares down (see Figure 6.17).

Now you might recall that sprites rotate to face the camera at all times—unless you change one of their angles to something other than zero. Open the object's Properties panel and where it says Rotate you should see (if you placed your sprite where I did) that X is set to 90.00 and Y and Z are set to 0.00. You want to tap the Y's arrow buttons once or type in **0.10** for the rotational angle. This will fix your sprite so it does not spin around to always face the camera. There are lots of images you might want to face the camera. For instance, trees on the horizon, the moon set in the night sky, or a halo image around a lamp are all good areas to let them rotate by themselves, but like the poster or signpost, our Christmas lights must hang in a fixed position.

While you have the Properties panel open, under the Properties tab, give the lights.bmp an Ambient setting of 100. Ambient makes objects appear lighter, even if they are in shadow.

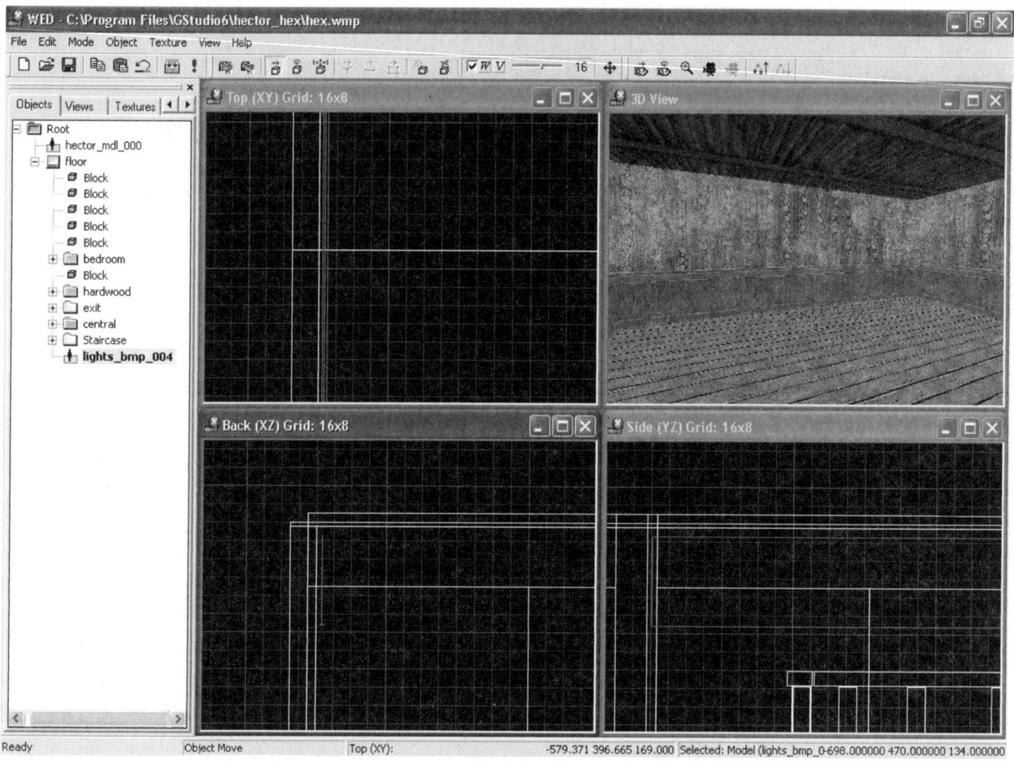

Figure 6.17
Placing your first sprite

The final thing we need to do with these lights is add static lights around them for realism. Go to Add Object > Add Light to create a static light in the game level; it will appear as a light bulb. Place two lights on either side of the lights.bmp, parallel to the sprite and to each other. We could go for realism and make tiny lights for every one of the Christmas light bulbs in the image, but because you cannot preview the image in WED and because that would be very difficult to manage, it would be inefficient. Two lights are just great.

Open each of the light's Properties panels one by one. Lights have different properties than most objects. You can set the color for the light, you can set the range for the light to illuminate in number of quants, and you can define whether or not you want its illumination to be Hi-Res. You can also change the file name, just like any other object, and position it.

The first light should be set to the brightest red and the second should be the brightest green. Both of them should have a Range set to 150.

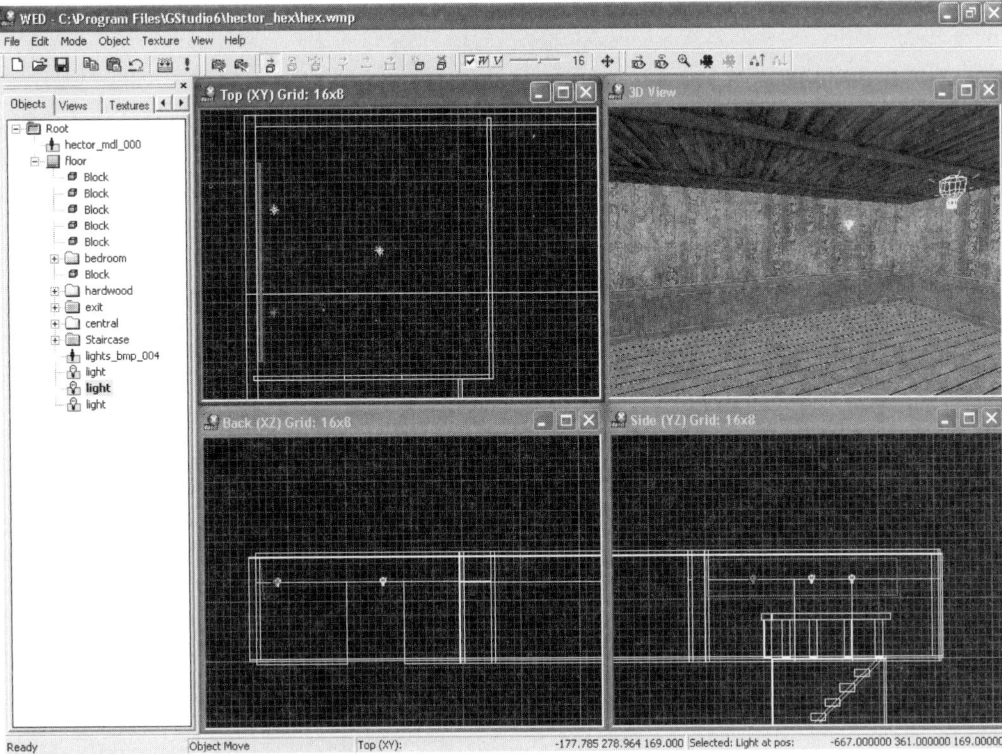

Figure 6.18
Adding lights to the Christmas lights

Create a third light set to a pale yellow color and a range of 300 and place it in the middle of the room. Make this light about one to two squares from the ceiling. It will be our room light and the main source of illumination in Hector's room (see Figure 6.18). See Figure 6.19 for the rendered view of what it will look like.

Let's move into the L-shaped hall outside of Hector's room. You are going to add a light source, colored white with Range set to 400, in front of each window in the hall, approximately in the middle of the corridor and one square off the floor. You should have five new lights when you get through.

In the Project window, right-click on one of the new lights you created, and choose New Group. Right-click on the new group, and open its Properties. Rename it **hallway lights.** Drag and drop each of the five new lights you've created into this group. You can keep the rest of your Project window tidy in this way, and it will improve your organization skills.

Figure 6.19
What room isn't better with Christmas lights?

Go to Object > Add Object > Add Model and find room_lamp.mdl. In its Properties panel, set the Scale to 2.00 and its Ambient to 20.00. Position the room_lamp.mdl over the pale yellow light source you placed in Hector's room, and make sure that its cord almost touches the ceiling.

Create a new group and call it **room lamp**, which you will drag and drop the room_lamp.mdl and the pale yellow light source into. This will become an amazing duo because you can use lights and the models that represent the light source as single groups; in many levels you can move and edit them together.

Now you are going to make another illuminating duo, but this time you are going to start with the model. Bring in wall_lamp.mdl and Scale it to 2.00 with an Ambient of 20.00. Place it in the large open area before you get to the room with the stairs. The wall_lamp.mdl does not hang from the ceiling. It has a base that has to rest against the wall, so make it flush with the wall and a few squares down from the ceiling (about head high on an adult; remember that Hector is not an adult yet, so proportions of the room must conform to that).

Next place a light source right in front of the wall_lamp.mdl. Set its Range to 200 and its color to bright orange.

Create a new group and name it **wall lamp**. Drag-and-drop your wall_lamp.mdl and the yellow light source into the new group. Presto! You now have a dynamic illuminating group that you can duplicate and place in multiple spots to light up the room (see Figure 6.20).

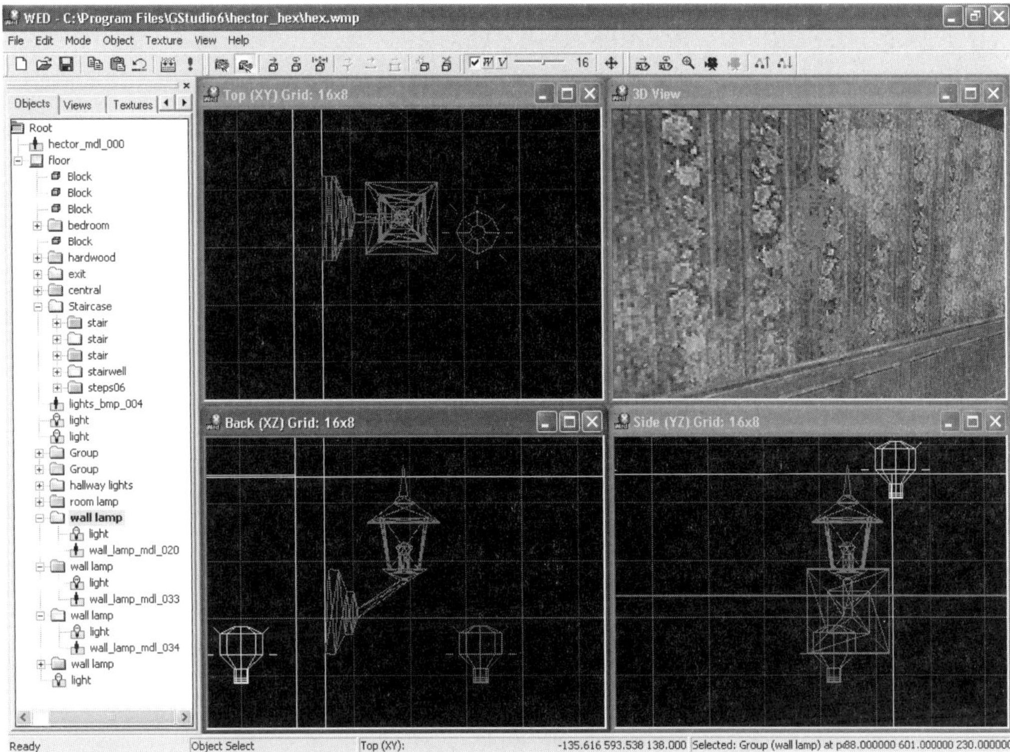

Figure 6.20
Decorative wall lamps add that "flipped this house" look.

Press CTRL + D to duplicate the wall lamp group, then move it around the room and at the head of the stairs in the room next to this room. You do not want more than four lamps lighting up this area; the more light sources you have, the more light will fill the space. Eventually you would get some really bright white areas that lose the immersive realism, and that would not be very good. Most developers will tell you, when in doubt err on the side of darkness. This is because darker rooms will create suspenseful immersion in games and covers a lot of modeling or design errors.

Place one more light source—this time set to a snot green color and Range to 500—in the middle of the large room about two squares off the floor. This will provide the wide room with as much illumination as needed.

You have learned about placing sprites as decals on walls, but now let's do a decal on the floor in the image of a rug. Go to Object > Add Object > Add Sprite and find rug.bmp. Load it into your level and open its Properties panel. Under the Position tab, place 90.00 in the Y-axis and 0.10 in the X-axis next to Rotate.

This will rotate the entire graphic so that it lies horizontally instead of standing vertically.

Place the rug in middle of the larger space on the floor or almost touching, anyway. Set its Ambient to 10.00. Also, in its Properties dialog box, make sure the Passable check box has a check mark next to it. This is simple to understand if you were to test-run the level without it. The engine would treat the rug as a wall, and when the player came to it, her character would be stopped in its tracks by an invisible force. With Passable turned on, the engine treats the sprite as a non-entity. The player can walk back and forth over the rug without impediment.

We need to place some other important sprites in this level—windows. The windows need a pane of glass set in them. Bring in the glasspane.bmp, and resize it as needed to fit one of the windows. If you need to, it can overlap the edges of the window frame of the wall, as long as there are no gaps around the edges. The glasspane.bmp should also fit well back in the window, providing a ledge on the inside; the outside won't matter, as the player will not be able to see outside.

We are going to set the glasspane.bmp to be transparent so that it appears more like glass. In its Properties panel, set a check mark next to Transparent, its Ambient to 20.00, and its Rotate Y-axis to 0.10 (to keep it in place). If you wanted to add further realism, you could place trees and other objects just outside the windows so there is something for the player to view, giving the illusion of a bigger world outside.

Duplicate the window pane four more times, and place the duplicates in the remaining windows.

Next we need to board up the windows. The downstairs floor might have windows in it, but they will have thick drapes covering them. Here, though, the family has not spent the money on drapery, and so boards will cover the windows to keep out most of the sunlight. Add the boards.bmp, and place the graphic over the front of the windows, just touching the wall on either side (to provide some fixture to nail the boards to, of course).

Set the boards.bmp to a Rotate Y-axis of 0.10 in the Properties panel so that they stay fixed.

Duplicate the boards sprite four more times and place the duplicates over the remaining windows so they are all covered up.

In the real world there is always some ambient light where no light shines directly but bounces off available objects. You can achieve this effect in WED by going to File > Map Properties, and clicking on the Sun tab. Ignore the Sun settings for now because this is purely an indoor level. Using Ambient you can adjust the level of ambient light for your level, which basically colors all your shadows. Remember, however, that the setting you choose here will pervade your entire level. You should never choose an ambient light that is too bright, or you won't have any shadows left! I have selected to define my own custom color, a kind of really dark bluish-purple.

You have copied a sounds folder into your directory. The sounds herein are titled so as to be self-explanatory. You can add static sounds (as long as they're WAV files) to your level as you progress. Keep in mind the overall effect and ambience these sounds will have. You will also be able to place music soundtracks directly into your level using WED. Try it. Go to Object > Add Object > Add Sound and find the WAV file worms.wav. Place it into your level, and in its Properties window you can change its settings.

Sounds have different value settings than other objects. You can edit their volume (in percentage rate) and the range of the sound source. For worms.wav, set its volume to 100% and its range (measured in quants) to 800. Place worms.wav in the very center of the level and up above the ceiling block. Because it is a static sound, the closer your camera gets to it the louder it will resonate, until it reaches the full volume that you set here in the Properties panel.

Place other sounds as you like. Do not go hog-wild with them, as they will loop and overlap; if you have all of them going at once and at full volume, you will merely create one noisy cacophony the player will want to avoid! The sound's range is similar to the light source's range but invisible to the naked eye when you run the engine. Attempt to discern quant distances by looking at the effect lights have and editing your sounds' Properties as needed.

Congratulations! You have successfully created a creepy second floor, complete with a rug, some Christmas lights, some lamps, wacky lights, and spooky stairs. Things are starting to look pretty good. Now you can use your own judgment from here on out. Add some other objects to this level, without making it look cluttered. Dress up Hector's room with posters, a bed, and a chair or side table. Place some picture frames on the hallway walls, opposite the windows. Add more details to the large empty room at the top of the stairs, if you like. You are free to use your imagination.

Use the Walk-Thru mode to test your level to make sure there isn't a major spot you have missed or a big gaping hole in your level that will make it look like the work of an amateur. Cover up and fix any problems that you discover.

Save your file when you are through before continuing.

Placing Props

We are going to need some weapons, obstacles, and power-ups along the path Hector will take. We have not implemented the main code that will run the game yet, so this part is practically impossible for us to test-run until we do. We will add the props that support the gameplay when we code the game in the next chapter. Just know that, though the level looks virtually empty now, it won't be when we get through.

Note

I create every game level in specific steps. If you skip steps or hurry ahead, you might find yourself more behind than ever. The typical progression for a game level developed in WED is as follows:

1. Set your Preferences and load your WADs using the Texture Manager.
2. Save your file as a unique filename, remembering to keep it under 20 characters with not a funny character in the lot besides maybe an underscore (_).
3. Build the basic geometry of your level, keeping your blocks tight together, and avoid "leaks." Keep the fencing tight. Create blocks for every contingent physical block, even if they have to be invisible blocks.
4. For details, don't use blocks because it will hog the compile time and cause slow-down in the engine. Use sprites, models, and textures creatively to add details to your level.
5. Light your levels as you go, paying careful attention to light sources.
6. Add sounds to your level as you go, keeping ambience in mind.
7. Save your file when you are done.
8. Build your level in the Map Compiler.
9. Run the level to test it.
10. Make adjustments as needed.
11. Script behaviors as needed.
12. Publish when you are through.

Test-Run the Level

Before you compile and test your level, you must make some changes to the program script. It is really very easy. The next chapter we will pay more careful attention to programming for our action game, but for now you want to run your level and make sure that you are satisfied with the build of it before continuing.

If your GameStudio version is older than 6.40, make sure you have the free, major engine update A6.405. Make sure that you have updated the engine, as well as the templates to the latest version. The engine can be updated by running the update6405.exe file, and the templates are updated by unzipping the template_640.zip file and copying its content inside your 3DGS folder, overwriting the existing files. When you are sure that you have the required toys to play with your level, move to the next step.

Go to File > Map Properties. Ignore the rest of what it says here in Map Properties for now, but note that under the Main tab you should see a line that says Script and beside it should be a blank field and three buttons. You can actually load and use pre-made script files, but for now click the New Script second button. A dialog box will pop up, asking you what sort of template files you wish to use for your level. You should select Shooter_Project. A6 provides you a lot of flexibility, including advanced physics, mirror effects, shaders, and more.

The map editor will automatically create a main script for your game based on the name you gave the level you have open. Because we called this level hex, the script file that is generated will be hex.wdl. See Figure 6.21 to compare. If you hit the New Script button and nothing happens—or if these buttons are grayed out—you have forgotten to save your level with a unique name such as hex.wmp. You must save your level file before you can create a script for it. Exit Map Properties when you are through.

Now in the Project window, click the arrow buttons at the top until you see the Resources tab appear. Hit the Resources tab, and you should get an updated list

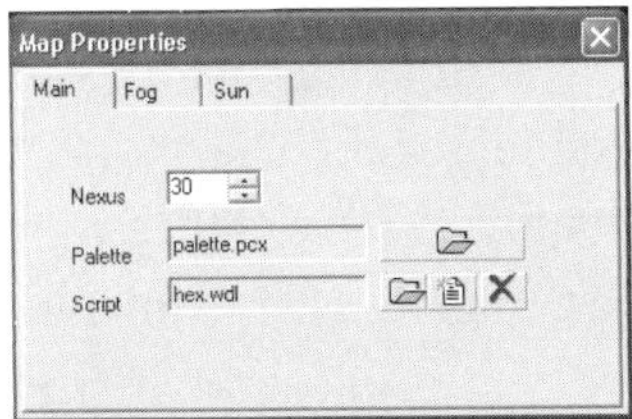

Figure 6.21
The ease of creating game scripts!

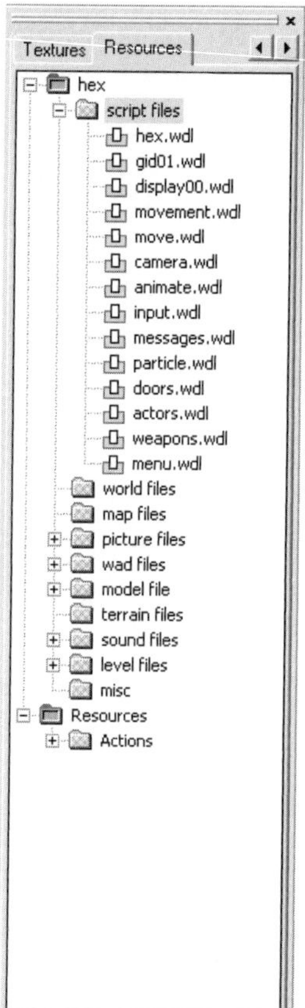

Figure 6.22
The Resources tab

of the build resources (such as program scripts) available for your level. Click the plus sign (+) beside the terms for an expanded list (see Figure 6.22). Under script files, you should find the script that we just created, hex.wdl. Double-click on the name hex.wdl (not on the blue icon beside it), and the script will open up in the Script Editor (SED) automatically.

Note that the script begins with path declarations. Paths set the directory structure for the game, much as you must do for Web site design. All game files—bitmaps, sounds, entities, or scripts—will first be searched for in the project folder you are currently working in and then in the paths given here. Note that backslashes (\) have to be given in C notation as double backslashes (for example, C:\\template). You can specify up to 32 paths, which will be searched in the sequence you write them in. In order to be able to copy your project to different locations, use relative paths for all files belonging to your project and absolute paths for all files that are on an absolute location on your hard disk (like the template scripts).

You should see the following paths already placed there:

```
path "C:\\Program Files\\GStudio6\\template_6";         // Path to A6 templates
directory
path "C:\\Program Files\\GStudio6\\template_6\\code";   // Path to A6 template
code subdirectory
path "C:\\Program Files\\GStudio6\\template_6\\images"; // Path to A6 template
image subdirectory
path "C:\\Program Files\\GStudio6\\template_6\\sounds"; // Path to A6 template
sound subdirectory
path "C:\\Program Files\\GStudio6\\template_6\\models"; // Path to A6 template
model subdirectory
```

You will add two new paths here underneath the other paths:

```
path "models";
path "sfx";
path "bmaps";
```

This tells the engine to search the hector_hex folder for subfolders named models, sfx, and bmaps. These came from the CD-ROM, and you copied and pasted them into your hector_hex folder. They contain the models, audio files, and images that you will use in your *Hector & Hex* game.

Without the path statement here, you couldn't test-run your level. It might spit out an error telling you that it could not find the models. The same is true for the bmaps folder, where you have placed all the sprites and other graphics you are going to use for the *Hector & Hex* game.

The string `level_str` tells the engine what level to load first. When making major edits in various levels of a single game, it's easy to test each of them. You simply edit this string command. Place the name of the level you want to test in the brackets. For now, you may leave this string line alone, as there is only one level to test.

The included files that follow are calling additional scripts from the given code script, and then continue scanning the original script file. In this way, pre-defined template scripts can be inserted. Up to 40 files can be included when generating the game. At the moment, you should see the following:

```
// Included files
include <gid01.wdl>; // global ids
```

```
include <display00.wdl>; // basic display settings
include <plSelect.wdl>;
include <cameraTarget.wdl>;
include <miscInput01.wdl>;
include <plBipedInput01.wdl>;
include <bipedPhy01.wdl>;
include <bipedAnim01.wdl>;
include <bipedSnd01.wdl>;
include <plBiped01.wdl>;
include <cameraSelect.wdl>;
include <camera1stPerson01.wdl>;
include <trigger00.wdl>;
include <particle00.wdl>;
include <fxa01.wdl>;
include <fxGore01.wdl>;
include <weaponfx00.wdl>;
include <weapons00.wdl>;
include <aiFPS01.wdl>;
include <plBipedWeap00.wdl>;
include <plBipedWeapHUD01.wdl>;
include <plBipedHUD01.wdl>;
include <lift01.wdl>;
include <saveLoad00.wdl>;
include <saveLoad01.wdl>;
include <menu01.wdl>;
```

These are fairly straight-forward script files that are preset to the Shooter_Project template.

We are through editing the script, so you can save the file and exit the Script Editor. Go back into the Level Editor and your hex.wmp. We have made some major changes to the script behind the level, so it is safer to refresh the level. Save the level (if you have not already done so) and open it up again. This will clear any residual memory files and reload the attached script file. Once it is through loading, select the hector.mdl (the player character) and right-click to open its Properties dialog box. Under the Behavior tab, you can select behaviors to be applied to the entity. The Action field identifies what action has been attached to the entity so far. Right now this field is blank or says "ndef" which stands for "no definition."

Click the folder icon on the right of this field, and you should be presented with the Choose Action dialog box, containing a list of available behavior actions (see Figure 6.23). Scroll down to view all of these actions. These are listed in

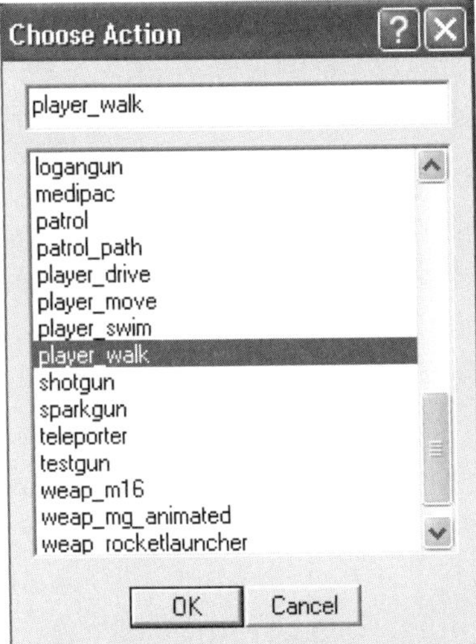

Figure 6.23
Choose Action dialog box

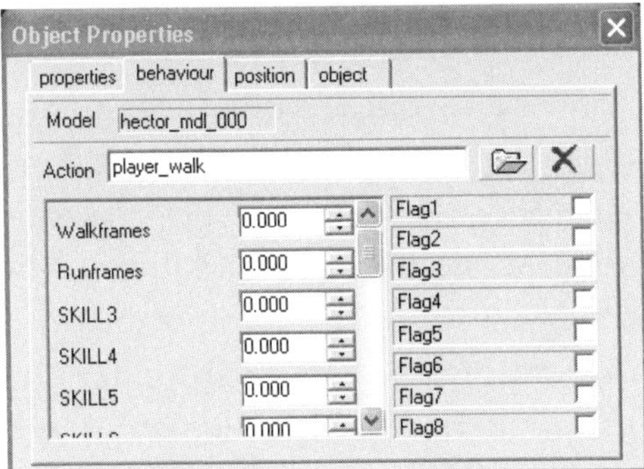

Figure 6.24
Chosen behavior

alphabetical order for easy use. Find and choose PlBiped01. This defines the model as the player character and allows the player to steer it through the use of the mouse and keyboard. You will notice that as soon as you choose PlBiped01 for the behavior, that the skills will change to fit the settings for the player (such as walk frames and such). Don't worry about them right now. Leaving them set at 0.00 or blank will keep them at their defaults (see Figure 6.24). Exit the Properties window when you are through.

Save your level file. Press the Build button (it reminds me of stairs or a door mat). Optionally, you could also go to File > Build WMB. The Map Compiler dialog box will open.

The build process calculates something called a BSP tree and converts your WMP file into a WMB file, without erasing or losing your original WMP file. The "B" in WMB stands for "binary"—because this is how the compiled version has to be for the machine to run it. This is known as *map compiling*. The Map Compiler allows you to build the level, build a map entity, update entities, update textures, or update lights. Choosing Default Build resets any changes to build settings you might have made. Visibility calculations and light calculations are the two worst and most time-consuming parts of compiling the level in the BSP tree, so there are options built-in here that allow you to nullify them somewhat if you are merely building a short level to test. Note that you can also tap the triple arrow button to expand the Map Compiler window and study all the available settings for compiling your level. You can actually use more than one CPU to build levels if you are creating titanic outdoor levels that are intended for a commercial game, for instance. Under Default Build, almost all the settings are set to Auto, which should be fine enough for us (see Figure 6.25).

Select Build Level. You can watch as the machine takes the compilation seriously. If your level exceeds certain threshold values, you will receive warning or error messages, such as "duplicate plane detected." The compiler runs through the level's individual portals, which can take time. Calculating visibility takes a long while because the compiler buffers portals multiple times. There will be occasions when you see the compiler freeze completely while calculating the visibility, but you know that you have built a really small tidy level. If that is the case—and it happens to everyone at least once—simply cancel and try again or try the Default Build. Eventually you will see the compiler clear the hurdle, and it will speed through the build.

When the compiler has completed its task—which on larger levels can take hours or even days—it will report to you the exact number of seconds it has taken to complete the task. Click OK to exit the Map Compiler.

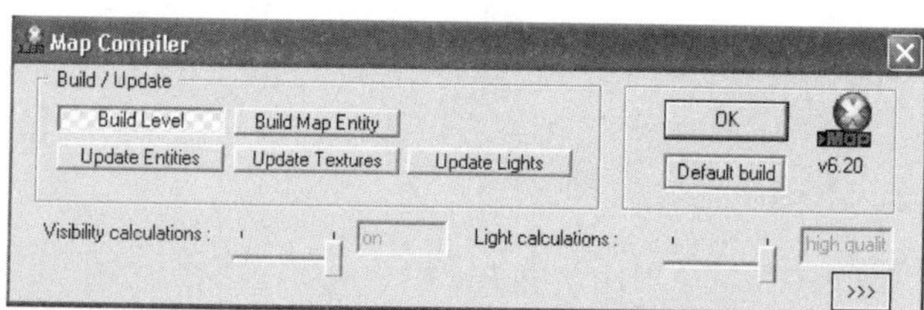

Figure 6.25
The Map Compiler dialog box

Now you are ready to test-run. To test-run your level, hit the red exclamation mark button right beside the Build button, or go to File > Run Level. It will give you a field where you can enter some command-line options. You can run the game level in a window mode (`-wnd`) or in a full screen mode. The default is toward the window mode. You can also select Hi-Res graphics (`-d hires`) or not; usually, you want to run Hi-Res unless you are on a slower system. If you run in window mode with Hi-Res on, you should enter this in the Engine Options field: **-wnd-d hires.** There are other command-line options you can use with 3D GameStudio for testing purposes. They are listed in your manual. Click OK when you are through.

You will see the loader open up. It will check your hardware devices, including video and sound, and it will modify itself to run on your system. If there are any bugs in your script or any files missing, they will appear during the Run phase.

Play through the level that you have created so far. You should have a basic heads-up display (or HUD) visible. Remember the default controls: press the WASD keys to move, use the mouse to control your camera, press the SPACEBAR to jump, and press the C key to crouch. If you need to go to the in-game menu, press ESC.

You should already have several weapons available to you. Press the Q key to bring them up and test them out. The first one is a doozy, however, so don't fire it too close to you or within a confined space. If you do, you will die; the screen will fade to black, and you will have to press ESC to start over.

There are some keys just intended for play-testing purposes, and though they can be helpful during the production process, I will show you how to remove their functionality later on before you let your friends play. When you are through testing out your level (or if you get stuck somewhere) you can quit by pressing F10 or by going through the menu screen (press ESC).

Did you see anything you think you should change? Were the colored lights effective, if you could preview them, or should you alter them again? Were there any "leaks" in your level, or any serious gaps or grotesque mistakes? Did you find yourself outside the level for any reason? Sometimes finding yourself stuck at the Zero Origin and unable to move is a problem caused by your forgetting to define the PlBiped01 behavior for your player character, so you might check and make sure that is not your problem.

How did playing your character model (Hector) work out for the first time (see Figure 6.26)? Do you think players will like playing the little ghoul? Did you spot any serious errors in any of his animation cycles? Is there anything we left out or

Figure 6.26
Hector boogying through his level.

that looks like it needs some tweaking in the avatar or the level he runs around in? Of course, you have not yet been able to test his death animation because he cannot be hurt quite yet, but what about his `walk`, `run`, `jump`, and `duck` states? Note that there are some issues when it comes to `jump`. Sometimes the entire `jump` cycle will not play unless the avatar is busy moving forward. Often the `duck` and `crawl` states will look funny. Anything you see that looks off, you can fix on your own time.

You've done a fine job! You are to be congratulated for creating your first level of your first game. Next we are going to look at adding additional levels and how that works.

Exercise 6.2: Building Mansion Floor 1

You have the second floor done. That's great. It is also easy to see where Hector will have to go. He leaves his bedroom, moves along the hall until he comes to the door, goes through the available doorway, and into a wider room to another door, which leads to the stairway down. We will stitch the levels together via the stairs. As soon as the player starts down the staircase, the player will hit an invisible switch that loads the next level. We just have to make the next level's insertion point appear predictable. That means we are going to have to start the player out at the bottom of the staircase. As we have already created this staircase, why not use it?

Flipping This Level

With hex.wmp open, save the file as **floor1.wmp** so you have a fresh building ground using the same elements as you had before. This is faster than starting from a clean slate.

Select the stairwell group (which should comprise the steps06, the stairwell box we had the steps go down into, and the railing). Raise it up so that the steps06 is above the floor. Scope Down and select the box surrounding the steps06 group. Scope Down again and remove the block just in front of the stairs, opening them up. Scope Up and raise the entire box to fit the room's height and keep the steps06 just touching the floor (see Figure 6.27). You should see that the bottom of the stairwell's box has now covered that hole in the floor!

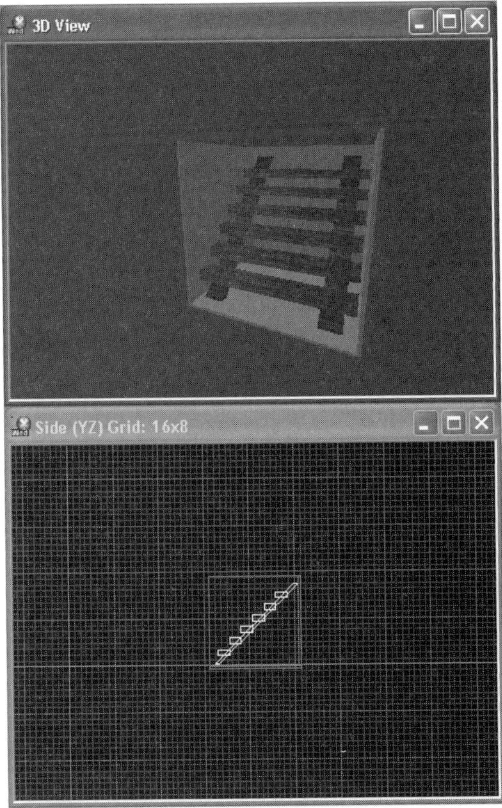

Figure 6.27
Creating a believable spawn point

Select the group of two walls, one with a door in it, that surrounded the staircase before. You want to rotate it 90 degrees counter-clockwise and move it into place so that the wall with the door in it touches the outside wall and the door frames the opening to the stairs. Scope Down and select the right-most block forming the wall without a doorway in it. Move it to the opposite side, and stretch it if need be. Scope Up to inspect your handiwork. You want to frame in that entire corner of the first floor.

Select the middle-most wall with the single door and door frame in it. Rotate it 90 degrees clockwise and move it up to touch the northern wall, forming one half of a hallway.

Next, grab the shorter wall that it used to attach to, the one that does not have a door or anything in it, and duplicate it (CTRL + D). The duplicate you can rotate 90 degrees clockwise and move down so it touches the original on one end and the outside wall on the other (use the Scale tool to stretch it if you have to). Next you'll need to scale it wider along the Y-axis in its object's Properties panel. This is more for variation than any design sense; I mean, who wants walls of the same thickness all throughout their house (see Figure 6.28)?

After you're finished with that, you should select the bedroom group and Scope Down. Load a medium cube, apply the Wood18 texture to it, and then resize it to be a perfect cube that would be big enough to fit through the door in here. Place it where it intersects the east wall, pretty far to the north along it, and when you are sure the height and width are relatively set correctly, select Edit > CSG Subtract to make a new door. Press DELETE to delete the cube when you are finished.

See how our path has come along? We now have redefined the second floor's layout to be the first floor's layout, and it has taken us fewer steps than our

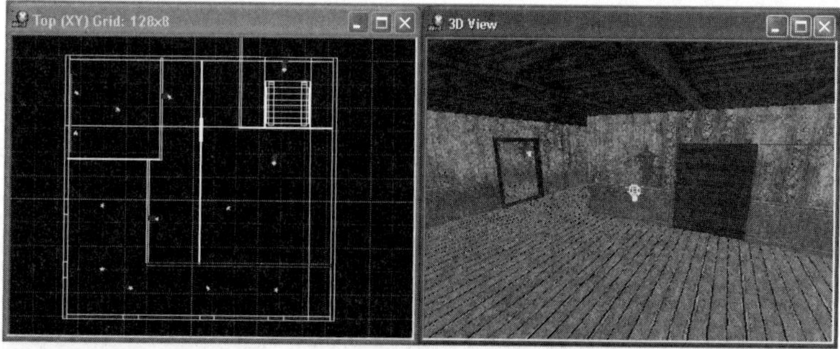

Figure 6.28
Flip this house!

predecessor. This is often the case in game design, which is evident if you play through enough of *Half-Life 2*'s sewer levels or *Doom 3*'s shadowy environs. You can build and save prefab constructions, like the wall with door at X position in it or the stairwell with railings, for later use and populate level after level with similarly based constructions. It saves you time and stress from having to make up new walls and objects all the time. However, it also gets old after a while, so you can make eight or nine levels of this size with these small variations before you need to change and do radical transformations.

Adding the Details

Now we need to reorganize our other objects—specifically our lights and models. Since we placed the wall lamps in neat and tidy groups, we can move them in whole sections without having to traffic with the light sources getting left behind or the models out of whack. So nab those puppies and move them so that they are flush to the walls and evenly spaced out again. You might also consider changing their apparent colors or ranges. I also had to duplicate one of them, so that I would have more. I placed three in the room just outside the stairwell. I placed two in the short hall just outside there. I moved the other light sources around, and the ones that used to simulate bright sunlight I dimmed because these windows, when I am through, will have heavy drapes covering them. Therefore, I also changed their color to appear dim red. I also added four other basic lights (no color—just gray) to take out the long corridors or add to too-dark corners. The only light source I did not move or change in any way was the room lamp in the bedroom. It will stay right where it's at for now.

It is time to delete the Christmas lights and other decorations that you might have placed in Hector's room, as well as the boards we placed on the windows in the hallway. I decided to change rugs and move other decorative elements and models I had placed around. You can reuse a lot of the same basic objects in unique ways, including the cobwebs, paintings, chests, and more. Take a stab at it. Use your creativity.

We are not going to place the physical appearance of stairs leading down to the next level (the basement). Instead, you are going to set a block at the end of the L-shaped hallway and give it a wood banded texture like wood017. Scale it and move it into position so that its texture looks like Figure 6.29, then in its Properties panel put a check in the check box next to Texture Lock to make sure

Figure 6.29
One trapdoor coming right up!

it's not going anywhere. This will provide an instant trapdoor you can use to show an entrance to the basement (and the final level of our short game).

Add the drapes.bmp to the level and resize so that the sprite covers the windows sufficiently. Remember to set 5.00 in its X- or Y-axis of Rotate in the Properties panel so that it remains stationary. Duplicate and cover the remaining windows.

Add the door13.bmp to the level and resize it so it matches the shapes of the door frames already existing. Set its X- or Y-axis (of Rotate in the Properties panel) to 5.00 to nail it. Then rotate it and move it flush against the east wall, between the lights set in the wall there. Duplicate it and move another against the north wall at the end of the short corridor. Duplicate it and move it against the west wall, inside the bedroom. You want these to provide for the player the appearance that she is only seeing a sampling of the first floor, that there is more out there if she could only get past these locked doors.

Now add other objects and details as you see fit. When you are through, and you have performed a short walkthrough, save your file (remember to save it as floor1.wmp).

Test-Run the Level

Enter hex.wdl in the Script Editor. In the string `level_str`, change the level in the brackets from hex.wmb to floor1.wmb. Save hex.wdl. You can do this multiple times as you create and test out new levels. The `level_str` identifies the first level to be loaded at run time; changing it changes the player's start point.

Go back to the Level Editor. Build the level so that you convert the WMP to a WMB (which we have just decided to call in the script file). Run your level to see what sorts of error messages (if any) you receive. Browse the whole first floor of your mansion. Pay particular attention to lights and sprites. If one of your doors is rotating to face the camera suddenly, it might be because you got in a hurry and rotated a duplicate—overwriting the 0.10 you placed in one of its angles. Simply open its Properties panel again and change the opposite angle to 0.10. If you merely change entities (like sprites or models), choose Update Entities when you build your level again; it will compile faster. If you merely change lights, choose Update Lights when you compile. Light and shadow maps are a fraction of the total level build to be had. The key to developing fast and wonderful levels is to nail your level geometry the first time around. Then the rest of the time you are just shifting entities or lights around, and their compile times are much shorter and less of a hassle.

Save your file when you test-run your level, and you know you have it right. Take a break! You've earned it!

Exercise 6.3: Building the Death-Match Arena

You have the first two levels constructed. Now all you need is the final level where Hector dukes it out with his sister Hex for possession of the teddy bear! This is meant to be a fight to the impasse. So Hector will use all his firepower, and Hex will use all hers. The level is built to be a death-match arena (see Figure 6.30), so it is windy and goes nowhere exactly, but it should create hazards and cover to hide behind.

Study the map provided for the mansion basement. Name the new file **DMarena.wmp** so that you will not get lost later when you program for it. I am not going to hold your hand and guide you step by step through this level's design. I want you to try it yourself. The family uses the basement as a wide makeshift library. It has all the moldy aspects of a library, but all the cobwebs, dust, and tattered rugs as the rest of their creepy mansion. Add bookcases, books, stacks of books to hide behind, couches, and so on. Put some creative thought behind it.

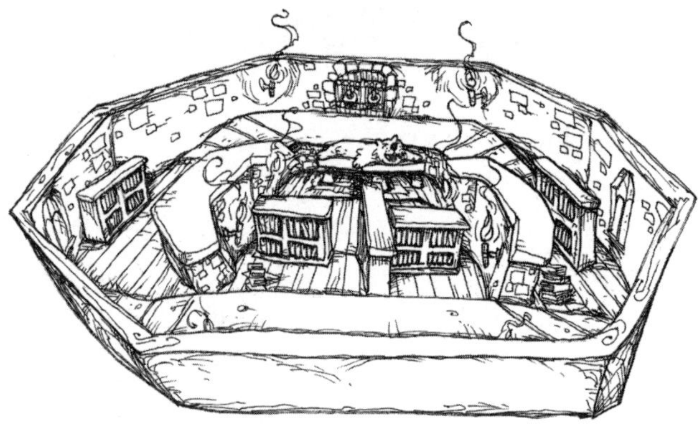

Figure 6.30
Map of the basement

In Summary

Our game *Hector & Hex* is really coming together and shaping up. Yet all we have created so far is one actor and the stage. How would you feel if you went to see Hamlet and one guy dressed in period garb strutted out on a stage and mocked lines in front of some painted boards for a couple of hours—without any other actors or single prop to support the play? You would probably want to nip out early for intermission, wouldn't you? Running your level now, you can see Hector strut his butt about the mansion's different floors, but he doesn't have a purpose or anything to do. In fact, none of these levels are even connected yet! So get buckled up and ready for it because we are going to turn you into a programmer. That's right. It is now time to add the scripts and other models and characters that will make this game really come to life!

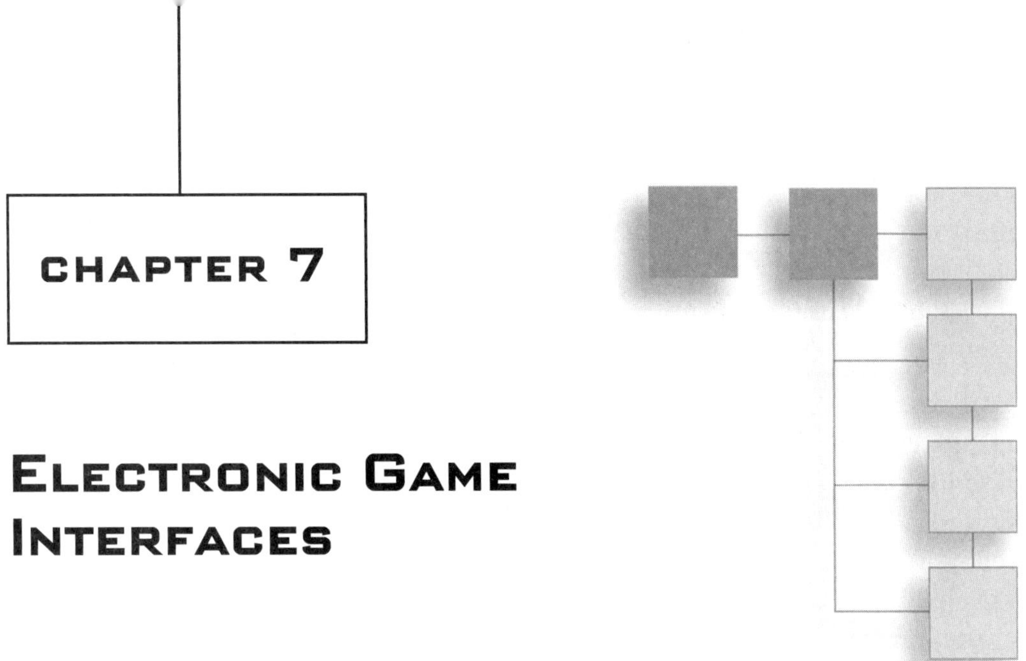

Chapter 7

Electronic Game Interfaces

Before you continue with programming your game, it is vital that you know what you are creating. A video game, first and foremost, is a fun entertainment product for use by a gamer. The gamer has to interact with the game through its interface. In the last chapter, we looked at ludic space and how this interaction is a dynamic field of controls and choice-making. What you do when you program a game is you morph this ludic space to fit the look and feel you intend for the game you are creating. This process can make a successful game or ruin a game that might have made it if it were only for the graphics. To be a game designer, you must understand the basic precepts of game interfaces and how you design them to fit your game.

Fleshing Out the "Gooey" Details

A graphical user interface (GUI, often pronounced "gooey") is a vehicle that allows for interacting with a computer that employs graphical images and widgets in addition to text messages to represent vital information to the player and available actions. Most of the time, but not always, the available actions are performed through manipulation of graphical elements or through keyboard commands.

Creating a detailed plan for your user interface in the game graphics section of your game outline or design document can really help drive game design. Fleshing out the little details of the game's look, such as in-game menu screens and the heads-up display (or HUD) will force many gameplay decisions to be made early on. It may even settle decisions for the direction the game's construction might take. Game developers can change the way an entire game is played based on their growing understanding of the scope of a game, which is exemplified in the user interface.

You are really lucky because 3D GameStudio has a built-in template interface that you can use. There is an in-game menu with options for adjusting sound and resolution, as well as help features and save/load features. The HUD can be turned on or off, as you please, with the call of a function—and this HUD resembles the popular first-person shooter HUD of games like *Quake*. You can use this HUD and alter the in-game menu with your own custom touches to create unique looks for your games, or you can code your own.

Listing Priorities for Your Interface

Before you go making game interfaces, you have to sit down and list your priorities. What are your goals through the game interface? What is your target audience? What mood, or atmosphere, are you planning to spread with the design look? Careful consideration over these serious details will make or break your game design. A game designed for children ages 3 to 5 that has to be simple and easy to use will have a vastly different interface than a gore-drenched action game intended to be M for Mature. The kids' game, for instance, would have bright saturated colors, big clear buttons that do not take a lot of skill or time to read, and intuitive decision-making. A GUI for adolescent gamers would have grungy panels, more text and information on the screen, and more options that befit a growing (yet gross) mind.

There are some other priorities that you should set straight early on. Creating game interfaces is simply underrated, and for good reason. Games look incredibly simple when they are finished, and the simpler they are, the more respect they get and the more addictive playtime are devoted to them. However, a lot of ground work—and even a little math—has to occur to achieve what looks so simple.

Figure 7.1 shows the mathematical model for simplicity and ergonomics in interactive design. This model, first published by Paul Fitts in 1954, has been used to show the correlation between where a person wants to go and how efficiently easy it is to get there. This is expressed by the person determining where she wants to go and using basic motor skills to get there.

$$T = a + b \log_2 \left(\frac{D}{W} + 1 \right)$$

Figure 7.1
Fitts' Law

T (or MT, as it has been traditionally expressed) stands for the average time taken to complete a single movement. D is the distance from the starting point to the center of the target. W is the width of the target. a and b are empirical constants. This equation shows a speed-to-accuracy tradeoff when it comes to point-targeting.

Since the advent of graphic interactive design, Fitts' Law has been used to express efficient interactivity and how to design a Web site or electronic interface. Fitts' Law takes into account visual cues and simple motor responses, such as positioning the mouse and clicking or using drag-and-drop. For this to work correctly, the user must be able to get where she wants to go (or do what she would like to do) with the shortest amount of work involved to get there. This makes for seamless interfacing and a smoother gaming experience.

For another thing, it is imperative to keep your game away from the dangers of feature creep. *Feature creep* is where you work too closely on a project and you end up mucking it up by tossing too many nifty-sounding features or game elements in that have no relationship or place in your game. A great game can become a train wreck if you put every amazing detail you like about games into it. For instance, if you are creating an urban action game, where the player is a gumshoe hot on the track of a killer, why would you decide to throw in melee weapons like swords? Magic potions? Alien artifacts? Or for that matter, contacts with ghosts or special superpowers that would only come from the four-poster comic book world? I am not trying to naysay genre mixture here; I am merely discouraging you from going off-track when developing a decent game. If you open up a *Pirates of the Caribbean* video game, you expect to have swords and cutlasses for weapons and a health bar or even a voodoo bar onscreen. You would not expect to pick up an AK-47 or have a spell bar for casting ritual magic; these elements would clutter a great game and are anachronisms anyway.

In the words of the immortal Judge Judy, "Keep It Simple Stupid!" A great game makes it to the top of the charts and wags the tongues when it is simple, neat, clean, and straight-forward, when lots of different people can play it without getting lost or confused, when it runs smoothly and still has room for upward mobility. Keep your design interface tidy. Hide unnecessary tools or icons. Reduce the screen windows, inventory windows, and character sheets. Make your choices legible and quick to read. Make your interface utterly transparent. Vital information must be easy to find. The best interface is the one that a player hardly notices, that never pulls the player out of his fantasy world or tells him, "Duh, this is just a game. What were you expecting?" This concept is referred to by designers as *scanability*, and with it you want to make every electronic interface fast, intuitive, dead-on and easy to scan. You want the player to find the most important information (whatever it is, such as health, mana, ammo) first and the less important information (such as journal notes, maps, and so on) secondary. You want the player to swim through your interface without having to stop and think about how it operates.

Scanability means the controls must be clear. The player should be able to jump right into a game without having to pore for an hour or so over your carefully crafted manual. The player should be able to understand at a glance what to do and when. In fellow designer Donald A. Norman's book, *The Design of Everyday Things*, he says, "Design must convey the essence of a device's operation; the way it works, the possible actions that can be taken, and, through feedback, just what it is doing at any particular moment." Sometimes this means you have to pay attention to and not deviate a whole lot from conventions of the game genre. For instance, most first-person shooters allow the player to see his health, armor, available ammo, and what gun he is holding at any particular time onscreen. You start taking away any of these details, and the player is liable to gripe. If there's a certain established convention or way in which a type of game is played, and it works and you like it—why change it at all? Einstein once said, "Make things as simple as possible, but no simpler."

Conceptualizing Your Interface

Once you have the priorities for your design set out, you can give consideration to the look of your interface systems (see Figure 7.2). Design a prototype of the interface fairly early on and, as designer Bob Bates says, "Keep noodling with it."

Giving the player more options and menus can be confusing at first, so you will have to get used to developing flowcharts of them, supplementing the image compositions. Flowcharts are just like the ones you create for the game story, algorithms for the programming, and decision-making trees for game paths. Charting is a craft all its own. You can use Microsoft Word or a program that is

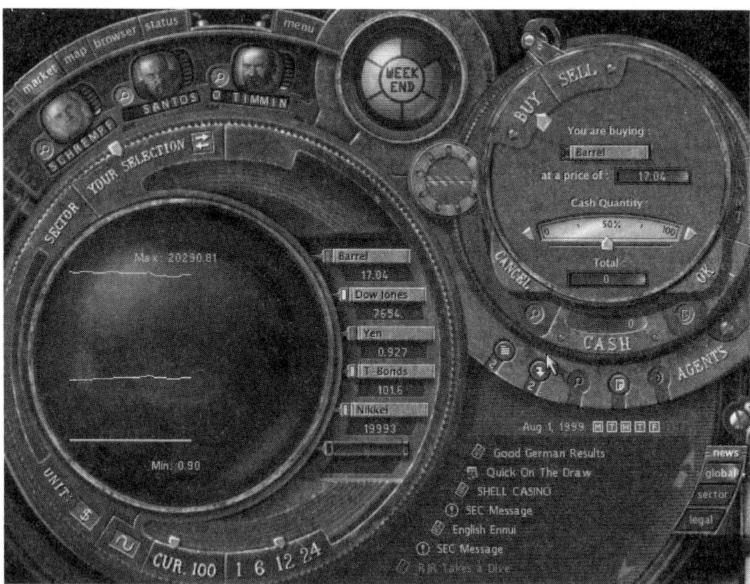

Figure 7.2
Wall Street Trader 99 (image courtesy of Monte Cristo Multimedia 1999)

built to handle making flowcharts, such as Visio, or you can use a vector art program like Adobe Illustrator or Fireworks. Typically, you would never want to use a raster program because vector allows for automatic resizing without loss of detail. Create nodes representing screen or window options, and place arrows that direct to other nodes, given player choices. Reflect all the player options.

Charting is only half the task when it comes to menu and interface creation, however. The majority of your preproduction work will be in creating compositions. Compositions often start with making thumbnails, which are very small sketches about a few inches wide. You generate pages of thumbnails, scribbling and sketching variations upon a theme, for each design element. Once you run through your standard set of ideas, you will be forced to make up even more and more creative ideas. When you have plenty of thumbnails to choose from, you pick the very best—the cream of the crop, as the old saying goes—and work them into serviceable mock-ups. A mock-up is sample art that is not the final product but a definitive visualization of the look and feel of the finished piece. It is similar to a rough draft. Choose the thumbnails you determine to be the best solutions, and work quickly in a paint program to produce a full-scale mock-up.

The mock-up should look practically finished, and it should include button schemes and logo images. Try to establish the look of the final product early on through your mock-ups. Generally, the mock-up is a trial stage for designing the finished piece, so do your best and keep in mind that you will be making edits later. The mock-up is also important for generating the color scheme and theme of the game.

Color is a vital ingredient in video games. What color are each of the buttons and elements of your game going to be? Answer this question early on. Keep your colors consistent with the theme. Colors have a dynamic effect on people's moods and the way they intuitively react to objects. The same is true of texture. Having elements that are bright red and covered in a rust texture will immediately cause the player to be apprehensive and afraid of getting hurt or dirty; this intuitive effect can be manipulated by a great game designer to set the course for a game. If you have never studied the color wheel or basic design principles, you should consider getting a book on it at your local library, or enroll in a class at your local college to pick these tools up because they will be invaluable to your arsenal as an artist.

Once you settle on a mock-up that you like, you can finalize the piece and pick it apart to see how you would code it into your game. Some custom interface pieces are easy to code. 3D GameStudio allows for a BMP or PCX image to be placed onscreen for any fixed amount of time, and it also gives you bonus features for layering the images so that you can have more than one image onscreen, and they will appear in a visible stack. This makes information screens immediate and versatile.

Types of Interfaces

There are many different types of interfaces that are becoming quickly standardized in gaming media. There are the player controls (generally in the physical sense as a keyboard and mouse or a console or joystick), which allow the player to move his character around onscreen and perform specific actions therein. There are feedback interfaces, such as the vibrations on consoles or noises and lights onscreen. There are also onscreen information panels—often referred to as the graphical user interface or just plain GUI (see Figure 7.3). In the GUI alone, there are many different types of interfaces, too. There are menu screens, loading screens, character screens, options screens, saving/loading screens, and so many more. Each can appear distinct. Some designers prefer that the artistic style applied to each screen remain consistently simple, such as the sheer blue interface

Figure 7.3
Scannable game interfaces are easy to navigate. (The *Elixir* beta version 0.9, image courtesy of Korpos Studios 2006)

of *City of Heroes*; many others prefer a thematic textural style that changes for every screen and represents the story world or mood of the particular game. If you are planning to go after the latter style, you will have to be skilled in 2D art and technology like Jasc Paint Shop Pro or Adobe Photoshop. A great example of this includes *Planescape: Torment* (Black Isle Studios), with its rusted metal and heavy grunge look.

Perhaps the most important GUI a design team must create is the heads-up display (HUD). The HUD shows the player at a glance the most vital information the player must know about the game. Most often this information includes the player character's health (which is often a number or a life bar that decreases or changes color whenever the player gets hurt), ability, magic or mana, and ammo. The HUD can (again) be simple and straightforward or it can be representative of the game world and artistic style. Some games have a HUD that covers up to an eighth of the entire screen size, although this is largely frowned upon because it takes up screen real estate.

In fact, the next generation of games are stretching for an almost transparent interface, including a nearly invisible or nonexistent HUD panel. Bethesda Softworks and Headfirst Games created *Call of Cthulhu: Dark Corners of the Earth* to have a nonexistent interface. Their original plan was to take the interface out altogether, to have the player so immersed in the story that the interface became purely intuitive so that the player had to check how much ammo by holding his pistol up by his face and looking at the rounds left in the gun. This ploy did not suit beta testers, however, so some conventional compromises had to be made. However, the character's health and sanity are still only recorded by how the feedback system is responding; the more insane or hurt a player character becomes, the more the picture onscreen will blur, fade, and flicker, the more the console device will vibrate, and the slower the player character will be able to move. This feedback system is considerately more realistic than most other games out right now.

You might not have the programming knowledge to take the interface to the next level. Never fear that this will harm the receptivity of your game, however. Most players share expectations that games will have certain conventional interfaces, and they will actually complain if the interface you design is radically different from the norm. For instance, most computer games use arrow keys or W, A, S and D keys for movement. Most games that require players to pick up and use inventory objects will have an inventory panel screen. Most games that require players to manage character traits and abilities will have character screens. Do not worry if you feel that the game you are distributing will have just another standard interface to it; the closer your interface is to industry standards, the more likely players are going to be able to sit down and play it without having to muddle through your player manuals and walkthroughs or get frustrated having to learn a totally new system.

3D GameStudio comes ready-made with menu screens, options screens, and saving/loading screens that you can add your own personal flair to. You can also program your own, once you learn how to code in C-script. Creating a HUD or a life bar for your players is also veritably easy, and you will learn how to do so later in this chapter. You can even code NPC dialog windows with ease in 3D GameStudio, similar to the pop-up windows favored in most role-playing games. Of course, probably the simplest interface would be a short text message, either when interacting with NPCs or when clicking on objects. I will show you different ways to accomplish these coding issues later in this book.

In Summary

Games would be pretty boring if the player could not interact with them and perform the actions they want to perform. Thus electronic interfaces are vital to the playing of video games. The development of these interfaces—their ease of use, intuitiveness, and overall performance—can prove the success of a best-selling game or lead to derision and disgruntled players.

What You Have Learned

A game supports gameplay through its clever interface between player and machine. The following are things you should have learned about electronic interfaces:

- You now understand the principles of GUI and HUD panels.
- You have learned that interfaces must be easily scannable.
- You have learned the many types of different game interfaces.
- You have a firmer grasp of how to come up with and design interfaces.

For Review

1. Play one of your favorite games or any popular game on the market. How does the game's interface enhance its play? Is it easy to use? What about it do you like? Are there some techniques you could use in your game?
2. Some games have a nearly transparent game interface, while others are much more complex, relying on the player to scroll through lists and open multiple panels to get to their object. The latter obviously doesn't follow Fitts' Law. Identify and describe two games (one that uses a transparent interface and one that has a more complicated one) and why you think the developers made them that way.
3. Your client wants you to design a GUI for their new game. It is meant to be a hardcore action game, featuring lots of aliens and monsters for the player to kill. Design some thumbnails on paper of what you would see the onscreen GUI (including HUD) being composed of. What sorts of color choices and textural effects would you apply?
4. Another client comes to you wanting you to develop a mock-up of a GUI for their game, which is similar to *Pajama Sam* and features a young boy who goes on amazing journeys through a wonderland world. The game's target market is for ages 3 and up. Design a rough draft or color mock-up for this game.

5. For the original game that you would like to develop, make a flowchart of menu actions and several thumbnails of potential GUI screens. Choose one of the GUI screen thumbnails and develop it into a full-color mock-up. Describe the textural effects, mood, and appeal you wish to foster with your design, and why you made the design decisions you did.

Exercise 7.1: Scripting Your Action Game

This exercise is intended to take the model of Hector and the levels you created of the mansion and make a 3D shooter game out of them, plugging in the basic template scripts and making custom scripts. The electronic game interface will be similar to *Half-Life 2* or *Doom 3*, and we will also allow for a third-person camera view. During the following lessons, you will also learn how to do the following:

- Create player and enemy entities
- Blow stuff up
- Create animated doors
- Play audio in your game
- Move from one level to the next
- Design a HUD
- Give the player power-ups
- Make entities interact with the player
- Design a nifty splash panel intro

When finished here, you will not be a true expert, but you will have a strong grasp of the most basic templates and options that 3D GameStudio offers. This will lay the groundwork for Part III of this book, where you will create puzzles and build an adventure game, as well as Part IV, where you will create a role-playing game. There you will learn more complicated scripts and how to program levels practically from scratch. You will also learn how to build outdoor levels, with weather and less simple enemy Artificial Intelligence programs.

Creating a Player and Enemy Entities

For now, let's open the Level Editor and go to hex.wmp level.

Note

To have a Behaviors list for entities, you must have a script attached to your level. To have a script attached to your level, you must save your level with a unique name while obeying proper file name conventions (no wild card symbols, spaces, hyphens, and the like). If you try to put an action to an entity and find no actions in the available list, the first thing you must check is that the level has a script attached to it by going to File > Map Properties. If there is a script attached, and there should be an A6 template script attached already, but there are still no actions, you might check that your script includes the other scripts we are going to be using (from the template folder), such as weapons.wdl and war.wdl.

Select your player model character (hector.mdl), then right-click and open his Properties panel. Under the Behavior tab, make sure that he has the PlBiped01 action selected. If not, you can click on the folder icon, scroll up or down the list, and find the PlBiped01 action in the handy alphabetical directory. If you scroll down a bit, you will see that there are many more skills (or parameters, if you like) that you can set individually, like the health and armor of the character. If you don't change anything, leaving the parameters at 0.00 or such, the default parameters are used, which are fine, unless you want to make the player more advanced.

The following are explanations of the player skills that can be set in the behaviors panel:

- **Health** and **Armor**—Sets (obviously) the amount of health and armor for your player. The default values are fine for our purposes, so you won't need to touch them.
- **ForceX**—Gives the forward and backward movement speed. Increase or decrease this value if you want the player to move faster or slower.
- **ForceY**—Sets the sideways movement speed (in other words, how fast the player strafes). Play with this value until the result fits your needs.
- **Pan**—Sets the player's rotation speed.
- **ForceMult**—Tells the player if it is supposed to slow down or accelerate while you press and hold the run/walk key (default key = SHIFT). The default value (0.5) sets the `always run` behavior that is used in most games, so you won't need to touch it for now.

- **Jump**—Sets the maximum jump height for the player.
- **Duck**—Sets the minimum height of the player while ducking (default ducking key = C).
- **WalkSwimDist**—Takes care of the animation speeds for walking (4) and swimming (040). A value of 15.040 makes your model look way better while walking, so let's use it.
- **RunCrawlDist**—Sets the animation speeds for running (6) and crawling (030). I recommend a new value of 22.030, which slows down the `run` animation, making it look good on the guard.
- **StandJumpTime**—Sets the animation speeds for standing (4) and jumping (020). I have used 20.030 here, slowing down the standing, as well as the jumping animations.
- **AttackDuckTime/DeathDamageTime**—Work similarly to StandJump-Time; you don't need to make any changes here at this stage.
- **RunThreshold**—Tells the player at which speed (quants / frame) it is supposed to change its animation from walking to running and back. The default value (12) is good, but feel free to play with it if you don't like it.
- **TriggerRange**—Sets the player's trigger range, which is used to trigger events. We don't know what to trigger yet, so let's ignore TriggerRange for now.

You can only have one player character in each level; the engine will not know what you mean to do if you place more than one player-controlled character in a single level. It is illogical to assume otherwise.

Now that you have a proper player character, you can move around the levels, observing your HUD for changes to your character statistics (such as health, armor, weapons, and ammunition). You also start with several weapons.

Let's go ahead and create an opponent for Hector to face in this level. Enemy AI is tricky to get just right, and the template AI needs some work, but we will focus on that later. Right now, you are just setting the stage and testing out the initial behaviors. So add the bot01.mdl to the level, place it in front of the room with the staircase, and in its Properties window assign it the `AIFPS01_Guard` action. You could theoretically use the other enemy code, `AIFPS01_Hover` action, but this code is meant for an aircraft that shoots its weapon at the hero and explodes in a fireball when beaten.

You will notice that after you have set the action for this entity that you can set skills for your opponents, too. The parameters work the same way as with the player. The only difference is that you can set the alertness, accuracy, and cowardice of an enemy AI. Alertness sets the range in which the enemy will notice the player (default is 1000 quants). The enemy won't notice the player if the player has not entered his line of sight: for instance, the enemy can't see through thick geometric blocks, and he won't see the player while he has his back to the player. If you want the enemy to be "blind," you can actually enter a negative number for alertness. For now, set alertness to 20.

The default value for accuracy is already set pretty high; the enemy's shooting will be hard for the player to miss as it is. If you enter a negative number, the enemy has perfect aim every time. With cowardice you can make the enemy run away when his health drops below a certain number. If you want the enemy to be stalwart and fight to the death, enter a negative number. The default lets the enemy run away when his health drops below 30.

Save your level, compile it, and run it to test your latest entities out (see Figure 7.4). You have not actually changed any level geometry, so when you hit Build you can select Update Entities to speedily compile your changes into a working WMB file

Figure 7.4
Testing your level

instead of performing a longer (default) build. Press the Q key to bring your weapons up, press the E key to cycle through your available weapons, and press the R key to reload any of them when needed. Click on the left mouse button to fire your weapons. Notice that when you get hit by the spider enemy, a red flash will light up the screen. Hit the spider model a few times and watch it die; `AIFPS01_Guard` sets it so that when the spider dies, it will display its death animation, have a blood puddle spread out from underneath it, and then slowly fade away. As soon as the spider is dead, the player can walk right through it because it is no longer read as a virtual object.

Script Terminology

All of the following information is repeated elsewhere within this guide, but here they are condensed for your ease of reference as you begin to code your game.

- **Expressions** set the parameters of given placeholders. Most expressions are just numbers or variables. Some expressions are switches that are either OFF or ON or TRUE or FALSE. These are used liberally through C-script to alter the effects of actions.
- **Variables** are place holders for information, and they can store numerical information for use as parameters in your game. Common variables used are `bg_color = 255` or `my._health = 100`. You can set your own variables by typing `var variable_name = #;` outside of a function or action, preferably at the beginning of your script just after the includes.
- **Paths** set your file structure and where your program looks for files you might reference. Paths can include a long directory structure, such as path `"C:\\Program Files\\GStudio6\\template_6\\models";` or a short directory structure, such as path `"..\\template";` However, you must always use \\ to represent folders.
- **Includes** call forth other scripts. You typically set includes at the start of your script, and they appear as include `<war.wdl>;` You can also call other operations inside functions and actions. These are sometimes referred to as includes, although they are not separate script files. Calls are written like `gun();`
- **Actions** set up behaviors that are ready at run-time. Any scripted action can be applied as a behavior to an entity in your level. Most actions call other actions or functions inside them or change the definitions of variables. An action is typically written as such and its routines are enclosed in brackets:

```
action my_player()
{       my.fat = off;
        my.narrow = on;
        my.trigger_range = 24;
        my._movemode = _mode_walking;
        my._force = 0.75;
        my.__trigger = on;
```

```
    my._health = 100;
    player_walk();
}
```

- Note that `player_walk();` calls that particular action within the `my_player` action.
- **Functions** are scripted behaviors that are not apparent at run time but can be called at any time by an action. Functions are typically written as such, and its routines are enclosed in brackets:

```
functionfade_dust()
{
      my.alpha -= 0.3 * time;
      if (my.alpha < 0) {my.lifespan = 0;}
}
```

Most of the custom scripts you create will have two parts: a function that relates the relevant parameter shifts and an action that sets up the conditions whereby the entity will react to the player's movements and call the function. Just remember to type the function before typing its action so that the program will know which function it is trying to reference when you call it.

Exit the test game, and open your hex.wdl script in the Script Editor. The easy way to do this without leaving WED is by clicking on the Resources tab in the Project window and expanding the hector and scripts directories. Find hex.wdl at the top of the scripts directory tree, and double-click on the file name (or right-click on it and select Open). Last time you added work paths to the script so that the machine would be able to find the model files. Now you are going to add some custom behavior scripts.

First, just after the includes, type this in:

```
include <camera3rd01.wdl>;
```

This will set up a third-person camera mode for your game. You merely have to press F7 while in the game to zoom out to a position behind the player character. You can still pull out weapons with the Q key, cycle through the available weapons with the E key, and reload with the R key—but now the weapons will be invisible, and the player character will be seen going through its attack animation when you fire a weapon by left-clicking the mouse.

Return a few lines after the includes, and type this in:

```
var video_mode = 8;
var video_depth = 32;
var video_screen = 1;
```

`Video_mode` sets the screen resolution. 6 = 640 × 480, 7 = 800 × 600, and 8 = 1024 × 768. `Video_depth` sets color depth. 32-bit resolution is the standard for almost all video cards. `Video_screen` (when set to 1) starts the game in full-screen mode; if it is set to 0 (the default), then the game will start in window mode every time.

Go down the script to the main function, and you should see this:

```
//+++ load starting values
```

Return a line directly under that, and type in the following (exactly as you see here):

```
fps_max = 70;
bg_color.blue = 5;
```

`Fps_max` is fairly obvious; fps stands for "frames per second" and 70 is a good round number.

Note

It was the late 1930s and Walt Disney had just started production on the first full-length animated feature film. It would be called *Snow White and the Seven Dwarfs.* There was a lot riding on this film, and for animators at the time, the project was a triumphant undertaking. Months before its release, critics said that a person watching a full-length animated film in a darkened movie theater could suffer damage to the optic nerve of the eye or have seizures. Being an ethical and honorable man, Disney hired a medical consultant to look into the matter. After close study, the optician determined officially there was no evidence of optical damage to the viewer whatever–that animated films were no different to observe than live action. Amazingly, the optician went on to report that the human eye could only see about half the scrolling frames anyway. Asked what he meant, the optician stated that although motion pictures at the time ran at 24 fps, the human eye only saw about 12 fps! Animation producers had been using 24 drawings for each second of recorded film at that time. Disney decided to put the optician's words to the test. The camera department pulled the last scene from *Snow White* and removed every other cel before reshooting the scene. When the two films were screened, no discernible difference could be made between them. Disney cut his production and the time it took his animators to draw the movies in half without compromising picture quality! TV typically runs at 60 frames interlaced. Computers run higher than that, and game engines can run even faster. However, the higher the fps of a program the more flicker the human eye will be able to detect, and so programmers insist on slowing down any given program by slowing the fps. Setting the fps of your game at 65, 70, or 75 is standard.

The last variable to set is `bg_color.blue`, which stands for the blue component of the game's background color. Whenever a game does not have a skybox set surrounding the environment (like this one), it is smart to set up a background color. Otherwise, the engine does not know what to fill the void with and interpolates between the last visible edges of your level geometry and the space beyond, which can look really weird. Background colors have three components—blue, green, red—that each correspond to the 0–255 color spectrum of the 3DGS engine. Setting your blue color component to 255 will be interpreted at run time as pure blue, and setting it to 5 will turn it black.

Any other scripting you wish to do can be inserted in a "safe zone" of the code, so as not to cause errors on rendering (see Figure 7.5).

Save your hex.wdl script, and test-run your level inside WED when you are through. You do not have to perform a new build of the level when you have only altered the script; the script is applied at run time externally and does not change anything but the available actions list in WED. The only time you have to worry about the level when you have altered the script is when you have added or

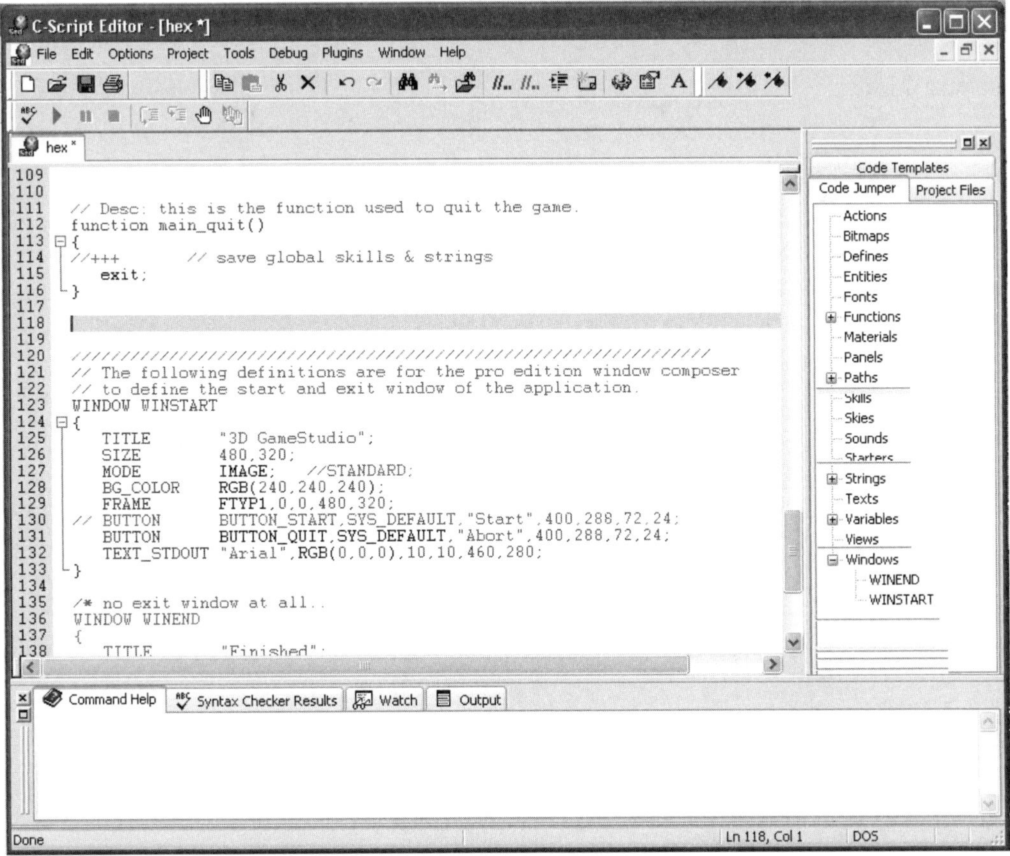

Figure 7.5
The "safe zone" where you can type new scripts

updated the actions; then you want to go to WED, save your level, and re-open it to refresh your available actions list for entity behaviors.. If you want to avoid the permanent refreshing, you can also set to Auto the Reload Externally Modified Files box under File > Preferences. All other script changes are applied instantaneously when you run the level.

Note

Watch for bugs; the de-bug script that should be running on start-up checks for broken items, buggy scripts, and missing links. The most common error is when you have misspelled a variable or action line–or when you have left off a semicolon at the end of an operation. If bugs are detected, 3DGS should report what line and what code script the bugs were found in individually by item. You can go to the script and look them up. Sometimes there will be only one semicolon out of place and you will get a cascade effect, which means that the bug report will show hundreds of errors. You can press ESC to abort the start-up at any time, then find the bug, and fix it before you try running the level again. Testing levels will become half your workload, and finding errors before they start a cascade will become your mission. Always remember to check your spelling and your code for errors before hitting Save, and it will save you a lot of time!

Test out your new third-person camera mode that you have created. Hit the F7 key to cycle back and forth between first-person and third-person mode.

You can customize the weapon models by finding them in the template_6 folder and replacing them, keeping the file names accurate. Another task would be to customize the crosshair used to fire on your opponent with; the crosshair is named crosshair_64 × 64.tga and is found in the template_6/images folder. Be aware that the crosshair is in TGA and has an alpha channel that handles its transparency. You can update the TGA file's alpha channel after changing the look of the crosshair, or you can save it as a PCX and update the code to display it. The PCX file will turn areas that are pure black transparent as well (see Figure 7.6).

You have created an opponent for the player and a weapon to fight with. You have trained in the ancient and violent art of making a shooter. Yet a shooter

Figure 7.6
An example of alpha transparency

Figure 7.7
Experimentation is the mother of all devastation!

would be pretty boring if all it possessed was one opponent and a single level to run and hide in. It's time for you to go for the jugular, so to speak (see Figure 7.7).

Blow Stuff Up

Yes, the exploding barrel is a cliché of games—but what would an action game be without shooting and blowing stuff up? Explosions cross media barriers between action films and action games and are observable standard expectations. So now let's look at how you can create an entity that can be destroyed without having health like the enemies do.

In hex.wmp, add the model barrel.mdl to the level. Place it in the larger room, beside the door to the stairwell. Open the barrel's Behaviors and select AIFPS01_Hover for the barrel. Change its Armor_003, Max_force_x_003, and Max_force_y_003 to 0.00 (zero). Change its Hearing_029 and its Fov_029 both to –10.00 (a negative number). These changes strip a normally active enemy AI of its abilities to react to attack.

Save your level and build, updating just the entities. Run the level. Now you should be able to walk up to the barrel, shoot it a few times, and it will explode in a massive fireball (see Figure 7.8). This will be great for making some parts of the level apparently impassible, until the player realizes that she can shoot barrels to clear her path.

Figure 7.8
What would a game be without exploding barrels?

Create Animated Doors

You could create a sprite image (either BMP or PCX) and add a script that makes it disappear when the player touches it (also playing a squeaky door sound effect when it does so) and in a flash the avatar seems to have opened up a doorway on touch. I have done this in games to popular effect before, and it is pretty easy to do. The same applies to creating trapdoors in the floors of your levels. However, 3DGS has a really nifty animated door behavior programmed right in. All you have to do is place an entity into the level (preferably a WMB or map entity) and give it the door action. Let me show you.

In hex.wmp, measure the smallest squares on your grid to see how wide and high your doorway is (the one in the middle of the wall at the south-most hallway, the one with the wooden doorframe around it). Measure the squares, writing them down if you have to. Then open WED in a new window and create a new file.

Remember to set your Preferences (Snap = 1, Hollow wall = 4) and load the Interior WAD file in the Texture Manager.

Add a cube. Scale it to the exact height and width of your doorframe in hex.wmp. The depth is totally up to you, but I usually make doors thin (about half of one grid square). Set it to the Wood18 texture. For an added bonus, you can place a smaller cube with a metallic texture on it about half-way up and to the right on the door for a doorknob; however, this is just a detail for dressing-up your level because the program is not dependent on the door having a doorknob to work.

Optionally, you can go to the Prefabs folder in GStudio6 and find Door1 in the Portals subfolder; this is what I used, but I had to rescale it to fit the doorway space I had in my level.

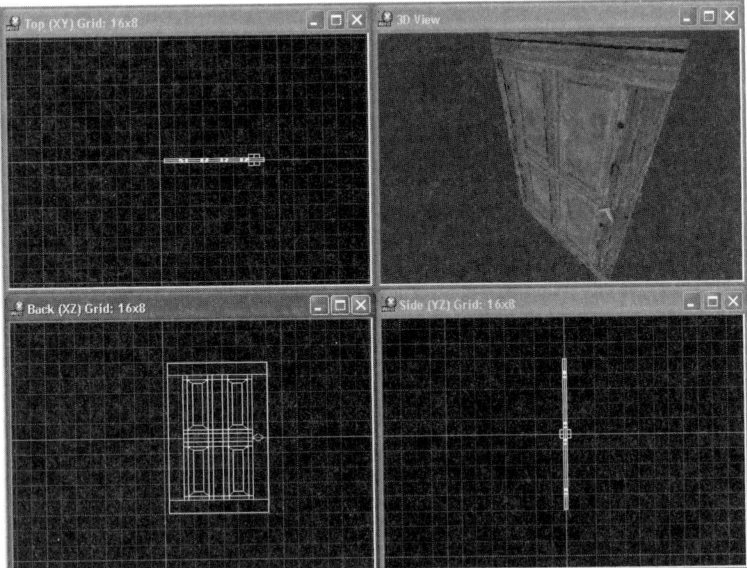

Figure 7.9
Creating a door map entity in WED

Position this door so that its edge is on the center origin. This is because WED interprets the X origin for the door's hinges when it runs the engine. See Figure 7.9 to understand where to properly place the door. When you have completed the positioning of the door block correctly on its origin line, save the file as **door1.wmp**. Build the level (it's not really an entire game level, since all there will be is a door, but this is necessary to create the WMB binary file that WED will interpret as a map entity), and then exit this level.

Back in hex.wmp, add the new map entity door1.wmb. You cannot stretch and scale map entities, which is why it was so vitally important that we got our measurements right from the start. Move the door into position in the doorframe you have just chosen.

Open File > Project Manager. This is the main window where you can manage all the A6 template scripts for your level. Under the Add tab, you should be able to drop down and review a list of scripts. Choose the one called Doors and Lids (01). The description dialog box just beneath the list menu should tell you that this script helps you "Make map entities into doors that react to activate scans." The box just beneath the description shows you the actions that Doors and Lids (01) will add to your available actions list. These include Door, Door Key, and Door01_TrekDoor.

Click Add New Script when you are ready and exit out of the Project Manager. The Project Manager has just made a dynamic change to your program script. Where you would have had to go into hex.wdl and add the line `include <door01.wdl>;` at the end of your list of includes, the Project Manager has done it for you.

If you have left hex.wdl open in a SED window, when you click back over to it, a message will tell you that the file has been modified outside the program and ask you if you want to reload it. Just click Yes.

In WED, select the door map entity and open its Properties panel. Under Behavior, select the action Door01 for the entity. Put a check in the boxes Use_absolute_00b and Use_sonar_00b. This will allow the player to walk up to the door and the door should automatically (depending on its origin) detect the player's presence and open.

Sometimes difficulties arise when using sonar alone to open a door in the game. It is far better to plan for this eventuality than to make compromises later. Open hex.wdl and scroll to the very bottom of it. You are going to write the following function:

```
function operate() // scan nearby doors or switches for operating them
{
	temp.pan = 120;
	temp.tilt = 120;
	temp.z = 150;
	scan_entity (camera.x, temp);
}
```

`function operate()` will scan for entities in front of the camera; if it detects any, and if those entities have scan enabled on them and are able to detect the player scanning them, then they will go through their subroutines (in this case, the door will detect the player and will open up for him).

Go back up to the main function in hex.wdl and type in the following after the `// +++ load starting values` line:

```
ON_CTRL = operate;
```

Note that you do not put parentheses () after `operate` here; to do so would alter the meaning of the call. Here I have shanghaied the CTRL key to do my bidding as a means of operating doors. You could use another key, if you like.

Save and build the level, updating the entities only, and then run it to test out your door. You merely have to walk up to a close distance to the door. The door should swing open on its hinges. When you get a door that you like, it is pretty simple to duplicate it and place it in multiple areas of your level. *Hector & Hex* has two levels that will require animated doors, so place them where you like.

Play Audio in Your Game

You can use noise other than sound effects in your game levels. For instance, you might want to use a sound track. You have determined what songs beforehand that you want to run in each of the levels, but only when you are in those levels. So we are going to use handles for each of the songs. You could use `media_play` or `media_loop` to play them. `Media_play` plays the streaming file once, and `media_loop` repeats it until told explicitly to stop. These media functions can handle all kinds of files, including AVI, MPG, WMV, WMA, WAV, MID, MP3, OGG, and more. You could also use `snd_play` to play sound files, as the example below shows. The files must exist in a path that you have already set at the onset of your script. You can also set individual audio volume of the stream, from 0 to 100 percent.

At the very bottom of hex.wdl, type this in:

```
SOUND my_song = "song1.wav";
function play_my_music ()
{
	my.event= NULL;
	wait(1);
	snd_play(my_song,50,0);
	ent_remove(me);
}

actiontrigger_music()
{
	my.INVISIBLE = ON;
	my.ENABLE_SONAR = ON;
	my.ENABLE_IMPACT = ON; // sensitive to plain touch
	my.event= play_my_music;
}
```

This effectively tells the machine to start playing the WAV song named song1.wav at half (50%) volume whenever they touch an entity that has the `trigger_music` action attached to it. You can add different songs for different game levels by duplicating this piece of code and renaming the action and function/event (plus the sound file used). Now to get this music to play, you add the versatile box.mdl which can be used as a prop for many different things, including invisible event triggers. Make the box.mdl twice its normal size, and move it to sit right in the center of the first doorway Hector will have to walk through. The sound is played and then the engine deletes the invisible trigger with the `ent_remove(ME);` snippet.

There are alternatives. Whenever you have the Commercial edition or higher, you can play music straight from a CD. This is highly effective if you want to play specific tracks burned to CD. All you have to do is type a bit of code like `cd_play` (# track to start with, # track to stop at).

Move from One Level to the Next

It is much faster, and easier on you and your processor, to build some small maze-like levels (as we have done here) and stitch them together fairly seamlessly through your coding rather than build one giganormous level that the Map Compiler has to churn through. I bear no ill will if you want to build large levels. Go right ahead. However, you might find yourself waiting for hours, or sometimes even days, while the level is compiled on your machine to the BSP tree. Calculating visibility of portals alone will take some doing, and God forbid that the compiler detects invalid brushes or planes!

Programming your game to jump the player through multiple levels, rather than letting him roam one giant outdoor level, is easier than the alternative. You are going to start by stitching together hex.wmb, floor1.wmb, and DMarena.wmb.

Open File > Project Manager, and click on the Add tab. Use the drop-down list to find Levels (00). The description box will tell you that this script "Allows multiple (up to 9) levels to be linked together. The player can pass between levels." Click Add Script to exit the Project Manager.

In the hex.wmp level, position the cube.wmb map entity inside the staircase. Apply the `Levels00_Exit_Pt` action to it. Make sure that Id_023 is set to 1.000 and Target_023 is set to 2.000. In floor1.wmp, go to where the bottom of the stairs are, where you want the player character to spawn, and place a cube.wmb map entity there. Apply the `Levels00_Entry_Pt` action to it, and make sure that its Id_023 is set to 2.000. If you had a player character set in floor1.wmp before, remove it.

Save, build (updating entities only), and run your level.

What you have just done is set up a gateway between one level and the next. You can use another script (teleport00.wdl) to create jump-gates within a single level, but to create gateways between two or more levels, you must use levels00.wdl.

Now back in WED, place another cube.wmb map enitity over the trapdoor, and attach the `Levels00_Exit_Pt` action to it, being sure to place its identity (Id_023) to 3 and its target (Target_023) to 4. You will create another spawn point in your last level, the death-match arena in the mansion's basement, and set its identity to 4.

Save your levels. Run your game. When you walk up to and touch the invisible cube, you trigger the function to load the next level. Run through each level, jumping to the next, to make sure that the code is working correctly. Now you have opened up an entire game of three levels, which you should fill with weapons, power-ups, and obstacles.

Design a HUD

3DGS has a built-in HUD panel that bears some resemblance to the hottest first-person shooter games' HUD panels (like *Quake*, *Deus Ex*, and *Doom*). This is brought to you in the script plBipedWeapHUD01.wdl and plBipedHUD01.wdl. Run your level again to see what this HUD offers.

It shows (from left to right) the player's health, armor, weapon type, ammunition, and reloads. It does so in pictographic as well as numeric readouts. The cross symbol beside the player's health is an animated HUD and represents the player's health state, changing colors the worse the player gets hurt, going from green to yellow to red. The player can glance to see if her health is going down—and if she wants to see the actual numbers, they will be there for her, too.

To customize the look of your player's HUD, you can open the original TGA image files, change them in a paint program, and save them with the same file names in your hector_hex folder. These TGA files are found in the Template_6/images folder and include healthHUD.tga, healthHUDicons.tga, ammo_hud.tga, and armorHUD.tga. Give each your personal flair (if you wish), as long as you recall that this file must retain the alpha channel (the pure black color) for alpha transparency. As you make changes, save them and test them out in the game level (there is no reason to rebuild your level, as you are only affecting changes to external files that the engine will load at run time only). This way you will know if you are making mistakes or getting your images out of proper alignment, and it will be easier to step back before you face disaster.

Give the Player Power-Ups

There are three types of power-ups common to every action game:

- Ammo
- Health
- Armor

Add the box.mdl to hex.wmp. Box.mdl is my catch-all model. It actually appears as a cardboard box, but it can become so much more! You can use the box.mdl whenever you need an object or want to try out a bit of code and don't have anything constructed ahead of time for it. This is potentially useful in many different ways. For one thing, I experiment with code a lot, and sometimes I will find just the snippet I wanted for a new object. Sometimes I won't. Using a catch-all object or stand-in model until I get the code just right saves me time and effort I might have applied to 3D modeling.

Once you've added the box.mdl to the level, right-click and under Behaviors you need to apply the `PlBipedWeap00_ArmP` action. `PlBipedWeap00_ArmP` is an armor pick-up item that will give your hero armor whenever she walks over it. You set the armor's effective armor range by adjusting its Amount_015 (which defaults to 35.000). Thus, if you type in 50.000, the armor entity will give the player a maximum of 50 points in armor.

You can also set up an armor station by using `PlBipedWeap00_AUnit` in place of the `PlBipedWeap00_ArmP`; the longer the hero character is within touch range of the entity, it will play a sound effect and raise the character's armor level until it becomes a "dud." Build and run your level to test the effectiveness of both of these armor types. Armor goes down before health does—so the more armor a player character has, the less health the player will lose if she happens to get smacked.

Next you want to revive Hector's health if he gets hurt by enemies or explosions, so you have to set up health items. Bring in a bottle.mdl and give it the `PlBipedWeap00_HlthP` action. When you build and run your level, take a little damage first and then run over to the bottle.mdl. Pick up the Boo-Coo health drink by running over it to restore some of your health (the exact amount is set by the Amount_015). You can set the fizzy health drink where it appears more realistic, like on the floor or on a table. Make details like these power-up items easy on the player, and place them where the hero can get to them.

You have created a health pick-up item. You can also create a health station, where as long as the player character is within touch range, she will raise her health until the station is tapped out (the actual amount is set, just the same as the health pick-up, in Amount_015). Instead of the `PlBipedWeap00_HlthP` action, use the `PlBipedWeap00_HUnit` action.

It is doubtful that you have played through your short game demo enough to run out of ammunition, but your player (especially of your finished games) might—so you need to set up ammo boxes throughout the levels. Place them where they would be found naturally. Don't even think about sticking ammo boxes in the center of oil tankers or out on mansion balconies. Place a box.mdl into your level to practice with. Apply the `PlBipedWeap00_AmmoP` action to it. The player will be able to run over this entity and pick it up, giving her added ammo for one of her weapons. The Type_015 setting determines which weapon the ammo is for. Experiment to get an idea of what ammo boxes could do for your game.

Make Entities Interact with the Player

Besides enemy AI alone, you can program objects that hurt the player's hero whenever the player is foolhardy enough to come too close to them. These are obstacles and can greatly enhance the game's challenges and difficulty (and conversely the player's sense of rising enjoyment). Streams of lava, toxic sludge, swinging pendulum blades, poison gases, and biting spiders are staples of many of the most popular games. The following are the two types of harmful objects we will code:

- Objects hazardous to touch
- Harmful objects in motion

You will use a bit of code reserved for the lava, toxic sludge, and other hazardous materials so that they will hurt if the player touches them. However, Hector is part vampire, so what you are going to make will be rays of sunlight in the first level's hallway. You have probably run the level enough times to see that the windows with the boards over them need dressed up a little bit more. Remove the boards sprite from every other window and add the model beam.mdl to your level. Beam.mdl is a cube that was made in MED and tilted at an angle to look like a ray of light. A bright gauzy texture map is applied to it.

Arrange beam.mdl to connect the window to the floor. You want the beam.mdl to extend a little past the window opening and through the floor, so some Scale might need to be added to it. Position it correctly, then in its Properties window, click on the check box next to Transparent. Build your level, updating entities only, and run it to see what your ray of light looks like. Each ray of deadly sunlight looks filmy and semi-opaque. This is perfect. Many designers would also place an animated sprite of dust motes inside the beam to further the illusion. You may do that later if you wish.

Next you need to create a `Behavior` action for the beam. You want it to hurt the player character whenever Hector runs into it. Open File > Project Manager and under Add, use the drop-down list to find Traps (00). Read what it says in the description dialog box before you continue. It says that Traps (00) "Allows' 'Traps' to be added to the level that can damage the player and AIs." Click Add Script to exit the Project Manager.

Select one of the rays of sunlight (the beam.mdl) and apply the action `Traps_ImpactDamage` to it. Do the same for the remaining sunbeams. Save and build your level (updating the entities). Run it to see how this works. When Hector gets near the sunbeams, a red flash will light up the screen and Hector's health will drop considerably; it will continue dropping the longer Hector stays in contact with it.

Exit the test run. You want to create some evil slicing blades that hang from the ceiling, don't you? Pendulum-swinging sabers are fascinating and difficult to navigate around. Most games that feature them time them just so the player can (with a little patience) run through them without getting hurt. I want you to attempt the same.

In hex.wdl, type this script in just after your dangerous action closes:

```
SOUND slice = "impact.wav";

function cut_player()
{
	ent_playsound(me,slice,200);
	IF (you == player)
	{
```

```
        your._health_003 -= 5; // player gets hurt 5
    }
}


action slicing_blades()
{
    my.enable_impact = on;
    my.enable_entity = on;
    my.enable_push = on;
    my.push = -5;
    my.event = cut_player;
    while (1)
    {
        my.skill20 += my.skill1 * time;
        MYmy.roll = ang(my.skill2 * sin(my.skill20));
        wait (1);
    }
}
```

Notice that the `while` statement sets the `while` parameter to 1; this would crash with a loop error if it were not ended with the `wait (1);` line at the end, before the bracket is closed. `wait (1)` determines the loop to pause until the next frame. Also notice that when the player gets hit or pushed by the blades, Hector's health will be dropped by 5 each time he's in contact with the swinging blades. Just like the sunbeam's code, you can change the number 5 into whatever you feel adequate, but experiment by testing it often in the Level Editor.

Add the map entity blades.wmb, and attach to it the action we just created, `slicing_blades`. In its Properties panel, adjust Skill 1 to 20, Skill 2 to 30, and Skill 20 to 5. This sets the script up because, if you noticed, the script depended on these skills to be set to positive integers to run correctly. Place the blades.wmb around the corner from where Hector first spawns, in the hallway there. The top of the blades.wmb should reach the ceiling. The blades.wmb should also be centered between the opposite walls of the hallway and rotated so that it looks ready to swing side to side. When you build and run the level, you should see that the blade swings crossways. If you duplicate blades.wmb so that there are three of them in a row and rotate the middle one 180 degrees, you should have enough randomness to make the player nervous. Test it out (see Figure 7.10). If you cannot get Hector past the slicing blades by crouching under them or by timing it and running past them, then rearrange your blades.wmb or adjust the script.

Figure 7.10
Slicing blades are such a cut-up.

Spinning saw blades in the floor are also common staples of action games. When the player touches them, he gets hurt. The player must avoid them at all costs. You can use the following snippet of code (with many thanks to George Pirvu) to make spinning saw blades that cross the floor, rebound off the walls, and cross the floor again. To keep the saw blades in place, the best thing to do is lower the floor that they are on. They are not programmed to go up steps or walls, so they will remain in place. If you mistakenly leave a leak in the room, they might sail out of the level, so be careful with them.

Also, notice that they have defined speed and use `c_move` for motion and `ent_animate` to animate through the `"walk"` cycle.

```
///////////////////////// DEADLY SAW BLADES IN FLOOR ////////////////////////
function hurt_them();
SOUND gotcha_wav = "gotcha.wav";
var saw_speed[3];
var in_front[3];

action deadly_sawblade()
{
     my.overlay=on;
     my.enable_entity = on;
     my.enable_impact = on;
     my.enable_block = on; // for further use
```

```
    my.event = hurt_them;
    while(1)
    {
          saw_speed.x = 8 * time;
          saw_speed.y = 0;
          saw_speed.z = 0;
          saw_speed *= time;
          in_front.x = my.x + 40 * cos(my.pan);
          in_front.y = my.y + 40 * sin(my.pan);
          in_front.z = my.z;
          if (content(in_front) == content_solid)
          {
                my.skill40 = my.pan;
                my.skill41 = 30 + random(90);
                while (my.pan < my.skill40 + my.skill41)
                { my.pan += 5 * time; wait (1); }
          }
          else // free to move
          {
                ent_animate(me,"walk", my.skill20, anm_cycle); // play the
"walk" animation
                my.skill20 += 10 * time;
                my.skill20 %= 100; // loop
                      result = c_move (me, saw_speed, nullvector,
ignore_passable | glide);
                IF (result == 0) // got stuck?
                {
                      saw_speed.x *= -1;
                      my.skill40 = my.pan;
                      my.skill41 = 30 + random(90);
                      while (my.pan < my.skill40 + my.skill41)
                      {
                            my.pan += 5 * time;
                            ent_animate(me,"walk", my.skill20, anm_cycle);
                            my.skill20 -= 10 * time;
                            my.skill20 %= 100; // loop
                                  c_move (me, saw_speed, nullvector,
ignore_passable | glide);
                      wait(1);
                }
                saw_speed.x *= -1; // restore the initial speed
          }
```

```
        }
        wait(1);
 }
 wait(1);
 }

function hurt_them()
{
        wait(4);
        if (you != NULL) // collided with an entity (the player, a monster, etc)?
        {
                snd_play (gotcha_wav, 50, 0);
                your._health__003 -= (5);
        }
}
```

Attach the `deadly_sawblade` action to your sawblade.mdl that you place in one of your rooms to try it out, and watch out! It will sweep across the floor of your game level; and if you happen to come into contact with it, you will hear a nasty noise and your health will drop considerably.

Design a Nifty Splash Panel Intro

Open the Project Manager again. Under the Add tab, find the Start up screen(s) script that describes that it can help you "Define the start screens (up to 2)." Add this script, and exit the Project Manager.

Run the game to see what it does. You will see two splash intro screens fade in and out before finally opening the first level of your game. This looks really professional. Now all you have to do is customize these screens. This uses the logodark.pcx picture in your Template_6/images folder for the initial start-up screen and logolite.pcx for the second screen. If you want to add your own pictures or information to either start screen, like the intros to most of the games out there (which usually display the developer's and producer's names before revealing the title screen), you can open logodark.pcx or logolite.pcx in any paint program and type your name and information, such as "Mike Duggan Presents. . . ."

Depending on whether or not you have the Commercial or Professional edition of 3DGS, you might be required to show the A6 logo somewhere during the startup of your finished game. It pays to show some pride in the game engine that has allowed you to complete these projects. Save the images locally in your hector_hex folder. You do this so that when the machine reads the script it finds the image in the nearest folder first (which is preferable to simply overwriting the file name completely, thereby destroying your only backup).

Run your level to see the new all-improved opening sequence. You might want to put other images in these start screens or even a quick play guide. If you wanted to, you could even play a song at start-up during this splash screen sequence. Use your imagination, and see what you come up with.

In Summary

Okay. From now on, you're on your own. You are now able to do more with 3DGS than you imagined when you started. But there is still so much more you can do. Some things I will show you when you learn how to make a role-playing game. Some things you can find online at the 3DGS community forum or at the company Web site or 3DGSUV site. Some things you will have to experiment with and try on your own. Remember to take the coding slow and test often. That way you always know what part of the code the machine did not like, and it makes troubleshooting that much easier.

Some of the template script behaviors that I did not cover but look really good in games (just not *Hector & Hex*) include the following:

- **FXA_LightBlink**—The entity will flair with light and blink rapidly, like a burning-out fluorescent light.
- **FXA_Smog**—The entity is invisible and sends out plumes of green smoke from its origin. This is great for urban chimney flues or parked car tailpipes.
- **FXA_ShortCircuit**—The entity attached to it is invisible and shoots out electric sparks in a particle shower while playing an electric buzz sound effect.
- **Door01_TrekDoor**—Senses the player's approach and raises the door through the ceiling like an electric door (also plays a sci-fi sound effect).
- **FXA_ExplosionTest**—The entity is invisible and bursts into fireballs and smoke over and over again; this is perfect for putting animated fire on burnt-out vehicles in a post-apocalyptic setting.

Check frequently for updates because new changes to the template scripts will appear all the time, and you might discover even neater game features at your fingertips!

Part III

Making a Role-Playing Game

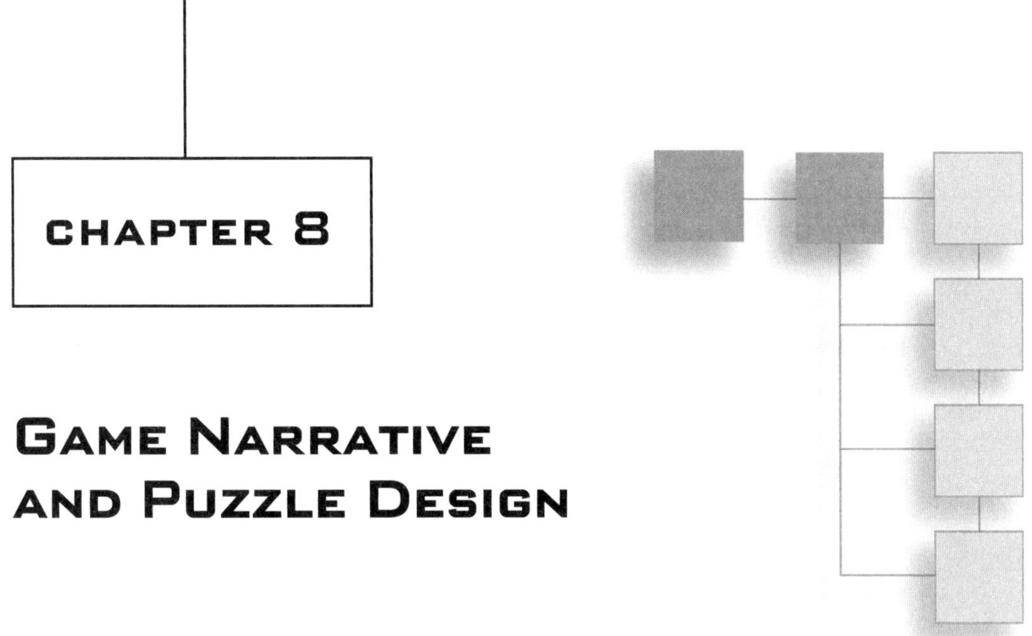

Chapter 8

Game Narrative and Puzzle Design

You have successfully created your first game (*Hector & Hex*) using 3D GameStudio software, so now you have a rough idea of what it takes to make character models, build indoor levels, and attach template behaviors to bring to life a fun action game. With this knowledge under your belt, you are proficient enough to delve into the cold caverns of one of the most venerable graphic computer game genres: the role-playing game!

History of Role-Playing Games

Your typical role-playing game (often seen as RPG or roleplaying game) is one of those pastimes that do not define winners and losers, as opposed to card and board games that were popular at the time RPGs were invented. In a role-playing game, several participants get together at a central location, often bringing snacks and rules system books, and collaboratively make up stories in which the characters they're playing take central stage. These participants determine the actions of their characters based on their characterization (what traits they possess), and their actions succeed or fail based on some outside luck-based system of rules, often printed in book format. Within the guidelines, the players can immerse themselves freely and do whatever they want (without "breaking character"). Their choices direct the outcome of these games. Thus role-playing games are closer to interactive or collaborative storytelling than to games—they depend largely on imagination, and interaction between the participants' imaginations is crucial.

One participant holds the fort down by assuming the role of Game Master; he does not actively participate in the game world but controls the environment, the enemies, and the obstacles the players must overcome. The Game Master sets the stage—he tells the players what their characters see, what they sense, and what happens to them. In many respects, the Game Master is the active computer interface that video games share.

Gary Gygax published the first commercially available role-playing game, Dungeons and Dragons, in 1974. He expected to sell only about 50,000 copies and was surprised when his game developed a cult following and a niche market. Dungeons and Dragons was the subject of controversy in the 1980s, when Christian extremists attacked it for having what they claimed was unsuitable content. The Tom Hanks movie based on the novel *Mazes and Monsters* did nothing to disparage this attack, but later academic research discredited all claims and proved to the contrary that RPGs were educational, honing both reading comprehension and arithmetic skills.

Computer games that started incorporating the settings and rules systems found in these role-playing games were referred to as CRPGs (or computer role-playing games). Due to the popularity of CRPGs, the term "role-playing game" became synonymous with its digital relative. As a result, the traditional tabletop non-digital pastimes of this sort (often referred to as *pen and paper* games) have shown a slight reduction in total number of sales.

Trends in Role-Playing Games

RPGs in the computer game market are booming. The popularity of such massive multiple-player online role-playing games (MMORPGs) as *EverQuest*, *World of Warcraft*, and *Knights of the Old Republic*, have given rise to several new innovative RPG systems. Online role-play has grown at an amazing rate and has expanded to other World Wide Web communities. Whether online or off, RPGs make up a significant portion of the video game market. They will be around for a long while.

Gameplay mechanics strongly associated with RPGs, such as statistical character development, have become widely adapted in other video game genres. For example, *Grand Theft Auto: San Andreas* has character traits and skills for how much body fat, muscle, lung capacity, weapon proficiency, and driving proficiency the player character has, and these change over the course of the game. These skill sets are often called *statistics* (abbreviated "stats") and are parameters within these games.

Through the course of an RPG, players are allowed to choose how they want to improve their character's performance. These improvements are given as rewards for overcoming obstacles (often in the form of *experience points*). The types of challenges that the player must face in order to win these improvements are sometimes focused on defeating enemies, while other games emphasize story through the completion of quests.

Regardless of the way in which a character improves, the player also has full freedom of movement. RPGs allow players to explore vast environments. Characters often have to travel long distances or wend their way through maze-like maps to complete their quests. Early games since *Akalabeth* featured two separate kinds of maps. When the player entered a city or dungeon level, the view was changed to the player view. While outside traveling the wilderness, the view was a bird's-eye one, and the player was a tiny dot whose every movement was restricted. This became the trend throughout most of the early RPGs, such as *Final Fantasy.* Today, however, players have more freedom to explore in fully 3D complex levels.

RPGs are not unlike adventure games because most RPGs have involved stories and plots, often in the form of quests. Often the player encounters several sub-plots or minor quests that allow her the option of gathering more experience and power.

Traits of Every Role-Playing Game

Every RPG has the same set of three major traits; a game would not be fair in the RPG industry without the designers giving each substantial consideration. When creating an original RPG, it is important to consider the following ingredients in this order:

1. **Setting**—Where does your RPG take place? Will it be in an abandoned Moon colony? In a far-flung jungle? In downtown New York City? The settings of most popular RPGs often take place in fantasy worlds filled with magic, but there are some that break the trend and are starting new foraging in the RPG future, such as *Knights of the Old Republic* which takes place in the intergalactic *Star Wars* universe, and *Vampire: Bloodlines* which is set in a dark gothic world of modern urban Los Angeles. Use your imagination.

2. **Roles**—What kinds of characters can the player choose from? Remember that for a role to fit and be serviceable, it must be a role that effects the

greatest change in the game's setting. The player must be the main character in the game narrative. Whether the player is the hero or villain is a matter of semantics. The typical RPG roles are rogue, fighter, wizard, ranger, and barbarian. Roles are determined by the setting chosen for the game, so these typical roles only really apply to fantasy settings. What about policeman, paramedic, news reporter, or hostage negotiator (if your setting were urban America)? What about space pilot, bounty hunter, or alien specialist (if your setting were in outer space)? Use your imagination and temper it with practicality to decide on the choice in roles.

3. **Skill sets**—Abilities, attributes, traits, stats, skills, and so on may all be synonymous, but RPGs use special parameters to define and track the development of the player character's role. To come up with skill sets, take a look at the roles you have decided on for your RPG. If you were to use a policeman, you'd need Firearms and Intimidation skills, but if you were a news reporter you might need Persuasion, Speech, and Appearance skills to get your job done. Additionally, most RPGs have some system for supernatural disciplines, such as magic spells, super powers, arcane tricks, and heroic abilities. Fantasy games commonly feature global stats like Charisma, Constitution, Dexterity, Intelligence, Strength, and Wisdom, and then have separate skills like Weapon Proficiency or Spell Casting that apply to specific roles only. What does your RPG have, and how does it relate to the setting and the roles of the people therein?

These are all very important traits, and without giving them thought, you would never get a proper RPG off the ground; but there are so many other elements that conventionally make up an RPG that you need to remember. For one thing, the players must be able to advance their characters, increasing their mastery in their role and raising their skill sets. This is done (as stated previously) through experience points or in-game training. Plus, a player character's skill sets does not a game make—the game must test the player character's skills all the time, motivating the player to make their character better all the time so they can hone their skills on these tests.

Role-playing games, by their very construct, allow the player more choices than other games; the best RPGs don't ever give the player the sense that she is "being led by the nose." The trick is to allow the player to choose the role for her character, what to spend her bonus points on to enhance her character, and even which alternative she wants to take in solving problems. When it comes to combat alone, some players will want to focus on stealth combat and scraping by under the cover of shadow. Some players will want to rush into hand-to-hand or melee combat and expect to face their enemies down. Some players may want to use only ranged combat, such as firearms or bows and arrows. Other players might want to use magic or their wits to get out of dangerous situations; these players will expect a varied list of spells or chances to use their charisma to bluff their way out of tight spots.

You have to take all of these player expectations into consideration and craft a multilayered game that whets their desires. Now this does not mean that you have to include EVERYTHING in one game. When Ion Storm made the *Thief* game, they wanted to make an incredibly realistic and fun game where the player has to play a sneaky cutpurse using ranged and stealth combat only; they did not waste their time on bluffing algorithms or magic spell-casting algorithms. They did what they did well, and the game became a sensation.

Figure out what you want to do, what you would find fun to build and play yourself, and do it well. You are bound to create a sensation, too.

Outline for a Role-Playing Game

The following game outline is also given in full description in Chapter 3, "Creating a Game Design." Some of the details and parameters of this game have been changed to fit the exercises that will follow and the length of time you will have to build the game.

Title: *Mama Kat*

Genre: Fantasy Role-Playing Game

Setting: The shrouded pirate city of Krawl.

Character: Kat, Mistress of Rogues (see Figure 8.1).

Premise: Considered a "monster" by others, you are a feisty girl who changes into a pirate cat every night. Try the unthinkable in the wharf-side sprawling city of Krawl—and become the Queen of Rogues! Use stealth, impish balance, pounce attacks, night sight, and your claws to take over Krawl and rule the Rogues' Guild!

Synopsis: The player starts out as the young freckle-faced redhead Katrina, as she is fished out of one of Krawl's canals by a trawling fisherman. She refuses to recall her past, but she mentions that a brute threw her in a potato sack and into the canal. The fisherman takes her home and takes care of her, but she soon runs away before he can learn that she is a cursed creature: a were-cat, able to change back and forth from young woman to able-bodied cat. By day she is a pretty redhead with an unruly attitude—and by night she is a slinky cat creature! She is missing one eye but wears an eye patch with a mouse skull on it; even with this handicap she has amazing abilities that allow her to escape down Krawl's winding alleys or over its rooftops. After exploring and getting into and out of several side quests, Katrina goes after the brute that threw

Figure 8.1
Mama Kat

her in the canal for dead—her father, the current Rogue Master who controls the guild of rogues. Her father ends up dead (one way or another) and Katrina becomes the new Rogue Mistress, having proven her merit and through inheritance.

For this particular game, you will construct a demo of one short mission—get the Ronal Ruby. Katrina the cat-girl has just discovered that a very important ruby has made its way into Krawl. It was aboard a plague ship, and her father the Rogue Master wants it BAD. However, before his minions could fetch it (because they were too freaked out to), the ruby was picked up by the crooked City Guards and taken to their barracks. Now Katrina decides to get the ruby for herself, before her nasty old daddy does.

Player Motivation: Enter the City Guards' barracks. Find the Ronal Ruby. Escape with life intact.

Target Audience: Players who love to explore will enjoy the many winding alleys and twisted walkways, nooks, and crannies of Krawl. Players who like puzzles and thinking will enjoy the locks that have to be picked, the goods that need rifled, and the fat merchants that need weaned from their golden tributes, all of which will take strategy. So the motivation for many players is already taken care of. When it comes to action, the game will keep players on the edge of their seats with adrenaline and suspense during chase scenes and swordplay.

On the demographic side, I imagined this game would attract those players who enjoy fantasy, do-it-yourself bravado, and the pirate theme. This applies to Generation-X as well as the Millennial Generation, with a brief nod to the Baby Boomers. That covers a wide scope.

Game Mechanics: The player's character would have resources like Health (which depletes whenever the player is hit by a weapon or singed by fire) and Weapons (such as blackjacks, garrote wires, tranquilizer darts, poisons, and explosives). Health could be regained by eating mice, which would have to be caught running around in game levels. Weapons could be found, bought, and upgraded, mostly through underground black market dealerships.

There would be parameters to playing the clever feline cat-burglar, and they consist of Life, Strength, Reflexes, Picklock, Charisma, and Grey Matter; the rates of these would go up as the player earns experience in them, and the only way the player earns experience is by reading Tomes of Lore or training in them.

Game Narrative (or How I Put a Story to Tetris)

Note

"When I design an adventure game, I start by telling a story. I bring together a plot, detailed characters, and a conflict. Then I allow for multiple paths through the story. Finally, I add puzzles."

—Bruce Balfour

A movie is about a decent guy having stones thrown at him. We (the audience) watch with anticipation to see what he'll do. Games, on the other hand, are unique in that we cannot sit back and watch the action: the audience is a player who is that guy and must decide what that guy will do when the stones start being thrown. In literature, this sort of interactive fiction is most commonly a choose-your-own adventure. As I mentioned before, if you go to www.projectaon.org you will find several online Fighting Fantasy books by Joe Dever that you can study, for example. So how do you set up the stone throwing in an electronic game? The answer is very carefully and with a versatile game script.

A versatile game script must illustrate all the story paths that are taken throughout the game. Some of those paths depend on what actions the players take. If the player decides on Choice A, one path might be taken; if a player decides on Choice B, another path might be taken. The actions players take could be anything from particular dialog choices to outright physical actions (such as engaging in combat or entering doorways). The paths in a game script are always going to be reflective of a game's interactivity because the paths are chosen by the players.

You can write these multiple paths into a comprehensive storyline on paper using a charting method (the same way you would chart an algorithm or an electronic interface). Creating a flowchart with nodes representing deviations in the player's path can help you illustrate the game in a way that you and the rest of the team will not have room for waffle or doubt; if there is ever a question about what contingency should be planned, you simply refer back to your flowchart. Some developers prefer making a walkthrough instead. A walkthrough appears as a text translation of a flowchart. It is not a chart, but it describes the major twists and turns in your game and where scripted events take place.

You might not know this, but there have been several debates in recent years about whether story or interactivity is more important in games. Some people feel that a game's narrative is more important, and it's the dramatic tension that motivates players to stay engrossed in the events taking place on screen. Others feel that the strategies players use to overcome challenges in the game are more important, and it is the "player control" that truly immerses players in the game, making players feel that they are a part of the game world. Both people are right. Overall, you must entertain, tell a decent story, and allow the player to collaborate with you to bring to life a really great game!

This is not easy, but it does not have to be hard either. I will show you some of the tricks of the trade, how to make a game that satisfies narrative while providing an interesting game challenge. You will learn what scripting is, how to design proper challenges, and what not to do.

Note

"There are only two or three human stories, and they go on repeating themselves as fiercely as if they had never happened before."

—Willa Cather

Narrative, placed in this context, means the story elements as communicated to the player through a video game. Note that not every game has to have a great narrative. Space Invaders did not have a narrative. Tetris did not have a narrative. Half of the FPS games out there have horrible or non-existent narratives. Players do not think to themselves, "I want to read a good story. I better pick up my game controller." People read books when they want a good story. They play games to be entertained for a variety of reasons (motivations we have already explored in an earlier chapter). Some game experiences, however, lend themselves to better storytelling than others. Adventure games, role-playing games, and even some first-person action games can all relate narrative within the confines of gameplay; and if there was no plot behind them, players snicker and call them flat or derivative. Before you apply game-specific story devices to a narrative, it's important to understand traditional story structure (see Figure 8.2).

Figure 8.2
Hark! Y'all listen and I'll tell you a story.

Some Brief Terminology

Game narrative shares some terminology with fiction writing, with minor alterations to the media. Following are the terms that will invariably crop up over and over again while developing game narrative.

- **Characters**—The actors on-stage in a game. The main character (or player character) is often referred to as the avatar, while secondary characters, such as monsters, enemies, villains, allies, and henchmen are often referred to as non-player characters (NPCs) or as the AI (although AI, which stands for artificial intelligence, actually refers to the finite-state machine algorithms applied to the characters).

- **Story**—What happens during the game. Clock Tower 3D's story can be summed up as "A young schoolgirl finds out her missing grandfather was obsessed with ghosts, who are now hunting her, so she must run, hide, and fight back." Story is separate from the game mechanics and overall design because it can easily be transported across media.

- **Setting**—The world the story takes place in and that the characters share as actors on the stage. Setting for most games determines the game mechanics because setting defines the reality, character professions and races, the physical laws and metaphysical laws (for example, magic spells, spaceships, laser blasters, and so on).

- **Plot**—The driving storyline of the game, the path that it takes (which in game media is never linear but branching). Plot takes on many guises in games. Where fiction has a major plot and several engaging subplots, games have quests (also called missions or goals) and several smaller quests, missions, or goals along the way. Where plot in fiction narrative is obscure to the reader, plot in games often comes across as transparent, and the smaller goals are straight-forward and obvious so that you don't lose the player.

- **Cut-scenes**—The short in-game movies (often displaying CG art) that serve as the vehicle for exposition you find in other media. Cut-scenes often reveal clues, reward the player, give the player a break to stop and breathe before continuing the action, and continue the game narrative. A string of cut-scenes with high polish are called *cinematics* and can ride the line between acceptable game narrative and machinima.

- **Backstory**—The history of all the events that have led up to the current action of the game. This can be as far-reaching as the creation myth of the world composing the game's setting, or the abduction of a perilous princess the night before the player character wakes up. Backstory is sometimes shown in a cut-scene before the game starts or through game artifacts.

- **Game artifacts**—Those objects in-game that enhance or reveal story elements. This includes dialog with NPCs, reading diaries and letters, and stumbling upon significant weapons or items. These items of information divulge the backstory and current events of the game narrative.

- **Story arc**—A description of the curve of action within the story, often of the transformation of the main character but also of the minor changes in difficulty and danger. A proper arc rises in tension throughout the course of the story, and finally at the end there is a major climax followed by a denouement. Appropriate pacing and game flow is essential to capturing the story arc.

- **Climax**—The final showdown, the last battle between the hero and the forces of darkness. Fiction reaches climax when the main quest is answered and the hero reaches the conclusion of all his desires. The climax is perceived by the audience and if it comes too early or does not fulfill their hopes, then it becomes a bungle. A proper climax thrills and surprises.

Note

The number one no-no in developing game narrative is to have a predictable story. Symptoms include a player figuring out plot twists or who is the murderer before she is ever expected to. If these symptoms crop up, then you have just lost the player completely. She might become so bored with your game as to never pick up the controller again. Make sure that the player's character is fairly up to speed on events along with the player (so that the player does not feel like she knows more than her character), and place well-crafted twists and turns designed to surprise and delight throughout your game. Never let your game get dull.

Purposes of Game Narrative

Games specifically satisfy the player's need for everything to make sense; in other words, the game story forms a web of information that makes connections between what happens in the game world and what the player has to do there. Narrative also leads to further game immersion (where the player is so involved in playing the game that he forgets about his real-life chores temporarily). All this should go without saying. Narrative can also put the mechanics into proper context so that the player can intuit the rules system. When a goal given to the player has a fantasy context (for example, the player isn't playing the Red Dot holding the Blue Square but is in fact a Crimson Knight told to hold the Cerulean Court before the invading horde by his King Pompous), then the goal is one that is certainly more appealing and one that the player will work harder for, in part because of the perceived stakes.

Lastly, game narrative can be its own reward. A player may not come to a game intentionally seeking an involved story, but the story devoted to the game can present the player with more depth and appeal. Game narrative provides the player with moments of emotional intensity and gameplay possibilities that go beyond the static choices (see Figure 8.3).

Scripting Game Narrative

Writing for video games is a skill that borrows a lot from screenwriting for movies, simply because a video game is essentially a visual medium. Scripts for games also borrow from choose-your-own adventure games and tabletop RPGs because of their branching fluid nature; great game scripts appear like walk-throughs or flowcharts because they do not have linear progression through scenes but remain dependent on the player's choices. Game scripts are not for the writers but are rather the players' stories, as the actions of the player will determine the outcome of the plot.

Figure 8.3
Elder Scrolls IV: Oblivion (image courtesy of Bethesda Softworks 2005)

There are four main rules to writing game scripts:

- Keep the gameplay and mechanics in mind at all times.
- Ensure the writing relates to the gameplay.
- Use the narrative tools (like in-game artifacts) to tell the story.
- Accept that most of the story will have to be revealed in backstory.

A great screenplay cannot become a great game overnight because the game mechanics must be represented at all times. This rule exists because a game narrative's primary purpose is to put the gameplay into context for the player. Keep the narrative short and to the point. Long scenes of dialog and exposition are ludicrous because they would slow down and complicate the game, leading to bored players. The players want to play a game, they want to play a game continuously, and they don't want to sit and read a book or get the impression they are unwitting viewers of a movie. Keep the cut-scenes and dialog short and to the point. Keep most of the backstory to game artifacts that the players can read or overlook, depending on how much immersive story the players want.

Note

Where is the writer in a game studio? Sometimes the actual writing is outsourced when needed to develop the game story for a particular project. Often due to the importance of gameplay and stable mechanics over narrative, traditional writers are not always in high demand in the game industry. This is unfortunate and might change soon as more developers are attempting to integrate storytelling with gameplay for a more cohesive game experience. Right now, it is not all that unusual for the game designer or director to write the story, or for the members of the design team to write the story and dialog for their respective game levels and missions.

Tips and Tricks: Game Writing

- **Play games in your chosen genre**, first and foremost. If you are making an action game, play lots of action games. Play good action games as well as the most popular ones. If you want to make RPGs, play as many different RPGs as you can, and get a feel for what is already out there. Whatever the genre of games you plan to make, you must get a really good feel for that genre's market. Study the story devices and consistent trends in your chosen genre. If your genre does not have game narrative (which many action games do not), then make one up. Think to yourself, "Gee, why would a Marine Commander be down here in this dark tunnel shooting all of these aliens?" Place a story to relatively bland or generic games; have fun, liven it up, and you just might accidentally create the next plot for your game!
- **Think creatively all the time**. When you watch a really good movie or read a really good book, stop and ask yourself, "Would this make a great game?" Come up with the game mechanics that would go with it. Look at the storyline from every angle. There might be just one scene from a movie that you think would make a great game (in and of itself). If you think about the gaming aspects of every medium you come across, you might just stumble across the find of the century and end up with a bestselling game.
- **Write constantly**. Carry a pen and notepad with you (or in this day and age, a laptop computer) everywhere you travel. Write down all the thoughts that come into your head. If you are waiting in line at the grocery store and see a tabloid magazine that sparks a great game idea in your head, it's best to whip out a pen and paper right then so you don't forget it.
- **Brainstorm with others**. Hang out with the friends who share the same likes and dislikes as you, and chat about game ideas. Bounce ideas off each other. Eventually, you might come up with some truly original (and fun-sounding) ideas, then write them down. A manic laugh session over some pizza at your favorite hangout might incidentally spawn a best-selling game. Then you'll have to take your friends out to eat again when the game sells!
- **Don't panic**. Don't fuss too much over the game plot or worry that your story might appear lackluster, particularly if this is your first attempt. Remember to play to the strengths of your medium—this is a game, and therefore the gameplay and the mechanics of it must come first! If you try to sacrifice the role of the player's character or the intrinsic fun of the gameplay for your narrative, you are essentially burning the bridge for firewood! Roll with the curves, ham it up, and just have fun. If you are having fun making a game, it is near as like that the player will have fun playing it!

Most Common Plots

A plot is a container holding all the events that will occur within your game. These events are often referred to as *plot points*. Plot is a cohesive force that binds the separate levels and game elements into a central active substance. There has to be something that happens, something that gets the player motivated. This something should have a level of tension to it as well. Imagine that you constructed a mission for the player that read like the following: "Go to Ornery Cave and get the Scepter of Sam." The player goes to that cave, conveniently marked on his map, and returns with the scepter. End of mission. How dull would that be? Instead, you have the player go to the cave, and fight or sneak his way past a gaggle of Killer Geese. Then when he gets the scepter, the walls begin to close in. When the player gets out of the Ornery Cave alive, he is beset by highwaymen trying to rob him of the scepter. And eventually the player finishes his mission with a sense of fulfillment and pride. That is the manner in which plot must be kept in pace with tension; anything less will end with the player scratching his head, wondering what the point to your game is supposed to be.

Quest Plots

A quest features a specific mission, one that can only be performed by the player character. Quests can even become epic, lasting over many smaller missions and leading toward final victory. Quests are fulfilling staples of RPGs and many other game genres because they keep the player moving toward a single goal while playing the game. A *quest plot*, as the name implies, is the player's search for a person, place, or thing, tangible or intangible. The search for the Holy Grail is one of the most well-known quest stories. Alfred Hitchcock used to talk about the MacGuffin in his films. The MacGuffin is an object that seems to be important to the characters but is really of little importance to the director—because it is not meant to seem that important to the viewer, consequently (see Figure 8.4). The MacGuffin of the popular films *Raiders of the Lost Ark* is the Ark of the Covenant; it appears to be what everyone is fighting and dying for, but in truth it is the backdrop that all the adventure takes place before. If you wish to create a quest plot, you first have to identify what the MacGuffin you are going to use will be. This type of quest leads to mostly linear levels, as the player progresses from one area to the next in an attempt to get the MacGuffin. Sometimes, once the MacGuffin is found, the player then must do something else with it. This can lead to a further climax or denouement. In other words, the finding of the MacGuffin was a false ending; don't try this trick too many times or your players might get frustrated with it.

Example of a Quest Plot

The player is a novice thief and has just joined the Thieves' Guild. He has been told by his guild master to prove his loyalty by stealing sensitive evidence proving that the City Guard has been accepting bribes from northern barbarians. This evidence is kept in the Guard Captain's office, hidden somewhere beyond the

Figure 8.4
Searching for the MacGuffin

Guard barracks. The player sets out to find the evidence and prove the City Guards' corruption. (The evidence is the MacGuffin.) The player thus sneaks through the city, into the Guard barracks, braves City Guards, traps, locked doors, and other challenges, and eventually reaches the Guard Captain's office. The thief must locate the evidence. Once he does, the game lets him know that an alarm has set off telling the City Guards that something is amiss and posts have been redoubled. The player must make it out of the barracks alive and take the MacGuffin back to his guild master.

Pursuit Plots

Note

> "The English country gentleman galloping after a fox—the unspeakable in full pursuit of the uneatable."
>
> —Oscar Wilde

Pursuit can become a mission or just one of the side-quests. There are two games that never get old on the playgrounds of schools everywhere: tag and hide-and-seek. Remember the glorious excitement of being hunted or hunting someone else? These were tests of speed, cleverness, and nerve. As we grow older, we grow more sophisticated in the types of games we play, but the thrill at heart of playing these ages-old games never wanes. Pursuit is the game version of hide-and-seek or tag. The player must chase down a target, steal the Titan's Orb, or find a lost cat. Or the player must escape from the City Dungeons or sneak into the broken-down Manor without getting caught. Another example of pursuit as a plot is the rescue, which is quite common as a motivator in games. Rescues involve helpless people in distress requiring the aid of the avatar to save them from some nameless evil. A rescue is dependent on a character triangle: the person in distress who needs saving, the player hero, and the antagonist.

Example of a Pursuit Plot

The player is the same thief as mentioned in the first plotline; he got the MacGuffin to his guild master, only to be betrayed by the guild master. The player was captured and thrown in the City Guard prison. Fortunately, the thief was able to hide and retain one lock pick and use it to unlock his prison bars. Now the player has a new mission: to escape the prison with his life intact. There is an added motivation of revenge, which can be similar to a quest plot, as the main character seeks one single objective: to get revenge for what the guild master did to him. Right now the main plot will be the pursuit plot because, as soon as the thief gets out of his prison cell and starts sneaking in the halls of the vast underground prison, the City Guard discover his absence and redouble their efforts to find him; and this time they will kill first, ask questions later. The player must focus on a hide-and-seek game that will lead him further into the backstory.

Riddle and Mystery Plots

Note

> "The mystery story is really two stories in one: the story of what happened and the story of what appeared to happen."
>
> —Mary Roberts Rinehart

It's elementary, my dear Watson. A riddle or mystery also makes for a decent plot in games. What child doesn't love riddles? What adult doesn't care for the brain teaser or murder mystery to solve? They delight us by challenging us. A riddle is invariably a deliberate and enigmatic question. The words or elements of the riddle form the solution, but we cannot interpret them without clues. The mystery is a paradox begging a solution. Things are not what they seem on the surface. Characters lie and clues lie within words and pieces of evidence. The player must solve the mystery or work out the riddle by exploring the game

Figure 8.5
The classic whodunit

environments, putting the clues together, and eventually reaching the startling conclusion. Riddles or mysteries are becoming quite common in games because they keep the player guessing the whole time and the writer can surprise the player with unique plot twists along the way. However, do not kid yourself into thinking that developing a great riddle or mystery will be easy. It requires a lot of cleverness and the ability to temporarily deceive the player (see Figure 8.5).

Example of a Riddle or Mystery Plot

The player—still playing the thief in the first two game plots—escapes from the City Guard and the winding prison tunnels. The player finds himself back in the city and bent on revenge against the guild master who betrayed him. A cut-scene plays, and the player discovers the guild master and the entire Thieves' Guild have been brutally murdered, their bodies mutilated, and the City Guard completely unconcerned. Shadowy figures were last seen at the home of the guild master and his daughter, who the player's character was kind of sweet on. The guild master's daughter has disappeared. The player must now overcome this mystery: "Who killed the Thieves' Guild?" Other questions that must be answered include, "Where has my sweetheart disappeared to? Is she in trouble?" and "Who paid the guild master to betray me? Is there some connection to the invading barbarians?" The player must use his wits now more than ever and interview countless NPCs, uncover clues, and read people's diaries and letters in an effort to find his answers.

Transformation Plots

Another plot that is becoming fashionable in the dawn of next-generation gaming is transformation—where the player must grow, metamorphose, and become a better person. We humans constantly change. Our shape reflects our inner psychological idiom and the process of becoming who we are today. We may not be able to detect the subtle changes in ourselves, but they are there nonetheless and impact our future choices. The study of humanity is a study in change. This shared common experience can become the basis for games. Essentially, the player character starts as raw or damaged goods: a young peasant, a page, or a criminal. Over the course of her adventures, the avatar is transformed by doing good deeds and gaining experience until the avatar becomes a renowned hero. This is one of the plots behind the game *Fable*.

Example of a Transformation Plot

The player has discovered all the answers to his earlier mystery plot. The Thieves' Guild was betrayed by the guild master, who was paid off by the Captain of the Guard, who in turn is really blood-related to the invading barbarians and wants to make takeover of the city easier. The player has learned that the guild master's daughter has also been taken by the barbarians and is now outside of the city somewhere. This point is where the transformation plotline starts. The player learns he cannot continue as a nervy cat burglar if he wants to save the city he has come to call home. Not only is the Thieves' Guild gone, but the role of the thief will not protect the player character any longer. The player must seek out Simon, an eccentric and wise shaman-warrior, who will teach the player how to become a magic-wielding fighter. This process changes the gameplay and the way the character sees himself; he becomes a changed man.

Love Plots

One of the most difficult literary devices that we have come to expect of film and books to transform into a game plot is that of love. Essentially, this plot would boil down to the classic boy-meets-girl story, and then situations come up that prevent the love affair from reaching its fullest potential. The viewer would pine while watching friction separate two people who are obviously meant to be together. Either social norms keep them apart or their own follies. However, this plot is as yet one of the hardest to translate into a compelling game. Games that have twisted versions of love, like the Leisure Suit Larry series, often fall prey to pursuit rather than true love. Developers have tried multiple times without a recorded success to inject games with love stories. Yet when you consider that a romance should work well within the confines of acceptable adventure game genres and that the rising majority of players are women, a love story should spark some interest in the game market. Consider the conventions of love and game media, and see what you can come up with.

Example of a Love Plot

The player character (who has gone from ignoble cutpurse to noble spell-warrior) has defeated the Captain of the Guard, saved the love of his life (the daughter of the Thieves' Guild master), and returned to the city triumphant. Things have become rocky. Gertrude, the one the player's character likes, has been changed by her time with the barbarians in the wilds. She no longer believes the way the city's citizens do; and though she loves the player's character, she believes him to be her father's killer. The player cannot proceed with the game until he can convince her he's innocent—and not only that but profess his love to her. If he cannot do that, then he will lose all motivation and self-respect and will end up a drunken lout when the barbarians invade the city. Romance will win his self-esteem back and give him something worth fighting for.

Housekeeping Plots

This reflects the dungeon delver's delight. The player must clean out an abandoned warehouse overrun by ghouls, a dark dungeon filled with bogeymen, or an old mansion that has been cursed by a foul sorcerer and is doomed to be haunted by lost souls until someone unlocks the door to the Velvet Parlor. . . . Okay, that last one was a bit of a stretch, but you understand what I am saying. This is not the most literary of plots but finds its way into many game genres. Essentially, the player's mission is wrapped around total annihilation of some evil. This plot is also area-dependent—the player is stuck within a set space, and that space is filled with nasty monsters to be destroyed. However, this type of game plot lacks some real finesse.

Example of a Housekeeping Plot

The player has won the heart of his life, Gertrude, and she has restored his self-esteem. Before the invading barbarians can overrun the city he has claimed as home and has become the hero of, the player must now go into the wilds outside the city and defeat the barbarians on their own turf. Using a combination of stealth, spell-casting, and warrior skills, the player must deal with the barbarian horde and rid their curse before it is too late. At the end of the game, the player can retire comfortably with his new wife and take on the role as the new Captain of the City Guard.

Figure 8.6
World of Warcraft (image courtesy of Blizzard Entertainment 2006)

Other Plots

There are many other possible game plots that I have not mentioned here; most are derivative of the ones I have listed, but there are those that are used only under special story conditions. For instance, there is the supplication plot, where the player character is approached to be an intermediary between a victimized public and a harsh despot and appeal to the despot to give up. You might make up a great storyline and weave missions for the player through it that bears no resemblance to the plots gleaned here. This does not make those plots wrong at all. The more unusual and well-told your game narrative, the better it will do when players sell it by word of mouth (see Figure 8.6).

String of Pearls Method of Scripting

Jane Jensen, creator of the Gabriel Knight adventure game series (see Figure 8.7), developed a method early in her career to help herself in game plot design. This method usually pertains to puzzles and quest-driven games but works pretty well for just about any sort of game you can imagine. This is called the String of Pearls Method, and if you want to you can incorporate it into scripting your story.

The String of Pearls Method is easy:

- First, picture each major plot point as the a pearl on a string. Each plot point begins on one side of the pearl, coming from the string.
- The player takes control of the action and explores the pearl. He or she uses what they know—what you the designer have told them—and there may be

Figure 8.7
Gabriel Knight created by Jane Jensen

as many as three to 15 little scenes or side-quests the player can trigger. Let the player trigger these in any order; this is important because the game ceases being a static Point A to Point B sort of a game and takes on the illusion of a free-roaming game.

- Then—once the player has triggered all these scenes—the game registers the fact and comes back to a central story point.
- There is often a cut-scene, and the next pearl on the string is begun.

Case Scenario

Here is an example of a game story based on Jane Jensen's String of Pearls Method. It is a case scenario from a typical survival horror game.

The hero (a mercenary named Janice) is trapped in downtown L.A. surrounded by zombies. She has a Jeep Grand Cherokee in the garage to escape in, but the Jeep is out of fuel and Janice can't find the ignition key. We have started a pearl, and the player knows her goal: to assemble the components needed in order to continue the adventure.

The hero's companion, Blake, thinks he left the keys in another part of the level. They split up, the hero looking for fuel and Blake going back for the keys. The hero finds a fuel station a few blocks away, but the pumps are turned off and the electronic door to get inside is out of order. She can easily see why: the electric control panel is missing a fuse. The player will move on with her search. She stumbles into a room upstairs of the filling station and finds some ammo—and several zombies to be put down! Just as she's leaving, her partner Blake radios her, needing some real help. Blake found the keys to the Jeep, but is now completely surrounded by zombies, without a weapon, and is begging Janice to come to the rescue! The hero races to rescue her companion, and tension mounts. . . .

Once Blake has been saved (notice the girl character had to save the guy for a change, which is good because it is uncharacteristic of old vintage games of damsels in distress and keeps the game "fresh"), the player returns to the filling station with a working fuse to open the electronic door, but the door only opens a little way, and then becomes stuck. Janice can fit under the door, but Blake must stay behind. The door suddenly shuts, and the player finds they are locked in the fuel station! Imagine she also felt sorry for her companion and gave him her gun, so now the player is trapped and defenseless, looking for a way to turn the gas pumps on all alone in a storehouse filled with zombies!

Finally, after a lot of hard work on the player's part, she gets the Jeep and goes back to the filling station to fuel up and takes off just in time. The pearl closes and a new one will open, as the player discovers that the Jeep has a flat tire while driving through some zombie-infested forest. This example shows how the String of Pearls Method, along with a very simple component-gathering puzzle, can turn a plodding horror story around for a much more suspenseful and appealing spin!

Making Players Make Choices

Games have made players solve puzzles since the earliest text parser games, such as Zork. Besides the fancy graphics and level designs, there are two main things that must be present in games to make them rise to the top:

- Difficult decisions that have to be made (by the player)
- Tangible consequences in the game for decisions that have been made

Note

"Our species can only survive if we have obstacles to overcome. You take away all obstacles. Without them to strengthen us, we will weaken and die."

–Captain Kirk, ***Star Trek*** ("Metamorphosis")

This is what it is all about. This is what separates a game from any other sort of media (see Figure 8.8). RPGs like Dungeons and Dragons are a form of pen-and-paper games whose influence on modern and next-generation video games cannot be overlooked or underestimated. However, the biggest difference between tabletop and video games is that the narrative for video games has to be completely decided on and programmed before letting the player toy with it, while tabletop games are run on the imaginations of the Game Master and sundry players in an ad hoc fashion; the narrative starts with suggested possibilities and remains open-ended. Video games do not have that luxury, as you

Figure 8.8
Decision making (*Curse of Monkey Island*, image courtesy of LucasArts 1997)

may be learning. On the other hand, there is some joint partnership between you, the developer, and your future players.

You essentially must pass off partial control of your game and its contingent story to the player who plays the game. Doing this is exciting. It is even more exciting when you are watching the testers for the first time playing through your game—or when you decide to play through it yourself. The decision process will either rectify the graphics and sounds you placed in your game—thereby producing a comprehensible game story—or it will destroy the experience for good. When you are creating decisions for the player to make, you must remember a couple of rules that can save your game.

First of all, a decision must never be an uninformed one. In other words, you must give the player all the right information to make a proper decision when faced with it; if you leave out the fact that if she chooses to keep the Sword of Eons, she will have to slaughter her only surviving sibling, then the player will throw a tantrum in frustration.

Another example is this: Jim makes a game where the player must get into a locked research laboratory. The easiest way to do so is to go all the way around to the other side of the building and come in through a back door that is not locked. The player has a map to show her how to get there. She fights several alien monsters along the way and arrives on the other side of the labs. She must make her way through an antechamber filled with poison gas. She succumbs to the gas and dies before getting to the lab door. Just as the player watches her character croak her last, she notices a gas mask on the wall opposite that was hidden from view. The player will lose her cool and might even stop playing because she feels that the designer abused the situation. She has every right. The designer should have left clues that the gas was toxic. The designer could have even left the gas mask in a locker outside the antechamber for the player to put on before entering. Or the designer could have built in some breadcrumbs telling the player that she needed to get a gas mask before going into the antechamber and could find one at X location on the other side of the laboratory, causing the player to sweat as she fights even more aliens to go get it! Any of these changes to the challenge would have solved the fairness issue, and the last one would have even improved the game.

A decision must be a real one to make; don't form a hollow decision on a whim and expect the player to go along with it. For instance, if you give the player (who is trying to make her way down a dangerous dungeon corridor) the option of choosing which branch of a tunnel to go down, and later she finds that both branches go to the exact same place without any difference, then there was really no true decision to be made. The player will feel cheated. Likewise, don't make up obvious decisions. If you ask the player whether she wants to pick up the pile of gold or not, and there are no repercussions except that the player gets richer by doing so, then the player will pick up the pile of gold and be shaking her head in wonder at the stupidity of the game designer for creating such an obvious and hollow decision.

The best choices of all to present the player with are difficult choices, especially if there is a perceived tension surrounding the outcome of the decision. The most common decision that players make in a game will be, "Oh no! I am coming around another corner, and I only have two bullets left. Should I wait to reload?" If you do your job as a game creator, this in itself will become a dramatically difficult decision.

Here is a case in point: Say that the player has one golden arrow, which she is led to believe might be the last one because golden arrows are extremely rare. The golden arrow is the only weapon that can hurt the evil Lord Bone-daddy. Now imagine you (the game's creator) have scripted it where the player's NPC ally gets hit with a poison cloud and lies there dying. The player is informed that the only antidote for the poison is a golden arrow melted down and mixed with bitter root and sea water (what if?). The player could choose to save her friend and lose the only weapon she has to slay Lord Bone-daddy. Or she could knock off Lord Bone-daddy and let the fate of her partner be on the winds. This could be an extremely tense decision to make if you scripted it right, with tangible results either way.

Players will make the big decisions like this because they hope for (and have come to expect) big rewards. Every game is essentially a Skinner box, and if you understand the psychoanalytic theory, you will go far in the making of electronic games. Players will scrounge around until they find the "feeder bar" in a game, and then they will continue to hit the feeder bar once they discover it. It is up to you to make every reward count for something. Don't let rewards come too often, or they will cease to matter. Every reward should appeal to the player because it gets him closer to winning the game or because it is a romantically desired object (such as magic weapons or shiny treasure).

As mentioned before, players expect rewards. They can also be trained to expect punishments. Sometimes a device as simple as a cut-scene where a non-player character runs out into an open field, hits a trip wire hidden there, and is killed is enough for the player to react. The player will expect that there are trip wires hidden all over the fields that might destroy him if he is not careful. Use these expectations wisely to create interesting tension in the game. Similarly, you can set up better challenges by thinking the way the player thinks, essentially stepping into the player's shoes. By understanding the player expectations, you will know what challenges to include when.

Types of Game Challenges

Note

> "Fairy tales do not tell children the dragons exist. Children already know that dragons exist. Fairy tales tell children the dragons can be killed."
>
> –G. K. Chesterton

Most of the time, challenges take the form of obstacles that must be overcome. Either the player faces a horde of hungry zombies shuffling along a grainy windswept city street, or the player is trapped within a ski lodge during a blizzard while a serial killer erases each of the player's in-game allies one by one. These habitually appear as lock mechanisms, and players are used to them (and the standard manner in which the lock mechanisms must be unlocked). Lock mechanisms by their very nature fence the player in, preventing access to some area or reward in the game until that moment when the player beats the mechanism and unlocks the next area or recovers the reward. Some of these lock mechanisms can appear as prosaic as the common lock: a locked door, jammed gateway, or elevator without power stand in the way of the player getting to Level Three. Some of these lock mechanisms may be in the form of puzzles or mysteries, requiring deductive reasoning and clue-finding to unravel. Some of these lock mechanisms may be enemies or gargantuan monsters barring the only path to Level Three, which must be whooped before the player can progress. Whatever the lock mechanism you use, it is a powerful and absolutely vital tool in your arsenal of game story devices, and it should be enacted with intelligence and creativity to work right.

The following are many types of challenges you could include in your games:

- Ordinary and unusual uses of objects
- Alchemical puzzles
- Cryptographic/clue-driven puzzles
- Mental deduction puzzles
- Timing/sequence challenges
- Social/dialog puzzles
- Mazes
- Monsters
- Traps

Ordinary and Unusual Uses of Objects

A door needs a key. The player finds a key. The player uses key on door. This is the oldest puzzle used in adventure games to date. Lock mechanisms used in games date back to the earliest RPGs (tabletop as well as computer varieties). However, it can be so old as to weary our player. Jazz it up a little. Perhaps the player can see a key lodged in the keyhole on the other side. If the player can find something small—like an ice pick—he can push the key out and unlock the door. Other ordinary uses of objects could also be put to use. The elevator might be missing its battery, so the player has to find and use a battery to get the elevator running, for instance. Take another example: the player can see a cliff face two stories up that she has to get to, but there does not appear to be any way open to reach it. She finds a floating platform, but it is not operational. She must find a switch somewhere in the level to turn the platform on and get up there to the cliff face.

Unusual use of an object involves recognition of an object's secondary nature. A diamond ring could (theoretically) be used to cut glass, because a diamond is sharp. A bleach detergent could be used to whiten fabrics, if a player has to make a ghost's costume and all he has is a brown burlap sack. But the error with unusual uses of objects in adventure games is that sometimes the game's creators can go overboard. One of the most annoying examples was in one of the *Secret of Monkey Island* games, where you had to pair up a monkey with a wrench to create a spanner to throw into the works. (Get it, a monkey wrench? No, neither did most of the players out there.)

Alchemical Puzzles

Alchemical puzzles require the player to take one or more objects and put them together to form something that they need to use. For instance, in *Resident Evil: Outbreak* the player must find parts to a bomb, the detonator and wire, and arm it before the timer runs out so as to blow up an entire city street full of zombies. But you have to tread carefully here as well: NEVER assume the player will guess what parts go together to make what. Leave clues that spell it out to the player in an obvious manner.

Some of the best Flash games on the web that do this well are universal in nature too: there are rarely any text messages to be read. Many of them feature the player character as a diner operator or sushi chef, and the player is expected to take orders and create food concoctions within a time limit. The player is shown one to six image icons that show her what food ingredients need to be combined and who the combination needs to be delivered to, and the player is expected to fix the problem in an ever-increasing tense environment. These sorts of alchemical puzzles are in the form of casual games and are really very good examples of the type (see Figure 8.9).

Cryptographic/Clue-Driven Puzzles

The player must supply a crucial bit of info, such as a password, a key code, etc., to pass by a guard, a locked door, or to open a locked briefcase. To figure out

Figure 8.9
Just a bit of this and a dollop of that . . .

what the code/password/other is, the player must hunt for clues. These clues are often left laying around in convenient journals, computer e-mail, or other documents. The player may have to figure out what something cryptic means in order to identify a clue, such as a cryptogram or rebus. It could even appear as a simple algorithm written on the back of a bathroom stall.

The most difficult part about this is that the designer cannot rely on a casual gamer or below-average gamer to catch on or figure out the puzzle. Therefore alternate puzzle answers or clues should exist. For a case in point, think about this: the player discovers that the key he needs to get to the next level is gnarled in the roots of a large thorny plant that—from some experiment gone wrong—is alive and carnivorous. Elsewhere in the level, the player has obtained two base chemicals and a mixing jar. There is a computation written on the back of a bathroom stall that says, 1R + 2Y = G. The player may be able to figure out that this means to combine one part red chemical with two parts yellow chemical to create a plant-killer. However, you couldn't allow a bottleneck to happen in the game if the player wasn't smart enough to figure that out. So you would have to provide some more straightforward clues as well, or you could time the player and, if he still doesn't get it, you could script it where an NPC steps onto the scene briefly and spills the truth about the creation of the plant-killer.

Mental Deduction Puzzles

Related to the cryptographic/clue-driven puzzles, mental deduction puzzles cause the player to put two and two together to work his way out of sticky situations. There must be a cause-and-effect relationship between at least two things for this to work. For instance, if the player knows that every time he pulls out his magic sword a demon who hates the color green will burst on the scene, and the player is facing a green door that is locked and he cannot find a key for it, the player can deduce that if he uses the magic sword, the demon might show up and bust down the door for him. He tries it and it works. Good for him—but this could be very difficult for you the creator to set up. Try to establish causal relationships in your game, and emergent game play will do the rest for you.

Timing/Sequence Challenges

The player must identify scripted events in the game and use them to his advantage. In some of the oldest platformer games, players would have to watch moving platforms and jump on them at just the right moment to get across a chasm. In role-playing games players might have to figure out the City Guard's shift change to sneak through the city gates at just the opportune moment. Other examples include the obvious ones littered throughout the *Prince of Persia* games. Fail to run past the spinning saw blades in time, and you die.

In movement puzzles, the goal to be reached (the exit) should be shown clearly to the player, and the means should be obvious. Pay attention to level geometry for precision and correct timing. Decreasing the time available for a player to pass an obstacle increases the difficulty and makes a challenge that much harder. This can work to your advantage. Also, the longer a player must act without a single pause in the action, the more difficult the challenge becomes. The player (as well as the game character) will want to take a deep breath after a complicated series of actions.

Reducing or altering a player's character control increases the difficulty and tension in a timing/sequence challenge. This is why so many platform games have slippery surfaces or quicksand. And longer, more complex patterns (such as multiple pendulums, each swinging at different rates or directions) will increase the player's difficulties.

Social/Dialog Puzzles

The player must encounter non-player characters and talk to each of them to find some that will help him past his hurtle. The player's choices will often take the form of complex dialog decisions, and it may even be dependent on outside parameters, such as the player character's charisma score. The help the player is seeking might not be in the form of a key, and it could take finding just the right thing to say to someone.

The non-player character (NPC) could be a guard, for instance, who has a card key to a secret laboratory the player needs to get into. The guard is tough and the player must tread carefully or else get swatted like a fly. The player finds out through reading an e-mail left open on a computer that the guard is sweet on a waitress next door. All the player has to do is convince the waitress to visit the guard, distract him with her big blue eyes, and the player can pickpocket the guard and get the card key he needs.

Mazes

Below-average gamers get lost in standard game levels, so making the level more difficult to get through by adding in lots of twists, turns, and dead ends might quickly make for a player headache. On the other hand, if you use an in-game map or set up a trail of breadcrumbs and some clever surprises along the way, a maze can become a wonderfully entertaining way to break the monotony of locked doors. Plus, it is easy to devise a series of maze levels in 3D GameStudio, apply the most basic templates to your code, and let the player get lost. Add to that a few obstacles, locked doors, and enemies to avoid, and you will find you have built a surprisingly simple fun game.

Monsters

Fighting games have progressive matches where the player must beat a tough opponent. First-person shooters have hordes of stinking zombies, war-time combatants or other sorts of dehumanized monsters running at the player, which he must mow down with fire power. Role-playing games have dungeons littered with monsters to tackle—and each drops treasure (no matter how unlikely that is). Battles with monsters typify the combat system of these games. There is always something to be gained by overcoming the monsters. Monsters should never get the short shrift. They scare us and titillate us, and they make for fearsome foes—even if they look like normal human beings in tanker gear. Either they block the door to escape or they carry the key to the next level. Many games will ramp up the difficulty by using an evolution of tougher and tougher monsters to fight. And the toughest of all are the "boss monsters" that guard the gates on the Gamers' Journey.

One monster is usually not enough for a single game. Every monster must be of a "type" and each "type" must be unique. You might have noticed that some games, like *Gauntlet: Dark Legacy*, will have several types, such as foot soldiers, kamikaze creatures with explosive barrels strapped to them, archers slinging arrows, magic-casting sorcerers, and so on. Then each level in *Gauntlet* will feature these types given unique traits, such as they will all be in various decomposition states of the undead in the farmyard level or they will all be wrapped-up mummies in the pyramid level. This is a classic example of various types of monsters. In some games, the only way to tell the types apart (for they are all the same model but given different skins) is the color of the monster.

Here is a better example of a monster challenge setup: use a giant aggressive anaconda. The player has stumbled into an old zoo that is closed at night. He starts to swim through a water-filled tank to reach a key that a technician dropped on a rampart on the other side, when this huge snake appears! First of all, this monster swims. Second, it has a powerful constricting body if it gets itself wrapped around the player character, so death will be practically instantaneous. It might also be immune to the player's dart gun because of its tough hide. So the player abandons her dart gun, gets out of the water tank to get away to safety, and must find a more suitable weapon to immobilize the anaconda. You might have to script it where the player must set up bait just outside a door to the exterior, and then find a way to open the door long enough for the snake to take the bait—letting the player get to the rampart and get the key she needs!

Creating better enemies for the player to avoid or contend with will always make for challenges in games.

Traps

Traps can combine the best of timing/sequence, cryptographic puzzle, and role-play. Traps are a hodgepodge of suspense, scenery, and intrigue. Good traps can have whole stories behind them, just like any other game challenge. Give some thought to each and every trap you place. Here are some things to keep in mind when creating traps for your game.

A trap in a high cleric's abbey may appear and work very differently from a trap set in a demon warlord's dungeon. Traps reflect the places and the people who built them, even if they share a common goal: to stop trespassers or thieves. There is usually more than one individual who put the trap together. It takes one person to want an area secured and often a team of personnel to design and build the traps. Some people may need to be informed or consulted about the making of the trap, which means they might know how to thwart it as well. Someone pays for it, someone makes it, and someone else may have to live with it. Keep that in mind when building traps in your game.

Traps do not have to indiscriminately appear lethal. Some may be designed to wound, harm, or hold a trespasser. Some others may raise an alarm, scare off, or deter a would-be invader. Some traps may not have actually been designed to be traps in the first place, but through age and disuse or negative natural conditions, accident-prone areas may have developed. A typical example is the rickety wooden bridge. Over the years, the boards may become ancient and the planks can rot. The rope holding it together may fray. A once-solid bridge may end up a death trap for the hero.

With a little ingenuity, natural hazards can be taken advantage of in making areas harder to penetrate or traps harder to perceive. Limestone in caverns means moisture and fog, which can limit visibility and make ledges slippery. Bodies of water can lead to drowning. And some areas where a trap is set may be home to natural predators, making them less navigable. Consider adjusting traps according to their immediate surroundings, including terrain, special features of the land, weather conditions, and even the expected intruder types (the traps might have been set to defend against an invading horde of tiny 3-foot humanoids rather than grown adventurers, so keep in mind that these traps might not work the same way).

Traps have two elements in order to work properly: a trigger (a means by which the trap monitors conditions and knows when to spring) and a response (a way to deliver its full effect). An example of a trap might involve a trip wire to detect intruders, a string (or pulley or gear mechanism) to transmit the response, and a wall of spikes to deliver the response. When creating traps you must think of the trigger, the transmitter, and the response as separate objects. In fact, when you program the trap later on, you will find that the trigger would be an invisible object with an action placed on it and the response would be dynamically called into action. You can even set it up where players can use their cleverness to overcome your traps:

- They could bypass the trigger. This leaves the trap intact for later.
- They could prevent the response, basically disabling the effectiveness of the trap.

- They could sever the connection between the trap and its response. The trap will spring, but nothing will happen.

Traps, like monsters, are one of the staples of popular games, ever since the days of pen-and-paper games like Dungeons and Dragons. A modern game called *Trapt* has the player using magic to set up and spring vicious traps on bad guys hunting her down. The player of this game earns additional points (leading to the ability to build bigger, more vicious traps later on) for mauling enemies in clever ways or doubling up traps. This game has taken a potential player obstacle and made it into a player skill with positive reactions.

I want to give you an example of a unique trap mechanism. You could script this (pretty easily) in 3D GameStudio. The player walks into a room with circular stone walls. In the center of the room is a tall metal pole with arms extending from it almost at random. The floor is wet with a drain hole near the pole. Pressure plates in the floor inside the room detect when the player has entered the room. The door swings closed. The metal pole with its wicked arms begins turning. Water starts gushing into the room, rising until the player is swimming. If the player is struck by the pole's arms at any time, the player loses considerable health. The player also runs the risk of drowning. The player must swim upward with the water, avoiding the spinning arms of the pole, and reach the top before she runs out of air. You can guess what happens if she doesn't. . . .

Problems to Avoid

Keep one of the Four Fs in mind when designing challenges in games: Fairness. Don't let a good game bottleneck because you put in a monster that is nearly unbeatable or a cryptogram only a professor could decipher. Along this same line of thought, avoid creating arbitrary puzzles or puzzles that only you, the creator, could solve. If players get stuck, they will turn to walkthroughs online. If players have to use a walkthrough to get through your game, you have done a poor job of designing it. So leave multiple clues or "bread crumbs" around in your games to fix confusion.

Never force a player to learn by dying. Always help the player to figure something out before slapping their wrists. This should be a game for them—not work! If there is a deadly trap just inside the Incan Temple door, splatter blood and body parts all around the trap spot, so that if the player *does* die, he'll say, "Stupid me!"—not "Stupid game designer!" Think for a moment of the player as a small

Figure 8.10
Dead ends

child and you as the parent taking him on a trip to the circus. You would not want to scold him every time he wanted to see the Big Tent act or buy some cotton candy, would you? Similarly, remember one of the suggestions I gave for level design: never create an area of the game that looks enticing that does not have something in it for the player; otherwise, she will struggle to get there only to find a dead end or (worse) get killed getting nowhere (see Figure 8.10).

Place the items the player is seeking or the answers to a puzzle within close proximity to the puzzle. Avoid wearing out the player, or more aptly the avatar's feet, by making her run throughout the entire level looking for one last item to solve the puzzle. This only causes tedium and frustration—two of the biggest no-nos in game design. If you develop player empathy and start looking at the world you create from the player's point of view, then you will learn to anticipate potential bottlenecks and avoid confusion.

Game challenges can quickly become tedious if monotony sets in. For instance, if you have the player go get the red key to open the red door to get the green key to open the green door to get the blue key to open the blue door to get some sword that is just as efficient as the one the player already owns, then the player will give your game a thumbs-down and word of mouth will kill your game before it's even started. This sort of monotony comes from the misuse of game challenges. Instead, imagine variety in your levels and avoid overusing the same types of challenges. Mix a maze with an alchemical problem with a cryptographic puzzle, and then post some monsters around with the clever attempt to spice up your game. All it takes to make a dull game a great game (earning an honorable mention in the *Game Informer* magazine) is to think intelligently when applying your game design!

Case Scenario of Creative Challenges

Ghosthunter, a little-known survival horror action game from Namco made in 2004, is an excellent demonstration of intelligent and varied design when it comes to in-game challenges. You play as Lazarus Jones, a rookie cop with a smart mouth and bad attitude. Your first night on patrol with your partner, you end up at an abandoned high school looking for prowlers and tangling with an ancient ghost. You seek to rescue your partner from the scar-faced phantom—while he high-tails it through various worlds of past, present, and future. You track him down each time by overcoming the game challenges, which involve capturing different psychotic ghosts and getting past obstacles like blocked doorways and submerged tunnels. Early on in the game, you realize that you are possessed by a spirit of a nightgown-dressed ghost girl, and she helps you out with her progressive abilities in the Nether World.

You may not realize it at all, but the blocked doorways, water-filled tunnels, and far-off switches are all lock mechanisms that the designers carefully planted to test you, the player. You must use your avatar's abilities as keys to unlock these mechanisms, but sometimes which ability to use is not terribly obvious and part of the challenge is your knowledge of which ghost ability you have to use. For instance, there's one area where you have to send forth your ghost's essence to glide through underwater corridors of a sinking British naval vessel. You find a water pump in the lower hold and must use a combination of abilities in the right order (including a Poltergeist power and a Haunt's power) to turn the water pump on and drain the water from the vessel's corridors. This challenge is effective because it draws on your personal attributes to put two and two together—and to identify the solution to the lock mechanism.

Creating a Classic Clue-Driven Game

First, let's evaluate the significant difference between making a clue-driven game as opposed to an action game. Think of some great evil to use in your adventure. It might be that the T-virus has leaked and everybody in the city has been killed or turned into zombies, or that the Blackness has come and taken everybody away into the Night Realm and the only ones still alive are trapped in a coma-like sleep. Whatever your evil is, it will have taken its greatest toll before the game starts out.

Now choose a roughly isolated place for the setting of your game. Stephen King was a master of isolating his characters, be it by a terrific storm or blistering blizzard (usually in a shunned hotel or grim rural town). Look at the first *Silent Hill* game: Harry wakes up in a small resort town named Silent Hill, where white fog and snow make visibility practically impossible. The streets come to dead ends, as if the whole town has been lifted off the planet. He meets a beat cop who tries to radio out, but she learns she cannot call for backup either. Isolating your players gives them an increased sense of suspense, plus it makes building and programming levels easier (because you have less content to create).

Make up all the key characters that might somehow be connected with the evil you designed in the first step. Write down their names, their positions, where they work or live, who else they might know, and what information they might have about the evil. All of this will be crucial to your next steps.

Make a time table of all the events that happened up to and just after the evil occurred. Make notes that include which key characters were involved and how. Using the notes you've made up, write some in-game artifacts that the player can discover and reveal the backstory. These can be pages of journals, e-mails, letters, memos, log entries, or just about anything else that the player can read and glean information from.

Now make a map for the setting you chose for this game. Split the map into more than one level the player has to explore. Include lots of empty rooms, examples of the destructiveness of the evil that you've thought up, and, if there are any survivors place them in centrally located areas.

Spice the map. This means that you should dress up the levels. Add weapons and power-ups (if you want to head the action route), or you can add traps, lock mechanisms, pick-up items, and so on. Be sure to add plenty of locked doors so that the player has to forage for ways to get around them. Whatever you do, don't clutter your levels with meaningless garbage unless your setting you've chosen is a garbage dump.

Place the in-game artifacts you created into the map in appropriate locations. Notes containing smaller or more obvious clues should come first, and more penetrating and thought-provoking clues should come later. Sometimes notes can appear in surprising locations instead of appropriate ones; often, they will show up after a run-in with an enemy or be left behind by a mysterious figure.

Add minor NPCs. These NPCs will know very little about the backstory. They will mostly be there to give the player tips, such as what traps to avoid or where to get keys to open locked doors. If you have to, make some of the NPCs incapacitated (so that even if they did know anything, they cannot communicate with the player). You can put them into comas, have them so badly wounded they are feverish and rest constantly, or you can put them where they have barricaded themselves into empty rooms and won't open the doors, even for the player. However, too many NPCs here will spoil the broth.

Add enemies. These are typically people corrupted by the evil you've imagined. The T-virus may have spawned walking dead. The Blackness may have borne stalking nightmares. The Sands of Time may have possessed all of the living and turned them into fierce scimitar-wielding villains. The madness may have turned everyone but the player into gibbering psychopaths. Whatever the case, place your enemies throughout the levels you have created so you keep the player on her toes.

Now you can bring the clueless player into your setting and make sure she can't get out again before she solves the mystery. Why must she be clueless, you ask? That is a really good question. For one thing, you are fostering an air of fear, suspicion, and mystery (and possibly even nameless horror). The player must not start with any information. Her character must not know anything about the evil that you have created. Oftentimes this leads to the creation of amnesiac heroes (a cliché that is hard to escape in game writing). The player's character may have stumbled into the setting by chance, having found it by accident, hearing great tales of its wealth, being called there by some psychic force, or simply being teleported there by some unseen being. The more the player character knows that the player does not, the more the player may bristle under the impression that she knows less than her avatar does about the approaching menace.

Most of the examples given here apply to mystery and survival horror games, but the lessons learned can also be applied to other adventure games (no matter the fiction genre).

Keeping It Real

Clues should be written on paper first and edited carefully before you put them into your game. In-game artifacts are a story device used in games to provide the player with backstory information and problem-solving knowledge—without appearing to. No player wants to pick up a journal page and read, "Journal Page No. 22. Jim was killed by the Thing at 13:00 hours. Safe combination is 08-02-12." That sort of bland in-your-face stack of details will certainly get the information across, but it kills the effective story immersion that you want to engender. You want to be careful, clever, and have a little flair when writing clues.

Remember that many clues will be in the form of written material, such as journal pages, diary entries, e-mails, instant messages, log entries, and so on. Each will have been written by a different sort of character. Write each in the character's own style. You don't want to write every clue to exhibit course language or accents. A character that speaks in Irish Brogue will certainly not write in it! You merely want to adopt the internal voice of the different characters.

Here's an example from a blog entry the player might find on a computer left on in one of the rooms: "December 2, Tuesday. A funny thing happened today. I was cleaning in Professor Albert's office when I fell and caught myself on the marble bust on the professor's desk. Well, I heard this noise and when I turned around I saw a doorway had opened in the back wall of his office! I never knew there was a door there; it must be some kind of secret passageway. The marble bust on his desk must've been the trigger. I never! Well, I heard someone cough behind me, and there was Professor Albert. He looked so pissed. He told me not to tell another living soul what I'd just seen. What's he into, anyway? He's a weird one, all right."

This note tells the player that there is a nasty-sounding professor somewhere who has an office and in it a desk with a marble statue on it. The statue operates a hidden door somewhere in that room. It also tells the player to watch out for the wrathful professor. On top of that information, the player has also been introduced to the writer of the blog: a cleaning lady who may or may not still be around. Reading the note, the player gets to hear her speak in her own voice and style.

Here is an example of a letter: "Dear Professor Tamry—I need you to do some research for me on the biology of the dorsi plant of Western Nigeria. There may be something in it that will answer your questions. I have been afraid myself. In fact, I would not mention this to anyone but you, but I believe that our Professor Albert has not been right in his mind. He pays considerably too much attention to his plant experiments, and he refuses to answer my inquiries about his current findings. Plus, I have heard strange noises coming from the arboretum after 11 every night. What am I to do? (Signed) George"

This heightens the player's suspicions and makes her wonder about that Professor Albert. Plus, though the information is thin at best (watered down by the writing), the player might want to find a library and read up on the dorsi plant of Western Nigeria—and at all costs, avoid the arboretum after eleven o'clock at night. As I said, these might be nearly intangible threads as clues, but the overall impact in the way they are written (the style and character's voice) impart much more.

Here is a different example, a memo scribbled on the back of a bookmark and placed inside a book lying on a bed in a room the player finds. When the player investigates the book, this bookmark falls out, and the player sees that there is something written on the back. It says, "Left door: Key M11, Right door: 3-8-7-7." This does not really carry the writer's inflection, but the player will understand that there are two doors somewhere and that they are probably opened by the means described in the memo. The left door probably needs a key to Room M11, while the right door probably has a keypad, and the combination to unlock the door is 3-8-7-7. This information may be vital, and it is clear and concise.

When considering how best to write your clues, try to give them each a distinctive voice, style, and appearance. No two should be just like the other (unless they are in a successive series). The more appropriate the notes appear, the less likely the player will wonder at their appearance at all and the more the player will focus on their content. At the same time, surprising the player or pulling tricks to deceive the player (especially if it fits with your game setting or the mood) are acceptable on occasion.

Note

"The best way to move game design forward is simply to develop, design, and construct a game. And make sure you finish it. No matter how bad, how simple, how slow your finished product is, you will learn an immense amount simply by building a game on your own . . . Read, experiment, design, develop, play, and most important of all, have fun. In the end, having fun is what games are all about."

—Ben Sawyer

In Summary

Adventure games in particular are reliant upon their stories. Narratives for games are needed for players to make sense of the gameplay and the mechanics, but the plotlines should never take the place of fun gameplay. Decide what you want your game to say, and keep its story paced right so that it never gets dull and the player is always on the edge of her seat.

What You Have Learned

The following are things you should have learned about game challenges and narrative:

- You now understand game narrative and its terminology.

- You have learned how to write game narrative and popular plots you can use.
- You now know the String of Pearls Method for scripting game story.
- You have learned the various game challenges you can set up.
- You know how to make the player's decisions dramatic and vital to story.
- You know what to avoid and how to plot a clue-driven game.

For Review

1. Play one of your favorite games or any popular game on the market. Does it have a narrative? Does the narrative reflect the gameplay, and if so, does this type of game genre usually have such evolved game narrative? What sort of plots does the game use for its missions, and do you believe the writing was crafted well? Is there anything that the writers left out or that the game developers could have done better?

2. Your client wants you to write a game for them. The player plays as a private eye in a futuristic setting, similar to the movie *Blade Runner*. The client tells you this will be an action-adventure game and must have a romantic interest and a government conspiracy. What sorts of plotlines jump to your mind? What game challenges could you make up for this game? Write a short summary for the client that details the game story you would design for their game.

3. A colleague comes to you in trouble. They have written a game narrative for an up-and-coming company, but there are some problems with it. The game is supposed to be a first-person shooter, where the player can assign his own character that he makes in an RPG-type panel; the character is not well-defined, but his goals are to run through a giant planet-size metal scrap yard labyrinth destroying giant rat creatures. The company has told your friend that they want it to be an intelligent shooter game and therefore to create an evolving storyline. Your friend does not know what sort of plots, missions, or objectives to create—or even who the player is supposed to be. What can you tell him that would save this game narrative?

4. You and your friend are writing a game that is going to be a third-person fantasy platformer heavy on running, jumping, escaping heavily armed

trolls, and solving puzzles. You have been told by the game's designer to include a tree house that is really beautiful to look at but when the player goes inside, the door slams shut behind her, and the house transforms into an evil dungeon filled with traps. What sorts of traps would you develop for this game—and how would you alert the traps' presence to the player without ruining the potentially dangerous surprises?

5. For the original game that you would like to develop, write a narrative that goes along with it. First, decide what the game genre and gameplay will be like. Then, based on the game mechanics, come up with a major plot and several sub-plots to form the game's missions and side-quests. Write a rough draft of the game's story.

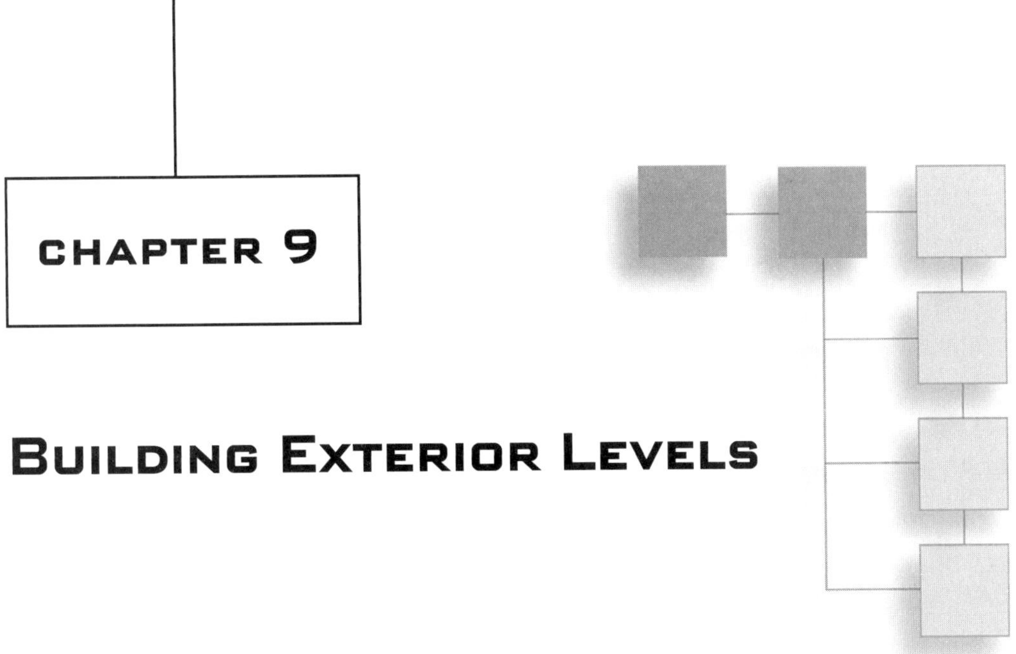

Chapter 9

Building Exterior Levels

You have learned how to make interior levels, which is fine for indoor and underground environments. You can use those principles to build apartment buildings, dungeons, sewer tunnels, and many other interior spaces. But the real proof of the pudding is making exterior levels. There is so much more that goes on in the outdoors, not the least of which is focusing on fencing in the player more, adding a sky cube or box, and creating natural-looking terrain. In this chapter, you will learn the principles of building exterior levels for the game *Mama Kat.*

Exercise 9.1: Building the City of Krawl

Krawl's description brings to the imagination a maze of dingy sea-swept streets, crooked vendors, and pirates and rogues rousting in taverns. Krawl should appear as tall as it is wide and taller in the middle, where the palace and Guard barracks will be. There should be a clever randomness to the look of it. If you can imagine a place that was never planned but built by settlers in a chaotic fashion of a mishmash of cultures, blueprints, and styles, then you will get some idea of the look of Krawl before you start to build.

Setting Up

Create a new folder in your GStudio6 folder. Call this new folder **mama_kat**. This will contain all your project files for this game that you are going to create.

On the CD-ROM provided, you will find the mama_kat folder; it has a bmaps, sfx, and a 3dmodels folder that you need to copy and paste to your mama_kat folder. Also copy and paste the Interior and Exterior WAD file from the WADs folder on the CD-ROM to your mama_kat folder.

Open a brand new level in WED. Go to File > Preferences to set Hollow Wall to 4. You can change this later to get variations in wall widths. You can also set Snap pretty low, but doing so may mistakenly make it harder to align blocks, increasing the compile time. Go to Texture > Texture Manager and find the Exterior.wad. Add this WAD. This has several outdoor-type textures, ground textures, and building textures in it.

Save your level as mamakat.wmp in your mama_kat folder that you created.

Right-click on Add Model to place the standin.mdl in your level. You do this to build proportion into the avatar's height and anatomy. Now your streets and doorways should follow his dimensions.

In the Map Properties, create a new script based on `WalkThru_Project` that will be called mamakat.wdl. This is the script file you will be using to test your levels as you build them, but we'll change it later.

Basic Geometry

The fantasy city of Krawl has a mixture of styles and architectures. Many different cultures (and races) of people live within it and have claimed these streets as their home. However, all of Krawl shares in a magic flair, as its people are often enchanted in their very nature. Its streets appear fairly regular and paved, and they are what you will start building. Once you get the pavement made, you can set up groups of blocks that make up houses along the road (see Figure 9.1). Placing them into organized groups will help you a lot in placing them correctly and being able to edit them without any more aggravation than necessary.

I found a picture on the Internet of the Sharoe Green Hospital in England, and it inspired me to create an important-looking building with a clock tower. See the image of the Sharoe Green Hospital in Figure 9.2. We are going to create a building that looks similar to this one. This building will appear as the outside of the City Guard barracks.

First add the ground cover. Go to Object > Add Primitive > Misc > Plate (large). This will place a large flat block into your new 3D space. Use the Scale tool to

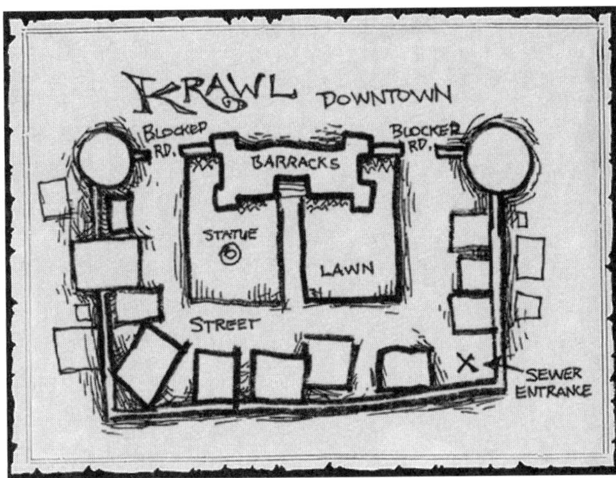

Figure 9.1
Map of downtown Krawl

Figure 9.2
An inspirational photograph

make it as thin as half of one square. You might have to fiddle with the Snap setting in the toolbar if you cannot seem to get the block to shrink. You want it to be as flat as a pancake. You must have a general thickness in quants for the player character to be able to walk on it, however; so if you accidentally make it too thin, the compile process may report errors or the physics will act wonky when you run the game later on. So leave the plate object thick enough that, when you compile, your machine will not slog away.

Still using Scale, you must stretch the plate object out to a very large size (approximately 32 × 32 of the larger squares). Texture it to look like concrete or dirt. This will be the ground block.

Duplicate (CTRL+D) this block and make it less than half the original width and length. Texture this block to appear like snow-covered grass. Raise it up so that it comes out of the concrete block less than half of a square unit. Using the Top View window, move this grass block over to your left so that it rests medially along the left side of the concrete block and away from the edge (see Figure 9.3).

Now duplicate (CTRL+D) this grass block and move it medially opposite from the first. Make sure that its height remains the same as the original grass block. Once you have both of them in place in the Top View window, nudge them until they almost meet in the center of the concrete block, with about twice the width of the standin.mdl between them. This will form the path leading up to the City Guard barracks (CGB) we will construct next. The grass blocks form the CGB's front lawn. See Figure 9.4 to make sure that you have gotten it right.

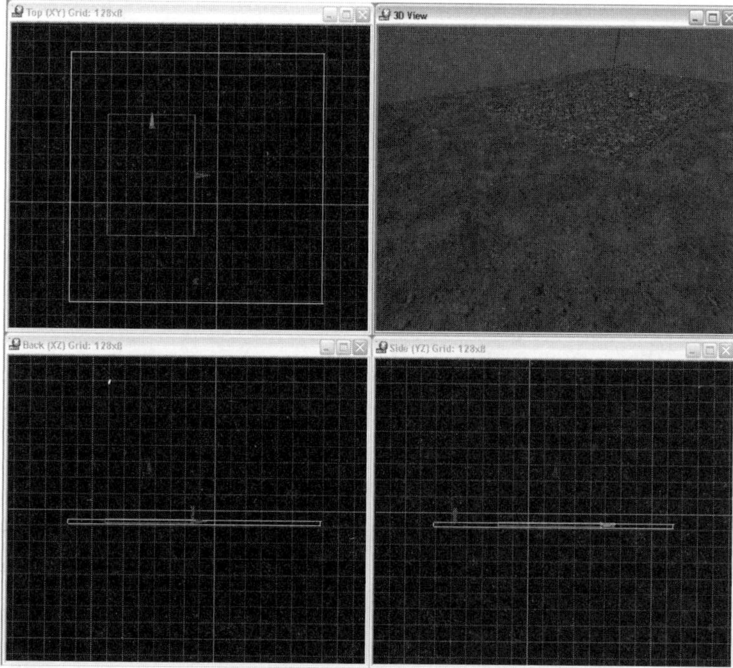

Figure 9.3
Creating one half of the lawn

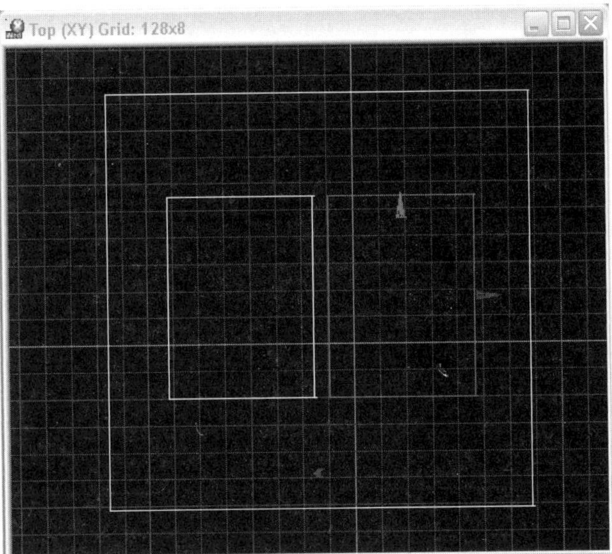

Figure 9.4
Completing the lawn

Add a large cube and scale it so that it stretches from nearly one edge of the lawn to the other, with a marginal space to either side. Add a building exterior texture to this cube, and align the texture on the surfaces so that the windows line up realistically. This is sometimes easier said than done and can take a lot of patience to get just right. Remember that you must lock the textures on this cube to keep the textures from wandering if you have to nudge the cube later. You can ignore the texture on the roof of this cube because you will be creating a real roof to go on the top of the building later.

Next, add a cube that you scale to the height of the CGB, but do not make it very wide. Give it a brick texture (one that matches the CGB cube at least a little bit). Place it on the corner of the CGB cube so that it appears to be an outcropping jutting away from the building. You are going to select the CGB cube and use it to CSG Subtract from the corner piece, but do not get carried away and delete the CGB cube; you still need to use it. Before you CSG Subtract, make sure that the CGB cube and the cube you wish to subtract from are both a distance in the air above the ground planes because you do not want to make the mistake of subtracting part of the lawn. Besides, you are going to set the CGB down on top of a foundation in a moment. Your finished corner piece should look like Figure 9.5.

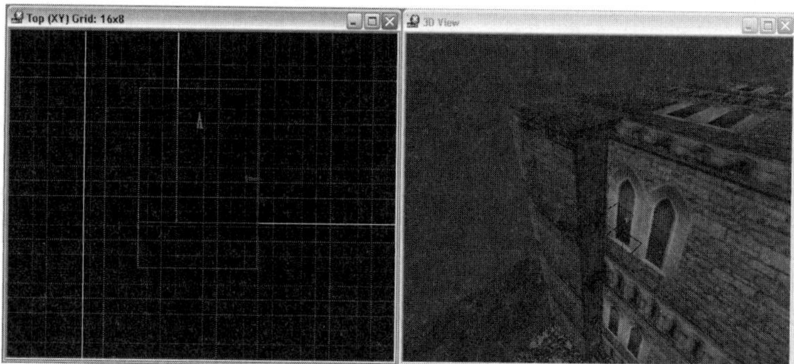

Figure 9.5
Corner piece of the barracks after CSG Subtract

Duplicate the corner piece and place one at all four corners of the CGB. Remember to use the Rotate tool to get some of them angled correctly.

To place a door on the CGB, create a smaller cube sized one story shorter than the CGB and place it front and center of the CGB cube, buried a depth to your liking inside the CGB cube. Add the same texture to it that you used on the CGB cube. Use CSG Subtract to remove a portion from the CGB cube, and then delete the cube you used to subtract with. Your CGB cube will now be in several block subsections. You might have to select some of the CGB cubes and use the Properties panel's Surface tab to rearrange the placement of the textures again. On the block that forms the central part of the CGB, where the door would be, open the Properties panel and go to the Surface tab. You will place a double door texture on it, resizing and scaling the texture to fit appropriately. Remember to compare it to the size of your standin.mdl for proper proportions.

In order for you to put a roof on the CGB, go to Object > Add Primitive > Misc > Trapezoid. The trapezoid primitive will need to be seriously scaled to fit over the entire top of the CGB, including the corner pieces. It will also need to rise steeply, and its lines should run parallel to the front of the building instead of sideways. This may take some time to get just right. When you have it proportioned accordingly (see Figure 9.6), then you add a roof-type texture to it. When most people think of roofs, they think of shingles, but you can do whatever you like.

You could add some gables or dormer-style windows coming off the roof for that added artistic style, but you can use your imagination and add your final touches later. Right now, all we have left to finish the CGB is to put it on a foundation (a large plate primitive scaled to fit would work just fine—just add a concrete or

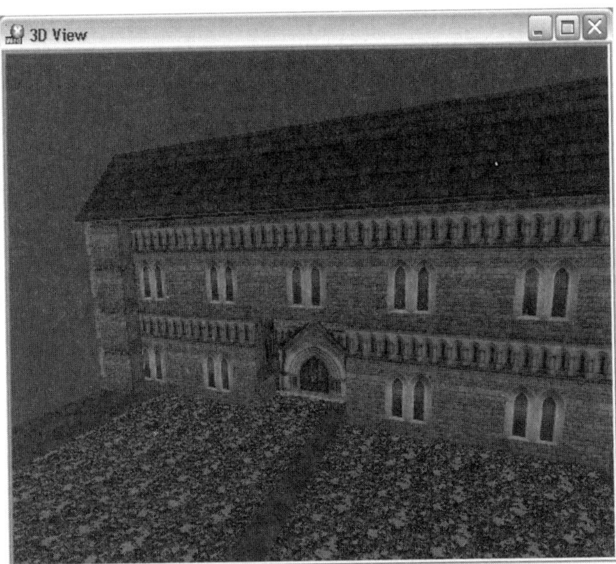

Figure 9.6
Putting a door and roof on

brick texture to it and make stairs so that the pretend people using the building can get up to the front doors); then put all of the blocks created so far into a new group called **CGB**.

If you have forgotten how to create new groups on the fly, remember to switch over to Objects in your Project window and right-click, selecting New Group. When the new group appears (in your Objects' directory tree), right-click on the folder name and open its Properties. Change the name to CGB and exit. Drag all of the blocks created in the process of the CGB's production into the new group by that name.

Adding a clock tower takes some ingenuity. Essentially, build it out of one or more cubes, rising sharply out of the center of the top of the CGB, and give it a convincing brick or stone texture. Put another trapezoid primitive with the same roof texture on the top of the clock tower. You can make arches in the clock tower's lower half by using CSG Subtract and cylinder primitives to subtract with. When you are through, add the sprite clock.tga to the level, and place it on the front of the clock tower. You might accidentally rotate it to face the wrong way; if so, you will notice this when you compile and run the level, and you can rotate it back the right way. See Figure 9.7 to get an idea how this will all look in the final render.

Figure 9.7
Clock tower

Place all the blocks (and sprite) that you used to construct the clock tower into a new group named **clockTower**. This will help you manage the clock tower separate from the building itself (and the surrounding environment).

Look again at the map of the hub level. There are meant to be some staggered buildings along the bottom half of the map, and some along the sides. You can do what I did: I opened a new level in WED and created a medieval-looking building, making sure I got its proportions and texture maps just right. I saved it as Hut1, and then compiled it into a WMB file, which I could load on the fly into mamakat.wmp as a map entity. You can do this to make four distinct buildings that you like the look of. Map entities are certainly easier because they make compiling the finished mamakat.wmp faster. Unfortunately, if you choose to use map entities, they do not affect static lighting and shadows in the game level, so you must take care and use them only when this does not matter.

When you have four map entities, you can drop them into your level and arrange them how you like, staggering them as you go. There are sure to be gaps between the buildings, but don't let this scare you. Fence the player in by running a single block, textured to look like a wood-plank fence, along the edge of the map. This fence can run through the buildings, if you like, so that the player cannot walk around to the other side of them.

Duplicate this wooden fence, and place it along each edge of the map so that the player cannot find a way to wander off it into the void. There are two areas (as identified on the map) which will appear to be streets leading out of the downtown square. You can place fence blocks there as well to keep the player from escaping the 3D environment, but make them invisible. You will place models in their location later to give the player a frame of reference as to why they cannot leave down these streets.

The last touch of geometry I would suggest you add to this level (although you might be able to imagine something else) is some environmental teasers. Place some houses (or parts of them) just outside your visible space, like over the other side of the fences. This will give the player a glimpse of a bigger city outside of the one you are letting her explore, increasing the sense of immersion and awe.

Creating Your Own Textures in 3DGS

You can create your very own textures (and texture packages) in 3D GameStudio. All you need is a paint program (like Adobe Photoshop) and some digital photographs.

Open your digital photograph in your paint program. Pick one area that you want to use to make a texture from (for example, a clean piece of brickwork, metal, or grass). Make sure that the lines and angles of the sample are facing straight toward the viewer; if they do not, you can use the Rotate, Skew, and Distort functions in Photoshop to move them around where they appear to face the viewer. Crop the image so that the sample is all that is visible. The image size must be a power of 2, so measurements of 64×64 or 128×128 are best.

Now the edges of the texture will not line up correctly with each other, believe it or not, and when you tile the texture on a geometric block, a visible edge will show up. To get rid of this, you can use a combination of the Offset Filter (go to Filter > Other > Offset) and the Clone Stamp tool.

If you have a large part of a wall that you want to texture, and you want the texture to be fixed and replace the detail of adding extra blocks, you can make one large texture that may only repeat once or twice. Be sure that your sides measure some numbers that are powers of 2, or else the game engine will kick out an error that you have a texture outside of size range.

Lastly, save your texture in an external folder as a 24-bit TGA file–do not use 32-bit TGA or else the engine will treat your textures as transparent! Open up WED, and expand one of the Textures windows in the Texture panel. Hold your mouse over the texture icons, right-click and select Add Texture from the dialog list. Browse to find the texture(s) you have made and import them into the current WAD; you will have to save the WAD to save your changes.

Alternatively, you can choose Extract Texture from the dialog list; alter the texture image in a paint program, and then select Add Texture to add it back in the WAD. In this way, you can change the look of textures from existing ones.

Adding a Sky

There are two methods in 3D GameStudio to create a visible and realistic sky. One is to apply the script sky00.wdl or sky01.wdl. These program scripts define a sky dome that surrounds the impassible terrain and can look really good. If you are going in through WED's Program Manager, you can attach the Basic Sky (01) template script, which calls sky01.wdl, debatably the best sky script. It sets the sky cube to appear as the skycube+6.tga image file, which you can edit in your paint program later.

The other way to add sky is build a sky box yourself in WED, sans scripting. This is the way that I will show you here.

Add a hollow cube and make it bigger than your current level. Then apply one of the sky textures to it from the Standard.wad. For personal reasons, Skyblue has always looked aesthetically pleasing. Right-click on Skyblue, and open its Settings panel. This texture image has a format of 256 × 128 × 16 and its name begins with "sky"; this is what makes the texture scroll like rushing clouds. Ostensibly, you could select any texture for your sky texture—as long as it begins with "sky" and contains two square images depicting sky and clouds. The texture would slide from the upper left to the lower right. However, the appearance may not look as "finished" and professional as this one does, unless you have layer channels and make the texture a TGA file before importing it. Notice that Skyblue has a unique look because its foreground layer appears to move faster than the background layer.

Once you have added the sky texture of your choosing to the sky box, you will not see it animated in the 3D View window. Do not be surprised by this. The animation will be perfectly visible when you save, build, and run your game level. It is sometimes easy to forget that the WED 3D View window is only a preview window and does not accurately show the final renderings that will come later when you compile the level.

You could use other geometric shapes besides a hollow cube for your sky box. You could use a many-sided shape or even a sphere, However, it will not look any different in the final render but drain the memory reserves when you go to compiling the level.

If you did not hollow it out first, when you run your level it will look fine, but you will notice that your characters are stuck inside the block and may react by "swimming" in it, which does not look realistic and may terrify your players.

Keeping the size of your levels small, and even leaving textures off of out-facing surfaces of the sky box, will restrict your compile time and give your machine better performance. To leave textures off of out-facing surfaces of the sky box, select the sky box group and Scope Down to select the individual blocks that make it up. In the Properties panel, hit the Surface tab and switch between available surfaces for the block. Find the one surface that faces out and away from the player, and turn its texture off, also making it invisible. When your Map Compiler starts up and you get an error message that there are surfaces without proper texture mapping and do you want to add the default texture to them, tell the Map Compiler to ignore them. These surfaces are not that important because the player will never actually see them in the finished game level.

The last thing that you need to do when creating a sky is to open the Map Properties. Click on the Sun tab. The Sun settings are unique. You can set the color of the sun by using the RGB fields. You can set the Ambient Lighting function in your level by using the RGB fields beside it. (The Ambient Light setting lightens and colors the shadows in your level. This is very touchy; try to keep Ambient Light considerably dark—almost black.) The sun is also governed by Azimuth (which are the sun's directions, north, south, east, and west) and Elevation (which is how high the sun is in the sky).

Elevation is what you need to pay particular attention to. I suggest setting it at 45 (this is a 45-degree rise from the ground plane). You can experiment with the sun's Value settings later.

If you have Lens Flares set to On (look in your Project Manager), you will see white rings descending from the sun's angle when you run the game level. If you are in first-person and look up toward the direction of the sun, these light flares will show up and add a neat cinematic touch to your level.

It is not necessary, but it is advisable to place a sprite entity into your game level to represent the sun but only if your sun is actually a moon. If you are constructing a night-time level, make sure that the Lens Flares are not on and not part of your project. You can set a silver color for the Sun setting in Map Properties, a 45-degree angle to the sun, and place a TGA file of a moon on a black background in the sky.

Adding Lights and SFX

Now you need to add light sources and sound effects (according to aesthetics). If you have an edition of 3D GameStudio that allows you to use colored lights, do so with impunity (recalling design lessons of color coordination and composition). Purposefully leave the level filled with shadows.

As for audio files, place sound sources for noise1.wav (a rabble sound) and crickets.wav (a night-time outdoors sound) around the level in a few different places. Depending on where you place these sound files—and what volume and range you give them—the Doppler effect will increase the sense of player immersion. Typically, put noise1.wav near the edges of the map, around houses or fences. Put crickets.wav on the lawn in front of the City Guard barracks.

Adding Final Touches

The last step to the level build is to put your final touches to it; these can include sprites, models, or map entities. The majority of the models you will place in this level will be tree1.mdl, tree2.mdl, and shrub.mdl. Each of these will need to be spaced out at random around the City Guard barracks (on the lawn). Do not put any on the street or the walkway up to the CGB. Keep your actual number of tree models used down below 100 because if you put too many visible models in one place, the end user's processor will have a hard time keeping up with showing so many polygons at once onscreen. This is not a forest that you are creating, only a town square, so don't go overboard.

Remember those two streets that you put invisible primitive objects in front of so the player would not assume they could wander out of bounds? You need to add the model closed.mdl to your level and duplicate it multiple times. Place these closed.mdl entities smack-dab in the middle of your invisible fence blocks. The blocks will not show up in the final render, but the 3D model will—and the player will understand why they cannot proceed in the directions they want to. (You can also stack invisible geometric blocks and 3D models together to give the players objects they can jump on top of and climb on.)

Other models you need to consider placing in mamakat.wmp are the bench.mdl (used to make it look like the pretend people in this level sit down occasionally) and the statue.mdl (placed somewhere on the lawn of the City Guard barracks to look "official").

Creating Terrain Height-Maps

Terrain height-maps are used by most modern 3D game engines to simulate the smooth and chaotic roughness of natural terrain by taking a topographical-type image of land and applying a depth to it. This application makes the map appear to rise higher in some areas and dip lower in others. Terrain height-maps are useful for aerial games, but they can also be used for outdoor terrain (if you have coded a decent gravity script for your player characters).

Terrain consists of one or several textures mapped onto a rectangular grid of height values. It is stored in an external HMP file. They can be created with MED or imported from RAW height maps or BMP or PCX height image bitmaps that are created with terrain builder programs.

Open up a new image file in Adobe Photoshop (or your choice of paint programs), and make sure its dimensions are set to a good average, like 512 × 512. Fill the image layer with pure black (0,0,0), and then select a range of gray colors to draw a topographical image. This can be done at random. The gray areas will appear at a higher elevation than the black ones. Save your image as a 24-bit bitmap file, such as roughterrain.bmp.

Open up MED, and select File > Import > Terrain from Picture to load the roughterrain.bmp file (you will have to select BMP types to open it). Your terrain height-map should automatically appear. Save it as a HMP file. You should add a new skin to it, making sure it is the same file size as the original BMP image. You can even use your roughterrain.bmp as a guideline to tell where the steeps and valleys are and paint roads or mountains accordingly.

Exercise 9.2: Building the Sewer Tunnels

The original game outline featured several alternatives to overcoming the obstacle of getting into the Guard barracks. You are going to program one of them. You can expand the game demo at a later date, on your own time, if you want to experiment with further alternatives. This will make your RPG more realistic and satisfy more players. For the sake of getting the game done in the shortest amount of time, you will set up the path the player will take to enter the Guard barracks through the subterranean tunnels. The player will start in the downtown square of Krawl, will find a sewer entrance, and then enter this level.

Setting Up

Start a new level. Define your Preferences.

In the Texture Manager, add the Interior.wad file. This has a lot of neat concrete and wall textures that will aid you in creating realistic tunnels.

Add the standin.mdl to define the size and proportion of your level creation.

In the Map Properties, browse to and set the script to be mamakat.wdl.

Save your file in the mama_kat folder as sewers.wmp.

Building Your Level

This will be an interior level. Look at the map in Figure 9.8. You have experience building interior levels from the exercises in Chapter 6, so I will not tell you how to go about constructing them here. You can do it yourself. Remember to build

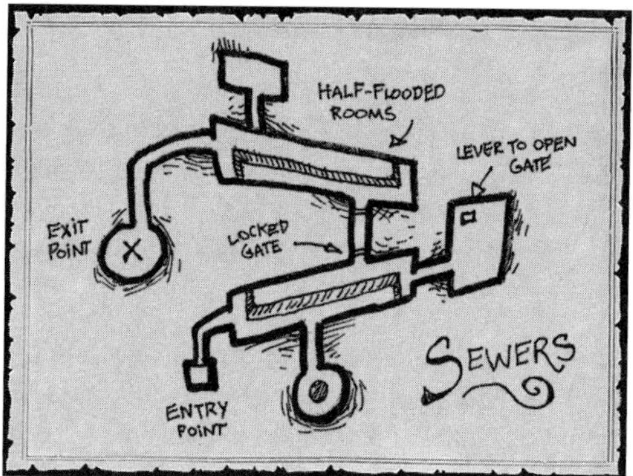

Figure 9.8
Sewer map

the basic geometry first, adding texture maps as you go. Put in some light and sound sources, and (last but certainly not least) flesh out your level with 3D models and sprite images. Keep the blocks tight that make up your level so that there are no level leaks. Place multiple blocks that form conduits into new groups, each of them named distinctly so that you can find your way through the Objects list better.

Exercise 9.3: Building the Guard Barracks

The Guard barracks rise sharply into the air, high over Krawl. There are few entrances and even fewer exits. The player must slip unnoticed to the top of the Guard barracks (in the clock tower) to the Captain's quarters and steal the Ronal Ruby. This could be the longest and most difficult part of the game to build; you could spend a lot of time on it, making the path increasingly harder as you go. The map, as shown in Figure 9.9, features the basement level of the barracks.

Setting Up

Open a new game level. In the Texture Manager, add the Interior.wad file. This has several wall and flooring textures that you will use to build the barracks interior.

Add the standin.mdl to define the size and proportion of your level creation.

In the Map Properties, browse to and set the script to be mamakat.wdl.

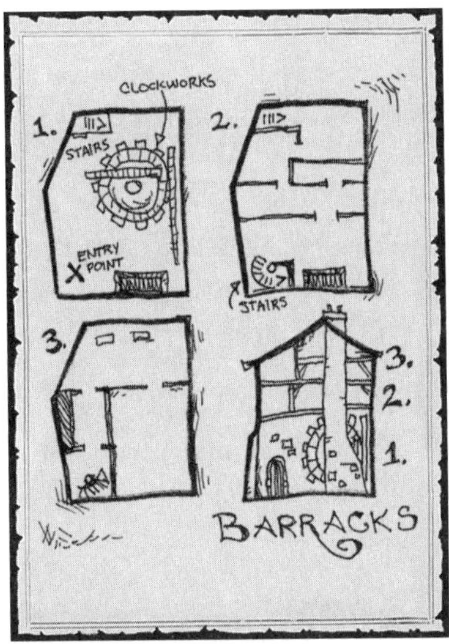

Figure 9.9
City Guard barracks map

Save your new files in the mama_kat folder as **guards.wmp** and **finish.wmp**. If you want to create more than one level to the City Guard barracks, use the guards.wmp and name them **guards2.wmp**, **guards3.wmp**, and so on.

Building Your Levels

Again, the City Guard barracks are interior levels. You can expand your proficiency at creating interior levels by making them yourself. Use the map as a blueprint to go by as you build. Use your imagination when adding colored lights, texture maps, and such.

Exercise 9.4: Adding Final Touches

The A6 template scripts are very comprehensive in giving you all that you need in terms of first-person, third-person, and isometric games (browse the scripts available for each in the Project Manager). For the *Mama Kat* game, you are going to use a different package of template scripts that will help you create a proper role-playing game. These are in the RPGplayer folder on the CD-ROM.

Creating an RPG Camera

The RPGplayer folder includes a camera script developed by David Lancaster; it is a popular third-person camera, as seen in such games as *Kingdom Hearts*, *Super*

Sunshine Mario, and *Beyond Good and Evil*. To view the RPG camera, you are going to have to attach the new template scripts to your game levels.

The new template package is called RPGplayer and is on the CD-ROM in the mama_kat folder under Project Files. Copy and paste the contents of the RPGplayer folder from there to your Template_6 folder in GStudio6. Be sure to copy all script files, as well as the subfolders 3d, sfx, and bmaps from there to your mama_kat folder. This will avoid dangerous error messages later.

Open mamakat.wmp in WED. From the CD's Project Files folder, where you find the RPGplayer package, copy the RPG_Project file and place it in your Template_6 folder in the GStudio6 folder of your hard drive. In Map Properties, click to add a new script, and from the available scripts screen select RPG_Project. If asked if you want to overwrite an existing script, select Yes. Exit Map Properties. Open the mamakat.wdl file and, under inclusive paths, tell it three more paths: paths to 3d, sfx, and bmaps. Save your mamakat.wdl file. You will have to open all the levels you built so far and make sure all of them have the mamakat.wdl script set for their master script under Map Properties.

Select your standin.mdl and apply the `RPGplayer` action to it. Save and build your level (updating only the entities).

When you are done making adjustments, test-run your game to experiment with the RPGplayer scripts. You should still be able to move with WASD keys and jump using SPACEBAR, but now the controls will seem more similar to console controls for the most popular video games today. Pan your camera all around the avatar with your mouse. You can attempt an attack by clicking with the mouse, but your character will not really hurt anything just yet. Run around the level to get a feel not only for the level you have spent quite a bit of time building, but also for the `RPGplayer` action that allows you to view your character and control it easily. You can also press the 0 key to switch between third- and first-person viewpoints.

You will not be able to see it yet, but one of the neatest new control options that comes with the RPGplayer package is that the avatar character will scan for enemies and target on one once it is found, turning to face it constantly until a maximum distance range is put between the player character and the enemy character or the player clicks the right mouse button. This can make attacks easier because the player doesn't have to fight with the camera pan to turn around and face enemies to get in a good hit; the avatar will automatically do it. This saves the player frustration, and makes your game that much more exciting.

Creating Entities

Add the Levels script to attach exit and entry points connecting all your levels. In the mamakat.wmp level, put the manhole.mdl in the center of the street next to the fence around the side of the City Guard barracks (refer to the level map to see where it is supposed to go). Place the cube.wmb map entity and position it on top of the manhole. Apply the `Levels00_Exit_Pt` action to it. Make sure that Id_023 is set to 1.000 and Target_023 is set to 2.000. In sewers.wmp, go to where the bottom of the stairs are, where you want the player character to spawn, and place a cube.wmb map entity there. Apply the `Levels00_Entry_Pt` action to it, and make sure that its Id_023 is set to 2.000. If you had a player character set in sewers.wmp before, remove it. Continue to place `Levels00_Exit_Pt` entities and `Levels00_Entry_Pt` entities in the rest of your levels, connecting them.

Place NPCs throughout the outside of the mamakat.wmp level, and attach communication behaviors (presented in Chapter 10, "Better Animation and AI"). In the barracks levels (except for in the Captain's quarters), place guard.mdl entities and place the RPGenemy behavior to them. In the sewers, you can find and place any monster models you like and put RPGenemy behaviors to them as well.

You might think up other entities to create. If so, go with your imagination but do not clutter the levels so badly that the player cannot find his way around for all the confusion.

Creating Weather

Open mamakat.wdl, and you will see an include that sets up weather conditions in game levels:

```
include <weather.wdl>;
```

Place a box.mdl entity in mamakat.wmp and attach the `Snow_Maker` action to it; this will cause the sky to snow in the exterior game level of Krawl City. Save mamakat.wmp, then build, and run the game to check out the cold weather effects. Later on you can change the look of the snowflakes, if that is your wish. They are set by the snow.pcx file that came in the bmaps folder of RPGplayer. Later you might wish to change this to look like falling leaves, and you can alter or duplicate the functions to make the sprites fall faster, making them appear like rain.

In Summary

You have learned to create more extravagant outdoor levels from map sketches, add a sky to outdoor game areas, and set up lighting and effects. You now also have a grasp of dressing your levels to appear like the player is really outside. Lastly, you set up a new script based on the RPG_Project template and experimented with entities and weather effects. You have a good understanding, overall, of what it takes to build exterior levels for 3D games. The next chapter will show you how to animate using a skeletal structure and how to program more advanced AI for bots!

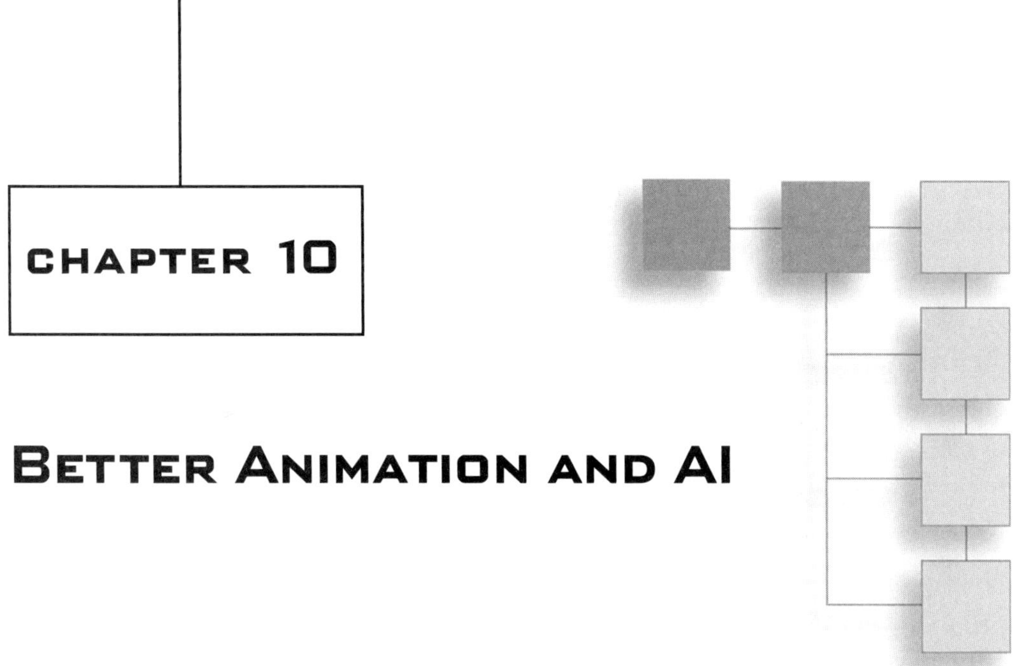

Chapter 10

Better Animation and AI

You have probably gotten sick and tired of the basic character models. In this chapter, you will learn about bones animation, creating better character models than you have previously with vertex animation, and you will also learn how to compose better AI (leading to faster, smarter, stronger, and more challenging enemies and monsters that the player will have to overcome).

You are going to take your skills up another notch by creating the mamakat.mdl used for the Mama Kat character—and by developing the Guards that Mama Kat has to avoid to get to the Ronal Ruby.

Exercise 10.1: Bones Animation

Bones animation refers to the "bones" that form the make-believe skeleton of a 3D model. These bones are used as an alternative method for vertex animation. A bone is defined by the following features:

- A hinge found at some fixed position on the model or attached to the end of the "parent" bone.
- A length.
- An orientation of pan, tilt, and roll.
- A set of vertices attached to the bone. (If the bone moves or rotates at all, the attached vertices move or rotate right along with it.)

A model can be animated by shifting either the orientation values or the length of a bone or set of bones in MED. MED allows users to create and connect bones, stick vertices to them, and record bones animations.

Animating Mama Kat

Open mamakat.mdl in the Model Editor. This model has been created—similar to the Hector model from your earlier exercises—in individual model parts and brought together in a single model file. There are no animations or realistic skins within this MDL file, but you are about to make them.

First open the Skin Editor and export the image to work up a skin in a paint program, then import it back into the Skin Editor. Use the Mama Kat character concept art as a basis for your skin.

Enter Bone mode by clicking the icon button bearing the yellow circle with the cross through it in the upper toolbar. Click on Animate down at the bottom of the Model Editor window until the Animate button turns yellow. You are ready to begin creating.

Enter bone creation by clicking the Create Bone button on the Bones toolbar at the bottom-right corner of the MED window (this icon will look like an identical circle with a cross through it, but it will be red and green instead of yellow). Clicking in one of the orthographic view panels creates a bone hinge point. The next click that you make connects the hinge point with the click point by a bone. Further clicks create a connected chain of "child" bones. If you mess up, don't worry. You can press DELETE to erase the last bone created. Pressing DELETE not only removes the last bone created, but it also initiates a new bone chain.

You can also create bones by clicking and dragging them. Clicking on an existing hinge point attaches the new bone to the previous bone. You can also merge two or more hinges by putting them together, selecting them, and clicking the Merge button. In this fashion, several child bones can be dutifully attached to a single parent bone.

With the Bone Mode selected in the upper menu bar, you can edit the bones you have created. Move mode allows you to move the bones by selecting and dragging their hinges around. When the Move Children button is selected, moving one of the parent bones moves all the child bones attached. Otherwise only the parent bone will be moved.

Using the Rotate tool, you can rotate a bone chain by clicking on a hinge and dragging it up or down. With Move Children selected, rotating a parent bone will also rotate all the child bones attached.

Once you have all the bones in Kat's skeleton created in simple-to-understand chains descending from the torso, you can apply the model parts. The way that you do that is by attaching vertices to the bones. Click the Apply Vertices Mode button. You should instantly see some changes: vertices already attached to bones will appear blue, and "free" vertices will appear yellow. Select a bone by clicking on its hinge point. Select some vertices near this hinge point, and click the Apply Vertices button. (If the Apply Vertices button—found in the bottom right of the MED window—is not apparent, it might be because you have the window minimized. Simply maximize or stretch the window out further, and all the buttons will be revealed.) The vertices are now attached to the selected bone and will move wherever the bone moves. You can remove vertices from a bone by clicking on the Remove Vertices button while the bone is selected. Continue until all the vertices of the model are blue.

Instructions for recording animation can be found in Chapter 5, "Modeling and Animating Characters," where you learned vertex animation. Recording bones animation is very similar to recording frame animation. Add a frame using the Edit > Manage Frames menu. Activate bones animation by clicking the Use Bones Animation button. Now select a bone by clicking on its hinge point. You can move or rotate the bone to its desired position. When you finish, add the next frame of animation and the next, tinkering with the bones in each one to produce the animation results you want. For instant replay of the animation that you have created, you can move the slider back and forth. Build animation cycles for every state of animation (walk, run, jump, and so on).

For more precise animation in each and every frame, click on the Bones Properties button (the icon that looks like a red circle is hiding behind a white page). You can change the following values for setting a bone's position and orientation in MED:

- **Position**—this moves the bone and its child bones to the desired position.
- **Rotate 1**—rotates the bone and its child bones around the bone's position.
- **Rotate 2**—rotates only the child bones around the bone's position.
- **Rotate 3**—rotates the bone and the child bones around the bone's origin.

If you wish to rotate without having the Bones Properties panel being open, you can switch between the three different rotations on the fly by pressing the number keys 1, 2, or 3. The current rotational mode is indicated in the status bar.

If you ever wish to reset the bone to its default position, you merely have to click the Remove Bones Animation button.

You never want to combine vertex and bones animation in the same animation frame. You can do this, and everything will look perfectly fine in MED, but when you see it rendered the vertex animations set in the same frames as the bones animations will be ignored. Also, if you decide to mix it up and have one bones animation and one vertex animation, the vertex frames must come first as a rule, followed by the bones frames. The only potential drawback to bones animation is that it needs more memory allocation per entity, and more render time than vertex animation; if you plan on using more than a few bones-animated models that will appear onscreen at any one time, you might consider going with vertex animation instead because it will load faster.

Once you are finished with mamakat.mdl, save your file and open mamakat.wmp in WED. You want to replace your standin.mdl with the mamakat.mdl while preserving its `RPGplayer` behavior. To do so, you can replace the source file in the object's Properties window. Save, build, and run your game to see your newly animated model in action.

Exercise 10.2: Artificial Intelligence

When the earliest computers were created, scientists wondered about their potential. Computers could do arithmetic faster than human beings? How fast or far could computers go? Could a computer possibly think like a human being? Could a computer become smarter than a human being?

These questions gave rise to a new research discipline in the field of computer science, called Artificial Intelligence (or AI). The goal of AI is to make computers do things that naturally sentient beings do: recognize objects by sensory organs, make logical decisions, and speak and understand languages.

In the 1950s, Arthur Samuels developed a program that could play checkers, although it could not beat a human expert. Eventually chess-and-checkers-playing programs became so powerful that no human could ever beat them. The best chess programs in the world are now totally unbeatable by anyone but a Grand Master. Commercial chess programs have deliberately limited intelligence so that the human beings playing them on their computers can have a chance against them. Chess and checkers are fairly simple games. After 50 years of study, computer programmers still haven't been able to build a computer that can conduct a general conversation with us so that—without knowing it was a computer—we couldn't tell the difference.

AI has mostly remained the domain of computer programmers and builders of robotic equipment. Game designers need not concern themselves with the depths of AI programming; what they need to do is to use AI to make their games appear more natural and responsive to the gamer. The common goals of Artificial Intelligence (AI) in games are

- To produce characters with "interesting" behaviors.
- To produce characters the player can relate to and interact with.
- To create challenges for the player (beating the game often equals beating the AI).

None of these goals includes making a perfect soldier, stunt driver, or insane clown. The perfection can come out of the computer because AI is byte-code derivative and can be made as perfect as you want; but you do not want to damage the player's self-esteem by ripping her away from the nice comfortable gaming experience. You merely want to challenge her. The supreme function of AI is to put up a good fight and then lose (see Figure 10.1).

Fundamental AI Structure

Most AI technologies share similar traits. They must be able to sense their environment, for one. For robots, this can mean a combination of infrared and motion-detection or camera perception (or lots of other sensory-simulated goodies). For the game characters, this means that they have to collect information about their understandings through algorithms. They must be able to perceive the following queries: Where is the player? Where is the player going? What is the basic geometry surrounding me? What is the shortest route I can take to get to where the player is right now? What weapons do I have?

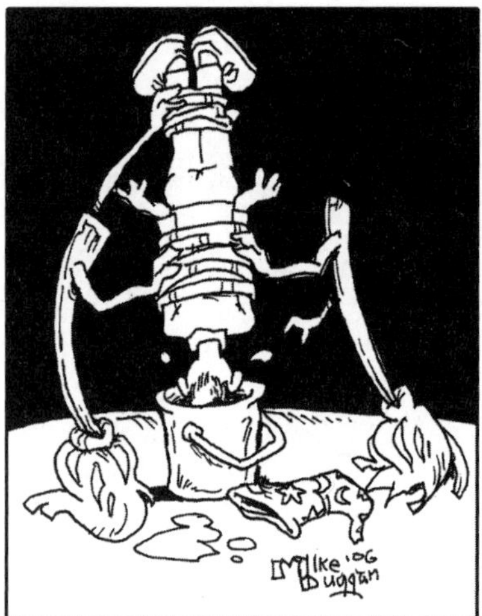

Figure 10.1
Alright, I give! I give!

AI must be able to keep track of important information that has been perceived. This may include the last known player position, the number of enemies he's up against, and the number of allies he's fighting with.

Finally, the AI must have an analysis or reasoning core—a "brain" if you will—set up through conditional statements that use sensory data and memory to make decisions about action. These define finite state machines and rule systems in the determination of the agent. The AI uses its reasoning core to achieve orders desired, and this is where the character's behavior or "personality" is displayed. Truly clever action routines can mimic intelligence.

Finite State Machines

This technique is the one most commonly used in games and is unlike most other techniques often used by the game designer. Finite state machines (or FSMs) are used in games to determine the behavior of some kind of artificial being and when and why its behavior changes. This being could be anything (an animal, person, robot, or any other virtual creature) and the finite state machine would be its brain.

This is the most important AI technique from the point of view of the game designer. A finite state machine isn't a physical machine at all. Don't think of wheels and gears. Rather it's a conceptual machine. Finite state machines are given that name because each one has a certain fixed number of possible states that it can be in. Let's look at an example of a real-life robot as it happens to be governed by an FSM.

In 1960, the researchers at Johns Hopkins University built a small robot they called the Hopkins Beast. The only thing this robot did was wander around the laboratory. When its batteries started to run low, it would search for an electrical outlet with its one photocell eye. Electrical outlets were the only objects in the laboratory the Beast could recognize. The Hopkins Beast would plug itself in until its batteries were fully recharged. Then it would set off wandering again. The Hopkins Beast had only three states: wandering, searching, and recharging. This robot was always in one of these three states. That's what FSM means.

Notice that just because the Hopkins Beast was in a fixed state doesn't mean that nothing was happening. While the robot was wandering, it was in motion and continually checking its internal sensors to determine the state of its battery level—to see if its battery was getting low. But at the most general level, these three things were what it did.

The states are one major part of an FSM. The other part of an FSM is the definition of how it changes from one state to another. These are called *transitions*. Transitions are shown by drawing thin arrows from one state to another with an explanation of what causes the change. The transition at the left that comes from nowhere indicates that wandering is the starting state. Most FSMs in real life don't always run in a loop like this, and it is possible to have more than one condition that causes them to change from one state to another.

Most FSMs create a set of states that represent AI configurations, such as `wait`, `attack`, and `escape`. There are a set of transitions that are conditions that have to be made to connect two states. For instance, the AI will stay in its `wait` state until it sees the player character, and then jump into its `hunt` state where in is running down the player character. When it gets near the player (near enough for melee combat), it switches to its `attack` state. FSMs are good for local behaviors, where only a few outcomes are possible in any given statement. They are also smart tools for sequential behaviors, where specific tasks follow other specific tasks, depending on extenuating circumstances.

Here is another example of a finite state machine. You have a virtual dog that the player will treat as a pet (similar to Nintendogs for the Nintendo DS). If there's a bone nearby and the dog is hungry, he eats it. If he's hungry and there is no bone, he will wander until he finds a bone. If he's not hungry, but he's sleepy, he will take a short nap. If he's not hungry and not sleepy, he'll yip and walk around acting playful and happy. This set of instructions can be programmed into a tidy algorithm. In 3D GameStudio it would look best in pairs of if . . . then/else subroutines.

AI Used in 3D GameStudio

You have already experienced the FPS template AI scripts, such as the FPS Guard, but there are other AI templates. The Dumb AI Bipeds (01) creates AI for testing and "background" AI. The `AIDumbBiped01` is a simple walking AI that can be killed. This is perfect for random NPCs who do not contribute anything but "warm bodies" to a game level.

The Fixed Place AI (01) governs AI for non-moving entities (gun turrets, search lights, and so on). The `AIFixed01_Turret` is literally a fixed weapon turret that continuously scans for the player and fires on him. This can be highly effective for creating high-security areas of a game level that you want to keep players out of.

Creating Better Character AI

Now that you know something about AI and have become more conversant on the underlying structure of AI as can be used in the GameStudio engine, I want you to expand what you know using the RPG_Project script.

Open each of your game levels you have built for the *Mama Kat* game. Apply the mamakat.wdl file in them as the master script file. Open the mamakat.wdl file and apply your skills to characters therein. If you want to have pedestrians milling around outdoors in the mamakat.wmp level, use guard.mdl, human1.mdl, warlock.mdl, witch.mdl, or inmate.mdl and add the Dumb AI Bipeds (01) script to the level. Attach `AIDumbBiped01` to these pedestrians, and change their individual settings so that not every single character has the same Force, Health, and so on.

If you have not done so yet, add the `RPGenemy` action to some of the guard.mdl and monster files in your sewers and barracks levels. You could even conceivably attach the Fixed Place AI (01) template script and put a few turrets into your levels. Use your imagination. You might be surprised at what you can come up with. If you want these AI to talk to the player, then continue on to Exercise 10.3.

Exercise 10.3: NPC Communication

You can program behaviors for objects to reveal a short text message or play a short audio clip when touched. These can be invisible triggers that disappear after they have finished their job, or they can remain as objects onscreen and present the text or audio messages every time the player avatar touches them. If you wish to use an animated entity, such as a non-player character (NPC), you can place a fixed but invisible entity around them and give them a behavior that shows the text message and remains. The character model used for the NPC, if it is not given a behavior, will endlessly loop through its animation frames.

George Pirvu at *Acknex Users Magazine* has created a tutorial called Morrowing which demonstrates the capabilities behind using text messages. If you are an advanced coder, you should download his tutorial and try out some of his tricks. I will demonstrate how you can play short audio clips or run raster images to demonstrate in-game discussions.

Play Audio on Contact

You can program NPCs to play a sound file (such as a WAV file). In this way, you can record voiceovers and play them throughout your game. You can reward players with funny and interesting results as NPCs start to really talk to them (see Figure 10.2). Try this: place a guard.mdl into the mamakat.wmp file, right in front of the City Guard barracks, and then place box.mdl over it. Scale

Figure 10.2
I knew that wouldn't work.

box.mdl up to surround the entire guard2.mdl. Apply the action listed below on it:

```
SOUND getaway = "goaway.wav";

functionGo_Away()
{
    if (event_type != EVENT_SONAR && event_type != EVENT_IMPACT) { return; }
    ent_playsound(me,getaway,100);
    wait(16);
}
action Gruff_Guard()
{
    my.INVISIBLE = ON;
    my.PASSABLE = ON;
    my.event = Go_Away;
    my.ENABLE_IMPACT = ON;
    my.ENABLE_SONAR = ON;
}
```

Save the level, compile it, and test-run it to see what the City Guard has to tell you. You can do this with other sound files and other characters to create an interactive environment. You can even program a randomizer to come up with random audio clips when the end user comes near the NPCs.

Show Journal Clues

Another in-game artifact is the classic NPC dialog window (traditional for RPGs) or the player finding journal entries that she can read onscreen. This can be done with bitmap panels that display on the computer screen, such as the following program script:

```
var diary_var;

BMAP diary1_map = "diary1.bmp"; // diary
PANEL diaryscreen = { bmap = diary1_map; }

BMAP diary2_map = "diary2.bmp"; // diary2
PANEL page2_screen = { bmap = diary2_map; flags =OVERLAY; }

BMAP diary3_map = "diary3.bmp"; // diary3
PANEL page3_screen { bmap = diary3_map; flags =OVERLAY; }

BMAP diary4_map = "diary4.bmp"; // diary4
PANEL page4_screen { bmap = diary4_map; flags =OVERLAY; }
```

```
function diary_pickup()
{
     wait(1);
          ent_remove(me);
          diary_var = 1;

}

function diary2_pickup()
{
       wait(1);
       ent_remove(me);
       diary_var = 2;

}

function diary3_pickup()
{
       wait(1);
       ent_remove(me);
       diary_var = 3;

}

function diary4_pickup()
{      wait(1);
       ent_remove(me);
       diary_var = 4;


}

///////////////// The Pickup Actions /////////////////

action diary()
{ my.ENABLE_CLICK = ON; my.event = diary_pickup; }

action diary2()
{ my.ENABLE_CLICK = ON; my.event = diary2_pickup; }

action diary3()
{ my.ENABLE_CLICK = ON; my.event = diary3_pickup; }

action diary4()
{ my.ENABLE_CLICK = ON; my.event = diary4_pickup; }
```

```
//////////////// Hide and Show Functions ////////////////

function show_diary()
{
        if (diary_var == 1) { diaryscreen.visible = on; }
        if (diary_var == 2) { page2_screen.visible = on; }
        if (diary_var == 3) { page3_screen.visible = on; }
        if (diary_var == 4) { page4_screen.visible = on; }
}

function hide_diary()
{
        if (diary_var == 1 )
        { diaryscreen.visible = off; bmap_purge(diary1_map); }
        if (diary_var == 2 )
        { page2_screen.visible = off; bmap_purge(diary2_map); }
        if (diary_var == 3)
        { page3_screen.visible = off; bmap_purge(diary3_map); }
        if (diary_var == 4)
        { page4_screen.visible = off; bmap_purge(diary4_map); }
}

ON_O = show_diary;
ON_P = hide_diary;
```

You will have to create four bitmap files (diary1.bmp–diary4.bmp) and type this code in at the bottom of mamakat.wdl verbatim for this code to work. Essentially, you are setting up four panels to display onscreen and a handler for them. Using this as a guide, you can elaborate or create as many screen images as you wish. Setting their flags to `overlay` will allow them to hide their pure black areas so you do not have to show a rectangle covering the entire screen and can achieve non-uniformity.

In Summary

You have learned to animate characters using bones animation, which makes for easier, more realistic bipedal animation but also costs memory reserves to render. You have also taken a journey into the intelligent arena of Artificial Intelligence and how finite state machines are used in 3D GameStudio to portray characters. You have gotten those characters to talk (in one way or another). You have spent enough time on non-player characters. Now it is about time to make your player's hero character tough, resilient, and destructive. The next chapter will show you how to create player avatars that please!

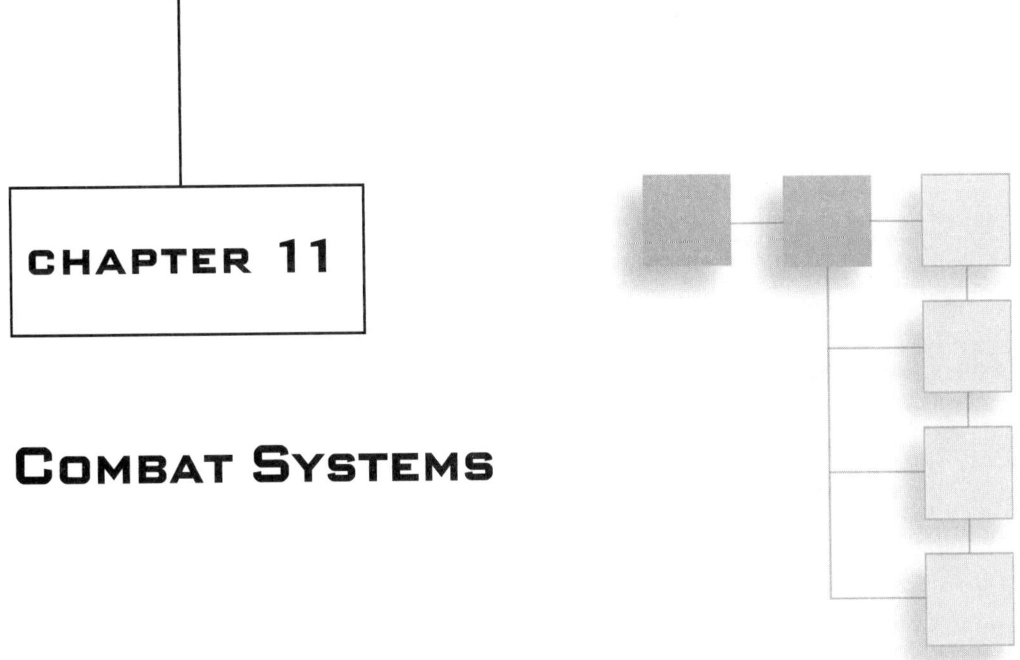

Chapter 11

Combat Systems

As the designer of a role-playing game, you must consider the player's options carefully. In the *Mama Kat* game, you are helped by the fact that the player's role is restricted to the feline rogue. You know what a rogue might do in a given circumstance and how to plan an encounter accordingly. In a game where you allow the player to choose the role they want to play before the game starts, you have little control over planning these circumstances. You will have to keep in mind the different roles and skills the player might want to apply to a situation, which you might not have planned in the first place. You must learn to adapt to player expectations in order to fully immerse her in a virtual world.

Exercise 11.1: Character Selection

Many role-playing games offer the player a choice of what role they want to play, such as a fighter, ranger, thief, or wizard. With the *Mama Kat* game, this is not necessary because the player can only choose the Kat character. She is still a versatile role to play, as she can go in many different directions, depending on the player's choices. The player can use melee, ranged, or stealth combat as well as join different factions.

If you wanted to create a selection screen at the start of the game, where the player chooses which character they want to play, you can do so by creating a dummy level at the start. This level will be a black texture-mapped hollow cube with a single 3D model floating in the center of it. You place the `rotate_model` action on this model. (See the code script below.) The `rotate_model` action allows the player to rotate around the 3D model and switch between the model's available skins. You will have to set more than one skin on each model for this to work; otherwise, there will be only the one skin available for each model. When the player has decided which character model he prefers, he presses ENTER to start the game. The game level must include an avatar with the behavior `player_choice` on it. `Player_choice` duplicates the basic player behavior, as well as mimics the player model and skin chosen.

It is a very short jump in theory to set specialized text messages that come up for each of the character models the player can flip between—telling him the names of the roles such as Warrior, Wizard, and Thief (see Figure 11.1). Then you can set `player_choice` to start with stat bonuses based on the character role chosen. You may even have to develop simultaneous games so that if the player chooses Wizard, only the game levels that pertain to Wizards will be loaded. Use your ingenuity to come up with other ways for players to select their starting characters.

The following is but one example. It uses three character models and three roles. It does not show text messages, as the character models are meant to be self-explanatory. The roles also do not start with stat advantages, but that is something that would be fairly easy to add.

```
var game_started = 0; // will be set to 1 when the player loads the playable level
var player_model = 0;
var player_skin = 0;
```

Figure 11.1
Him? Oh, he's just Typical Berserker Number 12.

```
var start_pos[3] = 100, 50, 30; // the player appears at x=100, y=50, z=30 in
the level
STRING dummy_wmb = "dummy.wmb";
STRING level_wmb = "level1.wmb";
STRING warrior_mdl = "guard.mdl";
STRING wizard_mdl = "warlock.mdl";
STRING thief_mdl = "thief.mdl";
function start_game(); // sets up function prototypes
function player_moves();// sets up function prototypes

action rotate_model() // this is the player select model
{
        my.skin = 1;
        my.light = on; // this model will glow with ambient light
        my.lightred = 155;
        my.lightgreen = 155;
        my.lightblue = 155;
        my.lightrange = 0;
        while (game_started == 0)
        {
               my.pan += 3 * time;
               if (key_cuu == 1)// if the player presses the up arrow key
               {
                     while (key_cuu == 1) {wait (1);}
                     my.skin += 1; // switch skin mapping
                     if (my.skin == 4) {my.skin = 1;}
               }
               if (key_cud == 1)// if the player presses the down arrow key
               {
                     while (key_cud == 1) {wait (1);}
                     my.skin -= 1; // switch skin mapping
                     if (my.skin == 0) {my.skin = 3;}
               }
               if (key_cur == 1)// if the player presses the right arrow key
               {
                     while (key_cur == 1) {wait (1);}
                     camera.pan -= 40; // camera will rotate
               }
               if (key_cul == 1)// if the player presses the left arrow key
               {
                    while (key_cul == 1) {wait (1);}
                    camera.pan += 40; // camera will rotate
            }
```

```
        camera.pan %= 360; // camera is limited to 360 degree rotation
        if (key_enter == 1) // if player presses ENTER, start the game
        {
                game_started = 1; // stop this loop
                player_model = camera.pan / 120 + 1;
                player_skin = my.skin;
                start_game();
        }
        wait (1);
    }
}

function start_game()
{
    me = NULL;
    level_load (level_wmb);
    wait (3);
    if (player_model == 1)// sets up the warrior
    { player = ent_create (warrior_mdl, start_pos, player_choice); }
    if (player_model == 2)// sets up the wizard
    { player = ent_create (wizard_mdl, start_pos, player_choice); }
    if (player_model == 3)// sets up the thief
    { player = ent_create (thief_mdl, start_pos, player_choice); }
}

function player_choice()
{
    my.skin = player_skin;
    RPGplayer(); // place your hero's behavior (from templates) here
}
```

Character Stats

For the *Mama Kat* game, we are not going to use a player select screen. Instead, we will jump right into creating a character by defining its character stats.

Setting Up

Find the WDL script file in your mama_kat folder called RPGadventure.wdl and double-click on it to open it up in SED. This is the master script for creating character stats. Scroll down to where you see this:

```
// use general purpose adventure text
STRING start1_str = "Boo-hoo-hoo...";
```

```
STRING level_info_str = "You made a level!
You may share bonus points!";

STRING bonus_info_str =
 "\n Divide Practice points! Done";

// Character stats
STRING char_pan_str = "

 Luck: / Charisma:

 Strength: / Gray Matter:

 Reflexes: / Current Level:

 Lockpick: Practice:

 Next Level:
 ";
```

This is the general adventure text, which you can replace depending on the setting and type of RPG you are designing. However, the blank spaces surrounding the characters that you see are vital to the performance of the character stats in-game; special values will appear therein, and if you change the text too radically, the letters may overlap or jump out of proper alignment. Therefore, take care when replacing the text and leave enough room for the values to appear in the proper places. You will get a preview of where they go when you run the game in a moment.

For now, I want you to notice that the character stats have already been carefully selected and input for the *Mama Kat* game; they include Luck, Strength, Reflexes, Lockpick, Charisma, and Gray Matter. The first three are variable stats. This means that they will go up and down frequently, as they can be taken away from and given back to, but never overriding their maximum values. Luck governs a lot of different tasks and is a catch-all category for overcoming trouble. Strength is used to see just how tough Kat is and how much damage she can perform. Reflexes are Kat's cat-like reflexes and control her level of agility and impish balancing.

The others are not so much variable attributes as they are fixed skills. Lockpick governs Kat's ability to pick locks. Charisma determines Kat's innate skill at demurely conning people into believing her. Gray Matter is Kat's skill at reading, writing, and comprehending concepts bigger than herself. If you continue scrolling down the script, you will see how these parameters are set and you can increase their integers. The script originally has them set very low to start, but you can change that by replacing the numbers in the code.

These character stats are not there merely for looks. Next we will look at making tests for each one and how they are appreciated in a balanced role-playing game.

Looting the Place

The first sort of character stat test we will look at is one of the most prevalent in RPGs: breaking into a locked place or locked treasure chest. This sort of task puts the Lockpick skill to the test. Scroll down to the bottom of RPGadventure.wdl and type the following:

```
/////// LOCKED TREASURE CHEST ///////
define lock_difficulty, skill1;
function pick_lock();
SOUND gottreasure = "box_open.wav";
SOUND sorry_locked = "locked.wav";

BMAP locked_map = "lockedbox.bmp"; // image of a locked box
PANEL lockedscreen = { bmap = locked_map; }
BMAP unlocked_map = "unlocked.bmp"; // image of an opened box
PANEL unlockedscreen = { bmap = unlocked_map; }

action treasure()
{       my.enable_impact = on; my.event = pick_lock; }

function pick_lock()
{
        wait (1);
        if (my.skill1 == 0) {my.skill1 = 5;}
        if (player_gew < my.skill1)
                {
                        snd_play (sorry_locked, 100, 0);
        lockedscreen.visible = on;
                         sleep(16);
                         lockedscreen.visible = off;
                }
        if (player_gew >= my.skill1)
                {
                           snd_play (gottreasure, 100, 0);
                           unlockedscreen.visible = on;
```

```
                        sleep(16);
                        unlockedscreen.visible = off;
                        ent_create("box.mdl", my.x, get_cash);
                        ent_remove (me);
                        wait(1);
                }
}
```

Note that the algorithm checks the value of `player_gew`, which is the code name for Kat's Lockpick skill. If the Lockpick skill is of a high enough value to match the chest's difficulty ranking (set by the entity's Skill 1, which you can set in WED), then Kat can open the treasure chest. The program removes the treasure chest and creates a box.mdl (our versatile catch-all model, which you can change by typing in a different file name here). This box.mdl is given the `get_cash` action. This is meant to reward Kat with money. Unfortunately, we haven't programmed that part. That's the next coding you must do.

Scroll up above the locked treasure chest code you just typed, and start writing:

```
////////// GET AND SPEND MONEY //////////
var cash = 0;
function add_money();
function buy_me();
BMAP cashmap = "cash.pcx";
SOUND gotcash_snd = "gotitem.wav";
SOUND spentcash_snd = "spentcash.wav";
BMAP item1_map = "item1.bmp"; // your first reward item
PANEL item1screen = { bmap = item1_map; }
BMAP item2_map = "item2.bmp"; // your second reward item
PANEL item2screen = { bmap = item2_map; }
BMAP item3_map = "item3.bmp"; // your third reward item
PANEL item3screen = { bmap = item3_map; }
BMAP item4_map = "item4.bmp"; // your fourth reward item
PANEL item4screen = { bmap = item4_map; }
BMAP item5_map = "item5.bmp"; // your last reward item
PANEL item5screen = { bmap = item5_map; }

PANEL cashpan =
{
      bmap = cashmap;
      layer = 20;
      pos_x = 550;
      pos_y = 5;
```

```
        digits = 40, 22, 4, standard_font,1, cash;
        flags = OVERLAY;
}

action get_cash()
{ my.enable_impact = on; my.event = add_money; }

function add_money()
{
        wait (1);
        if (my.skill1 == 0) {my.skill1 = 5;} // default =5 bucks
        if (cash == 0) { cashpan.visible = on; }
        cash += my.skill1;
        if (my.skill2 == 0) { item1screen.visible=on; sleep(16);
item1screen.visible=off;}
        if (my.skill2 == 1) { item2screen.visible=on; sleep(16);
item2screen.visible=off;}}
        if (my.skill2 == 2) { item3screen.visible=on; sleep(16);
item3screen.visible=off;}}
        if (my.skill2 == 3) { item4screen.visible=on; sleep(16);
item4screen.visible=off;}}
        if (my.skill2 == 4) { item5screen.visible=on; sleep(16);
item5screen.visible=off;}}
        snd_play (gotcash_snd, 70, 0);
        ent_remove (me);
}

action buy_items()
{
        my.enable_click = on;
        my.event = buy_me;
}

function buy_me()
{
        wait (1);
        if (event_type != event_click || cash < my.skill1) {return;}
        cash -= my.skill1;
        snd_play (spentcash_snd, 70, 0);
        ent_remove (me);
}
```

The first part of this program code (`get_cash` and `add_money`) gives the player a special item that is worth money and can be spent or bartered later on for other objects. Kat could fence these items later on in the game for favors (such as health pick-up items). You will have to supply the image and sound files for this script to work. You will need to make box_open.wav, locked.wav, lockedbox.bmp, unlocked.bmp, cash.pcx, gotitem.wav, spentcash.wav, item1.bmp, item2.bmp, item3.bmp, item4.bmp, and item5.bmp. The sound files you might be able to convert from files in the Audio folder on the CD. The image files can be small (under 60 × 60 pixels) or fill the screen—use your imagination.

The second part of the program code (`buy_items` and `buy_me`) is the part where Kat would barter for other objects. Right now they are essentially empty place-holders. The cash value is removed, without anything being given back. If you wanted, all you would have to do is copy and paste the `ent_create` line from the Lockpick test,changing the model created and the action given to the model to whatever it is you want Kat to get; type that in a line just after the `cash -= my.skill1;` in function `buy_me()`.

Both entities that you would place `get_cash` or `buy_items` on have an active placeholder in Skill 1. For `get_cash`, whatever is in Skill 1 gives the player an equal amount in money. For `buy_items`, whatever is in Skill 1 is the cost of the item. If Skill 1 in either case is left blank, then the system has a default set to 5 (in other words, 5 bucks).

Gaining Knowledge from Books

The game world of Krawl is filled with Tomes of Lore, the mere reading of which gains the user bonuses to her skills and understanding. You are going to program a Tome of Lore that gains the player advancements to one random character stat if properly learned. The learning of it is based on a test of the player character's Gray Matter (handled by the code name `player_int`). After the locked door functions you just input, begin writing this:

```
//////////////////// KNOWLEDGE FROM READING BOOKS //////////////////////
define reading_difficulty, skill1;
define learning = skill25;
function read_book();
BMAP book_map = "book.bmp"; // an image of an open book
PANEL bookscreen = { bmap = book_map; }
SOUND gotsmart = <"book2.wav">;SOUND sorry_dumb = <"book1.wav">;
action Reading_Book()
{       my.enable_impact = on;  my.event = read_book; }
```

```
function read_book()
{
    wait (1);
    if (my.skill1 == 0) {my.skill1 = 5;}
    if (player_int < my.skill1)
          {
                snd_play (sorry_dumb, 100, 0);
                bookscreen.visible = on;
                wait(-1);
                bookscreen.visible = off;
          }
    if (player_int >= my.skill1)
          {
                snd_play (gotsmart, 100, 0);
                bookscreen.visible = on;
                wait(-1);
                bookscreen.visible = off;
                if(my.learning==0){my.learning = 15 + random(35);}
    if(my.skill1==0){my.skill1=0;}
    if(my.learning<20) {player_mana += 2; }
    if(my.learning>=20 && my.learning<25) {player_str += 2; }
    if(my.learning>=25 && my.learning<30) {player_gew += 2; }
    if(my.learning>=30 && my.learning<35) {player_mut += 2; }
    if(my.learning>=35 && my.learning<40) {player_int += 2; }
    if(my.learning>=40 && my.learning<45) {player_hp += 2; }
    if(my.learning>=45) {player_bonus_pts += 3; }
                ent_remove (me);
                wait(1);
          }
}
```

You must create another bitmap image, book.bmp, for this script. The following is one of the most important lines of the code you can take away with you: `if (my.learning == 0) {my.learning = 15 + random (35) ;}`. It calls a random number from 15 to 50. First it sets a base number, which it does at 15. Then it adds a random integer from 0 to 35. The highest combination can be 50, while the lowest possible number would be 15. Then—because it loaded the result into a variable placeholder called `my.learning`—the next bit of code reads the results and tells the engine which character stat bonus to give the player. The very last one gives the player more bonus points, which the player can spend on any stats she wants, while the rest of the results selectively raise just one stat by 2 points, such as intelligence (see Figure 11.2).

Figure 11.2
Aw shucks. I dun got smarter!

Other Tests

What other sorts of character stat tests can you imagine taking place? Could Luck be the determining factor in Kat "just happening" to have the right Skeleton Key to unlock a lock mechanism? Could Charisma be the determining factor in Kat getting a City Guard to let her enter an area normally off limits to rogues? Plan for these tests ahead of time. Put your ideas to paper. Keep every character stat balanced so that not one of them becomes more usable and important than any other one. You want the player to sweat when she has bonus points to spend on advancing her player's character stats. If she doesn't wonder whether she should up her Gray Matter or up her Lockpick, then you have not done your job well enough or shown her the importance of using each character stat to its fullest potential.

Exercise 11.2: Melee Combat

In this chapter, you are going to focus on creating three different combat systems:

- Melee combat
- Ranged combat
- Stealth combat

The choice of most players (given the popularity of action games and the tendency for RPGs to focus on sword-fighting almost as much as spell-casting) is melee combat. Players who tire easily of the patience required for stealth combat or the slow uncertain aim of ranged combat delight in being able to rush an enemy and dash at them with sword, battle axe, club, and such. Whether slicing or bluntly bashing at an enemy at close range (or simply using fists), the player might prefer the honest fighting of RPG melee combat.

There are essentially two main ways that programmers have used 3DGS to create melee combat sequences. One is to create a "dummy" firearm weapon that operates similarly to a melee weapon. The template weapons could be altered slightly to be more harmful or less (depending) and can be applied to knives, axes, swords, or other melee weapons. The trick is to reduce their range of attack and turn off visible shooting. Then make them hit and give off sparks, and you are done.

Another way to create melee combat in 3DGS is to run a ray-trace. Ray-traces are performed by initializing a start point (usually a vertex on a 3D model) and running a ray from it to an end point (another vertex). If the trace detects collision along the ray with an enemy, it damages the enemy. Ray-tracing is fairly appropriate when creating a sword weapon, but it can become more difficult with larger, more complex models, such as two-handed war-axes. Yet the properties are the same. (See Figure 11.3.)

Figure 11.3
Nobody knew it, but on weekends Granny was a skilled operative for the Black Hand.

Exercise 11.3: Ranged Combat

The second most popular choice of players of role-playing games is to use strategy to overcome obstacles. Most players using strategy prefer a higher ground (and better advantage) to snipe at their enemies. They prefer keeping their enemies at a distance while still reducing their health. This is the realm of ranged combat. Ranged combat includes firearms as well as bows and arrows, depending (largely) on the game setting.

The easiest way to create ranged combat is to use the template scripts for weapons, but change the weapons models to appear however you want (including as crossbows or oak bows). There are several ranged weapons in the templates that work as comparatively well as any weapons you could code from scratch. You can theoretically alter any or all of these weapons (changing the pick-up messages, the look, and the usage effects) to represent any weapon you desire, within reason.

Another way to create ranged combat is to script it yourself from scratch. Because of the tricky nature of real-life bows and arrows, for instance, it is necessary to code it from scratch to get the weapon to look right.

First-Person Bow and Arrow Shooting

If you can enforce a first-person camera mode (not originally part of the RPGplayer package) you can use this quick-and-easy bow and arrow script that will give your player all the marksmanship she might need. You must use first-person because of the placement and appearance of the models herein. Anything else would just look funny.

```
function init_bowarrow();
function get_bow();
function move_arrow();
function hurt_you();
var arrow_fired = 0;
STRING arrow_mdl = "arrow.mdl"; // this is the model used for the arrows

ENTITY bow_entity =
{
	type = "bow.mdl"; // this is the model used for the bow
	layer = 10; view = camera;
	x = 30; y = 8; z = -10;
}
```

```
action bow() // attach this action to your bow & arrow model
{
        my.enable_impact = ON;
        my.event = get_bow;
        while (my != NULL) // rotates as long as it hasn't been picked up
        { my.pan += 3 * time; wait (1); }
}

function get_bow()
{
        wait (1); ent_remove (me);
        bow_entity.frame = 2; // show the arrow
        bow_entity.visible = on;
}

function init_bowarrow()
{
        while (1)
        {
                if ((mouse_left == 1) && (bow_entity.frame < 7))
                { bow_entity.frame += 2 * time; }
                else
                { if ((bow_entity.frame >= 7) && (arrow_fired == 0))
                       {
                     while (mouse_left == 1) {wait (1);}
                     vec_set (temp, player.pos);
                     temp.z += 20;
                     ent_create (arrow_mdl, temp, move_arrow);
                     arrow_fired = 1; // a single arrow
                }
                else // the player isn't shooting
                {
                     arrow_fired = 0;
                     bow_entity.frame = 2;
                }
        }
        wait (1);
    }
}

function move_arrow()
{
        wait (1);
        my.enable_entity = on;
```

```
        my.enable_block = on;
        my.event = hurt_you;
        my.passable = on;
        my.pan = camera.pan;
        my.tilt = camera.tilt;
        my.skill12 = 50;
        my.skill13 = 0;
        my.skill14 = 0;
        my.skill12 *= time;
        while (my.skill12 != 0) // moves until it hits something
        {
                if (vec_dist (my.x, player.x) < 100) {my.passable = on;}
                else {my.passable = off;}
                c_move (me, my.skill12, nullvector, activate_trigger);
                wait (1);
        }
    }
    function hurt_you()
    {

        if (event_type == event_entity)
        {
        my.skill12 = 0; // stop moving
        you._HEALTH_003 -= 80; // does damage = 80;
        wait(1);
        ent_remove (me);
      }
      if (event_type == event_block)
      {
            my.skill12 = 0;
            my.passable = on;
      }
}
```

This works really well, you'll find. The longer the player holds down the left mouse button, the longer the bow will keep the arrow strung and the more force will be applied to it when it is finally released, simulating medieval ranged combat.

Exercise 11.4: Stealth Combat

Ever since the original *Thief* game was released (see Figure 11.4), stealth has become a popular feature in many other video games, even those where it makes no sense. RPGs have been catering to the players who enjoy stealth and assassin tactics by offering stealth combat sequences. The game *Chronicles of*

Figure 11.4
Stealth in games can make play more like hide-and-seek. (*Thief: Deadly Shadows*, image courtesy of Eidos 2004)

Riddick: Escape from Butcher Bay took these tactics even further, offering the player all the power of stealth combat and the added ability to see in the dark using Riddick's unique night vision.

Players who delight in stealth combat enjoy being able to slink around dark halls and tunnels, keeping to the shadows, and using all their abilities of invisibility to get around obstacles. Where they cannot evade direct confrontations, they use assassination to silently kill their enemies—instead of going toe to toe with them in melee combat. Stealth combat takes skill and more than a little patience to get right.

The easiest method for creating stealth combat in a game is to define a variable where the player may become invisible as a target to his enemies; while invisible, the player can still move around and interact with the game environment but remains off the enemy's radar. As soon as the variable is turned off, the player character is once again visible to the enemy and a target for attack. This is how you will create the conditions for stealth combat.

Creating Stealth Mode

Type the following in at the very bottom of mamakat.wdl. This snippet controls the use of light and shadow to make the player appear visible or invisible.

```
//////////// SHOW AND USE LIGHT AND SHADOW //////////
var invisible_pl = 0;
BMAP back_pcx = "back.bmp";
BMAP cursor_pcx = "cursor.bmp";

PANEL back_pan =
{
      bmap = back_pcx;
      pos_x = 5; pos_y =505; layer = 3;
      flags = OVERLAY, VISIBLE;
}

PANEL cursor_pan =
{
      bmap = cursor_pcx;
      pos_x = 0; pos_y = 510; layer = 4;
      flags = OVERLAY, VISIBLE;
}

function player_light()
{
        while(1)
        {
              vec_set (temp, my.x);
              temp.z -= 1000;
              trace_mode = ignore_me + ignore_passable + scan_texture;
              trace (my.x, temp);
              nimbic_light = 10 + 0.38 * tex_light;
              cursor_pan.pos_x = nimbic_light;
              if(nimbic_light < 25){invisible_pl = 1;} // play with the value 25
              if(nimbic_light >= 25){invisible_pl = 0;} // 25 is repeated here
              wait (1);
        }
}
```

Place this line of code somewhere in the action that is attached to your player: `player_light();` This will turn on the function that checks for light ranges and return appropriate values. Note that—besides revealing the amount of light to the player in a visual onscreen panel—this code mostly turns the parameter `invisible_pl` on or off (1 or 0).

`invisible_pl` can be further set up within the RPGenemy.wdl script in the RPGplayer package to tell the enemy entity that, if `invisible_pl` is on (set to 1), to stop attacking the player. Open RPGenemy.wdl and look in the action `RPGenemy` for where the FSM is set to walk to the player's location. If you set `if(invisible_pl = 1) {return;}` in the code, you can stop the enemy from moving toward the player when the player is hiding in shadow. Of course, this can appear somewhat unreal when the player can walk right up on the enemy, and as long as the player is in a light variance of less than 25, the enemy will remain completely blind to the player. But it does allow for some wonderful assassination strategies. The key is to vary your levels. Pay close attention to the direction of static lights and shadows. Keep your ambient lighting very dark. Put pools of shadow in otherwise brightly lit areas, and make the player dart from darkness to darkness to sneak around enemies.

In Summary

You have learned the tricks behind making RPGs in 3D GameStudio. Who knows what the future might hold? Or what you can think of to build next? The two genres that I have shown you are a mere fraction of the overwhelming game genre market that exists right now in this booming industry. You may come up with a unique and original game that is so unconventional that it attracts attention. You may wish to sell this game online—or net the attention of a big-time game company and get an honored position with them. If so, then all there is left for you is . . . the conclusion.

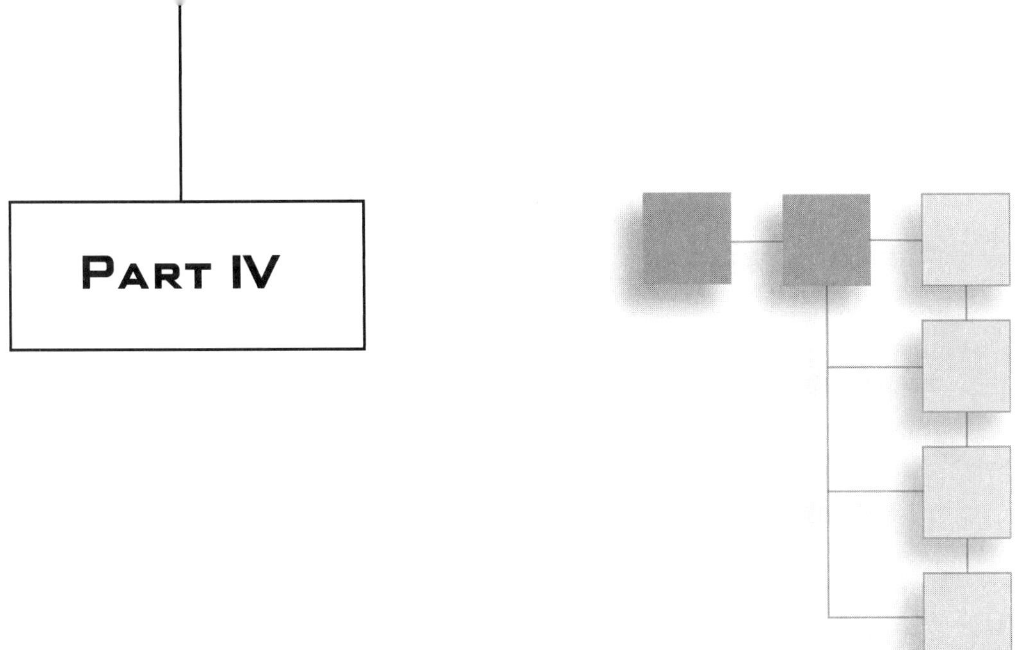

Part IV

Conclusion

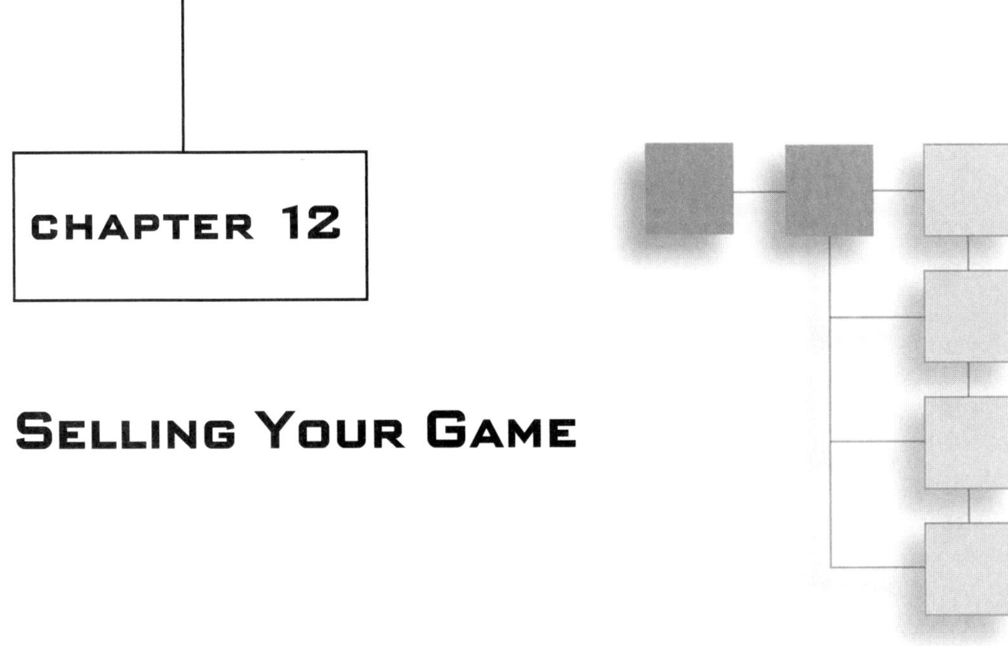

Chapter 12

Selling Your Game

Note

"The worst thing that could happen to you is that you've got a great game, but nobody's heard of it. We don't want that."

—Marc Taro Holmes, Obsidian Entertainment

You have become a game designer, and the skills you are learning now can service you if you prefer to continue along this path. The next chapter handles the details if you want to find higher education or enter the game industry from the inside. This chapter will give you all the details of starting your own game design studio and selling your own games online. Read on to learn the amazing world of independent game development.

Independent Game Development

Note

"Indie designers, targeting the gigantic market of casual users with low-end machines, are finding new paths beyond the usual Solitaire and Breakout clones. A golden age in any creative field typically requires a well-understood source of predictable, reliable, but modest and strictly limited income—along with a few strong visionaries leading a vigorous community that prizes originality. . . . The foundations of the golden age are almost in place. The next five to ten years will show what we can build."

—Allen Varney

Besides the big-name publishers, there are well over 1,000 video game development companies today. Many are small one- or two-person operations creating Flash games for the Web or games for cell phones. Other small companies work in their spare time to create independent games they publish themselves. There are also currently more than 250,000 independent hobby game developers. This is not a trend to overlook.

Justin Mette started his gaming career on the Atari 2600 and today is the president of 21-6 Productions. About independent game development he says, "I believe that the online distribution market for games is where most independent developers can get started and make a good living. Developing a game in 4 to 6 months with a small remote team means that your costs stay low and your return on your investment does not have to be as large as the box or console industry." He goes on to say that "it's a great time to be an indie. The Internet allows you to find amazing talent and work together without an office." He acknowledges that "a booming online game distribution market [lays] out the best opportunity in years for game developers to live their dreams." Imagine doing what you love to . . . and not having to go to work in an office. This is the dream that has inspired scores of game designers to become independent game developers.

Since 1999, the Game Developers' Conference, or GDC, has hosted the Independent Games Festival (IGF) to reward innovative games produced by small independent video game developers, as well as students in the field. The IGF was officially founded in 1998 by the Gama Network (the same people that run Gamasutra and *Game Developer* magazine) and was inspired by the Sundance Film Festival. There are awards from $500 to $20,000, and the Student Showcase displays 10 notable games submitted by students. The IGF is a great place to meet other independent game designers—and to get recognized.

Scratchware Manifesto

The Scratchware Manifesto originated from veteran game designer Greg Costikyan and starts by declaring, "The machinery of gaming has run amok." In it, Costikyan blames the game industry for running away with itself and leaving the independent or startup game studio in the dust. As Costikyan says, "Instead of serving creative vision, it suppresses it. Instead of encouraging innovation, it represses it. Instead of taking its cue from our most imaginative minds, it takes its cue from the latest month's PC Data list. Instead of rewarding those who succeed, it penalizes them with development budgets so high and royalties so low that there can be no reward for creators. Instead of ascribing credit to those who deserve it, it seeks to associate success with the corporate machine."

These are pretty harsh (but true) words and have left plenty of developers saying, "Here, here!" The game industry is one that focuses on money, which is true. It is a corporate venture where creative freedom is deliberately channeled to fuel an ever-expanding demand for game content. If you compare the actual number of music albums or videotapes sold at your local department store, you would find them sadly outnumbering the scope of video games sold at the same store. (This is on a wave of change, however.) Publishers fight with retailers and each other in order to get their products on the shelves and keep them there for as long as possible. They have a lot of money riding on the outcome of their sales, and this can indeed make any businessman nervous.

Costikyan's answer to this conundrum is for more developers to stand up to the big companies and self-publish. He calls this strategy "scratchware"—the games are made on a shoestring budget, practically by scratch, by one to three people who do everything they can out of their basement or garage. As Costikyan says, "They are made using normal software and hardware tools for the average computer system. They are made at night, on weekends, during vacations, or whenever one can. Tasks are delegated or shared. Anyone involved should have at least two of the following skills: writing, programming, art, game design, sound design, and/or music production." He goes on to say that scratchware games are primarily about 2D art, simply because he feels that 3D art is too costly and complicated (but you know that's not quite true today because the 3D GameStudio engine is a cost-efficient solution to making games).

Scratchware has never been made or attempted. The concept is still in it infancy, even though the idea has been around since the 1980s. Several Web sites do sell self-made games, but they don't call them scratchware. Most of these are run by adventure game developers. Adventure games, since they were surpassed by the 3D console market in the 1980s, have lurked in the background, and small teams of designers have continued to make them on relatively non-existent budgets. Costikyan acknowledges that the adventure game genre might become the first foray into scratchware.

Selling Hobby Games

Note

"Never be afraid to mislabel a product."

—Rule of Acquisition #239, Ferengi Rules of Acquisition

Scratchware is meant to be sold on an individual purchase basis and online for $10 to $25 per copy. As I mentioned at the start of this book, this might not sound like a lot, but if you were to accept royalties from a publisher on a game that you developed, you would not get that; royalties are typically 13 to 15 percent of all units sold to retailers, which may average about $5 dollars per game sold (if that). If you self-publish and do it well, you might be able to sell 1,000 units of your game in the first year, earning you a potential gross profit of $10,000 or $25,000. Most games sell at least 40,000 units in their first year. Think on them apples!

You might call this a hobby. It beats making pottery or knitting scarves. The trick is not so much the development of the game. I am sure you can use 3D GameStudio to make great computer games and publish them yourself. The trick is to promote yourself and sell your hobby games. Whether you decide to call them scratchware or not, creating personal imaginative entertainment products can be a fulfilling way to spend your time—and you can make a lot of money at it!

Starting a Studio

If you are going to be a game designer, you will need some supplies, hardware, and technology that support your imagination and creativity. This section contains all the information you need to set yourself up.

Before you can make any games, you will need to put together your game studio, a place where you can do your best work (see Figure 12.1). Your studio doesn't have to be a corporate office cubicle, a fancy study lined with books, or even an artist's loft. You can transform a section of your house, such as a bedroom, garage, or basement, into a working studio. The first step is to find someplace that offers some privacy and where you will feel comfortable creating. Be sure to let your family know that this will be your private work area and—if possible—ask them not to disturb you while you are working. Once you've located the ideal location for your game studio, check to make sure you have all the essential studio items.

- **Computer**—One of the most important features a game studio must have is a computer. You already have one that is compatible with the 3D GameStudio software, I hope, since you have made it this far in the book. If you were using a computer that belonged to someone else (such as a school), you

Figure 12.1
What your future game studio could look like. (Image courtesy of Illusion Softworks 2006)

will have to go out and purchase your own computer. Refer to this book's Introduction for computer requirements before making any purchases. As with any purchases you make for your game studio, this is a commercial purchase and part of a self-owned and self-operated business. You must keep all receipts for tax purposes.

- **Software**—You will need to have specific software installed on your computer, including 3D GameStudio, a paint program, Microsoft Word, a Web browser, a Web design program like Dreamweaver, an audio editor like Audacity, and any others that you can think of (or afford).
- **Scanner**—Every game artist needs access to a scanner bed for converting 2D art into digital art (for application to the game software).
- **Digital camera (optional**—Game artists find it beneficial to have a digital camera to take pictures of interesting locations (for developing into levels and background images), plus digital cameras can take shots of objects you want to use later as textures in your game.
- **Drawing table or desk**—You should have a good place to draw. Any kind of flat, sturdy surface will do: a card table, kitchen table, countertop, desk, or folding table. A light table would be ideal if you want to draw professionally because you can do tracings and clean-up work on it.

- **Art supplies**—Every game designer uses different art supplies, but some standards to consider include pens, brushes, and paper.
- **Lighting**—If your studio has a window, great. If that window has a view, then it's even better (as long as it doesn't distract you from working). However, a table lamp or two are essential for you to see the keyboard well enough and for detailed drawing.
- **A comfortable chair**—Finding a chair with good back support is extremely important. With a comfortable chair, you can withstand hours of sitting in front of your computer or drawing pictures. A cushion or pillow placed on the chair's seat might help as well.
- **Decorations (optional)**—Posters of your favorite games or game characters or pages from your favorite game magazines hung on the walls of your studio can help motivate your creativity. If you collect figurines, place them around your computer monitor. Just don't clutter your workspace so that you can't get anything done right.
- **Snacks (optional)**—Snacks can be great while working and can energize your creativity. When you need inspiration, a cookie or banana break can go a long way! Just be sure that any snacks you have are a safe distance from your computer keyboard or most prized artwork. And watch that you don't stuff your face and get out of shape.
- **Studio on the go**—If you have to leave for a trip or vacation and you want to work on your game, you can pack a portable studio and take it with you. The easiest way to do this is to take a laptop computer with all your software installed on it. Put your pens, pencils, and sketchbook into a box or bag so your work is protected from the elements. You could also pack a hard, but lightweight, drawing surface if you think that you'll need one (oversized books work really well).

The most important aspect of having a game studio is having fun while you are there. Unlike real work or doing your chores, you have the freedom to do as little or as much game creation as you want, whenever you want. Your success in the industry is totally up to you. But remember: real success takes time and dedication, so it's important to develop good work habits. Start by going to your studio every other day for thirty minutes to an hour at a go. Chances are, you'll have so much fun designing characters, levels, and challenges that you'll stay longer anyway and have to tear yourself away from work! When you are ready, try to devote more time to making games daily. Before you know it, time will be going by so quickly you won't even realize it.

What if it's not just you working out of your game studio? You might want to get some of your family or friends to help you make games. You might even find like-minded acquaintances over the Internet who want to help you make your visions come to life and sell them. If this is the case, go for it and have fun! You will have some serious decisions to make, involving legal issues, paying people, and sharing profits—not to mention the issues that might arise if you and your coworkers have a falling out or one of you backs out mid-production and still expects payback for work rendered. Take these issues seriously before they lead to legal action. Consider seeing a lawyer and starting your business out right with contracts that put everything in black and white for you and your team.

Video Game Marketing

It used to be a common practice for game studios to start advertising a few weeks before the initial shelf date because vendors did not see the sense in promoting something that the public couldn't yet buy. A new game had four to six months after its release to find an audience to purchase it. The game magazines focused on reviews rather than previews because they wanted to see the end product and the playability of the game before passing judgment. Likewise, there were no TV ads or Flash banner ads all over the Internet.

Today is a brand new era. Now game publishers usually don't publish games until they have enough unit pre-orders of a game. Chain stores prefer to turn their shelves often and are strict about games that do not sell soon after they are released. You can come under pressure to go right to markdowns (what lots of folks call *price protection*). Most people don't even realize that games that go into a retail outlet are not truly sold; the retailer has the right to return the games to the publisher for full credit if the games do not sell within a reasonable time. The retailer wants to carry only games that sell fast and make them money; publishers want all their games to stay on store shelves for as long as possible. This means that the public relations (including marketing and sales campaigns) must be set into motion months before the game even ships into stores. Before a retail vendor will pre-order a game, he must be shown that the game will sell well.

You are going to sell your own hobby games. It's called self-promotion for a reason: if you don't do it yourself, it doesn't get done! This may not sound all that exciting, but the more you sell yourself and your entertainment product, the more money you will make and the quicker your name will become known to the industry. Ludwig van Beethoven said what is on all of our minds: "There should be a single Art Exchange in the world, to which the artist would simply send his works and be given in return as much as he needs. As it is, one has to be half merchant on top of everything else, and how badly one goes about it!" The Internet may someday offer us a single Art Exchange (wouldn't that be nice?)—but right now you have to learn to sell your own work.

You can't wait to be discovered or for your site to be hit by the big cigar-chomping businessmen who want to give you a lot of dough for your hobby games. You can wait all your life and end up with resentment and regrets. It takes an incredible amount of energy and enthusiasm away from all the other things you have to do every week, but you know you should do it. You can do it. Because if you aren't marketing yourself, you've already fallen behind somebody else who is. Sure, you can make astounding game visuals and get noticed merely for your screenshots, but even super-successful celebrities have to promote themselves on a regular basis so the vibe stays high. This chapter is all about helping you sell your game.

First of all, ask yourself some serious questions. Do you want to make money? Do you want success? Do you want to make hobby games that people love to play? Is there a market for the kinds of games that you design? Do you think you can learn how to sell your games? Do you want to? If you have answered yes to all of these, then read on and learn the basics of promotion.

The Marketing Mindset

Note

"Never allow doubt to tarnish your lust for latinum."

—Rule of Acquisition #263, Ferengi Rules of Acquisition

You know people who promote themselves when you see them. Britney Spears, Madonna, Marilyn Manson, and Eminem are just a few who should be mentioned. They are excellent at taking risks, getting right up in people's faces, and being remembered. They are comfortable with promoting themselves. All of them are controversial, overexposed, and have that "look at me" aspect that you should learn to accept in yourself. It's not enough to be promotable—you have to know how to do it. Figuring that people who make it big were just lucky or had the right opportunities in life is a huge mistake. True, some of them had to be in the right place at the right time, but most of them mastered the marketing mindset or sought to hang around in the right place and do the right things that got them their current gigs.

You have to study the competition—then out-think, out-hustle, and outlast your competition. Visualize the end result, and work backward from there (in fact, creative visualization will help you in all aspects of your business). There is nothing "bad" or "wrong" about marketing yourself in a competitive market. Humbleness doesn't bring home the bacon. You have to do it; if not for yourself then for the games you work so hard creating. The great thing is that once you start selling your games, and you are witnessing the results of your efforts, it will become easier.

Some of these rewards will turn around and promote you, too. Winning an award for your game, getting a top spot on somebody's list, or having a record number of downloads on a popular Web site will all make you appear more remarkable to your target audience.

Set aside some time and money to market you. You might be wrapped in a big project or another game design right now, and you might think that you don't have the time to promote anything. Let me tell you: we all are too busy to promote our work. It doesn't matter because you have to find the time to do it. One hour a day is sometimes all the time you need to address your contacts and promote your game. Once you lay the groundwork, it may even take less than that. Consider that for a budding actor trying to enter the industry, it can cost a minimum of $5,000 just to get started in union dues, photo head-shots, videotape demos, a resume, and acting lessons alone.

The trick is to market you as cheaply as possible. If you have a computer and printer, you are already halfway there; if you can get friends to help you out—and you can engender word-of-mouth advertisement—all the better. Use offbeat schemes. The more original and offbeat your promotional campaign, the more likely you will get that word-of-mouth advertisement. If you can apply unconventional thinking to your marketing plans, you increase sales without having to plunk down a lot of extra money. I remember a mystery writer who decided to include her favorite recipes with her novels. A lot of her target audience liked to cook (as well as read mystery books). This offbeat plan helped sell cases of her books.

Be willing to go out, meet, and interview with your peers as well as your players. Get over being shy. You have to brush up your social skills and talk about your game in a natural and vibrant way. Whenever someone has a question, don't brush them off or stare at them like they are covered in dragon scales. The friendlier you can be, the more people will want to interview you and the more likely your studio will get recognition. If your hobby game becomes half as catchy as you hope it will, you will develop a fan base. Your cult following will want to meet you. Even if they are only three or four feet high, as J.K. Rowling's are with her Harry Potter series, they will be eager to meet you at conventions and trade shows and will be sorely disappointed if you turn out to be a jerk.

Develop a plan of attack. You don't want to cram your game down people's throats. Refine and define who you are, what your studio does, and what your games are about. The simpler it is for you to explain yourself and your entertainment products to people, the simpler you will find it is for you to sell them. Sometimes this can come out of defining your studio philosophy, what it is your game company is shooting for as a goal. Kristen Johnston once said her philosophy was, "I want to make a bad horror movie so bad I can taste it. I want to be in, like, panties and a T-shirt, brushing my teeth, asking 'Who's there?'" Dave Jaffe (creator of *God of War*) boasts that his team decided to throw out a lot of the conventional wisdom of game design when they built their signature game. He says, "If Terry Gilliam created a kid's pop-up book, what would it look like? We wanted that kind of magic in a game." Decide what it is you want to make, how you want your audience to feel. Sum it up in a direct statement like this one. Write it down. Make up adjectives to go in your statement and rewrite it in as many different ways as possible. You will be called upon—when submitting links to your Web site or in an interview later on—to discuss your personal statement, and you will know exactly what to say. You will also have a bulwark of stability that your studio can adopt.

Persistence: Todd McFarlane

Most people don't know this, but Todd McFarlane (creator of *Spawn* and a best-selling novelty toy line, as well as some of his very own brand video games) did not start out in the industry but got there from sheer hard work and persistence. He went over and above what the average person would do. He started out an avid comic book collector and fan. He wanted to make his own comics and taught himself to draw. He sent his drawings to many comic book publishers and received over seven hundred rejection letters. He didn't stop there, for he would not be deterred.

He mailed his portfolio package to companies for four straight months before Marvel Comics finally gave him work. "Editors knew my package was coming every month. After a while, they said, 'Just give him some work and shut him up.'" McFarlane showed everybody what he already knew: that he would not stop until he realized his dreams.

Remember that persistence pays off. The Black Knight in *Monty Python and the Holy Grail* kept trying to attack the other knight—even after he had all his arms and legs chopped off. "Come here; I'll bite you!" This is the kind of dogged perseverance you need when marketing yourself. You have to send other people the impression that "You can't stop me!" Drummer Tommy Lee of Motley Crue said once about their early days, "We were like a self-promotion machine. We went around with flyers and a staple gun and plastered everything." Many musicians in college towns everywhere do the same. You have to learn what it takes to get noticed and go after it, even if it means a lot of legwork and talking to people. Don't back down.

Don't take criticism personally (see Figure 12.2). Most of the time, people are criticizing your game or your work—not you directly (and if they are attacking you directly, then their criticisms are baseless and can be totally ignored). Step back and give their words an objective look. Find out whether what they are saying is because of their incomprehension or if they are valid criticisms. There can be ways to improve your work if you don't act defensive about their suggestions. Look at whether or not the people making the criticisms are experts in

Figure 12.2
Don't take it personally, but that DOES look like a skirt.

the field and might actually know what they are talking about; if they are, then you should probably give their opinions a second thought.

Occasionally, you will find that your worst critics are your friends and family. People could be telling you that you are no good—or that you will never make it. This, unfortunately, damages our esteem because it overlaps with the same words our hateful inner critic sometimes tells us. Don't let it get to you. Follow your dreams. If you know that what you are doing will be meaningful and that you have a chance of making something out of yourself, proceed with perseverance. People told Minoru Arakawa, the North American president of Nintendo, that he was crazy for wanting to import a funny little Japanese video game where players had to collect 150 tiny collectible monsters with funny names. Research panels Nintendo covered reported that the game would never make it and would be unpopular, but Arakawa went ahead anyway—and *Pokemon* took off as a million-dollar fad!

The Image You Represent

Most of the details you see in the mirror about your personal appearance cannot be changed, but there are more subtle details that you might not even be aware of that tell people more about you than you think. For some members of the public, the archetype of the game designer is full of negative images: nerdy, insecure, overweight, obsessive, scatterbrained, disorganized, lonely, unprofessional, flaky, neurotic, psychotic . . . and worse. Prove them wrong. If you see that your studio has an image problem, rearrange your image. Look your best with what you have. Destroy as many negative connotations as you can.

Usually, you want to keep your personal lifestyle out of the mix. No one has to know that you are married and have three kids or that you prefer fly-fishing in Aspen to video game arcades. Some people (like K.D. Lang, the Indigo Girls, and Ellen DeGeneres) have come out of the closet about their personal lifestyle choices. This has had a dramatic impact on how they are received by the public, but it is really not anyone's business. No matter what you do on the weekends, you have a professional image to keep as a game developer.

You can go for a signature look, like the U2 singer Bono's trademark sunshades or Gene Simmons' leather jackets. Signature looks help solidify a public image and can actually hide you when you go out in public without them. Ask yourself, has your look held you back? Are you losing street cred? Being too creative

Figure 12.3
What does your tribe wear?

with your look can repel people and ruin your prospects. Tone it down, be a little conservative, and project a positive and professional impression; it's just good for business. Dress to match your industry. What does your tribe wear? (See Figure 12.3.) Creative people (like game designers) are expected to dress differently from the rest, thank goodness! Find a happy medium between the inked nose-ring-wearing dyed-hair look and looking too uptight or dorky. Take your personal style and work it.

Here are some questions to get you thinking about the image you are representing to others:

- Do you look people in the eye and smile at them when talking to them, or do you habitually look down and away?
- How do you walk? Is it with a spring in your step? Head up or down?
- Is your handshake firm or flimsy?
- Do you slip quietly into a room, or do you make a big entrance wherever you go?
- Are you a good listener? What about conversation? Do you initiate discussions or clam up?

- Do you remember people's names, faces, or personalities?
- Do you dress conservatively or wild and artsy everywhere you go?
- When you sit, do you slouch or sit up straight? Do you cross your ankles or legs? Do you cross your arms? (Crossing any of your limbs is typically a sign of confrontation.)
- Do you talk clearly and enunciate, or do you whisper or talk with an accent?
- Do you like people, or do you try to avoid them at all costs?

As a business, you are not only selling yourself, you are selling the work that you make: your entertainment products. It is especially important to focus on the special niche where you have the assets and capabilities to succeed. Consider your game studio's image. Most companies out there have a Unique Selling Proposition that states exactly who (and what) they are. Domino's Pizza, for instance, uses this frequently cited Unique Selling Proposition: "Fresh hot pizza delivered to your door in 30 minutes or less, guaranteed." Notice that Domino's does not mention cheap, great-tasting, or nutritious. Domino's understands that they cannot be all things to all people all of the time. No one business can, otherwise we would all be shopping at The Only Store. Domino's does understand their image. The domino-shaped logo with its conventional red, blue, and white colors also helps their image.

Great Unique Selling Propositions have the following characteristics:

- They are contained in one clear, crisp sentence.
- They are credible.
- They describe the unique benefits associated with the company.
- They focus on the niche market.
- They state in measurable terms how the company satisfies customer needs.

Give your game studio a Unique Selling Proposition consistent with your personal philosophy and the kinds of games you can make. Then give your game studio a name that expresses your own unique style, for example Top Dog Games, Little Red Ware, or Big Brain United. If your studio is named Top Dog,

Figure 12.4
Top Dog Games

draw a funky-looking dog for your logo (see Figure 12.4). Put this into your computer and design it into a serviceable logo. Make a studio sign and hang it on the door to your basement, garage, bedroom, or wherever your studio is set up. Now you're in business!

Promotional Tools

Promotional materials might include posters, T-shirts, stickers, hats, mouse pads, and press kits. These can be given away or sold to prospective customers or retail stores. Promotional items may travel far and wide, and you never know where they will end up. One of the more popular promotions used for multi-player online games is the 10- or 30-day free trial period.

Game Demo

Game demos are important because they reflect the gameplay, mechanics, and graphics that audiences can anticipate from the final game product. Amazingly, demos are not shorter versions of their predecessor; they are complete projects in and of themselves, with a different purpose. Games provide the players with immersive long-lasting emotional entertainment. Demos sell the game to the players. Each demo must represent the game at its very best, showing off the highlights players can expect to see in the game when it hits store shelves. Following are some different varieties of game demos.

5 Seconds to 6 Minutes

A narrated looping video presentation may also have a music soundtrack. This type of demo shows some screenshots and examples of gameplay, which can be useful for buyers and trades people to "get" in a short amount of time. Many times these demos are used in press kits, Internet Web sites, and trade shows.

10 Minutes and Up

This is typically an interactive game demo of nearly one to three short game levels, featuring some of the game mechanics and most amazing cinematic cut-scenes. This type of demo is exhibited on magazine demo disks, downloadable online, or shown in store kiosks.

Hours Long

This game demo is reserved for larger games, to show players in-depth facets of the game. Many times these demos are set up as free trial periods, and after the player has gotten "hooked," she must pay to finish playing; this is common in shareware and massive multiplayer online games.

Flyers and Brochures

A flyer is a cheaper version of a poster. You can print up several flyers and staple them around your town. Band flyers often let people know about an upcoming music show. Events in your area usually advertise through the use of flyers. They are affordable and fairly easy to get. Being creative and an artist, you might be able to hand-draw a flyer that people will really want to stop and read. The purpose behind your flyer will be to announce the release part of your game (see below) or the upcoming sale of your game at a retail shop.

A brochure is normally a four-color production on high-quality paper stock. It requires a significant amount of time and expertise to lay out on a computer. Most companies design brochures to last a long time because they are not cheap. Brochures inform people of the company's history, Unique Selling Proposition, and best-known products. If people are interested in finding out recent news or what game projects you are working on at any time, don't put them on the brochure; have current information on your Web site. The usefulness of your brochure may also come into question. It is a nice addition with a press kit, and it informs folks about who you are and where you are coming from, but most of the time it won't get read (see Figure 12.5). Think carefully before investing in a brochure.

Screenshots and Wallpaper

It is often the case that the game with the best screenshots and desktop wallpaper will win the race. Don't snap a shot of random screen grabs; you might pick a boring location. To show off your game to its maximum selling advantage, you

Figure 12.5
Flyers are an efficient display—but don't go overboard.

must carefully choose just the right set of images. Sometimes the demand for screenshots, wallpaper, and other goodies can be nearly insatiable. Web sites that you are networking with will want your newest and most exclusive images; you will be pressured to provide as many as possible—long before you even finish with your game.

You can use Windows' own PRNT SCRN key function to capture a screenshot of the whole screen image and crop it using a paint program. You could also use programs like Camtasia to take professional screenshots. Whatever you choose to take your screenshots, you should use your concept artwork, screenshots, and video images to provide Windows wallpaper. Keep in mind that wallpaper must match computer screen resolution sizes, including 800 × 600 and 1024 × 768. It takes time and expertise to create the "right" sort of images, and if you are not careful with your promotional materials you might overexpose your game, that is, players might get bored by the time the game is released; they will have felt they have seen the whole game before it has even hit store shelves. (See Figure 12.6.)

Magazine Interviews

You might suffer from what many game developers do: you are too close to your product, and so you believe that its rewards should be self-evident to the public. You might not appear to be the perfect demonstrator of your game's benefits.

Figure 12.6
Game wallpaper for *Earthworm Jim 3D* (image courtesy of Interplay 1999)

Figure 12.7
Popular game magazine *Game Informer*

Nevertheless, game critics, trades people, and journalists prefer to interview the people actually making the games, so you should be prepared for this. When you do take your first interview, try to go over and beyond yourself. Show your game in its very best light. Give all the credit where credit is due, including the entire game studio team. Do not sit back and wait for magazines to contact you (see Figure 12.7). Do your research and send them e-mail to ask if they would care to do an interview with you. You must step up and do your own PR.

Your Game's Web Site

You will want to make a solidified attempt at an Internet Web site whose sole purpose is to sell the game. Do it yourself, do it for less. Unlike printed promotional materials, your Web site has to be updated regularly to encourage visitors to return often. You can add extra features that make it a hub of activity. You can also sell your game online through it, at relatively low cost to you.

Building the Web Site

You could attempt taking your blog or MySpace site and converting it into a studio site, but I advise you to start from scratch. Why? Two reasons: some places that you host personal Web pages do not appreciate you selling products on them, and you also want to keep your personal life out of your business one.

Plan your Web site out thoroughly on paper first. Consolidate the information that you want to present to players. Essentially you want to tell them about the characters, summary, and backstory. You want to include the information that will make them more curious about your game. Using your notes, develop navigation for your Web site based on the most important content. Navigation should be user-friendly and easy to scan. Look online at other people's Web sites that sell games or have amazing content. Many of the game studio Web sites offer interactive Flash content. Avoid copying other Web sites, however. Massage your Web site design. Put your content together, including images you want to show, downloads you want to provide, text that you write and spell check in Microsoft Word, etc. Put all of your content into a single folder on your computer.

After you have generated your content and outlined a navigation blueprint, it is time to sketch some thumbnails of what you want your Web site to look like. Of these thumbnails, you must narrow down your design decisions and choose one thumbnail to turn into a full-color mock-up. You can program your Web site in Dreamweaver, Microsoft FrontPage, or any other Web-design program. Of course, there are thousands of templates out there that you could use, but recognize that some have been overused and some people will know a template when they see it. Knowledge of Web design programs as well as markup languages (like HTML, XHTML, CSS, CSS2, PHP, and MySQL) can enhance your Web design and make it very professional-looking. You could also outsource the creation of your Web site to an expert design firm.

You have to register a desired domain name, such as www.mdduggan.com. A domain name is registered to your game studio and no one else. Pick a domain name that is descriptive, short, and memorable. Your studio name is always a good idea but not really required. If your studio name is not very descriptive, consider something a little more expressive, like www.reallyfungames.com. There are many places online where it's fast, easy, and relatively inexpensive to find and register your domain name, such as www.GoDaddy.com and www.Register.com.

Once the name is registered, the next step is telling the Internet where the Web site will reside at. In other words, there are millions of Web servers out there, but which one do you want to host the files that make up your site? This information is required to direct visitors to the correct place. Web hosts have constantly active Web servers that will house your Web site content for a fair price; a relatively low-cost one can be found at www.JiffyNet.net. Once you have a Web host and a domain name, you will have to publish your Web content to the server (often using FTP, or File Transfer Protocol). Your index.htm page will be the first page visitors go to when they type in your domain name in their address bar.

Advertise the Web Site

Once you have your Web site online, it is time to submit it to all the most popular search engines at DMOZ.org. The search engines will spider your Web pages and update their cache, which will take about 24 to 48 hours to propagate. When your site has established itself, it is time to promote it. Go online to games trade organization Web sites and push your Web site. Put your links everywhere you can. Conitec's Web site at www.3dgamestudio.com has a links section that demonstrates people's games that have been made using the 3D GameStudio engine. You should head there and email the Web manager with a link to your Web site.

Begin a personal network of contacts. E-mail everyone you can about your Web site. Send your contacts desktop wallpaper, screenshots of your game, and other goodies to get them to help you advertise your game. Send out press kits to game magazines and trade organizations. You can also advertise your game demo by having it available for download at various locations, such Downloads.net, Tucows.com, and GameSpy.com. Be prepared to answer the following:

- What is your game called?
- What genre is it?
- What is the platform your game is played on?
- What system requirements are needed to play it?

- What is your game about?
- What would you rank your game as if it had an ESRB rating?
- What is the target audience of your game?

Selling Games Online

You will find the setup and operation of an e-store or online shop increasingly easy and affordable. Businesses are finding the Internet a unique way to compete because shoppers can compare prices from dozens of online stores in less than a minute. Determine at what price you are willing to sell your game, figuring how much money it is costing you in terms of Web hosting, packaging, and other direct expenses. If you cannot sell your game for a low price (about $8 to $20), you might want to reconsider selling your games online. If you think that this marginal profit won't be worth it, then you are better off sending your games to publishers and getting one of them to pick it up for you. Otherwise, get ready to sell online.

Your Web site should tell people up front in clear and understandable words what they will be getting if they buy from you. Be sure to mention the system requirements for your game and that it will only run on Windows (sorry Mac users). If you leave even the slightest detail out, you run the risk of upsetting a customer and getting bad press.

Most Internet shoppers today expect shipment of their order within 24 hours, or at least 7 business days. Slower shipping than that frustrates them. Be prepared when you get a purchase order to have the game ready to ship right away. Sometimes you can find online services to handle your purchase orders and shipping. Some of them handle CD package shipments easier than others; all you have to do is upload the information meant to be burnt to CD, and their company will handle payments and shipping and send you your money at the end of the month, minus a small commission. If you go this route, you will find that your e-store will be a breeze (except you will earn less money). Otherwise you will have to burn your content to CDs and ship them yourself.

If you go the do-it-yourself way, here's what you need to do:

1. In WED, with your game open, hit Publish to provide a folder with your game and "cd" on the end of it.
2. Use an install wizard program, like Astrum Install Wizard, to organize the information in the folder so that the end user sees only startup icons and the

program has an "auto-run" file that tells it what you want to load first when the user puts the program into his computer.

3. When you have finished organizing the files with the install wizard (which is optional but suggested), burn the folder onto a blank CD. You will need another program, like Nero, to burn CDs, and you will need to have a CD burner on your computer.

4. After you burn the CD, test it to see if it runs all right. If there are any read errors, don't ship it out. You don't want to get a bad name in the industry for sloppy distribution.

5. Place the CD in a paper sleeve or plastic CD case. If you want, you can do something creative to dress these up. If you have the extra money, you can spend some on an actual box or package to place the CD case in, with custom artwork on the cover. People will excuse cheap packaging if it looks cool and is functional.

6. Enclose an invoice. This is a receipt that shows the shopper they are getting what they have ordered.

7. You might also want to enclose a game manual or sheet of paper that tells them how to install the game on their machine when they get it. Conscientious moves like these will get people talking.

8. Wrap the entire package in postal-correct materials so that the CD will not be damaged or erased by being set too close to a powerful magnet, and then ship it with your favorite shipping company.

If you are going the do-it-yourself route, you can have customers mail in their checks or money orders, but make sure they clear first before shipping. This is by far the safest (though slowest) purchase method. You might consider accepting credit and debit card payments. People who pay with plastic statistically purchase more. You could use one of the online payment companies like, PayPal, to handle the transactions for you because the process must be kept secure to thwart identity theft and credit card scamming.

Don't forget that sellers must generally collect, report, and pay sales taxes on shipments within their state, and various counties and other taxing jurisdictions may also want a piece of the action. This can become a real headache, especially when you are getting started. Learn what must be done in your area and do it. You can ignore sales taxes within the first few months of operation, but after things have settled down from opening your e-store, you will have time to run reports, fill out forms, and pay sales taxes that are due. Talk to an accountant (preferably a CPA) in your local area in order to find out what must be done.

Release Party

In South Korea, game studios make the release of a new computer game a big event. Even if the studio is made up of four guys working out of their garage, they open up the garage on the release date and invite the whole neighborhood in to play. The same thing happens on a larger scale all over South Korea, the most wired country in the world. If it can happen there, why can't you borrow the idea? Stage an event to promote your entertainment product.

Come up with an original theme for the event. If the event is taking place around a holiday, you could decorate and frame the event in the theme of the holiday. If your game is a fantasy one, you could invite out the Renaissance Festival players in their costumes. If your game is a western shooter, you and your friends could dress up as cowboys and dress up the location as an old-time saloon. The wilder and more imaginative you make the occasion, the more people will remember it. Make the event truly memorable. Use offbeat thinking to go above and beyond what people expect in a game release party. Get them talking about you, your studio, and your products with excitement and awe. People love a great party.

People expect freebies. Don't disappoint. Snacks are a must. Free samples—game demos, T-shirts, prize giveaways, and so on—are also well received. Give away something that attendees can wear or show other attendees and will prompt others to ask them where they got it. This can lead to a lot of free publicity, and your promotional materials might incidentally become a fashion fad. Bring plenty of your other promotional materials. Bring flyers, demo discs, posters, and such, and litter them around the computers so people will have something they can take home with them. Bring your press kits, and make it a point to hand them out personally to every single attendee if you have to. Don't be shy.

Make it a truly interactive experience. Have computers set up with playable game demos available on them. Have video screens playing samples of your work. Allow attendees to enter their names on a mailing list or sign up for a raffle or free giveaway. A short sales pitch or demonstration doesn't hurt either. Don't bore the attendees with 30 or 40 minutes of speeches, however. They are there to have a good time and to play your game.

Sticking Around

Once your game studio is a success and you are selling your games, you probably won't give it up any time soon. You will be running the Web site, handling tech support, and working on your next big project. Games follow in the trend set by the music industry, and you are playing a one-man band. Record companies hype one-hit wonders before their albums go on sale; but after they're through promoting their act, years will pass and no one will remember them. Fans' attention spans are not what they used to be, unless you can hit it off with a cult classic.

Right now it's "one strike and you're out." The way to survive longer is to have long-term fans or reinvent yourself and win new ones with the next game you put out. How? By capturing their emotions. Take the logic out of the equation. Give them a fun imaginative rollercoaster ride they can play any time on their computer, and people will pay and pay again to come back and ride again. Be so unique and avant-garde that you capture attention everywhere you go. Master your domain.

In Summary

For a lot of game developers—even veteran ones sick of the corporate industry—independent game development is where the money's at. You don't have to deal with deadlines, communication issues between you and countless teams of people in the pipeline, and being told what to do. You can make the games you dream of making, based on your personal vision, and you can sell them over the Internet to niche markets who snap them up like hotcakes. This is a path fraught with risks, but it can reap huge rewards.

What You Have Learned

The following are things you should have learned about promoting yourself and your games:

- You now understand the principles of independent game development.
- You have learned what scratchware and hobby games are.

- You have learned how to start your own game studio.
- You have learned the techniques of video game marketing.
- You now know how to start your Web store and sell your work.
- You have a better understanding of hosting a release party.
- You know how to make it as an independent game developer.

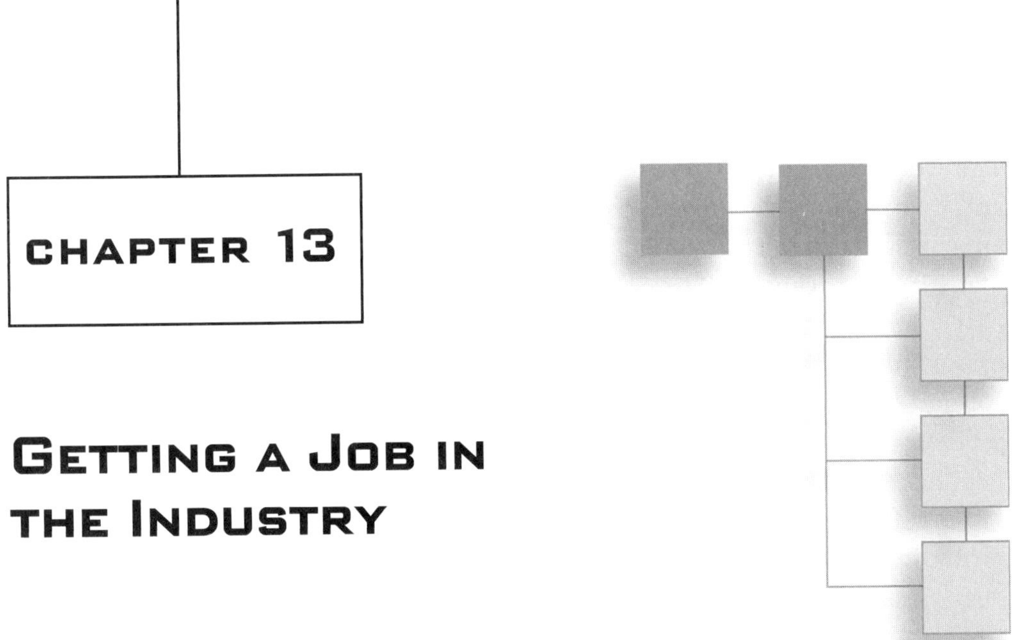

Chapter 13

Getting a Job in the Industry

Computer games are extremely sophisticated technical artifacts, unlike other media. Games require amazing 2D and 3D graphics, real-time programming to achieve smooth animation, and have artificial intelligence (originally reserved for robot technologies) featuring clever opponents to best the player. Games are aiming for a prized place currently occupied by TV, film, and literature, constantly raising expectations for a more in-depth theatrical experience, unlike other forms of media. Games have interludes of CG movies, requiring 3D artists to test the limits of the hardware. Today's computer games sit at the nexus of computer science, digital graphics, art, economics, social science, and mathematics. Increasingly evolving game artifacts are being built by the widest interdisciplinary teams. The rising complexity of games combined with their growing socio-economic and academic interest are surpassing the marginalized novelty level where games used to be and taking game design to the next level of awareness on an international scale.

Note

"Beyond their creative element, video games offer a major challenge in bringing together numerous core areas of advanced computer science, including artificial intelligence, graphical interfaces, modeling, algorithm design and, of course, programming. These programs are good academics."

—Gerard Medioni, Information Sciences Institute

The video game industry has grown to a whopping $11 billion a year business, and it is starting to eclipse standard entertainment media forms. It is creating an amazing demand for a significantly expanding work force. The Bureau of Labor Statistics confirms that computer software developers, including video game designers, is one of the fasting growing occupation fields, with "very good opportunities expected for college graduates with at least a bachelor's degree in computer engineering or science and with practical work experience." This prediction is part of a 67.9 percent growth between now and 2012. According to DigiPen, the release of next-generation games, including the Nintendo Wii, the Xbox 360, the Playstation 3, and their related software, has created an all-new hiring frenzy by video game companies, leading to much higher competition, salaries, and benefits.

That's not all. The Web has become a snare for multiplayer games, often built in Flash, Fusion Director, PHP (with a database back-end), and other leading software packages. These online games are explosive content, and businesses are seeking qualified individuals experienced in game design to work freelance or commission in the development of these games.

In comparison to other work fields where the average graduate with an arts degree starts at $30,000 per year, the video game industry has its recent arts degree grads starting between $35,000 and $50,000 a year! Plus the students entering this field are long-time gamers and get to do what they love, which (according to Dr. Phil and most other self-help gurus) is imperative to the quality of life. Developers may not get to play games all day long, but they get to make them and enjoy what they do.

Game Education

Note

"The industry is not about making children laugh or the cure for cancer, it is about making money, and we make money through innovation, new ideas, new content, and if you are going to innovate you have to have the understanding on how the technology works. The computer understands one thing and that is '1 and 0', or how to turn off and on. Those who can use that computer to create a *Halo* or *Metal Gear Solid*, those people are the innovators who will become industry leaders."

—Raymond Yan, DigiPen SVP of Operations

The industry is changing quickly and in order to serve the industry leaders and game companies, schools need to be prepared for those changes. The industry needs qualified employees with the skills to hit the ground running and propel their services into the future. Schools are working to insure that they are picking up software skills that will carry their students into these potential careers. Game design is practically propelling the educational market. In fact, Microsoft has been investing nearly $800,000 recently in the educational future with the Microsoft Research External Research and Programs group to sponsor and promote the development of game design educational programs through their Reality and Programming Together (or RAPT) program. This program's goal is to boost computer science enrollment in schools by increasing teenagers' interest in video games.

On top of the computer science angle, the program manager of the external research and programs of Microsoft Research, John Nordlinger, says that, "Whether a person is working toward a degree in computer science or developing the next multiplayer video game . . . one of the most important skills they can have is strong communication skills. As more and more technology classes are being added to class curriculums, the humanities courses are suffering. And the ability to communicate is what changes a person's career. At the end of the day, everyone's code is the same, but the ability to communicate an idea will set you apart in college, in an interview, or within your company." And to the mixture of arts, graphics, computer science, and physics taught in schools now, many of them are combining classes that focus on business skills, communication, and accounting. Video game design is a subject a lot of schools agree will be the future of the international business market.

Here are just a few of the colleges and universities offering degree programs in game design:

- Academy of Art University
- Al Collins College
- Art Center College of Design
- Boston University
- Brooks College
- Brown College
- California Institute of the Arts
- Carnegie Mellon University

- Collins College
- DeVry University
- Digital Media Arts College
- Ex'pression College for Digital Arts
- Florida Interactive Entertainment Academy
- Full Sail College of Florida
- Gnomon School of Visual Arts
- iD Tech Camps
- Institute of Technology
- ITT Tech
- John Hopkins University
- Keiser College
- Miami International University of Art and Design
- Minnesota School of Business / Globe College
- Platt College
- Pratt Institute
- San Francisco State University
- Sanford-Brown College
- Savannah College of Art and Design
- The Art Institute (located online and in many American cities)
- The Art Institute of Phoenix
- The Game Institute
- The School of Communication Arts
- University of Advancing Technology

- University of Southern California
- Vancouver Institute for Media Arts
- Westwood College Campus

As a comparison between DigiPen versus Full Sail, DigiPen offers a two-year associate's degree as well as a four-year bachelor's, and emphasizes the Macintosh/SNES. Their price tag is about $26,000-plus as of 2006. Full Sail offers a one-year associate's or two-year bachelor's degree, and emphasizes Windows/Linux. They have cutting-edge technology and more impressive classrooms, featuring an accelerated class structure 24/7. Their cost (as of 2006) is about $32,000-plus. DigiPen focuses on geometry and higher math, high-level programming, data structures, operating systems, computer graphics, and networking. Full Sail focuses on 3D modeling, C++, digital techniques, the rules of the game, and artificial intelligence.

Most colleges and universities are seeking to add game design degree programs or classes to their curriculum to meet the growing demand for game developers. Before choosing an educational institution, find out if they have an emphasis on the programming end or the graphics end, as most institutions focus on one or the other, but rarely both. If they do have an emphasis, decide which path you prefer—both are essential disciplines for game design.

Find out if the college's program is sponsored by one or more game companies. It doesn't hurt to know how long the program has existed and what its placement rate in the industry is like, either. Be sure to ask them what sort of hardware/software decisions they have made and what languages they focus on. Sometimes an educational institution may be sponsored by a game company for internships.

If you cannot find an institution that offers game design programs, you should try taking classes in computer science, programming, art, graphic or visual arts, animation, communications, business, and economics to get ahead in the video game development industry. One of the biggest advantages to getting a college education is that it helps you become a more well-rounded person. With education, you can bring a broader perspective to the job you might face some day. You will also be used to operating under deadlines. Schools also emphasize teamwork and collaboration on projects.

Not all employers are going to look at your schooling, however. Most of them want to see your skills. They want to see games that you have worked on before. If you have worked your way through this book, you will have at least three games under your belt and the potential to make so many more. This is what employers want to see.

Let me give you the bad news: there are lots of other people who have the same goal, who all want to join the game industry. Some of them may have better skills or more experience than you. Fellow students you meet at school will also offer you stiff competition.

The good news: the industry is huge and growing every day as the need for better video games is growing. The industry also has a high turnover rate. If you are talented, enthusiastic, skilled, and persistent (with the willingness to relocate anywhere the work is), you will almost certainly get on somewhere.

Breaking In to the Market

Note

> "Most newbies are overwhelmed by how much they have to work, the hours, the pressure. Some can't hack it."
>
> —Thomas Haegele

Be ready and willing to relocate. In the United States, most of the game industry is based out of California, with some strong rising communities in Texas, Washington D.C., Seattle, and smaller satellites throughout the country. If there is not a game company near you, you must be ready to pack up all your stuff and move where the work is.

There is a slow-growing trend in telecommuting in this industry. American McGee sees the future of game development handled by subcontracted work. A game company would be handled by a small but devoted team in-house, and the company would contract out to freelance artists and programmers to get a game built. These freelancers would not have to be in-house and could even work out of their home, posting into work every day online. This way, freelancers would be free to work on other projects at will. One of the economic setbacks for game companies today is that most of the team is off doing something other than their jobs; when the programmers are fine-tuning the game mechanics, the world-builders might not be doing anything or might be beta-testing the game (while drawing salaries and not able to move on to another project, per their non-disclosure agreement). That makes for some really expensive beta-testers for the

Figure 13.1
You need not be afraid of the work force.

game companies to have to pay! Unfortunately, as I said, the telecommuting and contract work is still a slow-growing trend and one of which many businesses are wary.

Finding Job Openings

The first step to entering the job market is to find job openings in the industry. The most obvious way to do that is to know the companies you would like working for (see Figure 13.1). Go to their Web sites and look for employment opportunities announcements, usually under a link like "Job Opportunities" or "Work for Us." If you cannot find announcements, locate the company's contact e-mail and send them a message requesting information. You should also browse Web sites covering industry news, like GameDev.net—they will often carry ads for job offers. You might have to sign up, giving your contact information, resume, and samples of your work, before browsing some of these sites. You can also go to job-finding sources online, like Guru.com or Monster.com, to sign up to receive free job offers. Be wary about job openings that offer you projected royalties or small investments in return for your work. It is really up to you what work you are willing to accept, but generally avoid opportunity offers that tell you "this will be a great resume builder but we cannot pay you at this moment."

Some companies—especially Microsoft, Electronic Arts, and Buena Vista Games—have intern programs. If you are attending a school in a game design program, inquire if the school has internship arrangements. If they don't, you can always write to the publisher of your favorite games and ask whether they have an internship they are willing to offer you. This is one way to get on the inside and possibly find work in the future.

Occasionally a "head hunter" or job placement personnel will browse forums online and make job offers available; for smaller game companies who cannot afford the high prices of advertisement on employment opportunities, this is a price-reducing manner to farm out work.

Last, consider doing a little research. If there is a small but growing game company that puts out really great games—and you would like to work for them—then you can look up their director, producer, tech lead, or art lead and e-mail them directly. Ask if there is anything that you could do to help. Be proactive, polite, and personable, and you will be amazed what doors might open for you.

Game designers are always eager to get help and are on the lookout for good employees who fit in and will do the work needed. If you prepare yourself, learn all you can about the industry, and demonstrate to potential employers that you have the skills they want, you will find your way into the industry.

Specializations

Note

"The biggest challenge is probably maintaining a coherent vision. For a game to work, it has to feel like the work of one mind (or at least a hive mind!)–but, in fact, games are (often) created by 30, 40, 100 people, or more. Communication is critical and, as in all human endeavors, communication is hard, hard, hard."

–Warren Spector

In theory a game would be created by one artist and one programmer—but in the end it takes a lot more than some programming and graphics to create a successful video game. Let's take a look at what is commonly referred to as "specialization" in the industry.

Chryssa Cooke, director of industry relations and career development in visual arts at Ex'pression College for Digital Arts, helps students prepare for the real world in the game industry. She says, "I think what the industry is looking for is generalists." Cooke appreciates that small game companies are more apt to look for generalists, while major studios remain specialized. A modeler who is familiar with UV mapping, texturing, rigging, and lighting, or someone who can model props as well as humanoids, has a bigger advantage against the specialists who only work on texturing props. People's opinions diverge widely when it comes to whether companies are looking for specialists or generalists. Tad Leckman, chair of VFX at the Savannah College of Art and Design (SCAD), believes that most companies want a compromise. Employers want employees who are sharp as tacks and have expertise at one specific task—but they must also be able to understand what they are doing and how it fits into the pipeline.

Most Influential People in the Industry

The following are the celebrities of the game industry, listed in alphabetic order.

American McGee–This guy is best known for his *Alice* goth-fantasy game, but he has partnered with Jerry Bruckheimer to create a new goth fantasy based on the *Wizard of Oz*.

Dave Jaffe–Jaffe created *God of War*, a post-modern remix of Greek myth.

Gabe Newell–Anyone know what a head crab is? Gabe is the founder of Valve and created *Half-Life* and *Half-Life 2*. *Half-Life* won 50 Game of the Year awards. The Counter-Strike MOD was so popular it was the first one that ever sold commercially.

Hideo Kojima–Hideo's signature game series–*Metal Gear Solid*–has been applauded for its amazing gameplay and cinematics.

Hironobu Sakaguchi–This man created the *Final Fantasy* games and had a hand in the creation of *Chrono Trigger*, *Chrono Cross*, *Mario RPG*, and the *Kingdom Hearts* games. He is the third person inducted into the AIAS Hall of Fame in 2000.

Jason Jones–Co-founder of Bungie Software, Jones created the Xbox signature games *Halo* and *Halo 2*.

John Carmack–Carmack created the first-person shooter because he worked on *Wolfenstein 3D*, *Doom*, and *Quake*. He is the owner and lead programmer of id Software. He started trends of user-modifiable games and engine licensing.

Nolan Bushnell–Bushnell was the force behind introducing the world to Pong and founded Atari. He sold Atari to Time Warner in 1976 and has since founded over 20 other companies, including one called Chuck E. Cheese Pizza.

Peter Molyneux–Known as the father of "god games," Molyneux is the founder of Lionhead Studios and is most notable for groundbreaking games like *Populous*, *Dungeon Keeper*, *Black and White*, and *Fable*.

Rockstar North–These guys created "emergent gameplay" and "sandbox games" and are best-known for the *Grand Theft Auto* series (but also for *State of Emergency*, *Manhunt*, and *Bully*). The team includes Sam Houser, Dan Houser, Terry Donovan, Jamie King, and Gary Foreman.

Shigeru Miamoto–He is the Steven Spielberg of video games. Miamoto joined Nintendo in 1977 as a young artist, and his first game was *Donkey Kong*. He went on to make *Super Mario Bros.*,

Legend of Zelda, Earthbound, Starfox, Pikmin, and *Metroid.* He is currently the General Manager of Nintendo and was the first person inducted into the Academy of Interactive Arts and Sciences' Hall of Fame in 1998.

Sid Meier—This co-founder of Microprose and FIRAXIS Games has been instrumental in the creation of *Civilization, Alpha Centauri, Railroad Tycoon,* and *Pirates!* He was the second person inducted into the AIAS Hall of Fame in 1999.

Tetsuya Mizuguchi—Mizuguchi has expanded the game market in areas it has never gone before with his rhythm-based games *Rez* and *Lumines.*

Tim Sweeny—This lead programmer at Epic Games wrote the Unreal Engine, one of the most flexible game engines in the industry.

Tom Bean—He started the first Christian game design company and currently works on Adventure in Odyssey games for Focus on the Family. His company includes programmers from such great games as *Oregon Trail* and *Carmen Sandiego.*

Toru Iwatani—He created *Pac-Man* in 1980, inspired by a partially-eaten pizza. *Pac-Man* was originally called "Puck Man" in Japan.

Warren Spector—This founder of Ion Storm Games brought emotional drama and great stories to the game market through games like *Deus Ex* and *Thief.*

Yu Suzuki—Credited with the first simulation game (called *Hang On,* a motorcycle game), he is best known for creating *Virtua Fighter,* the first 3D fighting game.

Every discipline of game design has its own requirements to get noticed and get ahead. You have to experiment with them all and decide which discipline appeals to you before you even consider specialization in any one area.

Artist

Artists create the art involved in games. If you cannot draw, it is not advisable to attempt to become a game artist. If you can draw—and you can work within a tight deadline and take directions well—then art is for you. Technological tools that you should consider working with include Adobe Photoshop, Jasc Paint Shop Pro, Flash, Maya, 3D Studio Max, and MilkShape. Art and technology are more intertwined than ever before. Besides the technology, you must know standard artist tools, like drawing and painting with pen and ink, charcoal, paint, and canvas. Learn anatomy and figure drawing, color design, layout, composition, and perspective.

There are basically four specializations in art: drawing (analog and digital), modeling, texturing, and animation. There are lots of different applications for this art, including characters, props, weapons, vehicles, backgrounds, interiors, exteriors, environments, cinematics, cut-scenes, interfaces, and special effects. 2D artists focus on applying two-dimensional art to games, especially concept artwork or texture maps. 3D artists create and refine three-dimensional models and environments.

Note

"For game art, the choice between Maya and 3D Studio Max is a toss-up. At this time, game-quality models are simple triangulated polygon meshes somewhere under 4,000 polys, and closer to 2,000–so using Maya to do in-game work is like cutting cheese with a laser. If you're doing pre-rendered cinematics and want to work more seamlessly between your game assets and some inflated higher resolution version, then Maya might pull ahead. . . . For 2D, Adobe Photoshop rules all. It's a powerful, flexible tool for concept artwork, texturing, and illustration. There are those who prefer Painter for high-end illustration, but if you want to keep your team on the same platform, Photoshop is the more flexible tool."

–Marc Taro Holmes, Obsidian Entertainment

Programmer

Game programming can involve anything from creating the game physics of the core engine to the graphics, audio, and world-building tools that other team members can use during production. Programmers are the best paid and most likely applicants to be accepted into the game industry. You are expected to know math, physics, geometry, and programming languages like C, C++, Visual Basic, Java, and Actionscript. Get a computer science degree and consider learning as many programming languages as possible, including networking and database languages (because games are quickly moving online and becoming even more versatile than ever before).

John Ahlquist was one of the creators of Macromedia Fireworks (now Adobe Fireworks). He also developed the tools and engine for the popular games *Command & Conquer: Generals* and *The Lord of the Rings: The Battle for Middle-earth* (see Figure 13.2). John says, "My first responsibility is to analyze what the designers and artists need the game engine and tools to do—and I design and implement efficient solutions. There are two keys to efficiency: the first is to develop the code quickly, since we are always longer on features and shorter on time. The second is runtime performance for the engine."

World Builder

The only way you can prove to studios you have the skill it takes to make game levels is to build as many as you can (interior, exterior, and outdoor) and show

Figure 13.2
The Lord of the Rings: The Battle for Middle-earth (image courtesy of EA Games 2006)

them in a demo reel. There is no formal training for level designers. Nevertheless, using game engines like 3D GameStudio or your favorite game's map editor, you can practice and get the experience needed to become a genius world builder. Map editing tools are usually proprietary, built in-house by studio tool programmers to fit their production schedules. When they release them to the public, they do so under a limited end-user agreement. This means that you can use their map editors (like the Aurora Toolset from *Neverwinter Nights* or the Valve Hammer Editor from *Half-Life 2*), but you cannot publish and make money off games made with them. Joining an online MOD community offers you a testing ground for your development skills with these map editors. In the meantime, you can learn visual arts and 3D modeling at college.

Tester

Play-testing is the one area where newbies get hired rather quickly, but the turnover rate is outstanding. You need not have any experience to apply; it helps you if you've participated as a tester on an open beta-test before, but it's not a requirement. Companies are always looking for beta-testers and expect good communication and writing skills, as well as thoroughness. Game testing involves playing a game before its release in order to determine whether or not it is playable. By *playable*, I mean that it must be bug-free, consistent, and entertaining. Starting out as a tester is comparable to starting out in the mailroom of a movie studio.

Quality assurance (QA) is not to be confused with testing. QA involves process monitoring, product evaluation, and auditing—ensuring that the game meets the documents, outline, and code standards set by the game designer and producer. Compliance is even more important in console game development and licensed game production (due to legal/contractual agreements).

Sound Engineer

Breaking into the industry as a music composer, musician, sound specialist, or sound effects technician is really difficult. Most game companies do not have an in-house audio department and outsource the audio services, such as music, sound effects, and dialog. Game companies receive more demo tapes and CDs from sound people every month than any other submission. Many of them never get listened to. Persistence pays off, but most of the sound engineers working in the industry started out as professionals working in the film or television industry. The best advice is to network. Form personal contact lists. E-mail producers directly. Keep sending them your demos.

If you want to get your feet wet (or wetter, as the case may be) with game audio, there are some popular audio creation tools you should investigate. They include Digidesign's ProTools, Microsoft's DirectX Audio, and SoundMAX Smart Tools. Many of these allow sound engineers to create interactive and non-repetitive audio content so that game sounds do not sound the same at every single interval of playback.

Designer/Producer

No one starts out in the industry as a game designer or producer. People who are currently in these job roles got there in the most roundabout ways. Mostly, people start in another position with the game company, work up from the ground floor, become proficient at making games, and take on more and more responsibility until they find themselves at the top floor. Along the way, you need to learn what everyone in the team does. Study the pipeline carefully. Become a generalist of sorts, and work on your communication skills. Become an art or tech lead and move up from there.

The game designer focuses on gameplay, levels, interfaces, and the "vision" behind the game in its entirety. They work tirelessly to iron out game concepts, complex storylines, and mechanics in order to bring a coherent game world together. Most of them are technically called "directors" rather than designers, due to the confusion the public has about the difference between game designer and game artist. As Chris Avellone of Obsidian Entertainment tells us, "Overall, I'm responsible for keeping the vision for the game, the game mechanics, and the 'fun' of the game; the overall story (and any specific elements about the game designed to propel the overall story, such as companions, key locations, etc.); and then breaking down the remaining elements into digestible chunks for the other designers in terms of area briefs and area overviews."

The producer is someone who "makes things happen." Producers are responsible for finding funding, making sure the game is released on budget and under deadline, and following through to keep everyone doing what they are supposed to. Producers report to upper management. They take care of staff, schedules, pay periods, and due dates. Frank Gilson at Blizzard says, "Part of my role as producer involves business development. We need to look to the future to determine what projects the company should finance, and who should develop them.... Once a project exists, I manage the relationship between my company, a publisher, and the game developer."

The Demo, Cover Letter, and Resume

Once you have chosen the profession that is best for you and you have found a career opportunity, you will have to show the human resources person or employer that you have what it takes to work at their company. This is done with a solid demo, cover letter, and resume.

Demo

A portfolio is often a half-inch three-ring binder with clear sheet protectors in it filled with your most striking artwork (if you are an artist). Keep the amount of work in the portfolio short and to a minimum (20 pages max). Put your material on your Web site as well for prospective employers or clients to peruse. Add your name, address, and contact information on the cover.

It doesn't hurt to make a booklet or pamphlet to leave with interviewers that also displays your artistic nature and style. Make the information portrayed therein relevant and concise.

Showing a great demo reel (often referred to as the *digital portfolio*) is the single fastest way for you to get hired in this business. Game companies are more interested in your capabilities right now than your past credentials. You are far better off showing what you can do than talking about it. This is true in almost every industry. Creating a demo shows your prospective employers a lot of things, including

- You can do the work required.
- You can take initiative.
- You can get it done.
- You are enthusiastic about what you do.
- You are good at what you do.

If your digital portfolio does not exhibit even one of these items, you might not show your full potential, and you might not get picked up by an employer. Show off only your very best work. Use only your best material. Update your demo as your talents improve. Don't pick up stale out-of-date work and toss it into your demo because you are lazy. Show the highlights—the very best of your work—up front or within the first five minutes of your demo reel (see Figure 13.3). Don't make the menu selection or navigation layout more exciting than the work because most people that preview demos will guess that you used a wizard of some kind to make that part.

Depending on the job you are trying to get and the skill set you are trying to show off, you might want to include animation shorts, music videos, audio effects,

Figure 13.3
The demo reel should spotlight your best work.

cinematic sequences, or short game demos (like the ones you have made in this book). Make sure that your CD portfolio does not have any copyrighted or plagiarized material, as this will make you look really bad.

Have your demo reel do more for you: prepare it for interviews and boardroom presentations because you never know when an opportunity presents itself for you to display what you can do. It pays to be prepared. Thus ensure the cross-compatibility and automatic startup of your demo reel. You don't want someone to give up on you because they could not get their computer to run your disc.

Cover Letter and Resume

Your resume should consist of your applicable skills listed in detail, your education and what degree(s) you might possess, and what related job experiences you might have had. If your resume fulfills the following outline, you will do much better at getting people to read it:

1. **Objective**—What job positions you are applying for and what you feel you will contribute if you are brought to the table on it.
2. **Education**—Your measure of learning in the field.
3. **Skills**—What you can do. List everything that would apply or is required for the job position you are trying for, without exaggerating or lying about any of it.
4. **Experience**—Mention related jobs you have had in the past.
5. **References**—People they can contact for more information about you and your teamwork capabilities.

Notice that I say over and over again that you should only mention what is related to the job position you are trying to fill. This is because a job application (in the form of digital portfolio/demo reel, contact letter, and resume) must not seem generic but should be focused toward the company and the opportunity you are seeking. This goes for any industry you might work in.

References are often written as "Available upon request." This is accepted, but it is often more enlightening if you can get a really good reference or two from past employers or college instructors because this will show prospective employers you actually have some and that you are up front about everything.

The Job Interview

Be open, friendly, and personable. Isn't that what every counselor and job interview book will tell you? It is 100 percent true. Here are some other things to keep in mind: use a confident walk. Put a spring in your legs, walk on the balls of your feet, toes facing forward, tummy sucked in, arms swinging free at your sides, hands relaxed, shoulders rolling and always facing forward. Use a firm handshake timed just right. Lean in toward the person you are speaking to. Watch your body language. Don't compare your shortcomings to someone else's endowments. Admit when you do not know something and ask for answers or further clarification.

In regard to your speech patterns, you should use humor, respect, affinity, professionalism, diplomacy, patience, discretion, and firmness. Don't catch yourself using uncertainty, generalizations, manipulation, sneak attacks, or cutting words. The reason for this is that words you habitually choose also affect how you communicate with yourself, and therefore what you experience. Realizing that the power of your words commands everything you think and do, you can simply choose to use more positive words. Take pleasure in finding the *right* words. Find positive synonyms and drop the mediocre or hateful words. In fact, it is highly possible to adopt someone else's habitual vocabulary and end up adopting their emotional/behavioral patterns as well. This is one of the reasons why we become more like—and bond quicker with—those individuals we habitually hang out with. As Mary Catherine Bateson said, "Few things are more debilitating than a toxic metaphor."

Every company and every interviewer have a unique way of conducting interviews, some of them quite unconventional, so you have to be ready for variations and adapt well. Prepare for your job interview the same way you would a test in class. Try to find out ahead of time as much as you can about the company you are going to interview at. Play some of its most recent games. Check the game industry news sites for recent stories on it, and visit the company's own Web site for current events (if you haven't already).

Some companies will want to give you a test before you arrive, or it may be part of the interview process. Others don't do any sort of testing at all. These tests may be anything from task competency tests to personality tests to an academic test meant to test your knowledge. Even if you are not aware of any test being given, the interviewer probably has subtle cues and nonverbal tests that he or she is watching carefully for to see how well you perform.

Find out what you should wear to the interview ahead of time. Some places appreciate it if you wear what they call "dress casual," while others determine that you are dirt if you don't wear a dress or tie. Finding out something like this beforehand will help you immensely. And whatever you do, take the care to perform some basic hygiene before going into your interview. This is difficult around the core game programmers and artists crowd, who usually do not care as much about the personal appearance as they do the projects they are working on, but your first impression will suffer somewhat if you don't pay attention to the social niceties.

Be on time to your job interview. Even if your own personal philosophy is to do everything "on Indian time," get to your job interview on time. The reasons should be obvious. Not only will your interviewer grade you on your timely arrival, getting to the interview on time and looking good doing it shows them deep personal respect and that you care what they think. If you really don't care what they think and consider your antisocial ways endearing, you should consider working as an independent game developer or freelancer and cross your fingers when approaching clients.

Most interviews follow a standard list of questions. If they have already previewed your demo or digital portfolio, they may ask specific questions about how you put it together, what you feel your best work is, and where you want to go from here. You might even hear them ask extremely specific technical questions. If you don't know what they are talking about, or they leave your depth of field, don't fake it—tell them so. The more up front and honest you are about yourself and your skills, the further your interview will take you.

Group interviews are more difficult to handle. The purpose of a group interview is to see how well you fit in with the other personalities at the company and if you are comfortable working with a team. Questions within a group setting are more likely to be softer-edged, like "What's your favorite game?" "What do you like to play?" and "What movie do you like that's out right now?" There's no use trying to fake your way here or tailor each and every response to put you in a better light. If you are giving a presentation of your demo in front of the group, be ready for questions immediately following. Speak clearly and directly. It is fine to have a sense of humor, but if you sense that no one is getting your humor, drop the jokes and remain professional. If the interview is done over lunch, which happens on occasion, order only bite-sized portions of food so that you can concentrate on talking rather than eating.

Every interviewer will get to a point where they stop and ask you if you have any questions. This will put you on the spot, and if you don't have anything, you will invariably feel like a dolt. Don't let this creep you out. Be prepared ahead of time. Remember that you are supposed to do as much research about the company as possible. Memorize a few questions to ask about their upcoming projects, the corporate culture, the work load, or the management style of the company. If you are from out of town and considering relocating, show the initiative and ask about housing, traffic conditions, and where's a good place to get something to eat. If you recall that there was some recent news about the company, ask about it and how it's affected the lives of the employees. If nothing else, ask the interviewer where they see the company going or what their mission statement is again.

If you haven't received the most important information that usually comes out of an interview (the job they might hire you for, the company's benefit package, and the salary requirements) ask about them. Don't accept the job offer on the spot (unless it appears to be a really good one) because you don't want to appear needy or desperate. Allow yourself at least 24 hours to think it over, ask any questions you might have forgotten to ask during the interview, and discuss it with your spouse or family, especially if accepting the job means changes in your relationships with them.

Typical Work Expectations

Mentioned previously was that salaries of new graduates entering the game design industry are between \$35,000 and \$50,000 per year. The highest salary earners are not the producers or the designers, however–they are the game programmers. Male programmers earn an average of \$53,000 a year. Female programmers (which are estimated at only 9 percent of the current population) earn less–about \$48,000 a year. No one on salary earns overtime, except for the beta-testers. Each employee is assigned to a particular project and will have numerous tasks in support of that project. A 9- to 10-hour work day is not that uncommon. Crunch periods to get games in before deadline can be anywhere from two to six months at a go and can average 80- to 140-hour work weeks (which works out to 20-hour days). It is estimated that about one-third of all game designers who enter the industry for the first time burn out and quit before seeing their first game finished.

There have been cries for quality-of-life reforms. Interns who were overworked and never paid by a United States branch of EA Games recently got paybacks for their hard work. There are even rumors that game companies are going to start outsourcing to freelance studios. This could be a boon to smaller independent game developers.

After the interview, send a thank-you letter within 24 hours. Show your follow-up skills in a positive light. Keep them thinking about you. Write directly to an individual. If you met multiple individuals, get their business cards so that you have proper spellings and job titles. Restate in your letter why you are the candidate that they should choose. Remember to spell check it.

Networking

Conferences and trade shows are the number-one places to network with people inside the industry. There are several major game conferences you might want to check out or head to here in the United States:

- Game Developers Conference (GDC) in March (www.gdconf.com)
- Electronic Entertainment Expo (E3) in May (www.e3expo.com)
- Austin Game Conference in September (www.gameconference.com)

When you go to one of these conferences, be prepared to research, talk to lots of professionals in the industry, listen to what they have to say, and take notes. Get names or business cards. You never know what sort of connections you will be able to make. If you form any promising leads at a conference, don't be shy about following up.

IGDA is the International Game Developers Association. It pays to join. IGDA is working to improve the quality of life for game designers everywhere; if you want to, you can think of them as your own personal union. IGDA works against government censorship and regulation. IGDA has helped develop standards of curriculum in game schools. It provides GDC scholarships to 25 college students every year. It also provides its members with Special Interest Groups (SIGs) that they can belong to—including SIGs focusing on AI, preservation, independent game development, mobile games, online games, student affairs, casual games, women developers, and writers. You can find out more about IGDA and sign up on their Web site at www.igda.org.

What Do You Want to Do With Your Life?

Ask yourself the following questions:

- What am I happy about in my life?
- What am I excited about right now?

- What am I most proud of right now?
- What am I most grateful for right now?
- What am I most committed to (what do I make a priority)?

At the end of the day, ask yourself

- What have I contributed to my family or my society today?
- What have I learned today?
- How has today added to the sum quality of my life experiences?
- Where should I go from here?

These are all very tough questions. Do not hastily judge them to be "cheesy" (see Figure 13.4). They can enlighten you. What you love doing most might have no physical relation to what you commit yourself to every day. You might, for instance, be stuck working in a cubicle doing tax preparation day in and day out while the love of your life is getting home to play *World of Warcraft*. You might even be content with that irony. Or you might have never taken the time to think through these important details, and you might find that you have wasted most of your life experiences taking the trash out. There's an old adage that says, "When someone says you have potential, it means you haven't done anything with your life . . . yet!"

Figure 13.4
Hang on—it's not that cheesy!

We all act consistently with our views of who we think we truly are, whether that view is entirely accurate or not. The reason is that one of the strongest forces in the human organism is the utter and complete need for consistency. As Ralph Waldo Emerson once pointed out, "A foolish consistency is the hobgoblin of small minds." We all have a need for certainty in our lives. Most folks fear the unknown because uncertainty implies the potential for pain. As we develop new beliefs about who and what we are—and what we are capable of—our behavior and destiny will change to support the new identity.

Right now you can make a decision that weaves your fate; if you truly decide to, you can do almost anything. Decide what you want to do, and then do it. Making a true decision means committing yourself to achieving a result (even if it might be failure). Fear not, for you will find a way. It's your decisions about what to focus your will on, what things mean to you, and what you are going to do about them that will ultimately determine your destiny. We don't have to allow the programming of our past to control our present or our future.

Self-help and personal instructor Anthony Robbins says that there is an Ultimate Success Formula, consisting of only four steps:

1. Decide what it is you want.
2. Take immediate action.
3. Notice what is working or not.
4. Change your approach until you get the desired outcome.

Robbins' approach is amazingly similar to the scientific method, except your livelihood is the experimental subject. Success is truly the result of good judgment. Good judgment is the result of experience, and experience is often the result of bad judgment. In order to succeed, it's imperative to have long-term focus. Mistakes along the way are to be expected, as they will instruct you on how to reach your success faster. The one thing to make a habit is never to leave the scene of a decision-making session without first taking a specific action toward its realization.

Your focus determines your reality. Very few things in life are absolute, but over 100 percent of everything is relative. So focus on where you want to go, not your fear of failure (see Figure 13.5). How you do this is exactly the same way you would alter a photo image in Adobe Photoshop—you shift the brightness/contrast

Figure 13.5
You could be the next video game celebrity!

or the hue/saturation to make the image more intensive, you spotlight on the details to affect the impression you want to impart to the viewer, and you alter its "mood." Life is identical to this process. You can get a lot of things done you never knew were possible if you only tweak your focus. Like the Buddha said, "We are what we think. All that we are arises with our thoughts. With our thoughts, we make our world."

In Summary

No matter what it is about game design that entices you, there is some niche for you to break into the business. This explosive new major entertainment medium is currently looking for its next big celebrities. You too could become the next Miyamoto or Warren Spector. Don't let anyone—not even your inner critic—convince you otherwise.

What You Have Learned

Getting into the game design industry takes skill, courage, cleverness, and more than a little luck.

- You now understand the many different roles in a game company.
- You have learned what it takes to sell yourself.

- You have learned how to develop a demo reel.
- You have a firmer grasp of cover letters and resumes.
- You understand what to do on a job interview.
- You have a better understanding of getting what you want in life.
- You know the Ultimate Success Formula.

For Review

1. What roles in a game development team are particularly specialized, and which ones are more generalized? Why do you think that they are so? How does this affect the game production?
2. Using one popular electronic game, find and discuss three examples of how art is used throughout the game. Does the game utilize 2D or 3D art productively?
3. Put together a game design team for your original game idea. How many artists, programmers, designers, producers, world builders, sound engineers, and testers will you have on your team, and why? Would you want any of those members to specialize in one area of emphasis or be generalists, and if so why?
4. Say that a make-believe game company Whirligig Studios is looking to hire someone in your field. Consider what you would have to do to get hired there. Write a cover letter and resume, and make a list of what you would prepare for before the job interview. What sorts of questions would you ask the interviewer? What would you put together in your demo reel or digital portfolio?
5. What would you like to do with your life? Make up your mind about what you love and what you want to do with the rest of your life. Construct a goal plan that covers the next three years.

INDEX

B

C

F

H

I

Q

R

X–Z

License Agreement/Notice of Limited Warranty

By opening the sealed disc container in this book, you agree to the following terms and conditions. If, upon reading the following license agreement and notice of limited warranty, you cannot agree to the terms and conditions set forth, return the unused book with unopened disc to the place where you purchased it for a refund.

License

The enclosed software is copyrighted by the copyright holder(s) indicated on the software disc. You are licensed to copy the software onto a single computer for use by a single user and to a backup disc. You may not reproduce, make copies, or distribute copies or rent or lease the software in whole or in part, except with written permission of the copyright holder(s). You may transfer the enclosed disc only together with this license, and only if you destroy all other copies of the software and the transferee agrees to the terms of the license. You may not decompile, reverse assemble, or reverse engineer the software.

Notice of Limited Warranty

The enclosed disc is warranted by Thomson Course Technology PTR to be free of physical defects in materials and workmanship for a period of sixty (60) days from end user's purchase of the book/disc combination. During the sixty-day term of the limited warranty, Thomson Course Technology PTR will provide a replacement disc upon the return of a defective disc.

Limited Liability

THE SOLE REMEDY FOR BREACH OF THIS LIMITED WARRANTY SHALL CONSIST ENTIRELY OF REPLACEMENT OF THE DEFECTIVE DISC. IN NO EVENT SHALL THOMSON COURSE TECHNOLOGY PTR OR THE AUTHOR BE LIABLE FOR ANY OTHER DAMAGES, INCLUDING LOSS OR CORRUPTION OF DATA, CHANGES IN THE FUNCTIONAL CHARACTERISTICS OF THE HARDWARE OR OPERATING SYSTEM, DELETERIOUS INTERACTION WITH OTHER SOFTWARE, OR ANY OTHER SPECIAL, INCIDENTAL, OR CONSEQUENTIAL DAMAGES THAT MAY ARISE, EVEN IF THOMSON COURSE TECHNOLOGY PTR AND/OR THE AUTHOR HAS PREVIOUSLY BEEN NOTIFIED THAT THE POSSIBILITY OF SUCH DAMAGES EXISTS.

Disclaimer of Warranties

THOMSON COURSE TECHNOLOGY PTR AND THE AUTHOR SPECIFICALLY DISCLAIM ANY AND ALL OTHER WARRANTIES, EITHER EXPRESS OR IMPLIED, INCLUDING WARRANTIES OF MERCHANTABILITY, SUITABILITY TO A PARTICULAR TASK OR PURPOSE, OR FREEDOM FROM ERRORS. SOME STATES DO NOT ALLOW FOR EXCLUSION OF IMPLIED WARRANTIES OR LIMITATION OF INCIDENTAL OR CONSEQUENTIAL DAMAGES, SO THESE LIMITATIONS MIGHT NOT APPLY TO YOU.

Other

This Agreement is governed by the laws of the State of Massachusetts without regard to choice of law principles. The United Convention of Contracts for the International Sale of Goods is specifically disclaimed. This Agreement constitutes the entire agreement between you and Thomson Course Technology PTR regarding use of the software.